THE POSTAL SERVICE GUIDE TO U.S. STAMPS

16TH EDITION

1990
STAMP VALUES

UNITED STATES
POSTAL SERVICE

W9-ANQ-294

UNITED STATES
POSTAL SERVICE
WASHINGTON, D.C.
20260-6755
ITEM NO. 0864

EXPLANATION OF
CATALOG PRICES

The United States Postal Service sells only the commemoratives released during the past few years and current regular and special stamps and postal stationery.

Prices in this book are called "catalog prices" by stamp collectors. Collectors use catalog prices as guidelines when buying or trading stamps. It is important to remember the prices are simply guidelines to the stamp values. Stamp condition (see pp 11-12) is very important in determining the actual value of a stamp.

The catalog prices are given for unused (mint) stamps and used (cancelled) stamps, which have been hinged and are in Fine condition. Stamps in Superb condition that have never been hinged may cost more than the listed price. Stamps in less than Fine condition may cost less.

The prices for used stamps are based on a light cancellation; a heavy cancellation lessens a stamp's value. Cancelled stamps may be worth more than uncancelled stamps. This happens if the cancellation is of a special type or for a significant date. Therefore, it is important to study an envelope before removing a stamp and discarding its "cover."

Listed prices are estimates of how much you can expect to pay for a stamp from a dealer. If you sell the same stamp to a dealer, he may offer you much less than the catalog price. Dealers pay based on their interest in owning that stamp. If they already have a full supply, they will only buy more at a low price.

Prices in regular type for single unused and used stamps are taken from the *Scott 1990 Standard Postage Stamp Catalogue, Volume 1* © 1989, whose editors have based these values on **actual retail values** as they found them in the marketplace. Prices quoted for unused and used stamps are for "Fine" condition, except where Fine is not available. If no value is assigned, market value is individually determined by condition of the stamp, scarcity and other factors.

Prices for Plate Blocks and First Day Covers are taken from *Scott's Specialized Catalogue of U.S. Stamps,* 1989 Edition, © 1988. The Scott numbering system for stamps is used in this book.

Prices for Souvenir Cards are taken from *Brookman Price Guide of U.S. First Day Covers, Souvenir Cards, USPS Panels and Pages,* published by Brookman Stamp Company. Prices for American Commemorative Panels are from The American Society of Philatelic Pages and Panels, an organization specializing in Commemorative Panels. Prices for Souvenir Pages are from Charles D. Simmons of Buena Park, California.

			Un	U	PB/LP	#	FDC	Q
2407	25¢	New Orleans, Mar. 3	.00	.00	0.00	( )	0.00	000,000,000

Scott Catalog Number — Denomination — Description — First Day of Issue — Unused Catalog Price — Used Catalog Price — Plate Block Price or Line Pair Price — # of stamps in Plate Block — First Day Cover Price — Quantity Issued

2407

TABLE OF CONTENTS

Celebrate Stamps That Honor America

- Every U.S. commemorative stamp issued during the year
- Large-format, informative booklet for displaying stamps
- Clear acetate mounts to protect stamps

It's a Celebration of America and Americana

And it's a very special trip through America's past—the people, places, ideals and events that highlight our history.

Fun, Informative and Valuable

Commemorative Mint Sets gather the year's honorees in one convenient, collectible and colorful package. The current Set contains all 1989 commemoratives, including the new additions to the Black Heritage Series (A. Philip Randolph), the American Sports Series (Lou Gehrig) and the Literary Series (Ernest Hemingway).

The 1989 Set also features the five commemoratives issued as part of the Constitution Bicentennial Series and the exciting stamp issued for WORLD STAMP EXPO '89™. And, you will trace our country's westward growth with the statehood stamps for Montana, North Dakota and Washington. The 1989 Commemorative Mint Set is available for $12.50 through March 10, 1990, then for $14.50 in the softbound edition. A deluxe, hardbound edition is available for $21.50.

To Obtain
A Commemorative Mint Set

The 1989 Set, and some earlier sets, are available at your local post office or Philatelic Center. Or fill out the postage-paid request card in this book. Also, you can write directly to:

USPS GUIDE
COMMEMORATIVE MINT SETS
PHILATELIC SALES DIVISION
UNITED STATES POSTAL SERVICE
POST OFFICE BOX 9997
WASHINGTON DC 20265-9997

Past Sets Include:
1988 Commemorative Mint Set

Includes the Cats Quartet, Winter and Summer Olympics, Australia Bicentennial, Antarctic Explorers, Knute Rockne, New Sweden, seven statehood bicentennial stamps, Classic Cars pane of five and Carousel Animals block of four. ($14.50 softcover; $21.50 deluxe, hardcover)

1987 Commemorative Mint Set

Consists of all 41 commemorative issues, including Christmas and Love stamps; a booklet pane of 10 Special Occasions stamps; Drafting of the Constitution and more. ($12.95 softcover; $20.95 deluxe, hardbound)

I took the starting lever in one hand and the stopping one in the other, pressed the first, and almost immediately the second. I seemed to reel; I had a nightmare sensation of falling; and, looking around, I saw the laboratory exactly as before. Had anything happened? For a moment I suspected that my intellect had tricked me. Then I noted the clock. A moment before, as it seemed, it had stood at a minute or so past ten; now it was nearly half-past three!

So begins the tale of the Time Traveller in H.G. Wells' *The Time Machine*.

Wells was fascinated by the concept of time as the fourth dimension (length, width and breadth comprising the other three). But traveling through the fourth dimension—unlocking the secrets of the past and opening the door on the future—is just science fiction fantasy. Or is it?

While the wondrous wanderings of Wells' hero required the use of a time machine, collecting stamps lets you summon the people, places and events of our past, our present and even our future every time you open a stamp album.

Postage stamps are windows on time where you can view the scope and splendor of our country's history, celebrate our heros and heroines, chronicle wars, acknowledge contributors to mankind and learn about architects and aviation, basketball and banking, cars and commerce—on through an entire alphabet of fascinating trips through time.

So, pack your bags and board our version of a time machine— U.S. postage stamps.

WHAT IS PHILATELY? Collecting stamps is easier than pronouncing the technical word that describes the hobby. **Philately** (fi-lat-el-lee) is the collecting and study of postage stamps and other postal materials. The name is derived from the Greek words *philos*, which means "loving," and *atelos*, which means "free of tax." In their most basic form, stamps are signs that the postal fees have been prepaid.

Stamp collectors are called **philatelists**. The key to enjoying philately is to save the types of stamps you like best. **General collecting**—saving as many stamps as possible—is a good way to start. Many new collectors find it interesting to have a wide range of stamps. To help build your "time machine," check your mailbox daily for letters, postcards and packages with used stamps on them. Have your family and friends save envelopes they receive in the mail. And ask people who write you to use interesting stamps.

Longtime collectors often will help new philatelists by giving them some duplicates (extra stamps). Neighborhood businesses that get a lot of mail— banks, stores, travel agencies, utility companies—may be sources of stamps for you as well.

Definitive

Commemorative

Special

Topical collecting is another popular way to collect stamps because it lets people tailor their collections to their own interests. Simply choose one or two specific themes that really interest you—art and history, science and technology, architecture, sports and transportation are just a few of the possibilities.

If, for example, you love animals, you can get your topical collection off to a great start by finding some of the many U.S. stamps with animal subjects issued within the past five years.

You could begin with the pane of 50 North American Wildlife stamps issued in 1987, then add blocks of four of horses (1985), dogs (1984) and cats (1988). And you can create a special animal category in your collection with

the addition of the Prehistoric Animals block of four (1989).

Whatever stamps you choose to collect, there are additional sources where you can obtain them. Some stamp clubs meet at schools, YMCAs and community centers. If you are fortunate enough to have one of these in your area, it may be a great place for stamps and philatelic advice. If you do not know of a stamp club in your area, the people at Linn's Club Center can help you locate clubs near your ZIP Code. Just write to them:

LINN'S CLUB CENTER
POST OFFICE BOX 29
SIDNEY, OH
45365-0029

For information on the popular Benjamin Franklin Stamp Club program for elementary school students, read the accompanying article that begins on page 18.

Another good source of stamps is the classified ads in philatelic newspapers and magazines available at your library. (See page 25 for a listing of philatelic publishers who are willing to send you a free copy.) After reviewing these periodicals, you may wish to subscribe.

Stamps are classified into several major categories according to their intended use:
• **Definitive** stamps are found on most mail in denominations ranging from 1¢ to $5. Their subjects frequently are former Presidents, statesmen, other prominent persons and national shrines. Printed in unlimited quantities for specific postal rates, definitives are available for several years.
• **Commemorative** stamps honor important people, events or special subjects of

Booklet

Coil

Airmail

national appeal and significance. They usually are larger and more colorful than definitives. Printed in limited quantities, commemoratives are available only for two to three months at most post offices and for about one year by mail order from the Postal Service's Philatelic Sales Division.

• **Special** stamps include issues that supplement the regular stamps, such as Christmas and Love stamps.

• **Airmail** stamps are used for sending mail overseas.

• **Booklet** stamps are issued in small folders containing one or more panes of 3 to 20 stamps each. Each stamp has one, two or three straight edges.

• **Coil** stamps are issued in rolls. Each one has two straight and two perforated edges.

CARING FOR YOUR COLLECTION

Your stamps are just that—*your* stamps. You can do whatever you want with them. You can save entire envelopes and store them anywhere, from shoe boxes to special albums. Or you can try to peel the stamps off the envelopes.

However, the proper way to remove stamps from envelopes is to soak them.

Stamps are delicate little pieces of paper; so, be careful. Tear or cut off the upper right-hand corner of the envelope, or cover. Place the stamp face down in a small pan of warm water. After a few minutes the stamp

will float off the paper and sink to the bottom.

Allow a few more minutes for any remaining gum to dislodge from the stamp, then lift it out using tongs—a metal grasping device with flat ends, similar to tweezers—if you have a pair. (Although many collectors touch stamps with their fingers, it is better to handle them with tongs. Even if your hands are clean, oil from your skin can damage stamps.)

To keep a stamp from curling while it

dries, put it between two paper towels and apply pressure with a heavy object, such as a book. Leave the stamp there overnight, and it will be flat the next day. Stamps with dry, "invisible" gum are trickier to dry because they tend to retain gum after soaking and stick fast to paper when drying.

Dry these stamps face down with nothing touching the back side, and flatten them later if they curl. To learn more about soaking stamps, look for a detailed handbook on stamp collecting at your local library.

ORGANIZING YOUR COLLECTION

You will want to protect your stamps so they do not get damaged or lost. As they accumulate, it is a good idea to put them in some kind of order.

You can attach your stamps to loose-leaf paper organized in a simple three-ring binder. Or, arrange them in a more formal album available in stores.

Some stamp albums feature specific categories with pictures of the stamps that are supposed to appear on each page. It is usually best to select an album with loose-leaf pages so you can add pages easily as your collection grows.

A stock book is an album with plastic or paper pockets on each page; there are no pictures of stamps, so you can organize it *your* way.

It is best to use a small strip of thin plastic, gummed on one side, to put stamps in your album. Called a hinge, this strip is available either folded or unfolded.

If you use a folded hinge, lightly moisten the short end and press it to the back of the stamp with the fold about ⅛″ from the top.

Then hold the stamp (with your tongs) and lightly moisten the long end of the hinge. Place the stamp where you want it in the album and secure it by pressing down. Using your tongs, gently lift the stamp's corners to make sure none have stuck to the page.

By using a hinge—instead of tape or glue—you can peel the stamp from the page, if you wish, without damaging it.

Collectors may use mounts instead of hinges to prevent air and dirt from damaging their stamps and to keep excess moisture from disturbing the gum.

A mount is a small, clear (usually plastic) sleeve into which an entire stamp is inserted. Mounts are more expensive than hinges, but many collectors believe the extra protection is well worth the price. With your first "window" in place, you will be ready to add more to your time machine of stamps.

With used stamps and a few inexpensive accessories, such as a small album and a package of hinges, even collectors with a limited budget can have a great time. Remember to mention stamps, stamp albums and hinges to your friends and relatives before Christmas and your birthday!

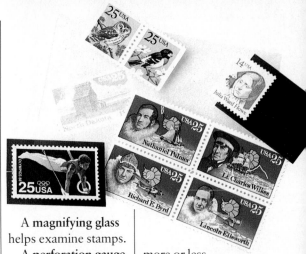

TOOLS OF THE TRADE

In addition to the tongs, hinges and mounts previously described, other equipment that can aid stamp collectors includes:

Glassine (glass-een) **envelopes** are used to store and keep stamps that you have yet to add to your album. Glassine is a special thin paper that keeps grease and air from damaging stamps.

A **stamp catalog** is a handy reference with many illustrations that can help identify stamps; it also provides information such as values for used and unused stamps.

A **magnifying glass** helps examine stamps.

A **perforation gauge** measures the jagged cuts or little holes, called *perforations*, along the edges of stamps. Size and number of perforations are sometimes needed to identify stamps. "Perfs" make stamps easy to tear apart.

A **watermark tray** and **watermark fluid** are used to make more visible the designs or patterns (called *watermarks*) that are pressed into some stamp paper when it is manufactured.

STAMP CONDITION

Like an old book, the value of a stamp depends largely on two factors: how rare it is and what condition it is in. You can get an idea of how rare a stamp is by the price listed for it in a catalog. Depending on its condition, however, a stamp may sell for more or less than the catalog price. A very rare stamp may be quite expensive even though it is in poor condition.

At first, you'll probably be collecting stamps that are not very expensive, but you still should try to get them in the best condition you can find. Here are some things to look for when judging stamp condition:

Examine the front of the stamp. Are the colors bright or faded? Is the stamp dirty, stained or clean? Is the stamp torn? Torn stamps are not considered "collectible." Is the design in the center of the paper, or is it a little crooked or off to the side? Are the edges in good condition, or are some of the perforations missing? A stamp with a

Superb

Light Cancel—Very Fine

Very Fine

Medium Cancel—Fine

Fine

Heavy Cancel

Good

light cancellation mark is in better condition than one with heavy marks across it.

Now look at the back of the stamp. Is there a thin spot in the paper? It may have been caused by careless removal from an envelope or a hinge.

Stamp dealers put stamps into categories according to their condition. Look at the examples to see the differences in these categories.

A stamp listed as mint is in the same condition as when purchased from the post office. An unused stamp has not been canceled but may not have any gum on it. Stamps in mint condition usually are more valuable than unused stamps.

Catalog prices listed in *The Postal Service Guide to U.S. Stamps* are for used and unused stamps in Fine condition that have been hinged. A stamp that has not been hinged and has excellent centering and color may cost more; a stamp in less than Fine condition that has been heavily canceled may be worth less than the catalog listing.

Choosing Subjects for Stamps

In addition to being powerful devices for education and communication, stamps often function as a public service, stimulating people to take worthwhile action. Similar to the mass media—television, radio, magazines and newspapers—postage stamps bring important messages to a large audience.

Who decides what subjects will be honored on stamps?

The USPS's Citizens' Stamp Advisory Committee receives hundreds of suggestions every week, but just a few can be recommended because of the limited number of stamps issued each year.

Established more than 30 years ago, the Committee meets six times a year. It consists of historians, artists, business people, educators, philatelists and others interested in American history and culture. Keeping all postal customers in mind, they use a set of eligibility guidelines to aid in their difficult task.

Once a recommended subject receives the "stamp of approval," a Committee design coordinator assists in selecting a professional artist to design the stamp. The Committee reviews preliminary artwork and may request changes before a final version is approved.

If you think a story should be told on a stamp, submit your idea at least 36 months before its logical date of issuance. Send suggestions, along with helpful background information, to:

United States
Postal Service
Citizens' Stamp
Advisory
Committee
Room 5800
475 L'Enfant
Plaza West SW
Washington DC
20260-6352

It is recommended that artwork *not* be submitted; unsolicited artwork is seldom used because stamp designing is an exacting task requiring extraordinary skill.

Other Postal Collectibles

In addition to their regular form, stamp designs are printed or embossed (made with a raised design) directly on envelopes, postal cards and aero-

grammes. Available at post offices, these **postal stationery** products are particularly popular among some serious collectors.

Stamped envelopes are made in several sizes and styles, including the window type. First issued in 1853, more than 600 million stamped envelopes now are printed every year.

Postal cards are made of a heavier paper than envelopes. Plain and simple, one-color postal cards were first issued in 1873, and the first U.S. multicolored commemorative postal card came out in 1956. Several different postal cards usually are issued during a year

and approximately 800 million are printed annually.

Aerogrammes (air letters) are flat sheets of paper that are letters and envelopes all in one. They are specially stamped, marked for folding and already gummed. Meant for foreign airmail only, aerogrammes will carry your message anywhere in the world at a lower postage rate than regular airmail.

There are other philatelic items to collect, too, including:

Blocks of Four used or unused, unseparated stamps that have two stamps above and two below.

Plate Blocks, which usually are four stamps from a corner of a pane with the printing plate number in the margin, or selvage, of the pane. The USPS began a new plate numbering system in 1981.

Each color plate used first in stamp production is represented by a number 1 in the group of numbers in the margin. When a plate wears out and is replaced, a number 2 takes the place of the 1. The color of the number is the same as the color of the plate it represents.

Copyright Blocks, which feature the copyright symbol © followed by "United States Postal Service" or "USPS" and the year in the margin of each pane of stamps. The USPS began copyrighting new stamp designs in 1978.

Booklet Panes are panes with three or more of the same stamps. One or more panes of stamps are affixed inside a thin folder to form a booklet. Booklet pane collectors usually save entire panes.

First Day Covers (FDCs) are envelopes with new stamps on them that have been postmarked on the first day of sale at a city designated by the USPS. Collecting of First Day Covers is now honored by the U.S. Postal Service and the American First Day Cover Society

with an annual First Day Cover Collecting Week. The fourth annual week will occur September 18 to 24, 1989.

Souvenir Cards are issued as keepsakes of stamp exhibitions. Although they cannot be used for postage, some souvenir cards are available canceled. Of special interest is the annual souvenir card for National Stamp Collecting Month each October, which was first issued in 1981.

Souvenir Programs from first day ceremonies now are available through mail order subscription from the Postal Service. The programs also are given to people who attend the ceremonies. Produced by the Postal Service, Souvenir Programs contain a list of participants and biographical or background information on the stamp subject and have the actual stamp(s) affixed and postmarked with the first day of issue cancellation.

Many stamp collectors also enjoy the variety of **postmarks** available. Some collect

or each new postal issue, the USPS selects one town or city, usually related to the stamp's subject, as the site for the first day dedication ceremony. First day covers (FDCs) are envelopes with new stamps canceled with the "FIRST DAY OF ISSUE" date and city.

The fastest way to receive a first day cover is to buy the stamp yourself (new stamps usually go on sale the day after the first day of issue), attach it to your own cover and send it to the first day post office for cancellation. You may submit up to 50 envelopes. Write your address in the lower righthand corner of each first day envelope, at least ⅝" from the bottom; use a peel-off label if you prefer. Leave plenty of room for the stamp(s) and the cancellation. Fill each envelope with cardboard about the thickness of a postal card. You can tuck in the flap or seal it.

Put your first day envelope(s) inside another, larger envelope and mail it to "Customer-Affixed Envelopes" in care of the postmaster of the first day city. Your envelope(s) will be canceled and returned. First day envelopes may be mailed up to 30 days after the stamp's issue date.

Or, you can send an envelope addressed to yourself, but without a stamp attached. Put the self-addressed envelope(s) into another, larger envelope. Address this outside envelope to the name of the stamp, in care of the postmaster of the first day city. Send a check, bank draft or U.S. Postal money order (made out to the United States Postal Service) to pay for the stamp(s) that are to be put on your envelope(s). Do not send cash.

If a new stamp has a denomination less than the First-Class Rate, add postage or payment to bring each first day envelope up to the First-Class Rate. Do not send requests more than 60 days prior to the issue date.

The first formal stamps appeared in England in May of 1840. America's first adhesive stamp was issued a year and a half later by City Despatch Post, a private carrier service in New York City run by Alexander Greig. Although valid only in New York, the delivery service was so successful that it was bought by the U.S. Post Office six months later. The first two official U.S. postage stamps, featuring Benjamin Franklin and George Washington, date back to July 1, 1847. Before long, these small, pictorial squares had become the world's windows on America.

cancellations from every city or town in their respective counties or even states. Remember, a stamp collection is whatever you, personally, want to make it.

TIME TRAVEL
THROUGH STAMPS
Whatever your age, the USPS welcomes you to the fascinating world of time travel through stamps. We hope this introduction has provided you with the basics to get under way. You are about to embark on a wonderful trip through time with American philately, and we're sure your experience will be enjoyable and long-lasting. Stamp collecting is the most popular hobby in the world, and you are just beginning on the road to discovery and adventure.

Nearly 1 in 10 Americans collects stamps for one primary reason—for the fun of it! Join them on their exciting journey.

Milestones in Philately

• Includes block of four mint-condition commemorative stamps mounted on 8½" x 11¼" high-quality paper

Quality, Elegance and Value

Since the American Commemorative Panel series began in 1972, collectors have recognized these keepsakes as significant milestones in philatelic history. Because they are printed in limited editions, Panels are available on an advance subscription basis.

Accompanying the acetate-mounted block of four mint stamps are intaglio-printed reproductions of historical steel line engravings and informative articles on the stamp subject.

For Subscription Information

For more information, use the postage-paid request card in this book or write to:

**USPS GUIDE
COMMEMORATIVE PANEL PROGRAM
PHILATELIC SALES DIVISION
UNITED STATES POSTAL SERVICE
POST OFFICE BOX 9993
WASHINGTON DC 20265-9993**

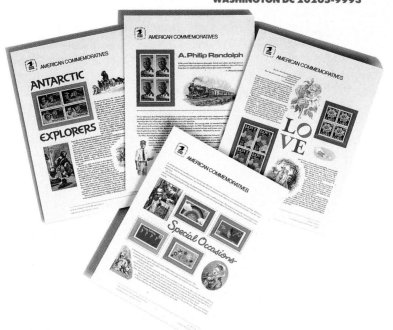

Stamp Clubs for Young Collectors

Time travel with stamps has no age limit. From children to grandparents, it makes no difference to the time machine. Statistics show, however, that most of America's 19 million philatelists were introduced to stamps before they were 16 years old, with the vast majority exposed to stamps before age 12. And where better for children to learn from stamps—and *about* stamps—than in school?

The United States Postal Service (USPS) currently supports more than 35,000 Benjamin Franklin Stamp Clubs (BFSCs) in public and private elementary schools and libraries throughout the nation. And the number is growing!

Named after our first Postmaster General and leader in organizing the U.S. postal system, the Benjamin Franklin Stamp Club Program was established in 1974 to create an awareness of stamps and to demonstrate their educational and entertainment benefits to students in the fourth through seventh grades.

Stamp collecting is an enjoyable experience that teaches important skills applicable to everyday life (for example: organization, appreciation of valuable objects, the value of money and how to manage money).

American educators agree that studying stamps is a great way to learn. Stamps have been used as teaching tools in schools for more than 100 years. The National Association of Elementary School Principals calls stamp collecting "a unique teaching tool."

The BFSC program, celebrating its 15th year, has introduced more than seven million students and teachers to the fascination and pleasures of the hobby of philately.

HERE'S ALWAYS SOMETHING EXCITING GOING ON IN THE ENJAMIN FRANKLIN STAMP CLUB

Sign Up Sheet

lb...Join the fun today!

BFSC ACTIVITIES
The Postal Service supplies materials that enable teachers to use stamps as educational aids for such subjects as mathematics, English, reading, social studies, geography and science. These materials are provided as a public service to all teachers and students.

At the beginning of each school year, clubs receive a Ben Franklin Organization Kit and copies of *Introduction to Stamp Collecting*, a reprint of selected sections of *The Postal Service Guide to U.S. Stamps*.

Two BFSC newsletters, *Stamp Fun* (for club members) and *Leader Feature* (for teachers), are sent five times during the school year; they suggest activities, such as games, puzzles and class projects.

In addition to the newsletters, there are films (on a loan basis from the Postal Service) and stamp activity guides available to club members and leaders. Some students even listen to guest speakers who teach them the Hows and Whys of stamp collecting.

STARTING A BFSC
Teachers or administrators interested in starting clubs may call their local postmaster, or for more information on the BFSC Program, they may write to:

U.S. POSTAL SERVICE
BEN FRANKLIN STAMP
CLUB PROGRAM
WASHINGTON DC
20260-6755

Benjamin Franklin Stamp Clubs are fun *and* educational. Committed, enthusiastic teachers and an interested student body are big first steps in getting started.

BFSC members across the nation—more than one million of them—share the excitement of traveling in time with stamps, and many of them will stick with stamps as they mature—because once you get stuck on stamps, you're stuck for good!

Treasury of Stamps Album
School Year 1989

For the Armchair Collector

- Receive the new stamps,
  stationery and/or philatelic
  products *you* want via
  mail order
- Quality guaranteed

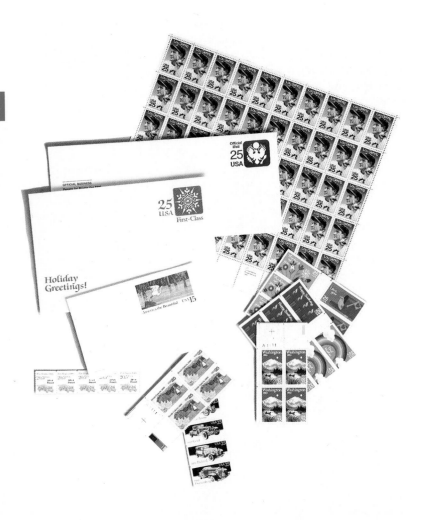

Automatic and Convenient

The armchair collector need never leave the comfort of home to use the U.S. Postal Service's Standing Order Service subscription program. Sign up once and make an advance deposit, and all postal items you desire will be shipped to you automatically on a quarterly basis.

Exceptional Quality Guaranteed

Subscribers to the Standing Order Service receive mint-condition postal items of exceptional quality—the best available centering, color and printing registration. If you are not completely satisfied with an item, return it within 30 days for a full refund or replacement.

All products are sold at face value—there are no markups, extra fees or shipping and handling charges. Just make an advance deposit based on the items and quantities you plan to select. You will be notified when you need to replenish your deposit account.

For Subscription Information

Send in the postage-paid request card in this book or write to:

USPS GUIDE
STANDING ORDER SERVICE
PHILATELIC SALES DIVISION
UNITED STATES POSTAL SERVICE
POST OFFICE BOX 9974
WASHINGTON DC 20265-9974

STAMP COLLECTING
WORDS AND PHRASES

Accessories   The tools used by stamp collectors, such as tongs, hinges, etc.

Adhesive   A gummed stamp made to be attached to mail.

Aerophilately   Branch of collecting airmail stamps and covers and their usage.

Album   A book designed to hold stamps and covers.

Approvals   Stamps sent by a dealer to a collector for examination. Approvals must either be bought or returned to the dealer within a specified time.

Auction   A sale at which philatelic material is sold to the highest bidder.

Block   An unseparated group of stamps, at least two stamps high and two stamps wide.

Booklet Pane   A small sheet of stamps specially cut to be sold in booklets.

Bourse   A marketplace, such as a stamp exhibition, where stamps are bought, sold or exchanged.

Cachet (ka-shay')   A design on an envelope describing an event. Cachets appear on first day of issue, first flight and stamp exhibition covers, etc.

Cancellation   A mark placed on a stamp by a postal authority to show that it has been used.

Centering   The position of the design on a postage stamp. On perfectly centered stamps the design is exactly in the middle.

Coils   Stamps issued in rolls (one stamp wide) for use in dispensers or vending machines.

Commemoratives   Stamps that honor anniversaries, important people or special events.

Condition   The state of a stamp in regard to such details as centering, color and gum.

Cover   An envelope that has been sent through the mail.

Definitives   Regular issues of postage stamps, usually sold over long periods of time.

Deltiology   Postcard collecting.

Denomination   The postage value appearing on a stamp, such as 5 cents.

Duplicates   Extra copies of stamps that can be sold or traded. Duplicates should be examined carefully for color and perforation variations.

Error   A stamp with something incorrect in its design or manufacture.

Face Value   The monetary value or denomination of a stamp.

First Day Cover (FDC)   An envelope with a new stamp and cancellation showing the date the stamp was issued.

Gum   The coating of glue on the back of an unused stamp.

Hinges   Small strips of gummed material used by collectors to affix stamps to album pages.

Imperforate   Indicates stamps without perforations or separating holes. They usually are separated by scissors and collected in pairs.

Label   Any stamp-like adhesive that is not a postage stamp.

Maximum Card   A postcard that has an illustration, stamp and cancel with a common theme.

Miniature Sheet   A single stamp or block of stamps with a margin on all sides bearing some special wording or design.

Mint   Indicates a stamp in the same condition as when it was issued.

Overprint   Additional printing on a stamp that was not part of the original design.

Pane   A full "sheet" of stamps as sold by a Post Office. Four panes make up the original sheet of stamps as printed.

Perforations   Lines of small holes or cuts between rows of stamps that make them easy to separate.

Philately   The collection and study of postage stamps and other postal materials.

Plate Block (or **Plate Number Block**)   A block of stamps with the margin attached that bears the plate number used in printing that sheet.

Postage Due   A stamp issued to collect unpaid postage.

Postal Stationery   Envelopes, postal cards and aerogrammes with stamp designs printed or embossed on them.

Postmark   A mark put on envelopes or other mailing pieces showing the date and location of the post office where it was mailed.

Postmaster Provisionals Stamps made by local postmasters before the government began issuing stamps.

Precancels Cancellations applied to stamps before the stamps were affixed to mail.

Reissue An official reprinting of a stamp that was no longer being printed.

Revenue Stamps Stamps not valid for postal use but issued for collecting taxes.

Selvage The unprinted paper around panes of stamps, sometimes called the margin.

Se-tenant An attached pair, strip or block of stamps that differ in design, value or surcharge.

Surcharge An overprint that changes the denomination of a stamp from its original face value.

Tagging Chemically marking stamps so they can be "read" by mail-sorting machines.

Tied On Indicates a stamp whose postmark touches the envelope.

Tongs A tool, used to handle stamps, that resembles a tweezers with rounded or flattened tips.

Topicals Indicates a group of stamps with the same theme—space travel, for example.

Unused Indicates a stamp that has no cancellation or other sign of use.

Used A stamp that has been canceled.

Want List A list of philatelic material needed by a collector.

Watermark A design pressed into stamp paper during its manufacture.

Coils

Overprint

Precancel

Imperforate

Perforate

Surcharge

Se-tenant

FOR YOUR INFORMATION...

Here's a list of philatelic resources that can increase your knowledge of stamps as well as your collecting enjoyment.

ORGANIZATIONS

Please enclose a stamped, self-addressed envelope when writing to these organizations.

American Air Mail Society
Stephen Reinhard
P.O. Box 110
Mineola, NY 11501
Specializes in all phases of aerophilately. Membership services include Advance Bulletin Service, Auction Service, free want ads, Sales Department, monthly journal, discounts on Society publications, translation service.

American First Day Cover Society
Mrs. Monte Eiserman
Dept. USG
14359 Chadbourne
Houston, TX 77079-8811
A full-service, not-for-profit, noncommercial society devoted exclusively to First Day Covers and First Day Cover collecting. Offers information on 300 current cachet producers, expertizing, foreign covers, translation service, color slide programs and archives covering First Day Covers.

American Philatelic Society
Keith A. Wagner, Exec. Dir.
P.O. Box 8000
State College, PA 16803-8000
A full complement of services and resources for the philatelist. Membership offers: American Philatelic Research Library; educational seminars and correspondence courses; expertizing service; estate advisory service; translation services; a stamp theft committee that functions as a clearing house for stamp theft information; intramember sales service; and a monthly journal, The American Philatelist, sent to all members. Membership 57,000 worldwide.

American Society for Philatelic Pages and Panels
Gerald Blankenship
539 North Gum Gully
Crosby, TX 77532
Focuses on souvenir pages and commemorative panels, with reports on news, varieties, errors, oddities and discoveries; free ads.

American Topical Association
Donald W. Smith
P.O. Box 630
Johnstown, PA 15907-0630
A service organization concentrating on the specialty of topical collecting. Offers handbooks on specific topics; an exhibition award; Topical Time, a bimonthly publication dealing with topical interest areas; a slide and film loan service; information, translation, biography and sales services; and an heirs' estate service.

Black American Philatelic Society
c/o Walt Robinson
9101 Taylor Street
Landover, MD 20785-2554
For collectors interested in the study of Black Americans on postage stamps.

Booklet Collectors Club
Larry Rosenblum
1016 E. El Camino Real, #107-U
Sunnyvale, CA 94087-3759
Devoted to the study of worldwide booklets and booklet collecting, with special emphasis on U.S. booklets. Publishes The Interleaf, a quarterly journal.

Bureau Issues Association
P.O. Box 1047
Belleville, IL 62223-1047
Devoted to the study of all U.S. stamps, principally those produced by the Bureau of Engraving and Printing.

Errors, Freaks and Oddities Collectors Club
CWO James McDevitt, USCG (Ret.)
1903 Village Road, W.
Norwood, MA 02062-2524
Studies stamp production mistakes.

Junior Philatelists of America
Central Office
P.O. Box 701010
San Antonio, TX 78270-1010
Publishes a bimonthly newsletter, The Philatelic Observer, and offers auction, exchange, penpal and other services to young stamp collectors. Adult supporting membership and gift memberships are available. The Society also publishes various brochures on stamp collecting.

Mailer's Postmark Permit Club
Florence M. Sugarberg
P.O. Box 5793
Akron, OH 44372-5793
Provides listings and information on mailers' precancel postmarks.

Mobile Post Office Society
Andrew C. Koval
P.O. Box 502
Bedford Park, IL 60499
A nonprofit organization concentrating on transit markings and the history of postal transit routes. The Society is engaged in documenting and recording transit postal history by publishing books, catalogs and monographs, as well as a bimonthly journal.

Modern Postal History Society
Terence Hines
P.O. Box 629
Chappaqua, NY 10514-0629

National Association of Precancel Collectors
Glenn V. Dye
5121 Park Blvd.
Wildwood, NJ 08260-0121
Publishes Precancel Stamp Collector, a monthly newsletter that contains information on pre-canceled stamps.

Perfins Club
Ralph W. Smith, Secretary
RR 1 Box 5645
Dryden, ME 04225
　Send SASE for information.

Philatelic Foundation
21 E. 40th Street
New York, NY 10016
　A nonprofit organization known for its excellent expertization service. The Foundation's broad resources, including extensive reference collections, 5,000-volume library and Expert Committee, provide collectors with comprehensive consumer protection. It also publishes educational information. Slide and cassette programs are available on such subjects as the Pony Express, Provisionals, Confederate Postal History and special programs for beginning collectors.

Pictorial Cancellation Society
Robert Hedges
P.O. Box 306
Hancock, MD 21750
　Studies and catalogues USPS pictorial cancellations.

Plate Block Collector Club
P.O. Box 937
Homestead, FL 33090-0937

Plate Number Society
9600 Colesville Road
Silver Spring, MD 20901-3144

Postal History Society
Diane Boehret
P.O. Box 61774
Virginia Beach, VA 23462
　Devoted to the study of various aspects of the development of the mails and local, national and international postal systems; UPU treaties; and means of transporting mails.

Post Mark Collectors Club
Wilma Hinrichs
4200 SE Indianola Road
Des Moines, IA 50320-1555
　Collects and preserves postmarks on U.S. and foreign letters.

Precancel Stamp Society
P.O. Box 160
Walkersville, MD 21793

Souvenir Card Collectors Society
Robin M. Ellis
P.O. Box 4155
Tulsa, OK 74159-4155
　Provides member auctions, a quarterly journal and access to limited-edition souvenir cards.

United Postal Stationery Society
Mrs. Joann Thomas
Box 48
Redlands, CA 92373-0601

United States Possessions Philatelic Society
Geoffrey Brewster
141 Lyford Drive
Tiburon, CA 94920-1661
　Nonprofit organization devoted to the collection and study of the postal history of Guam, Hawaii, U.S. Trust Territories, Puerto Rico, U.S. Administration of Cuba and the Philippines, D.W.I./Virgin Islands, Ryukyu Islands and the Canal Zone. Quarterly journal. Annual dues: $10.

Universal Ship Cancellation Society
David Kent
P.O. Box 127
New Britain, CT 06050-0127
　Specializes in naval ship cancellations.

FREE PERIODICALS

The following publications will send you a free copy of their magazine or newspaper upon request:

American Stamp Dealers' Association
Joseph B. Savarese
3 School Street
Glen Cove, NY 11542
　Association of dealers engaged in every facet of philately, with 11 regional chapters nationwide. Sponsors national and local shows. Will send you a complete listing of dealers in your area or collecting specialty. A #10 SASE must accompany your request.

Council of Philatelic Organizations
P.O. Box COPO
State College, PA 16803-8340
　A nonprofit organization comprised of more than 400 national, regional and local stamp clubs, organizations, societies and philatelic business firms. The objective of COPO is to promote and encourage the hobby of stamp collecting. Membership is open only to organizations; COPO uses a variety of methods to promote stamp collecting, including an ongoing publicity campaign, a quarterly newsletter and joint sponsorship (with the USPS) of National Stamp Collecting Month.

Linn's Stamp News
P.O. Box 29
Sidney, OH 45365-0029
　The largest weekly stamp newspaper.

Mekeel's Weekly Stamp News
P.O. Box 5050
White Plains, NY 10602

The Minkus Stamp Journal
P.O. Box 1228
Fort Mill, SC 29715-1228
　Quarterly. Articles of importance to collectors as well as complete listings of worldwide new issues.

Philatelic Sales Catalog
United States Postal Service
Washington, DC 20265-0001
　Published bimonthly; includes every philatelic item offered by the USPS.

Stamp Collector
Box 10
Albany, OR 97321-0006
　For beginning and advanced collectors of all ages.

Stamps Magazine
85 Canisteo St.
Hornell, NY 14843-1544
　The weekly magazine of philately.

Stamps Auction News
85 Canisteo Street
Hornell, NY 14843-1544
　The monthly financial journal of the stamp market.

Stamp Collecting Made Easy
P.O. Box 29
Sidney, OH 45365-0029
　A free, illustrated 96-page booklet.

Stamp Club Center
P.O. Box 29
Sidney, OH 45365-0029
　Write for the name and address of the stamp club nearest your ZIP code.

MUSEUMS, LIBRARIES AND DISPLAYS

There is *no charge* to visit any of the following institutions. Please contact them before visiting because their hours may vary.

American Philatelic Research Library
100 Oakwood Ave.
State College, PA 16803-8000

Cardinal Spellman Philatelic Museum
235 Wellesley St.
Weston, MA 02193-1538
　America's only fully accredited museum devoted to the display, collection and preservation of stamps and postal history. The museum contains three galleries of rare stamps, a philatelic library and a branch post office/philatelic counter.

The Collectors Club
22 East 35th St.
New York, NY 10016-3806
　Bimonthly journal, publication of various reference works, one of the most extensive reference libraries in the world, reading and study rooms. Regular meetings on first and third Wednesdays each month at 7:30 p.m., except July and August. A number of study groups also meet at the Club.

Hall of Stamps
United States Postal Service
475 L'Enfant Plaza
Washington, DC 20260-0001
Located at USPS headquarters, this exhibit features more than $500,000 worth of rare U.S. stamps, a moon rock and letter canceled on the moon, original stamp design art, etc.

National Philatelic Collection
National Museum
of American History
Third Floor
Smithsonian Institution
Washington, DC 20560
Houses more than 16 million items for exhibition and study purposes. Research may be conducted by appointment only on materials in the collection and library.

San Diego County Philatelic Library
4133 Poplar St.
San Diego, CA 92105-4541

Western Philatelic Library
Sunnyvale Public Library
665 West Olive Ave.
Sunnyvale, CA 94087

Western Postal History Museum
Box 40725
Tucson, AZ 85717-0725
Regular services include a library, philatelic sales and a Youth Department. Membership includes subscription to a quarterly journal, *The Heliograph.*

Wineburgh Philatelic Research Library
University of Texas at Dallas
P.O. Box 830643
Richardson, TX 75083-0643

LITERATURE

Basic Philately
Stamp Collector
Box 10
Albany, OR 97321-0006

Brookman Price Guide of United States Stamps
Arlene Dunn
Brookman Stamp Company
25 S. River Road
Box 429
Bedford, NH 03102-5457
Illustrated, 144-page, perfect-bound catalog.

Brookman Price Guide of U.S., U.N. & Canada Stamps
Arlene Dunn
Brookman Stamp Company
25 S. River Road
Box 429
Bedford, NH 03102-5457
Illustrated, 240-page, spiral-bound catalog.

Brookman Price Guide of U.S. First Day Covers, Souvenir Cards, USPS Panels & Pages
Arlene Dunn
Brookman Stamp Company
25 S. River Road
Box 429
Bedford, NH 03102-5457
Illustrated, 128-page, spiral-bound catalog.

Catalogue of United States Souvenir Cards
Washington Press
2 Vreeland Road
Florham Park, NJ 07932-1587

1988 Commemorative Cancellation Catalog
General Image, Inc.
P.O. Box 335
Maplewood, NJ 07040

Compilation of U.S. Souvenir Cards
P.O. Box 4155
Tulsa, OK 74159-4155

First Day Cover Catalogue (U.S.-U.N)
Washington Press
2 Vreeland Road
Florham Park, NJ 07932-1587
Includes Presidential Inaugural covers.

Fleetwood's Standard First Day Cover Catalog
Fleetwood
Cheyenne, WY 82008-0001

Minkus US Specialized Catalog 1988
P.O. Box 1228
Fort Mill, SC 29715
A complete updated catalog of all U.S. and Possessions stamps, including a complete list of federal and state Duck stamps.

19th Century Envelopes Catalog
Box 48
Redlands, CA 92373-0601

Noble Official Catalog of United States Bureau Precancels
P.O. Box 931
Winter Park, FL 32789-0931

Postage Stamp Identifier & Dictionary of Philatelic Terms
Washington Press
2 Vreeland Road
Florham Park, NJ 07932-1587

Precancel Stamp Society Catalogue of U.S. Bureau Precancels
P.O. Box 926
Framingham, MA 01701

Precancel Stamp Society Town and Type Catalogue of U.S. Local Precancels
P.O. Box 926
Framingham, MA 01701

Scott Stamp Monthly
P.O. Box 828
Sidney, OH 45365-0828

Scott Standard Postage Stamp Catalogue
Box 828
Sidney, OH 45365-8959

Scott Specialized Catalogue of United States Stamps
Box 828
Sidney, OH 45365-8959

Souvenir Pages Price List
Charles D. Simmons
P.O. Box 6238
Buena Park, CA 90622-6238
Please send self-addressed, stamped envelope to receive current listings.

Stamps of the World Catalogue
Stanley Gibbons Publications.
Available through dealers only.
All the stamps of the world from 1840 to date. Over 1,900 pages feature more than 200,000 stamps (47,900 illustrations) from over 200 issuing countries.

Standard Handbook of Stamp Collecting
Harper & Row
10 East 53rd St.
New York, NY 10022-5299

20th Century Envelopes Catalog
Box 48
Redlands, CA 92373-0601

U.S. Postal Card Catalog
Box 48
Redlands, CA 92373-0601

A Popular Collectible Returns

- An opportunity to complete your 1987 and 1988 collections in a very special way
- Contains 47 definitive stamps
- Includes four-color album with text and illustrations

Start a New Tradition

From 1980 through 1984, Definitive Mint Sets were offered to collectors. The 1987-1988 Definitive Mint Set now presents an opportunity to continue a collecting tradition.

This compilation of definitive issues contains 47 stamps, including 19 from the Transportation Series, 10 from the Great Americans Series, 4 Flag stamps, 3 Wildlife, 3 Special and 2 Airmail issues. Honored by definitives are such notables as artist Mary Cassatt, civil rights activist Julia Ward Howe, educator Mary Lyon, aviator pioneer Igor Sikorsky and American Indian Chief Red Cloud. A handsome, illustrated booklet with clear acetate stamp mounts is included.

To Obtain Your Set

The 1987- 1988 Definitive Mint Set is available from your local post office or Philatelic Center for $13.95. For more information about mail order, use the postage-paid request card in this book or write to:

USPS GUIDE
DEFINITIVE MINT SETS
PHILATELIC SALES DIVISION
UNITED STATES POSTAL SERVICE
POST OFFICE BOX 9997
WASHINGTON DC 20265-9997

PHILATELIC CENTERS

In addition to the more than 20,000 postal facilities authorized to sell philatelic products, the U.S. Postal Service also maintains more than 435 Philatelic Centers located in major population centers throughout the country.

These Philatelic Centers have been established to serve stamp collectors and make it convenient for them to acquire an extensive range of all current postage stamps, postal stationery and philatelic products issued by the Postal Service.

Centers listed are located at Main Post Offices unless otherwise indicated.

Alabama
351 North 24th Street
Birmingham, AL 35203

615 Clinton Street
Huntsville, AL 35801

250 St. Joseph
Mobile, AL 36601

Downtown Station
135 Catoma Street
Montgomery, AL 36104

Alaska
Downtown Station
3rd & C Streets
Anchorage, AK 99510

Downtown Station
315 Barnette Street
Fairbanks, AK 99707

Arizona
2400 N. Postal Blvd.
Flagstaff, AZ 86004

Osborn Station
3905 North 7th Avenue
Phoenix, AZ 85013

General Mail Facility
4949 East Van Buren
Phoenix, AZ 85026

1501 South Cherrybell
Tucson, AZ 85726

Arkansas
30 South 6th Street
Fort Smith, AR 72901

100 Reserve
Hot Springs National
Park, AR 71901

310 East Street
Jonesboro, AR 72401

600 West Capitol
Little Rock, AR 72201

724 West Walnut
Rogers, AR 72756

California
Holiday Station
1180 West Ball Road
Anaheim, CA 92802

Cerritos Branch
18122 Carmencita
Artesia, CA 90701

General Mail Facility
3400 Pegasus Drive
Bakersfield, CA 93380

2000 Allston Way
Berkeley, CA 94704

135 East Olive Street
Burbank, CA 91502

6330 Fountains Square Dr.
Citrus Heights, CA 95621

2121 Meridian Park Blvd.
Concord, CA 94520

2020 Fifth Street
Davis, CA 95616

8111 East Firestone
Downey, CA 90241

401 W. Lexington Ave.
El Cajon, CA 92020

Cotten Station
3901 Walnut Drive
Eureka, CA 95501

1900 E Street
Fresno, CA 93706

313 East Broadway
Glendale, CA 91209

Hillcrest Station
303 East Hillcrest
Inglewood, CA 90311

5200 Clark Avenue
Lakewood, CA 90712

300 Long Beach Blvd.
Long Beach, CA 90801

300 N. Los Angeles St.
Los Angeles, CA 90012

Terminal Annex
900 North Alameda
Los Angeles, CA 90052

Village Station
11000 Wilshire Blvd.
Los Angeles, CA 90024

El Viejo Station
1125 "I" Street
Modesto, CA 95354

565 Hartnell Street
Monterey, CA 93940

Civic Center Annex
201 13th Street
Oakland, CA 94612

211 Brooks
Oceanside, CA 92054

1075 North Tustin
Orange, CA 92667

281 E. Colorado Blvd.
Pasadena, CA 91109

1647 Yuba Street
Redding, CA 96001

General Mail Facility
1900 W. Redlands Blvd.
Redlands, CA 92373

1201 North Catalina
Redondo Beach,
CA 90277

Downtown Station
3890 Orange Street
Riverside, CA 92501

2000 Royal Oaks Drive
Sacramento, CA 95813

Base Line Station
1164 North E Street
San Bernardino,
CA 92410

2535 Midway Drive
San Diego, CA 92199

7th & Mission Streets
San Francisco, CA 94188

1750 Meridian Drive
San Jose, CA 95125

St. Matthews Station
210 South Ellsworth
San Mateo, CA 94401

Simms Station
41 Simms Street
San Rafael, CA 94901

Spurgeon Station
615 North Bush
Santa Ana, CA 92701

836 Anacapa Street
Santa Barbara,
CA 93102

120 W. Cypress Street
Santa Maria, CA 93454

730 Second Street
Santa Rosa, CA 95404

4245 West Lane
Stockton, CA 95208

15701 Sherman Way
Van Nuys, CA 91408

Channel Islands Station
675 E. Santa Clara St.
Ventura, CA 93001

396 South California St.
West Covina, CA 91790

Colorado
1905 15th Street
Boulder, CO 80302

201 East Pikes Peak
Colorado Springs,
CO 80901

1823 Stout Street
Denver, CO 80202

222 West Eighth Street
Durango, CO 81301

241 North 4th Street
Grand Junction,
CO 81501

5733 South Prince Street
Littleton, CO 80120

421 North Main Street
Pueblo, CO 81003

Connecticut
141 Weston Street
Hartford, CT 06101

Meridian & Waterbury Tpk.
Marion, CT 06444

11 Silver Street
Middletown, CT 06457

50 Brewery Street
New Haven, CT 06511

27 Masonic Street
New London, CT 06320

469 Main Street
Ridgefield, CT 06877

421 Atlantic Street
Stamford, CT 06904

Stratford Branch
3100 Main Street
Stratford, CT 06497

135 Grand Street
Waterbury, CT 06701

Delaware
55 The Plaza
Dover, DE 19801

Federal Station
110 East Main Street
Newark, DE 19711

11th & Market Streets
Wilmington, DE 19850

District of Columbia
Headsville Postal Station
National Museum
of American History
12th & Constitution, NW
Washington, DC 20560

National Capitol Station
North Capitol Street &
Massachusetts Avenue
Washington, DC 20002

Pavilion Post Office
Old Post Office Bldg.
1100 Pennsylvania, NW
Washington, DC 20265

USPS Headquarters
475 L'Enfant Plaza, SW
Washington, DC 20260

Florida
824 Manatee Ave. West
Bradenton, FL 33506

100 South Belcher Road
Clearwater, FL 33515

Downtown Station
220 North Beach Street
Daytona Beach, FL 32015

1900 West Oakland Park
Fort Lauderdale, FL
33310

2655 North Airport Rd.
Fort Myers, FL 33906

401 S.E. 1st Avenue
Gainesville, FL 32601

1801 Polk Street
Hollywood, FL 33022

1110 Kings Road
Jacksonville, FL 32203

210 North Missouri Ave.
Lakeland, FL 33802

118 North Bay Drive
Largo, FL 33540

2200 NW 72nd Avenue
Miami, FL 33101

1200 Goodlette
Naples, FL 33940

1111 E. Nebraska Ave.
New Port Ritchey, FL 34653

400 Southwest First Ave.
Ocala, FL 32678

1335 Kingsley Avenue
Orange Park, FL 32073

46 East Robinson Street
Orlando, FL 32801

1400 West Jordan St.
Pensacola, FL 32501

99 King Street
St. Augustine, FL 32084

3135 First Avenue North
St. Petersburg, FL 33730

Open Air Postique
76 4th Street North
St. Petersburg, FL 33701

1661 Ringland Blvd.
Sarasota, FL 33578

2800 South Adams Street
Tallahassee, FL 32301

5201 W. Spruce Street
Tampa, FL 33630

801 Clematis Street
West Palm Beach,
FL 33401

Georgia
115 Hancock Avenue
Athens, GA 30601

Downtown Station
101 Marietta Street
Atlanta, GA 30301

Perimeter Branch
4400 Ashford-
Dunwoody Road
Atlanta, GA 30346

Downtown Station
120-12th Street
Columbus, GA 31908

3470 McClure Bridge Road
Duluth, GA 30136

364 Green Street
Gainesville, GA 30501

451 College Street
Macon, GA 31201

5600 Spaulding Drive
Norcross, GA 30092

2 North Fahm Street
Savannah, GA 31401

Hawaii
3600 Aolele Street
Honolulu, HI 96819

Idaho
770 South 13th Street
Boise, ID 83708

220 East 5th Street
Moscow, ID 83843

730 East Clark Street
Pocatello, ID 83201

Illinois
909 West Euclid Ave.
Arlington Heights, IL
60004

Moraine Valley Station
7401 100th Place
Bridgeview, IL 60455

1301 East Main Street
Carbondale, IL
62901

Loop Station
211 South Clark Street
Chicago, IL 60604

433 West Van Buren St.
Chicago, IL 60607

1000 East Oakton
Des Plaines, IL 60018

1101 Davis Street
Evanston, IL 60204

2359 Madison Avenue
Granite City, IL 62040

2000 McDonough St.
Joliet, IL 60436

1750 W. Ogden Avenue
Naperville, IL 60566

901 Lake Street
Oak Park, IL 60301

123 Indianwood
Park Forest, IL 60466

5225 Harrison Ave.
Rockford, IL 61125

211-19th Street
Rock Island, IL 61201

Schaumburg Station
450 W. Schaumburg Rd.
Roselle, IL 60194

2105 E. Cook Street
Springfield, IL 62703

Edison Square Station
1520 Washington
Waukegan, IL 60085

1241 Central Avenue
Wilmette, IL 60099

Indiana
North Park Branch
4492-B 1st Avenue
Evansville, IN 47710

Fort Wayne
Postal Facility
1501 S. Clinton Street
Fort Wayne, IN 46802

5530 Sohl Street
Hammond, IN 46320

125 West South Street
Indianapolis, IN 46206

2719 South Webster
Kokomo, IN 46901

3450 State Road 26, E.
Lafayette, IN 47901

424 South Michigan
South Bend, IN 46624

30 North 7th Street
Terre Haute, IN 47808

Iowa
615 6th Avenue, SE
Cedar Rapids, IA 52401

1165 Second Avenue
Des Moines, IA 50318

320 6th Street
Sioux City, IA 51101

Kansas
1021 Pacific
Kansas City, KS 66110

6029 Broadmoor
Shawnee Mission,
KS 66202

434 Kansas Avenue
Topeka, KS 66603

Downtown Station
401 North Market
Wichita, KS 67202

Kentucky
1140 Carter Avenue
Ashland, KY 41101

1088 Nadino Blvd.
Lexington, KY 40511

St. Mathews Station
4600 Shelbyville Road
Louisville, KY 40207

Louisiana
1715 Odom Street
Alexandria, LA 71301

750 Florida Street
Baton Rouge, LA 70821

General Mail Facility
1105 Moss Street
Lafayette, LA 70501

3301 17th Street
Metairie, LA 70002

501 Sterlington Road
Monroe, LA 71201

701 Loyola Avenue
New Orleans, LA 70113

Vieux Carre Station
1022 Iberville Street
New Orleans, LA 70112

2400 Texas Avenue
Shreveport, LA 71102

Maine
40 Western Avenue
Augusta, ME 04330

202 Harlow Street
Bangor, ME 04401

125 Forest Avenue
Portland, ME 04101

Maryland
1 Church Circle
Annapolis, MD 21401

900 E. Fayette Street
Baltimore, MD 21233

Chevy Chase
Financial Unit
5910 Connecticut Ave.
Bethesda, MD 20815

215 Park Street
Cumberland, MD 21502

201 East Patrick Street
Frederick, MD 21701

6411 Baltimore Avenue
Riverdale, MD 20840

500 N. Washington St.
Rockville, MD 20850

U.S. Route 50
& Naylor Road
Salisbury, MD 21801

Silver Spring Centre
Finance Station
8455 Colesville Road
Silver Spring, MD 20911

Massachusetts
McCormick Station
Post Office &
Courthouse Bldg.
Boston, MA 02109

120 Commercial Street
Brockton, MA 02401

7 Bedford Street
Burlington, MA 01803

Center Station
100 Center Street
Chicopee, MA 01014

2 Government Center
Fall River, MA 02722

881 Main Street
Fitchburg, MA 01420

330 Cocituate Road
Framingham, MA 01701

385 Main Street
Hyannis, MA 02601

Post Office Square
Lowell, MA 01853

212 Fenn Street
Pittsfield, MA 01201

2 Margin Street
Salem, MA 01970

Main Street Station
1883 Main Street
Springfield, MA 01101

462 Washington Street
Woburn, MA 01888

4 East Central Street
Worcester, MA 01603

Michigan
2075 W. Stadium Blvd.
Ann Arbor, MI 48106

90 South McCamly
Battle Creek, MI 49106

26200 Ford Road
Dearborn Heights,
MI 48127

1401 West Fort Street
Detroit, MI 48233

250 East Boulevard Dr.
Flint, MI 48502

225 Michigan Avenue
Grand Rapids, MI 49501

200 South Otsego
Jackson, MI 49201

General Mail Facility
4800 Collins Road
Lansing, MI 48924

735 West Huron Street
Pontiac, MI 48056

1300 Military Street
Port Huron, MI 48060

30550 Gratiot Street
Roseville, MI 48066

200 West 2nd Street
Royal Oak, MI 48068

1233 South Washington
Saginaw, MI 48605

6300 North Wayne Road
Westland, MI 48185

Minnesota
2800 West Michigan
Duluth, MN 55806

100 South First Street
Minneapolis, MN 55401

Downtown Station
102 South Broadway
Rochester, MN 55904

The Pioneer
Postal Emporium
133 Endicott Arcade
St. Paul, MN 55101

Mississippi
2421-13th Street
Gulfport, MS 39501

La Fleur Station
1501 Jacksonian Plaza
Jackson, MS 39211

401 E. South Street
Jackson, MS 39201

500 West Miln Street
Tupelo, MS 38801

Missouri
920 Washington
Chillicothe, MO 64601

Columbia Mall Station
Columbia, MO 65203

315 Pershing Road
Kansas City, MO 64108

Northwest Plaza Station
500 Northwest Plaza
St. Ann, MO 63074

Pony Express Station
8th & Edmond
St. Joseph, MO 64503

Clayton Branch
7750 Maryland
St. Louis, MO 63105

500 W. Chestnut Expwy.
Springfield, MO 65801

Montana
841 South 26th
Billings, MT 59101

215 First Ave., North
Great Falls, MT 59401

1100 West Kent
Missoula, MT 59801

Nebraska
204 W. South Front St.
Grand Island, NE 68801

700 R Street
Lincoln, NE 68501

300 East Third Street
North Platte, NE 69101

1124 Pacific
Omaha, NE 68108

Nevada
1001 Circus Circus Dr.
Las Vegas, NV 89114

200 Vassar Street
Reno, NV 89510

New Hampshire
15 Mount Forest Avenue
Berlin, NH 03570

50 South Main Street
Hanover, NH 03755

955 Goffs Falls Road
Manchester, NH 03103

80 Daniel Street
Portsmouth, NH 03801

New Jersey
1701 Pacific Avenue
Atlantic City, NJ 08401

Veterans Plaza
Bergenfield, NJ 07621

3 Miln Street
Cranford, NJ 07016

229 Main Street
Fort Lee, NJ 07024

Bellmawr Branch
Haag Ave. & Benigno
Gloucester, NJ 08031

Route 35 & Hazlet Ave.
Hazlet, NJ 07730

Borough Complex
East End & Van Sant Ave.
Island Heights, NJ 08732

69 Montgomery Street
Jersey City, NJ 07305

160 Maplewood Avenue
Maplewood, NJ 07040

150 Ridgedale
Morristown, NJ 07960

Federal Square
Newark, NJ 07102

86 Bayard Street
New Brunswick,
NJ 08906

Nutley Branch
372 Franklin Avenue
Nutley, NJ 07110

194 Ward Street
Paterson, NJ 07510

171 Broad Street
Red Bank, NJ 07701

757 Broad Avenue
Ridgefield, NJ 07657

76 Huyler Street
South Hackensack,
NJ 07606

680 Highway 130
Trenton, NJ 08650

155 Clinton Road
West Caldwell,
NJ 07006

41 Greenwood Avenue
Wykoff, NJ 07481

New Mexico
1135 Broadway NE
Albuquerque,
NM 87101

200 E. Las Cruces Ave.
Las Cruces, NM 88001

415 N. Pennsylvania Ave.
Roswell, NM 88201

New York
Empire State
Plaza Station
Rockefeller Plaza N.E.
Albany, NY 12220

General Mail Facility
30 Old Karner Road
Albany, NY 12212

115 Henry Street
Binghampton,
NY 13902

Bronx General P.O.
149th Street &
Grand Concourse
Bronx, NY 10451

Parkchester Station
1449 West Avenue
Bronx, NY 10462

Riverdale Station
5951 Riverdale Avenue
Bronx, NY 10471

Throggs Neck Station
3630 East Tremont Ave.
Bronx, NY 10465

Wakefield Station
4165 White Plains Rd.
Bronx, NY 10466

Bayridge Station
5501 7th Avenue
Brooklyn, NY 11220

Brooklyn General P.O.
271 Cadman Plaza East
Brooklyn, NY 11201

Greenpoint Station
66 Meserole Avenue
Brooklyn, NY 11222

Homecrest Station
2002 Avenue U
Brooklyn, NY 11229

Kensington Station
421 McDonald Avenue
Brooklyn, NY 11218

1200 William Street
Buffalo, NY 14240

1764 Route 9
Clifton Park, NY 12065

40 Main Street
Cooperstown, NY 13326

Downtown Station
255 Clemens Center Pkwy.
Elmira, NY 14901

1836 Mott Avenue
Far Rockaway, NY 11691

41-65 Main Street
Flushing, NY 11351

Ridgewood Station
869 Cypress Avenue
Flushing, NY 11385

Broadway & Maple St.
Glenham, NY 12527

16 Hudson Avenue
Glens Falls, NY 12801

185 West John Street
Hicksville, NY 11802

88-40 164th Street
Jamaica, NY 11431

300 East 3rd Street
Jamestown, NY 14701

Ansonia Station
1980 Broadway
New York, NY 10023

Bowling Green Station
25 Broadway
New York, NY 10004

Church Street Station
90 Church Street
New York, NY 10007

Empire State Station
350 Fifth Avenue
New York, NY 10001

F.D.R. Station
909 Third Avenue
New York, NY 10022

Grand Central Station
45th St. & Lexington
New York, NY 10017

Madison Square Station
149 East 23rd Street
New York, NY 10010

New York General P.O.
33rd and 8th Avenue
New York, NY 10001

Rockefeller Center
610 Fifth Avenue
New York, NY 10020

Times Square Station
340 West 42nd Street
New York, NY 10036

Main & Hunt Streets
Oneonta, NY 13820

Franklin & S. Main Sts.
Pearl River, NY 10965

10 Miller Street
Plattsburgh, NY 12901

Branch Office
407 East Main Street
Port Jefferson, NY 11777

55 Mansion Street
Poughkeepsie, NY 12601

1335 Jefferson Road
Rochester, NY 14692

250 Merrick Road
Rockville Centre,
NY 11570

29 Jay Street
Schenectady, NY 12305

25 Route 11
Smithtown, NY 11787

550 Manor Road
Staten Island, NY 10314

New Springville Station
2843 Richmond Ave.
Staten Island, NY 10314

5640 East Taft Road
Syracuse, NY 13220

10 Broad Street
Utica, NY 13503

108 Main Street
Warwick, NY 10990

100 Fisher Avenue
White Plains, NY 10602

78-81 Main Street
Yonkers, NY 10701

North Carolina
West Asheville Station
1300 Patton Avenue
Asheville, NC 28806

Eastway Station
3065 Eastway Drive
Charlotte, NC 28205

301 Green Street
Fayetteville, NC 28302

Four Seasons Station
Four Seasons Town Centre
High Point Road
Greensboro, NC 27427

310 New Bern Avenue
Raleigh, NC 27611

North Dakota
657 2nd Avenue North
Fargo, ND 58102

Ohio
675 Wolf Ledges Pkwy.
Akron, OH 44309

2650 Cleveland Street
Canton, OH 44701

Fountain Square Station
5th & Walnut Street
Cincinnati, OH 45202

301 W. Prospect Ave.
Cleveland, OH 44101

850 Twin Rivers Drive
Columbus, OH 43216

1111 East 5th Street
Dayton, OH 45401

105 Court Street
Hamilton, OH 45011

200 North Diamond St.
Mansfield, OH 44901

200 North 4th Street
Steubenville, OH 43952

435 S. St. Clair Street
Toledo, OH 43601

99 South Walnut Street
Youngstown, OH 44503

Oklahoma
101 East First
Edmond, OK 73034

115 West Broadway
Enid, OK 73701

102 South 5th
Lawton, OK 73501

525 West Okmulgee
Muskogee, OK 74401

129 West Gray
Norman, OK 73069

320 SW 5th Street
Oklahoma City,
OK 73125

116 East 9th Street
Shawnee, OK 74801

333 West 4th
Tulsa, OK 74101

12 South 5th
Yukon, OK 73099

Oregon
520 Willamette Street
Eugene, OR 97401

751 N.W. Hoyt
Portland, OR 97208

1050 25th Street S.W.
Salem, OR 97301

Pennsylvania
442-456 Hamilton St.
Allentown, PA 18101

535 Wood Street
Bethlehem, PA 18016

115 Boylston Street
Bradford, PA 16701

229 Beaver Drive
Du Bois, PA 15801

Griswold Plaza
Erie, PA 16501

115 Buford Avenue
Gettysburg, PA 17325

238 S. Pennsylvania
Greensburg, PA 15601

10th and Markets Sts.
Harrisburg, PA 17105

111 Franklin Street
Johnstown, PA 15901

Downtown Station
48-50 W. Chestnut St.
Lancaster, PA 17603

980 Wheeler Way
Langhorne, PA 19047

Lehigh Valley Branch
Airport Rd. & Route 22
Lehigh Valley, PA 18001

Monroeville Mall Branch
348 Mall Circle Drive
Monroeville, PA 15146

1 W. Washington Street
Kennedy Square
New Castle, PA 16101

28 East Airy Street
Norristown, PA 19401

B. Free Franklin Station
316 Market Street
Philadelphia, PA 19106

30th & Market Streets
Philadelphia, PA 19104

Penn Center Station
2 Penn Center Plaza
Philadelphia, PA 19102

William Penn Annex
9th & Chestnut Streets
Philadelphia, PA 19107

Castle Shannon Branch
307 Castle Shannon Blvd.
Pittsburgh, PA 15234

Seventh Avenue
& Grant Street
Pittsburgh, PA 15219

McKnight Branch
McKnight & Seibert Rds.
Pittsburgh, PA 15237

59 North 5th Street
Reading, PA 19603

North Washington Ave.
& Linden St.
Scranton, PA 18503

237 South Frazer Street
State College, PA 16801

7th & Ann Streets
Stroudsburg, PA 18360

300 South Main Street
Wilkes Barre, PA 18701

Center City Finance Station
240 West Third Street
Williamsport, PA 17703

200 S. George Street
York, PA 17405

Puerto Rico
General Post Office
18 Roosevelt Avenue
Hate Rey
San Juan, PR 00918

Plaza Las Americas Sta.
San Juan, PR 00938

Rhode Island
320 Thames St.
Newport, RI 02840

24 Corliss Street
Providence, RI 02904

South Carolina
4290 Daley Avenue
Charleston, SC 29402

1601 Assembly Street
Columbia, SC 29201

600 West Washington
Greenville, SC 29602

South Dakota
500 East Boulevard
Rapid City, SD 57701

320 S. 2nd Avenue
Sioux Falls, SD 57101

Tennessee
General Mail Facility
6050 Shallowford Road
Chattanooga, TN 37401

Tom Murray Station
133 Tucker Street
Jackson, TN 38301

530 East Main Street
Johnson City, TN 37601

501 West Main Avenue
Knoxville, TN 37901

Colonial Finance Unit
4695 Southern Avenue
Memphis, TN 38124

Crosstown Finance Unit
1520 Union Avenue
Memphis, TN 38174

555 South Third
Memphis, TN 38101

901 Broadway
Nashville, TN 37202

Texas
2300 South Ross
Amarillo, TX 79105

300 East South Street
Arlington, TX 76010

Downtown Station
300 East 9th
Austin, TX 78701

General Mail Facility
8225 Cross Park Drive
Austin, TX 78710

300 Willow
Beaumont, TX 77704

1535 Los Ebanos
Brownsville, TX 78520

2201 Hilltop Drive
College Station, TX 77840

809 Nueces Bay
Corpus Christi, TX
78408

400 North Ervay Street
Dallas, TX 75221

5300 East Paisano Dr.
El Paso, TX 79910

251 West Lancaster
Fort Worth, TX 76101

401 Franklin Avenue
Houston, TX 77201

411 "L" Avenue
Lubbock, TX 79408

601 East Pecan
McAllen, TX 78501

100 East Wall
Midland, TX 79702

Downtown Station
615 East Houston
San Antonio, TX 78205

10410 Perrin Beitel Road
San Antonio, TX 78284

1411 Wunsche Loop
Spring, TX 77373

2211 North Robinson
Texarkana, TX 75501

221 West Ferguson
Tyler, TX 75702

800 Franklin
Waco, TX 76701

1000 Lamar Street
Wichita Falls, TX 76307

Utah
3680 Pacific Avenue
Ogden, UT 84401

95 West 100 South
Provo, UT 84601

1760 West 2100 South
Salt Lake City, UT 84119

Vermont
204 Main Street
Brattleboro, VT 05301

1 Elmwood Avenue
Burlington, VT 05401

151 West Street
Rutland, VT 05701

Sykes Avenue
White River Junction,
VT 05001

Virginia
111 Sixth Street
Bristol, VA 24201

1155 Seminole Trail
Charlottesville,
VA 22906

1425 Battlefield Blvd., N.
Chesapeake, VA 23320

700 Main Street
Danville, VA 24541

Merrifield Branch
8409 Lee Highway
Fairfax, VA 22116

809 Aberdeen Road
Hampton, VA 23670

300 Odd Fellows Road
Lynchburg, VA 24506

Denbigh Station
14104 Warwick Blvd.
Newport News,
VA 23602

600 Granby Street
Norfolk, VA 23501

Thomas Corner Station
6274 East Virginia
Beach Boulevard
Norfolk, VA 23502

1801 Brook Road
Richmond, VA 23232

419 Rutherford Ave. NE
Roanoke, VA 24022

1430 North Augusta
Staunton, VA 24401

501 Viking Drive
Virginia Beach,
VA 23450

Washington
11 3rd Street N.W.
Auburn, WA 98002

Crossroads Station
15800 N.E. 8th
Bellevue, WA 98008

315 Prospect Street
Bellingham, WA 98225

3102 Hoyt
Everett, WA 98201

3500 West Court
Pasco, WA 99301

424 East 1st Street
Port Angeles, WA 98362

301 Union Street
Seattle, WA 98101

West 904 Riverside
Spokane, WA 99210

1102 A Street
Tacoma, WA 98402

205 West Washington
Yakima, WA 98903

West Virginia
301 North Street
Bluefield, WV 24701

Lee & Dickinson St.
Charleston, WV 25301

500 West Pike Street
Clarksburg, WV 26301

1000 Virginia Avenue, West
Huntington, WV 25704

217 King Street
Martinsburg, WV 25401

Wisconsin
325 East Walnut
Green Bay, WI 54301

3902 Milwaukee Street
Madison, WI 53707

345 West St. Paul Ave.
Milwaukee, WI 53203

235 Forrest Street
Wausau, WI 54401

Wyoming
150 East B Street
Casper, WY 82601

2120 Capitol Avenue
Cheyenne, WY 82001

FOREIGN CENTERS

Australia
Max Stern & Co.
Port Phillip Arcade
234 Flinders Street
Melbourne 3000

France
Theodore Champion
13 Rue Drouot
75009 Paris

**Federal Republic
of Germany**
Hermann W. Sieger
Venusberg 32-34
D-7073
Lorch/Wurttemberg

Great Britain
Harry Allen
Langwood House
Rickmansworth
Herts WD3 1EY

Japan
Japan Philatelic Co., Ltd.
Post Office Box 2
Suginami-Minami
Tokyo 168-91

Netherlands
J.A. Visser
Post Office Box 184
3300 Ad Dordrecht

Sweden
Bo Follin
Frimarkshuset AB
S-793 01 Leksand

Switzerland
De Rosa International S.A.
Av Du Tribunal
Federal 34
CH-1005 Lausanne

31

WE CAME IN PEACE FOR
ALL MANKIND

These words, etched on a
plaque that now sits on
the moon, represent the
spirit of the space program—human-
kind's best instincts brought to life
in the pursuit of a dream.

Twenty years ago—on July 20,
1969—Neil Armstrong made his
small step and ushered in a new era.
By setting foot on the moon, we had
finally achieved a new age in history.
To mark this special anniversary, the
U.S. Postal Service recently issued

a $2.40 Priority Mail-rate stamp depicting astronauts planting the American flag on the moon.

The race is on! The launching of *Sputnik* by the Soviet Union in 1959 set in motion the people and resources required to land a man on the moon within a mere 10 years. The seven original Mercury astronauts—chosen with much fanfare and media attention—were America's space pioneers. When Alan E. Shepard in *Mercury 3* was launched for a brief moment in space and John H. Glenn in *Mercury 6* actually orbited Earth, the United States was firmly on the path to reaching its goal.

"There will certainly be no lack of human pioneers when we have mastered the art of flight...we shall prepare for the brave sky travelers, maps of the celestial bodies—I shall do it for the moon, you, Galileo, for Jupiter."

—LETTER TO GALILEO, Johannes Kepler, 1610

Many of the early "firsts" in space were achieved by the Russians. Yuri Gagarin was the first man in space; *Vostok 3* and *4* were the first craft to fly "in formation" in space; Valentina Tereshkova was the first woman in space; and the *Voskhod 2* mission was the first to feature a walk in space. Not deterred, the Americans raced to catch up and eventually pass the Russians. At some point, the race became one not between Americans and Russians but between man and the constraints of Earth holding him back from the heavens.

Heroic pursuits are not without peril, however, and just three months separated a tragic "first" for both space programs: In January 1967 a fire in the *Apollo* capsule on the launch pad claimed the lives of American astronauts Gus Grissom, Ed White and Roger Chaffee; and in April the Russian spacecraft *Soyuz 1* made a fatal crash landing in Asia.

But this is a story of many more successes than setbacks. The *Mercury* program was followed by the Gemini program, which concentrated on acclimatizing man to work in space—inside and outside the spacecraft. The first American Extra Vehicular Activity (EVA), or walk in space, occurred in June 1965. The Gemini flights were, almost without exception, characterized by successful completion of appointed missions.

cination with the stars and the planets—visible to the eye, but too far away to reach. Of such things are imaginative poems made.

Early on, the moon was associated with various gods and goddesses. Pythagoras (582-500 B.C.) was the first to believe that the moon was a sphere, and Galileo (1564-1642) made detailed drawings of the moon's rough mountains, craters and canyons from his telescopic observations. Johannes Kepler (1571-1630) believed that the moon influenced our

subject to intense heat and cold (he was partially right) and that it was populated by prehistoric lizards (he was wrong).

The moon inspired other science-fictional musings: Cyrano de Bergerac in the 17th century imagined a voyage to a moon settled by lunar giants; Jules Verne's *From the Earth to the Moon* (1865) at least had a scientist as its hero; while H.G. Wells, in 1901, imagined the *First Man on the Moon*. Just one year later, in 1902, Georges Melies produced a motion picture called *A Trip to the Moon*—complete with lots of special effects.

"We had the sky, up there, all speckled with stars, and we used to lay on our backs and look up at them, and discuss about whether they was made, or only just happened."

—HUCKLEBERRY FINN, Mark Twain, 1884

The voyage of *Apollo 11* was the outgrowth of man's continual fas-

tides (he was right), that the moon was

The first breakthrough in developing the technology that would lead to real space travel came about the same time as Wells and Melies were fancifully creating fictional trips. The Russian Konstantin E. Tsiolkovsky designed a rocket that used liquid fuels—hydrogen and oxygen. This technology was the precursor of the propulsion and fuel systems used today. For his work, Tsiolkovsky is called the father of astronautics.

It took World War II and the need for ever more powerful weapons for the German to make another breakthrough—this time it was the V-1 and V-2 rockets, dreaded airborne bombs that were the early relatives to today's rockets, which are used for peaceful exploration. The American space program can truly be characterized as a team effort with leaders who were giants in their field: Robert H. Goddard and Wernher von Braun, the catalyst for the moon program, among others.

And it took another giant—the 36-story-tall *Saturn V* rocket—to launch the *Apollo* program. The *Saturn's* engines produce 7.6 million pounds of thrust and use 30,000 pounds of propellants *per second.* The *Saturn* rocket launched several memorable flights—the Christmas Flight of *Apollo 8* with the crew reading a special Christmas message to the world (#1371); the tense, troubled *Apollo 13* flight, which

THE SECRET SPACE STAMP

Early in the space program, the Mercury *flights captured the nation's interest. It was an exciting time—and unpredictable.*

Prior to America's first orbit of Earth in February 1962, the Postal Service prepared a commemorative stamp. But, not knowing whether the mission would succeed, the Postal Service kept the stamp's existence a secret. Sealed pouches containing the stamps were distributed in the late fall of 1961 to post offices across the country with strict instructions not to open them until permission came from headquarters.

John Glenn's successful journey into space prompted issuance of the stamp, which sold out that day at many

post offices. The Project Mercury *stamp (#1193) pictured a lone* Mercury *capsule hurtling through space —making history for the U.S. and acknowledging man's desire to conquer the unknown.*

UPU
COMMEMORATIVES
LOOK AT MAIL
TRANSPORTATION OF
THE PAST AND
FUTURE

During 1989 the Postal Service is commemorating the 20th Universal Postal Congress by issuing a block of four 25-cent commemorative and a block of four 45-cent airmail stamps that explore mail transportations—past and future. The United States is proudly hosting the Congress in Washington, D.C., the first time in 92 years it has been held in this country.

The designs for these stamps were unveiled at special ceremonies in Berne, Switzerland, headquarters for the Universal Postal Union. The UPU, a specialized agency of the United Nations, is comprised of 169 member nations. It regulates the exchange of mail between nations. The UPU makes it possible for us to affix the proper postage on a letter and send it almost anywhere in the world with the assurance that it will reach its intended recipient in a timely fashion.

These 1989 United States commemoratives develop this theme of

tested man's ability to improvise in space; and the famous moon landing mission of *Apollo 11.*

world, and 600 million people watch as Armstrong, his breathing magnified by the microphone in his

Houston: *"30 seconds."*

Eagle: *"Drifting right. Contact light. Okay, engine stop."*

Houston: *"We copy you down, Eagle."*

Eagle: *"Houston, Tranquillity Base here. The Eagle has landed."*

This transmission on July 20, 1969, signalled the world that the race was won—man had reached the moon. Then the fuzzy, black-and-white television pictures began transmitting from a camera mounted beside the *Eagle's* exit ladder. Astronaut Neil Armstrong comes flickering into view on living room consoles and giant screens set up throughout the

space helmet, gingerly tests his footing, takes his "small step" and then presses his boot firmly into lunar soil. Buzz Aldrin joins him on the moon's surface while Michael Collins in the *Columbia* orbits above them.

The poetry over, the astronauts get to work setting up a TV camera, flag, a laser reflector, a solar wind sheet

transporting mail any-
where and everywhere.
The historical set of
25-cent stamps depicts
various colorful, early-
American modes of
moving the mail—
stagecoach, biplane,
steamboat and auto-
mobile. The futuristic
set of airmail stamps
looks to new worlds
and new modes of car-
rying mail: hypersonic
airliner, space shuttle,
rover vehicle on a space
colony and hovercraft.
Both sets of stamp
designs also are being
issued in imperforate
souvenir sheets. (The
UPU Mint Set, which
the Postal Service is
producing, contains
both blocks of four
stamps and the souve-
nir sheets as well as the
WORLD STAMP EXPO
'89™ commemorative.)

In the unveiling cer-
emony for the futuris-
tic stamps, Associate
Postmaster General
Edward E. Horgan Jr.
noted that "by improv-
ing international com-
munications, the UPU
has made the world a
little smaller and a lot
friendlier." The 20th
Universal Postal Con-
gress commemoratives
represent a glance back
and an exciting look
forward to the vital
contributions of this
international
organization.

From an early rocket launching (#976) to a celebration of man's many space achievements (#1912-1919), the U.S. Postal Service has chronicled the exploration of the final frontier. Issues include the early Mercury *flights, space walks and the* Apollo-Soyuz *spacecraft docking. The history of man in space is colorfully depicted on U.S. stamps.*

Scott #	Description	Issue Date
976	3-cent Fort Bliss	1948
1173	4-cent Echo I—Communications in Space	1960
1193	4-cent Project Mercury	1962
C69	8-cent Robert H. Goddard	1964
1331	5-cent Space-walking Astronaut	1967
1332	5-cent Gemini 4 (#1331-1332: Accomplishments In Space Issue— se-tenant pair)	1967
1371	6-cent Apollo 8	1969
C76	10-cent Moon Landing	1969
1434	8-cent Earth, Sun, Moon	1971
1435	8-cent Lunar Rover & Astronauts (#1434-1435: Space Achievement Decade Issue—se-tenant pair)	1971
1529	10-cent Skylab	1974
1556	10-cent Pioneer/Jupiter	1975
1557	10-cent Mariner 10	1975
1569	10-cent Apollo Soyuz	1975
1570	10-cent Spacecraft (#1569-1570: Apollo Soyuz Space Issue— se-tenant pair)	1975
1759	15-cent Viking Missions to Mars	1978
1912-1919	18-cent Space Achievement Issue (#1912-1919: se-tenant block of eight)	1981
2419	$2.40 20th Anniversary of Moon Landing	1989
C122-125	45-cent Future Mail Transportation	1989

and a sun-powered seismometer. They gather lunar samples—a big hit for years to come at museums throughout the world—and fulfill the mundane tasks of their mission. And then, after blast-off from the moon and rendezvous with *Columbia*, the astronauts head home.

Left on the moon is the descent stage of the lunar module. On it is a plaque that reads: "Here Men from the Planet Earth First Set Foot upon the Moon. July 1969 A.D. We Came in Peace for All Mankind."

The *Apollo* program was a large and event-filled chapter in man's exploration of the heavens. And the book is far from finished... space shuttle flights, space colonies and interplanetary travel are the new goals—stepping stones in man's eternal quest for discovering the new, the unknown.

*"There can be no thought of finishing,
for aiming at the stars, both literally
and figuratively, is the work of
generations, but no matter how much
progress one makes there is always
the thrill of just beginning."*

—Robert H. Goddard, 1922

SPACE MAIL ON THE *CHALLENGER*

As the Space Shuttle Challenger *launched into orbit in August 1983, it carried with it very special philatelic treasures: Space Mail Flight Covers.*

The U.S. Postal Service and the National Aeronautics and Space Administration (NASA) combined to give collectors an opportunity to acquire stamps and cacheted envelopes that had flown in space with the Challenger *crew.*

The $9.35 Express Mail stamp (#1909)—issued at the Kennedy Space Center just days before the launch—proudly pictures an eagle with the moon in the background. The cover's front contains a reproduction of the "patch" design for the flight; the reverse carries NASA's 25th anniversary logo. Cancellations include the dates of the launch and the return to Earth.

The Space Mail Flight Covers hold a special poignancy because the vehicle that carried them exploded in flight less than three years later. The nation still mourns the loss of the crew of the Challenger *in January 1986.*

The world of philately is coming to Washington, D.C., as the U.S. Postal Service sponsors the first international stamp show in its 214-year history.

WORLD STAMP EXPO '89 will take place November 17-20 and November 24-December 3, 1989 during the 20th Congress of the Universal Postal Union at the Washington Convention Center.

Come visit us at WORLD STAMP EXPO '89 and discover a spectacular exhibition, ranging from rare stamps to new issues from around the world. More than 100 foreign postal administrations and 150 stamp dealers will be on hand with items to tempt new and experienced collectors.

EXPO visitors will find stamp collecting information at their fingertips. A special touch-screen computer system will provide complete information on daily show activities, booth and exhibit locations and Postal Service products available at the exposition.

Budding stamp collectors will have their own very special area at WORLD STAMP EXPO '89. Designed for children 16 years of age and younger, the Youth Area will feature a dinosaur theme based on the new Prehistoric Animals stamps issued by the Postal Service. Youngsters will test their skills with philatelic computer games, obtain free starter kits and an international assortment of stamps and receive special tours of the Court of Honor and Post Office of the Future.

Even noncollectors will enjoy seeing the "crown jewels of the stamp kingdom." The elite WORLD STAMP EXPO '89 Court of Honor will include some 250 frames of philately's most spectacular items, including portions of the royal collections of the Prince of Monaco and the Prince of Thurn and Taxis.

First day of issue enthusiasts will have a field day because 11 ceremonies are planned for new U.S. stamp and stationery items during the 14-day show. Several foreign postal administrations, including Canada, the People's Republic of China and the Soviet Union, also plan to hold first day events.

New stamps won't be the only innovations on display at WORLD STAMP EXPO '89. We plan to showcase the latest in retail services and postal technology in the Post Office of the Future. Visitors will get a glimpse of tomorrow in stamp production and mail processing.

From helpful hints for new collectors to specialized advice from philatelic experts, there will be many opportunities to learn more about the world's most popular hobby. An assortment of informative seminars and lectures are scheduled during WORLD STAMP EXPO '89.

On 10 evenings, the Sheraton Washington Hotel will be the site for official WORLD STAMP EXPO '89 auctions, with millions of dollars worth of rare and unusual stamps going to the highest bidders.

Award-winning philatelic collections... stamp dealers and auctioneers with offerings from around the world...educational and entertaining activities for young hobbyists...a look at innovations in automation and stamp technology in the Post Office of the Future... all this awaits you at WORLD STAMP EXPO '89, the stamp celebration of universal proportions.

41

A Club Just for You...
The Collector

- Includes a Commemorative Stamp Club Album that contains illustrations and mounting areas for individual issues
- Advance announcements about *every* commemorative stamp
- Stamps and custom-printed album pages mailed directly to you

A Special Trip through History

The Commemorative Stamp Club provides a convenient, comprehensive and attractive method to collect and save U.S. stamps. Your membership means an exciting trip to the places, people, events and ideals of America's past through commemorative stamps.

And if you're ready for a side trip, you can expand your horizons by choosing to receive definitive stamps, as well as album pages and annual commemorative sets issued in past years.

Other Membership Benefits

You'll receive clear acetate mounts to hold and protect your stamps and a *free* one-year subscription to the *Philatelic Catalog*, a bi-monthly publication with full-color illustrations of all stamps, postal cards, aerogrammes, stamped envelopes and other collectibles available through mail order.

Get Your Ticket
To Collecting Adventure

A no-risk, money-back guarantee assures your satisfaction. If you discontinue your membership within 90 days, simply return the album pages and stamps with a label from one of your shipments, and we'll send you a complete refund; the album is yours to keep. Annual membership in the Commemorative Stamp Club for 1989 costs just $21.95.

To Join

For more detailed information, use the postage-paid request card in this book or write to:

USPS GUIDE
COMMEMORATIVE STAMP CLUB
PHILATELIC SALES DIVISION
UNITED STATES POSTAL SERVICE
POST OFFICE BOX 9983
WASHINGTON DC 20265-9983

1¢ Franklin Types I-V of 1851-57

5

Bust of **5**

Detail of **5, 18, 40** Type I
Has curved, unbroken lines outside labels.
Scrollwork is substantially complete at top, forms little balls at bottom.

Detail of **5A** Type Ib
Lower scrollwork is incomplete, the little balls are not so clear.

Bust of **5**

Detail of **6, 19** Type Ia
Same as Type I at bottom but top ornaments and outer line partly cut away.
Lower scrollwork is complete.

Bust of **5**

Detail of **7, 20** Type II
Lower scrollwork incomplete (lacks little balls and lower plume ornaments).
Side ornaments are complete.

Bust of **5**

Detail of **8, 21** Type III
Outer lines broken in the middle.
Side ornaments are substantially complete.

Detail of **8A, 22** Type IIIa
Outer lines broken top or bottom but not both.

Bust of **5**

Detail of **9, 23** Type IV
Similar to Type II, but outer lines recut top, bottom, or both.

Bust of **5**

Detail of **24** Type V
Similar to Type III of 1851-56 but with side ornaments partly cut away.

3¢ Washington Types I-IIa of 1851-57

10

Bust of **10**

Detail of **10, 11, 25, 41** Type I
There is an outer frame line at top and bottom.

Bust of **10**

Detail of **26** Type II
The outer frame line has been removed at top and bottom. The side frame lines were recut so as to be continuous from the top to the bottom of the plate.

Bust of **10**

Detail of **26a** Type IIa
The side frame lines extend only to the bottom of the stamp design.

5¢ Jefferson Types I-II of 1851-57

12

Bust of **12**

Detail of **12, 27-29** Type I
There are projections on all four sides.

Bust of **12**

Detail of **30-30A** Type II
The projections at top and bottom are partly cut away.

10¢ Washington Types I-V of 1851-57

15

Bust of **15**

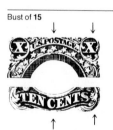

Detail of **13, 31, 43** Type I
The "shells" at the lower corners are practically complete. The outer line below the label is very nearly complete. The outer lines are broken above the middle of the top label and the "X" in each upper corner.

Bust of **15**

Detail of **14, 32** Type II
The design is complete at the top. The outer line at the bottom is broken in the middle. The shells are partly cut away.

Bust of **15**

Detail of **15, 33** Type III
The outer lines are broken above the top label and the "X" numerals. The outer line at the bottom and the shells are partly cut away, as in Type II.

Bust of **15**

Detail of **16, 34** Type IV
The outer lines have been recut at top or bottom or both. Types I, II, III, and IV have complete ornaments at the sides of the stamps and three pearls at each outer edge of the bottom panel.

Bust of **15**

Detail of **35** Type V
(Two typical examples). Side ornaments slightly cut away. Outer lines complete at top except over right "X". Outer lines complete at bottom and shells nearly so.

15¢ Columbus Landing Types I-III of 1869-75

118

Vignette of **118**

Detail of **118** Type I
Picture unframed.

Vignette of **118**

Detail of **119** Type II
Picture framed.

Vignette of **118**

129 Type III. Same as Type I but without fringe of brown shading lines around central vignette.

Comparison of Issue of 1870-71: Printed by the National Bank Note Company. Issued without secret marks (134-141, 145-152, 187) and **Issues of 1873-80: Printed by the Continental and American Bank Note Companies.** Issued with secret marks (156-163, 167-174, 178, 180, 182-184, 186, 188-190, 192-199).

134   135   136   137   138

Detail of **134, 145**

Detail of **136, 147**

Detail of **138, 149**

Detail of **156, 167, 182, 192**
1¢. In the pearl at the left of the numeral "1" there is a small crescent.

Detail of **158, 169, 184, 194**
3¢. The under part of the upper tail of the left ribbon is heavily shaded.

Detail of **160, 171, 196**
7¢. Two small semi-circles are drawn around the ends of the lines which outline the ball in the lower right hand corner.

Detail of **135, 146**

Detail of **157, 168, 178, 180, 183, 193**
2¢. Under the scroll at the left of "U.S." there is a small diagonal line. This mark seldom shows clearly.

Detail of **137, 148**

Detail of **159, 170, 186, 195**
6¢. The first four vertical lines of the shading in the lower part of the left ribbon have been strengthened.

139   140   141   143   206   207

Detail of **139, 150, 187**

Detail of **161, 172, 188, 197**
10¢. There is a small semi-circle in the scroll at the right end of the upper label.

Detail of **206**
1¢. Upper vertical lines have been deepened, creating a solid effect in parts of background. Upper arabesques shaded.

Detail of **140, 151**

Detail of **162, 173, 198**
12¢. The balls of the figure "2" are crescent-shaped.

Detail of **207**
3¢. Shading at sides of central oval is half its previous width. A short horizontal dash has been cut below the "TS" of "CENTS".

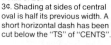

Detail of **141, 152**

Detail of **163, 174, 189, 199**
15¢. In the lower part of the triangle in the upper left corner, two lines have been made heavier, forming a "V". This mark can be found on some of the Continental and American (1879) printings, but not all stamps show it.

208   209

Detail of **208**
6¢. Has three vertical lines instead of four between the edge of the panel and the outside of the stamp.

Detail of **143, 154, 165, 176**

Detail of **190**, 30¢. In the "S" of "CENTS," the vertical spike across the middle section of the letter has been broadened.

Detail of **209**
10¢. Has four vertical lines instead of five between left side of oval and edge of the shield. Horizontal lines in lower part of background strengthened.

**2¢ Washington
Types I-III of 1894-1898**

248

Triangle of **248-250, 265**
Type I
Horizontal lines of uniform
thickness run across the triangle.

Triangle of **251, 266** Type II
Horizontal lines cross the
triangle, but are thinner within
than without.

Triangle of **252, 267, 279B-
279Be** Type III
The horizontal lines do not cross
the double frame lines of the
triangle.

$1 Perry Types I-II of 1894

261

Detail of **261, 276** Type I
The circles enclosing $1 are
broken.

Detail of **261A, 276A** Type II
The circles enclosing $1 are
complete.

**10¢ Webster
Types I-II of 1898**

282C

Detail of **282C** Type I
The tips of the foliate ornaments
do not impinge on the white
curved line below "TEN CENTS."

Detail of **283** Type II
The lips of the ornaments break
the curved line below the "E" of
"TEN" and the "T" of "CENTS."

**3¢ Washington Types I-IV
of 1908-19**

333

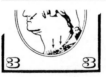

Detail of **333, 345, 359, 376,
389, 394, 426, 445, 456,
464, 483, 493, 501-01b** Type I
Top line of toga rope is weak
and rope shading lines are thin.
Fifth line from left is missing.
Line between lips is thin.

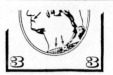

Detail of **484, 494, 502,
541** Type II
Top line of toga rope is strong
and rope shading lines are heavy
and complete. Line between lips
is heavy.

Detail of **529** Type III
Top row of toga rope is strong
but fifth shading line is missing
as in Type I. Toga button center
shading line consists of two
dashes, central dot. "P", "O" of
"POSTAGE" are separated by
line of color.

Detail of **530, 535** Type IV
Toga rope shading lines are
complete. Second, fourth toga
button shading lines are broken
in middle; third line is continuous,
with dot in center. "P", "O" of
"POSTAGE" are joined.

2¢ Washington Types I-VII of 1912-21

406

Detail of **406-406a, 411, 413, 425-25e, 442, 444, 449, 453, 461, 463-63a, 482, 499-99f** Type I
One shading line in first curve of ribbon above left "2" and one in second curve of ribbon above right "2". Toga button has only a faint outline. Top line of toga rope, from button to front of the throat, is very faint. Shading lines of face end in front of ear with little or no joining to form lock of hair.

Detail of **482a, 500** Type Ia
Similar to Type I but all lines are stronger.

Detail of **454, 487, 491, 539** Type II
Shading lines in ribbons as in Type I. Toga button, rope and rope shading lines are heavy. Shading lines of face at lock of hair end in strong vertical curved line.

Detail of **450, 455, 488, 492, 540, 546** Type III
Two lines of shading in curves of ribbons.

Detail of **526, 532** Type IV
Top line of toga rope is broken. Toga button shading lines form "DID". Line of color in left "2" is very thin and usually broken.

Detail of **527, 533** Type V
Top line of toga is complete. Toga button has five vertical shading lines. Line of color in left "2" is very thin and usually broken. Nose shading dots are as shown.

Detail of **528, 534** Type Va
Same as Type V except third row from bottom of nose shading dots has four dots instead of six. Overall height of design is 1/3 mm shorter than Type V.

Detail of **528A, 534A** Type VI
Generally same as Type V except line of color in left "2" is very heavy.

Detail of **528B, 534B** Type VII
Line of color in left "2" is continuous, clearly defined and heavier than in Type V or Va but not as heavy as Type VI. An additional vertical row of dots has been added to upper lip. Numerous additional dots appear in hair at top of head.

2¢ Washington Types I-II of 1923-29

599

Detail of **599, 634** Type I
No heavy hair lines at top center of head.

Detail of **599A, 634A** Type II
Three heavy hair lines at top center of head.

COMMEMORATIVE AND DEFINITIVE STAMPS

1847-1875

1   2   3   4

5   11

12   14   17   30   37   38

39

		Un	U
	Issues of 1847,		
	Printed by Rawdon, Wright, Hatch & Edson,		
	Imperf., July 1, Unwmkd.	Un	U
1	5¢ Benjamin Franklin	4,000.00	500.00
2	10¢ George		
	Washington	*17,500.00*	1,400.00

Issues of 1875,
Reproductions of 1 & 2

3	5¢ Franklin	850.00	—
4	10¢ Washington	1,000.00	—

Reproductions. The letters R. W. H. & E. at the bottom of each stamp are less distinct on the reproductions than on the originals.

5¢. On the original, the left side of the white shirt frill touches the oval on a level with the top of the "F" of "Five." On the reproduction, it touches the oval about on a level with the top of the figure "5."

10¢. On the reproduction, line of coat at left points to right of "X" and line of coat at right points to center of "S" of CENTS. On the original, line of coat points to "T" of TEN and between "T" and "S" of CENTS.

On the reproduction, the eyes have a sleepy look, the line of the mouth is straighter and in the curl of hair near the left cheek is a strong black dot, while the original has only a faint one.

Issues of 1851-56,
Printed by Toppan, Carpenter,
Casilear & Co., Imperf.

5	1¢ Franklin, type I	200,000.00	17,500.00
5A	1¢ Same, type Ib	7,500.00	2,500.00
	#6-9: Franklin (5)		
6	1¢ dark blue, type Ia	20,000.00	6,500.00
7	1¢ blue, type II	450.00	85.00
8	1¢ blue, type III	5,500.00	1,500.00
8A	1¢ pale blue, type IIIA	2,000.00	600.00
9	1¢ blue, type IV	300.00	75.00
10	3¢ orange brown		
	Washington, type I (11)	1,000.00	40.00
11	3¢ Washington, type I	130.00	7.00
12	5¢ Jefferson, type I	10,000.00	1,300.00
13	10¢ green		
	Washington, type I (15)	9,000.00	700.00
14	10¢ green, type II (15)	2,000.00	300.00
15	10¢ Washington, type III	2,000.00	300.00
16	10¢ green, type IV (15)	11,500.00	1,500.00
17	12¢ Washington	2,000.00	250.00

Issues of 1857-61, Perf. 15

	#18-24: Franklin (5)		
18	1¢ blue, type I	800.00	375.00
19	1¢ blue, type Ia	10,000.00	2,500.00
20	1¢ blue, type II	425.00	150.00
21	1¢ blue, type III	4,500.00	1,400.00
22	1¢ blue, type IIIa	700.00	250.00
23	1¢ blue, type IV	1,850.00	300.00
24	1¢ blue, type V	110.00	22.50

		Un	U
	#25-26a: Washington (11)		
25	3¢ rose, type I	650.00	27.50
26	3¢ dull red, type II	45.00	2.75
26a	3¢ dull red, type IIa	110.00	20.00
	#27-29: Jefferson (12)		
27	5¢ brick red, type I	*8,500.00*	800.00
28	5¢ red brown, type I	1,350.00	250.00
28A	5¢ Indian red, type I	*10,000.00*	2,000.00
29	5¢ brown, type I	750.00	200.00
30	5¢ Jefferson, type II	750.00	900.00
30A	5¢ orange brown		
	Jefferson, type II (30)	450.00	175.00
	#31-35: Washington (15)		
31	10¢ green, type I	5,250.00	525.00
32	10¢ green, type II	1,750.00	185.00
33	10¢ green, type III	1,750.00	185.00
34	10¢ green, type IV	*17,500.00*	1,750.00
35	10¢ green, type V	175.00	50.00
36	12¢ blk. Washington (17)	325.00	75.00
37	24¢ Washington	600.00	235.00
38	30¢ Franklin	775.00	300.00
39	90¢ Washington	1,250.00	*3,500.00*
	90¢ Same, with pen cancel		1,000.00

Note: Beware of forged cancellations of #39. Genuine cancellations are rare.

Issues of 1875,
Government Reprints, Printed by the
Continental Bank Note Co.,
White Paper, Without Gum, Perf. 12

40	1¢ bright blue Franklin (5)	*500.00*	
41	3¢ scarlet Washington (11)	*2,500.00*	
42	5¢ orange brown		
	Jefferson (30)	*1,000.00*	
43	10¢ blue green		
	Washington (15)	*2,000.00*	
44	12¢ greenish black		
	Washington (17)	*2,250.00*	
45	24¢ blackish violet		
	Washington (37)	*2,500.00*	
46	30¢ yellow orange		
	Franklin (38)	*2,500.00*	
47	90¢ deep blue		
	Washington (39)	*3,500.00*	
48-54 not assigned			

Following the outbreak of the Civil War, the U.S. Government demonetized all previous issues.

Issues of 1861,
Printed by the National Bank Note Co.,
Thin, Semi-Transparent
Paper, Perf. 12

		Un	U
55	1¢ Franklin	*20,000.00*	
56	3¢ Washington	500.00	
57	5¢ Jefferson	*14,000.00*	
58	10¢ Washington	*6,000.00*	
59	12¢ Washington	*40,000.00*	
60	24¢ Washington	*6,500.00*	
61	30¢ Franklin	*17,500.00*	
62	90¢ Washington	*22,500.00*	
62B	10¢ dark green		
	Washington (58)	*6,000.00*	450.00

#55-62 were not used for postage and do not exist in a canceled state. Paper of the following issues is more opaque.

Issues of 1861-62

63	1¢ blue Franklin (55)	125.00	15.00
64	3¢ pink Washington (56)	4,000.00	300.00
65	3¢ rose Washington (56)	65.00	1.00
66	3¢ lake Washington (56)	1,650.00	
67	5¢ buff Jefferson (57)	5,000.00	375.00
68	10¢ yellow green		
	Washington (58)	250.00	30.00
69	12¢ black		
	Washington (59)	475.00	55.00
70	24¢ red lilac		
	Washington (60)	575.00	80.00
71	30¢ orange Franklin (61)	475.00	70.00
72	90¢ blue		
	Washington (62)	1,300.00	250.00

Issues of 1861-66

73	2¢ Andrew Jackson	110.00	22.50
74	3¢ scarlet		
	Washington (56)	*4,500.00*	
75	5¢ red brown		
	Jefferson (57)	1,300.00	225.00
76	5¢ brown Jefferson (57)	325.00	52.50
77	15¢ Abraham Lincoln	500.00	67.50
78	24¢ lilac Washington (60)	275.00	50.00

#74 was not regularly issued.

Grills on U.S. Stamps

Between 1867 and 1870, postage stamps were embossed with grills to prevent re-use of canceled stamps. The pyramid-shaped grills absorbed cancellation ink, making it virtually impossible to remove a postmark chemically.

Issues of 1867,

With Grills		Un	U
Grills A, B, C: Points Up			
A. Grill Covers Entire Stamp			
79	3¢ rose Washington (56)	1,750.00	425.00
80	5¢ brown Jefferson (57)	*40,000.00*	
81	30¢ orange Franklin (61)		*32,500.00*
B. Grill about 18 x 15 mm.			
82	3¢ rose Washington (56)		*45,000.00*
C. Grill about 13 x 16 mm.			
83	3¢ rose Washington (56)	1,750.00	400.00
Grills, D, Z, E, F: Points Down			
D. Grill about 12 x 14 mm.			
84	2¢ black Jackson (73)	3,500.00	1,000.00
85	3¢ rose Washington (56)	1,500.00	450.00
Z. Grill about 11 x 14 mm.			
85A	1¢ blue Franklin (55)		
85B	2¢ black Jackson (73)	1,300.00	350.00
85C	3¢ rose Washington (56)	4,000.00	950.00
85D	10¢ grn. Washington (58)		25,000.00
85E	12¢ blk. Washington (59)	1,650.00	575.00
85F	15¢ black Lincoln (77)		
E. Grill about 11 x 13 mm.			
86	1¢ blue Franklin (55)	800.00	250.00
87	2¢ black Jackson (73)	350.00	70.00
88	3¢ rose Washington (56)	250.00	10.00
89	10¢ grn. Washington (68)	1,300.00	175.00
90	12¢ blk. Washington (69)	1,500.00	190.00
91	15¢ black Lincoln (77)	3,250.00	450.00
F. Grill about 9 x 13 mm.			
92	1¢ blue Franklin (55)	350.00	100.00
93	2¢ black Jackson (73)	135.00	25.00
94	3¢ red Washington (56)	95.00	2.50
95	5¢ brown Jefferson (57)	900.00	225.00
96	10¢ yellow green		
	Washington (58)	700.00	110.00
97	12¢ blk. Washington (59)	700.00	120.00
98	15¢ black Lincoln (77)	700.00	135.00
99	24¢ gray lilac		
	Washington (60)	1,350.00	475.00
100	30¢ orange Franklin (61)	1,500.00	375.00
101	90¢ bl. Washington (62)	4,400.00	950.00

A Reminder: Beginning with this edition, catalog values for all stamps listed reflect (as accurately as possible) actual retail values as found in the marketplace.

55 56 57 58 59

60 61 62 73 77

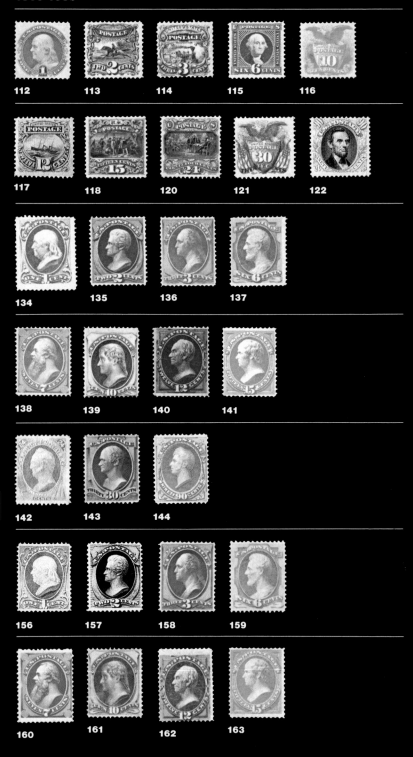

112   113   114   115   116

117   118   120   121   122

134   135   136   137

138   139   140   141

142   143   144

156   157   158   159

160   161   162   163

54

	Issues of 1875, Reissue of 1861-66 Issue, Without Grill, Perf. 12	Un	U
102	1¢ blue Franklin (55)	*500.00*	*800.00*
103	2¢ black Jackson (73)	*2,500.00*	*4,000.00*
104	3¢ brown red		
	Washington (56)	*3,250.00*	*4,250.00*
105	5¢ brown Jefferson (57)	*1,800.00*	*2,250.00*
106	10¢ grn. Washington (58)	*2,100.00*	*3,750.00*
107	12¢ blk. Washington (59)	*3,000.00*	*4,500.00*
108	15¢ black Lincoln (77)	*3,000.00*	*4,750.00*
109	24¢ deep violet		
	Washington (60)	*4,000.00*	*6,000.00*
110	30¢ brownish orange		
	Franklin (61)	*4,500.00*	*7,000.00*
111	90¢ bl. Washington (62)	*5,750.00*	*18,500.00*

	Issues of 1869, With Grill Measuring 9½ x 9 mm.		
112	1¢ Franklin	225.00	60.00
113	2¢ Post Rider	160.00	25.00
114	3¢ Locomotive	135.00	5.50
115	6¢ Washington	775.00	100.00
116	10¢ Shield and Eagle	850.00	95.00
117	12¢ S. S. Adriatic	750.00	90.00
118	15¢ Columbus		
	Landing, type I	1,750.00	300.00
119	15¢ brown and blue		
	Columbus Landing,		
	type II (118)	850.00	150.00
119b	Center inverted	*145,000.00*	*17,500.00*
120	24¢ Declaration		
	of Independence	2,500.00	450.00
120b	Center inverted	*125,000.00*	*16,500.00*
121	30¢ Shield,		
	Eagle and Flags	2,250.00	225.00
121b	Flags inverted	*120,000.00*	*45,000.00*
122	90¢ Lincoln	7,000.00	1,200.00

	Issues of 1875, Reissue of 1869 Issue, Without Grill, Hard, White Paper		
123	1¢ buff (112)	325.00	225.00
124	2¢ brown (113)	375.00	325.00
125	3¢ blue (114)	2,750.00	*10,000*
126	6¢ blue (115)	850.00	550.00
127	10¢ yellow (116)	1,400.00	1,200.00
128	12¢ green (117)	1,500.00	1,200.00
129	15¢ brown and blue,		
	type III (118)	1,300.00	550.00
130	24¢ grn. & vio. (120)	1,250.00	550.00
131	30¢ bl. & car. (121)	1,750.00	1,000.00
132	90¢ car. & blk. (122)	5,500.00	*6,000.00*

	Issue of 1880, Reissue of 1869 Issue, Soft, Porous Paper	Un	U
133	1¢ buff (112)	200.00	135.00

	Issues of 1870-71, With Grill, White Wove Paper, No Secret Marks		
134	1¢ Franklin	500.00	57.50
135	2¢ Jackson	350.00	37.50
136	3¢ Washington	285.00	10.00
137	6¢ Lincoln	1,650.00	250.00
138	7¢ Edwin M. Stanton	1,100.00	225.00
139	10¢ Jefferson	1,450.00	400.00
140	12¢ Henry Clay	*12,000.00*	1,500.00
141	15¢ Daniel Webster	1,850.00	700.00
142	24¢ Gen. Winfield Scott		*9,500.00*
143	30¢ Alexander		
	Hamilton	4,500.00	825.00
144	90¢ Commodore Perry	6,000.00	750.00

It is generally accepted as fact that the Continental Bank Note Co. printed and delivered a quantity of 24¢ stamps. They are impossible to distinguish from those printed by the National Bank Note Co.

	Without Grill, White Wove Paper, No Secret Marks		
145	1¢ ultra. Franklin (134)	165.00	6.50
146	2¢ red brown		
	Jackson (135)	57.50	4.50
147	3¢ grn. Washington (136)	120.00	.50
148	6¢ carmine Lincoln (137)	225.00	12.00
149	7¢ verm. Stanton (138)	325.00	50.00
150	10¢ brown Jefferson (139)	225.00	12.00
151	12¢ dull violet Clay (140)	525.00	60.00
152	15¢ bright orange		
	Webster (141)	500.00	60.00
153	24¢ purple Scott (142)	600.00	80.00
154	30¢ black Hamilton (143)	1,000.00	95.00
155	90¢ carmine Perry (144)	1,350.00	175.00

	Issues of 1873, Without Grill, White Wove Paper, Thin to Thick, Secret Marks		
156	1¢ Franklin	55.00	1.75
157	2¢ Jackson	150.00	7.00
158	3¢ Washington	45.00	.15
159	6¢ Lincoln	200.00	9.00
160	7¢ Stanton	400.00	55.00
161	10¢ Jefferson	225.00	10.00
162	12¢ Clay	600.00	65.00
163	15¢ Webster	575.00	60.00
164	not assigned		
165	30¢ Hamilton	650.00	60.00
166	90¢ Perry	1,350.00	185.00

Issues of 1875,
Special Printing,
Hard, White Wove Paper, Without Gum,
Secret Marks, Perf. 12   Un   U

Although perforated, these stamps were usually cut apart with scissors. As a result, the perforations are often much mutilated and the design is frequently damaged.

		Un	U
167	1¢ ultra. Franklin (156)	7,500.00	–
168	2¢ dark brown		
	Jackson (157)	3,500.00	–
169	3¢ blue green		
	Washington (158)	9,500.00	–
170	6¢ dull rose Lincoln		
	(159)	8,500.00	–
171	7¢ reddish vermilion		
	Stanton (160)	2,100.00	–
172	10¢ pale brown		
	Jefferson (161)	7,750.00	–
173	12¢ dark violet		
	Clay (162)	2,750.00	–
174	15¢ bright orange		
	Webster (163)	7,750.00	–
175	24¢ dull pur. Scott (142)	1,850.00	–
176	30¢ greenish black		
	Hamilton (143)	7,000.00	–
177	90¢ vio. car. Perry, (144)	7,000.00	–

Yellowish Wove Paper

178	2¢ vermilion		
	Jackson (157), June	160.00	5.00
179	5¢ Zachary Taylor, June	175.00	9.00

Special Printing, Hard, White Wove Paper,
Without Gum

180	2¢ carmine vermilion		
	Jackson (157)	19,000.00	–
181	5¢ br. bl. Taylor (179)	32,500.00	–

Issues of 1879,
Printed by the American Bank Note Co.,
Soft, Porous Paper, Thin to Thick

182	1¢ dark ultramarine		
	Franklin (156)	120.00	1.20
183	2¢ verm. Jackson (157)	55.00	1.20
184	3¢ gr. Washington (158)	42.50	.10
185	5¢ blue Taylor (179)	225.00	7.50
186	6¢ pink Lincoln (159)	450.00	12.00
187	10¢ brown Jefferson (139)		
	(no secret mark)	750.00	14.00
188	10¢ brown Jefferson (161)		
	(with secret mark)	475.00	15.00
189	15¢ red orange		
	Webster (163)	165.00	14.00
190	30¢ full blk. Hamilton, (143)	475.00	30.00
191	90¢ carmine Perry (144)	1,000.00	150.00

Issues of 1880,
Special Printing, Printed by the American
Bank Note Co., Soft, Porous Paper,
Without Gum   Un   U

		Un	U
192	1¢ dark ultramarine		
	Franklin (156)	10,000.00	–
193	2¢ black brown		
	Jackson (157)	6,500.00	–
194	3¢ blue green		
	Washington (158)	15,000.00	–
195	6¢ dull rose Lincoln		
	(159)	10,500.00	–
196	7¢ scarlet vermilion		
	Stanton (160)	2,100.00	–
197	10¢ deep brown		
	Jefferson (161)	9,750.00	–
198	12¢ blackish purple		
	Clay (162)	4,500.00	–
199	15¢ orange		
	Webster (163)	9,250.00	–
200	24¢ dk. vio. Scott (142)	3,000.00	–
201	30¢ greenish black		
	Hamilton (143)	7,500.00	–
202	90¢ dull carmine		
	Perry (144)	8,500.00	–
203	2¢ scarlet vermilion		
	Jackson (157)	18,000.00	–
204	5¢ deep blue		
	Taylor (179)	32,500.00	–

Issues of 1882

205	5¢ yellow brown		
	Garfield, Apr. 10	120.00	4.00

Special Printing, Soft, Porous Paper,
Without Gum

205C	5¢ gray brown (205)	18,500.00	–

Issues of 1881-82,
Designs of 1873 Re-engraved

206	1¢ Franklin, Aug. 1881	32.50	.40
207	3¢ Washington,		
	July 16, 1881	40.00	.12
208	6¢ Lincoln, June 1882	225.00	45.00
209	10¢ Jefferson, Apr. 1882	75.00	2.50

Issues of 1883

210	2¢ Washington, Oct. 1	32.50	.08
211	4¢ Jackson, Oct. 1	140.00	7.50

Special Printing, Soft, Porous Paper

211B	2¢ pale red brown		
	Washington (210)	750.00	–
211D	4¢ deep blue green		
	Jackson (211) no gum	15,000.00	–

179   205   206   207   208

209   210   211   212

219   220   221   222   223   224

225   226   227   228   229

Issues of 1887	Un	U
212 1¢ Franklin, June	60.00	.65
213 2¢ green		
Washington (210), Sept. 10	22.50	.08
214 3¢ vermilion		

Issues of 1890-93	Un	U
219 1¢ Franklin,		
Feb. 22, 1890	18.50	.10
219D 2¢ lake Washington		
(220) Feb. 22, 1890	150.00	.45

230

231

232

233

234

235

236

237

238

239

240

241

242

243

244

245

	1893 continued	Un	U	PB	#	FDC	Q
	Columbian Exposition Issue, Printed by the American Bank Note Co., Jan. 2 (8¢ March), Perf. 12						
230	1¢ Columbus Sights Land	17.50	.25	350.00	(6)	3,500.00	449,195,550
231	2¢ Landing of Columbus	16.00	.06	300.00	(6)	2,600.00	1,464,588,750
232	3¢ The Santa Maria	38.50	12.50	650.00	(6)	6,000.00	11,501,250
233	4¢ ultramarine Fleet of Columbus	55.00	5.00	950.00	(6)	6,000.00	19,181,550
233a	4¢ blue (error) (233)	8,000.00	3,250.00				
234	5¢ Columbus Seeking Aid	62.50	6.00	1,350.00	(6)	6,250.00	35,248,250
235	6¢ Columbus at Barcelona	55.00	16.50	1,050.00	(6)	6,750.00	4,707,550
236	8¢ Columbus Restored to Favor	45.00	7.00	650.00	(6)		10,656,550
237	10¢ Columbus						
	Presenting Indians	90.00	5.00	3,000.00	(6)	7,500.00	16,516,950
238	5¢ Columbus						
	Announcing His Discovery	150.00	45.00	4,750.00	(6)		1,576,950
239	30¢ Columbus at La Rabida	210.00	65.00	7,000.00	(6)		617,250
240	50¢ Recall of Columbus	300.00	110.00	9,500.00	(6)		243,750
241	$1 Isabella						
	Pledging Her Jewels	1,050.00	475.00	20,000.00	(6)		55,050
242	$2 Columbus in Chains	1,150.00	400.00	22,000.00	(6)	18,000.00	45,550
243	$3 Columbus						
	Describing His Third Voyage	1,950.00	700.00	45,000.00	(6)		27,650
244	$4 Isabella and Columbus	2,750.00	1,000.00	90,000.00	(6)		26,350
245	$5 Portrait of Columbus	3,000.00	1,300.00	100,000.00	(6)		27,350

RE-CREATION OF COLUMBUS' VOYAGE PLANNED

October 12, 1992 will mark the 500-year anniversary of the arrival of Columbus in America (#230-245). To commemorate the event, Spain plans to re-create the voyage with replicas of the historic ships, which already are under construction. Among the crew will be Cristobal Colon the 18th, a Spanish naval lieutenant named for his famous ancestor.

Bureau Issues Starting in 1894, the Bureau of Engraving and Printing at Washington has produced all U.S. postage stamps except #909-921, 1335, 1355, 1410-1418, 1789, 1804, 1825, 1833, 2023, 2038, 2065-66, 2073, 2080, 2087, 2091, 2093, 2102, 2110, 2137-41, 2153, 2159-64, 2167, 2203-04, 2210-11, 2220-23, 2240-43, 2250, 2283, 2337-39, 2343-44, 2369, 2371-75, 2377, 2386-89, 2395-98.

	Issues of 1894, Perf. 12, Unwmkd.	Un	U	PB	#
246	1¢ Franklin, Oct.	15.00	2.00	300.00	(6)
247	1¢ blue Franklin (246)	37.50	.85	600.00	(6)
248	2¢ pink Washington, type I, Oct.	17.50	2.00	200.00	(6)
	#249-252: Washington (248)				
249	2¢ carmine lake, type I	85.00	.95	1,250.00	(6)
250	2¢ carmine, type I	14.00	.15	300.00	(6)
251	2¢ carmine, type II	110.00	1.50	2,250.00	(6)
252	2¢ carmine, type III	70.00	2.00	1,350.00	(6)
253	3¢ Jackson, Sept.	55.00	4.25	1,000.00	(6)
254	4¢ Lincoln, Sept.	60.00	1.75	1,250.00	(6)
255	5¢ Grant, Sept.	52.50	2.50	875.00	(6)
256	6¢ Garfield, July	95.00	12.00	1,500.00	(6)
257	8¢ Sherman, Mar.	80.00	8.00	1,100.00	(6)
258	10¢ Webster, Sept.	115.00	5.00	2,400.00	(6)
259	15¢ Clay, Oct.	175.00	30.00	3,750.00	(6)
260	50¢ Jefferson, Nov.	225.00	50.00	6,000.00	(6)
261	$1 Perry, type I, Nov.	550.00	160.00	*15,000.00*	(6)
261A	$1 black Perry, type II (261),				
	Nov.	1,200.00	325.00	*25,000.00*	(6)
262	$2 James Madison, Dec.	1,400.00	400.00	*35,000.00*	(6)
263	$5 John Marshall, Dec.	2,250.00	750.00	*15,000.00*	(3)
	Issues of 1895, Wmkd. (191)				
264	1¢ blue Franklin (246), Apr.	3.50	.10	185.00	(6)
	#265-267: Washington (248)				
265	2¢ carmine Washington,				
	type I, May 1	15.00	.40	350.00	(6)
266	2¢ carmine, type II	13.00	1.75	325.00	(6)
267	2¢ carmine, type III	3.00	.05	135.00	(6)
268	3¢ purple Jackson (253), Oct.	22.50	.65	575.00	(6)
269	4¢ dark brown				
	Lincoln (254), June	34.00	.75	600.00	(6)
270	5¢ chocolate				
	Grant (255), June 11	22.50	1.20	600.00	(6)
271	6¢ dull brown				
	Garfield (256), Aug.	42.50	2.50	1,100.00	(6)
272	8¢ violet brown				
	Sherman (257), July	30.00	.65	700.00	(6)
273	10¢ dark green				
	Webster (258), June	40.00	.80	1,150.00	(6)
274	15¢ dark blue Clay (259), Sept.	110.00	5.50	3,000.00	(6)
275	50¢ orange Jefferson (260), Nov.	160.00	14.00	6,000.00	(6)
276	$1 black Perry, type I (261), Aug.	375.00	45.00	*10,000.00*	(6)
276A	$1 black Perry, type II (261)	825.00	92.50	*20,000.00*	(6)
277	$2 bright blue				
	Madison (262), Aug.	600.00	200.00	*18,500.00*	(6)
278	$5 dark green				
	Marshall (263), Aug.	2,000.00	425.00	*60,000.00*	(6)

246 248 253 254 255 256

257 258 259 260 261 262

263

USPS

282C   **283**

285   **286**   **287**

288   **289**   **290**

291   **292**   **293**

294   **295**   **296**

297   **298**   **299**

	Issues of 1898-1900, Perf. 12, Wmkd. (191) (279Be issued in 1900, rest in 1898)	Un	U	PB	#	FDC	Q
279	1¢ deep green Franklin (246), Jan.	6.00	.06	175.00	(6)		
279B	2¢ red Washington, type III (248)	5.50	.05	160.00	(6)		
279Be	Booklet pane of 6, Apr. 16, 1900	350.00	200.00				
280	4¢ rose brown Lincoln (254), Oct.	20.00	.45	650.00	(6)		
281	5¢ dark blue Grant (255), Mar.	22.50	.40	650.00	(6)		
282	6¢ lake Garfield (256), Dec.	35.00	1.40	900.00	(6)		
282C	10¢ Webster, type I, Nov.	100.00	1.20	2,500.00	(6)		
283	10¢ Webster, type II	60.00	1.00	1,500.00	(6)		
284	15¢ olive green Clay (259), Nov.	85.00	4.50	2,250.00	(6)		
	Trans-Mississippi Exposition Issue, June 17						
285	1¢ Marquette on the Mississippi	20.00	3.75	325.00	(6)	4,500.00	70,993,400
286	2¢ Farming in the West	17.50	1.00	300.00	(6)	4,000.00	159,720,800
287	4¢ Indian Hunting Buffalo	100.00	16.00	1,700.00	(6)		4,924,500
288	5¢ Fremont						
	on the Rocky Mountains	87.50	14.00	1,500.00	(6)	5,000.00	7,694,180
289	8¢ Troops						
	Guarding Wagon Train	125.00	30.00	2,650.00	(6)	7,500.00	2,927,200
290	10¢ Hardships of Emigration	140.00	17.50	3,500.00	(6)		4,629,760
291	50¢ Western Mining Prospector	500.00	150.00	20,000.00	(6)	9,000.00	530,400
292	$1 Western Cattle in Storm	1,325.00	475.00	52,500.00	(6)	12,500.00	56,900
293	$2 Mississippi River Bridge,						
	St. Louis	1,950.00	725.00	115,000.00	(6)		56,200
	Issue of 1901, Pan-American Exposition Issue, May 1						
294	1¢ Great Lakes Steamer	13.50	2.50	275.00	(6)	3,750.00	91,401.500
294a	Center inverted	10,000.00	4,500.00	44,000.00	(3)		
295	2¢ An Early Locomotive	13.50	.75	275.00	(6)	3,250.00	209,759,700
295a	Center inverted	45,000.00	13,500.00				
296	4¢ Closed Coach Automobile	70.00	12.50	2,500.00	(6)	4,250.00	5,737,100
296a	Center inverted	13,000.00		67,500.00	(4)		
297	5¢ Bridge at Niagara Falls	82.50	12.50	2,750,00	(6)	4,500.00	7,201,300
298	8¢ Sault Ste. Marie Canal Locks	100.00	50.00	4,750.00	(6)		4,921,700
299	10¢ American Line Steamship	150.00	22.50	7,500.00	(6)		5,043,700

		Un	U	PB/LP	#	FDC	Q
	Issues of 1902-07, Perf. 12, Wmkd. (191) (all issued 1903 except #300b, 301c, 306, 308)						
300	1¢ Franklin, Feb.	6.50	.05	185.00	(6)		
300b	Booklet pane of 6, Mar. 6, 1907	400.00	250.00				
301	2¢ Washington, Jan. 17	7.50	.05	200.00	(6)	2,750.00	
301c	Booklet pane of 6, Jan. 24	350.00	250.00				
302	3¢ Jackson, Feb.	30.00	2.00	850.00	(6)		
303	4¢ Grant, Feb.	30.00	.60	850.00	(6)		
304	5¢ Lincoln, Feb.	35.00	.65	950.00	(6)		
305	6¢ Garfield, Feb.	37.50	1.50	1,000.00	(6)		
306	8¢ M. Washington, Dec. 1902	25.00	1.25	700.00	(6)		
307	10¢ Webster, Feb.	30.00	.70	1,150.00	(6)		
308	13¢ B. Harrison, Nov. 18, 1902	25.00	5.00	650.00	(6)		
309	15¢ Clay, Mar. 27	87.50	3.75	3,000.00	(6)		
310	50¢ Jefferson, Mar. 23	250.00	17.50	6,750.00	(6)		
311	$1 David G. Farragut, June 5	450.00	35.00	14,500.00	(6)		
312	$2 Madison, June 5	600.00	125.00	25,000.00	(6)		
313	$5 Marshall, June 5	1,650.00	450.00	62,500.00	(6)		
	For listings of #312 and 313 with Perf. 10, see #479 and 480.						
	Issues of 1906-08, Imperf. (All issued 1908 except #314)						
314	1¢ blue green						
	Franklin (300), 1906	16.00	13.00	275.00	(6)		
314A	4¢ brown Grant (303), Apr.	17,500.00	9,000.00				
315	5¢ blue Lincoln (304), May 12	375.00	150.00	4,750.00	(6)		
	#314A was issued imperforate, but all copies were privately perforated at the sides.						
	Coil Stamps, Perf. 12 Horizontally						
316	1¢ blue green pair						
	Franklin (300), Feb. 18	50,000.00		60,000.00	(2)		
317	5¢ blue pair Lincoln (304)	5,500.00		8,000.00	(2)		
	Perf. 12 Vertically						
318	1¢ blue green pair Franklin						
	(300), July 31	4,250.00		6,250.00	(2)		
	Issue of 1903, Perf. 12, Shield-shaped Background						
319	2¢ Washington, Nov. 12	4.00	.05	100.00	(6)		
319g	Booklet pane of 6	90.00	20.00				
	Issue of 1906, Washington (319), Imperf.						
320	2¢ carmine, Oct. 2	17.50	11.00	300.00	(6)		
	Issues of 1908, Coil Stamps (319), Perf. 12 Horizontally						
321	2¢ carmine pair, Feb. 18	60,000.00					
	Perf. 12 Vertically						
322	2¢ carmine pair, July 31	5,500.00		8,000.00	(2)		
	Issues of 1904, Louisiana Purchase Exposition Issue, Apr. 30, Perf. 12						
323	1¢ Robert R. Livingston	17.00	2.75	275.00	(6)	3,000.00	79,779,200
324	2¢ Thomas Jefferson	15.00	.90	275.00	(6)	2,750.00	192,732,400
325	3¢ James Monroe	60.00	22.50	950.00	(6)	3,750.00	4,542,600
326	5¢ William McKinley	65.00	14.50	1,100.00	(6)	5,500.00	6,926,700
327	10¢ Map of Louisiana Purchase	115.00	20.00	2,500.00	(6)	8,500.00	4,011,200

300 301 302 303 304

305 306 307 308 309 310

311 312 313 319

323 324 325

326 327

328   329   330

331   332   333   334

335   336   337   338

339   340   341   342

	Issues of 1907	Un	U	PB/LP	#	FDC	Q
	Jamestown Exposition Issue, Apr. 26, Perf. 12						
328	1¢ Captain John Smith	11.50	1.90	300.00	(6)	*3,750.00*	77,728,794
329	2¢ Founding of Jamestown	15.00	1.50	425.00	(6)	*5,500.00*	149,497,994
330	5¢ Pocahontas	67.50	15.00	2,750.00	(6)		7,980,594
	Issues of 1908-09, Wmkd. (191)						
331	1¢ Franklin, Dec. 1908	4.50	.05	80.00	(6)		
331a	Booklet pane of 6	165.00	*35.00*				
332	2¢ Washington, Nov. 1908	4.25	.05	75.00	(6)		
332a	Booklet pane of 6,						
	Nov. 16, 1908	100.00	*35.00*				
333	3¢ Washington, type I,						
	Dec. 1908	20.00	1.75	350.00	(6)		
334	4¢ Washington, Dec. 1908	23.50	.55	390.00	(6)		
335	5¢ Washington, Dec. 1908	30.00	1.50	600.00	(6)		
336	6¢ Washington, Jan. 1909	32.50	3.50	900.00	(6)		
337	8¢ Washington, Dec. 1908	26.00	1.75	475.00	(6)		
338	10¢ Washington, Jan. 1909	42.50	1.00	1,000.00	(6)		
339	13¢ Washington, Jan. 1909	25.00	14.00	475.00	(6)		
340	15¢ Washington, Jan. 1909	40.00	3.75	650.00	(6)		
341	50¢ Washington, Jan. 13, 1909	175.00	10.00	*7,500.00*	(6)		
342	$1 Washington, Jan. 29, 1909	300.00	50.00	*12,500.00*	(6)		
	Imperf.						
343	1¢ green Franklin (331), Dec. 1908	4.50	2.75	80.00	(6)		
344	2¢ carmine						
	Washington (332), Dec. 10, 1908	6.50	2.00	145.00	(6)		
	#345-347: Washington (333)						
345	3¢ deep violet, type I, Mar. 3, 1909	12.00	10.00	300.00	(6)		
346	4¢ orange brown, Feb. 25, 1909	21.00	12.00	400.00	(6)		
347	5¢ blue, Feb. 25, 1909	37.50	27.50	650.00	(6)		
	Issues of 1908-10, Coil Stamps, Perf. 12 Horizontally						
	#350-351, 354-356: Washington (333)						
348	1¢ green						
	Franklin (331), Dec. 29, 1908	17.50	9.25	175.00	(2)		
349	2¢ carmine						
	Washington (332), Jan. 1909	30.00	5.00	275.00	(2)		
350	4¢ orange brown, Aug. 15, 1910	67.50	50.00	800.00	(2)		
351	5¢ blue, Jan. 1909	75.00	67.50	850.00	(2)		
	Issues of 1909, Coil Stamps, Perf. 12 Vertically						
352	1¢ green Franklin (331), Jan.	32.50	20.00	325.00	(2)		
353	2¢ carmine						
	Washington (332), Jan. 12	30.00	5.00	300.00	(2)		
354	4¢ orange brown, Feb. 23	87.50	37.50	850.00	(2)		
355	5¢ blue, Feb. 23	95.00	55.00	900.00	(2)		
356	10¢ yellow, Jan. 7	1,300.00	400.00	7,500.00	(2)		

	Issues of 1909, Bluish Paper, Perf. 12, Wmkd. (191)	Un	U	PB/LP	#	FDC	Q
357	1¢ green Franklin (331), Feb. 16	75.00	65.00	1,150.00	(6)		
358	2¢ carmine						
	Washington (332), Feb. 16	70.00	55.00	1,100.00	(6)		
359	3¢ deep violet, type I	1,500.00	1,250.00	17,500.00	(6)		
360	4¢ orange brown	17,500.00		65,000.00	(3)		
361	5¢ blue	2,900.00	3,000.00	37,500.00	(6)		
362	6¢ red orange	1,150.00	750.00	12,000.00	(6)		
363	8¢ olive green	17,500.00		65,000.00	(3)		
364	10¢ yellow	1,200.00	800.00	12,500.00	(6)		
365	13¢ blue green	2,000.00	1,100.00	18,500.00	(6)		
366	15¢ pale ultramarine	900.00	600.00	10,000.00	(6)		
	Lincoln Memorial Issue, Feb. 12, Perf. 12						
367	2¢ Bust of Abraham Lincoln	4.25	1.40	160.00	(6)	350.00	148,387,191
	Imperf.						
368	2¢ Bust of Abraham Lincoln	19.50	15.00	275.00	(6)	5,000.00	1,273,900
	Bluish Paper, Perf. 12						
369	2¢ Bust of Abraham Lincoln	170.00	165.00	4,250.00	(6)		637,000
	Alaska-Yukon-Pacific Exposition Issue, June 1						
370	2¢ William H. Seward	7.00	1.10	300.00	(6)	1,800.00	152,887,311
	Imperf.						
371	2¢ William H. Seward	27.50	19.00	375.00	(6)		525,400
	Hudson-Fulton Celebration Issue, Sept. 25, Perf. 12						
372	2¢ Half Moon & Clermont	9.50	3.25	350.00	(6)	900.00	72,634,631
	Imperf.						
373	2¢ Half Moon & Clermont	30.00	21.00	400.00	(6)	2,000.00	216,480
	Issues of 1910-11, Wmkd. (190) #376-382: Washington (333)						
374	1¢ green						
	Franklin (331), Nov. 23, 1910	5.00	.06	85.00	(6)		
374a	Bklt. pane of 6, Oct. 7, 1910	110.00	30.00				
375	2¢ carmine						
	Washington (332), Nov. 23, 1910	5.00	.05	85.00	(6)		
375a	Bklt. pane of 6, Nov. 30, 1910	95.00	25.00				
376	3¢ dp. vio., type I, Jan. 16, 1911	11.50	1.00	175.00	(6)		
377	4¢ brown, Jan. 20, 1911	17.50	.30	225.00	(6)		
378	5¢ blue, Jan. 25, 1911	17.50	.30	265.00	(6)		
379	6¢ red orange, Jan. 25, 1911	24.00	.40	450.00	(6)		
380	8¢ olive green, Feb. 8, 1911	70.00	8.50	1,250.00	(6)		
381	10¢ yellow, Jan. 24, 1911	65.00	2.50	1,300.00	(6)		
382	15¢ pale ultramarine, Mar. 1, 1911	175.00	11.50	2,750.00	(6)		
	Issues of Jan. 3, 1911, Imperf.						
383	1¢ green Franklin (331)	2.25	2.00	65.00	(6)		
384	2¢ carmine Washington (332)	3.50	1.75	200.00	(6)		
	Issues of Nov. 1, 1910, Coil Stamps, Perf. 12 Horizontally						
385	1¢ green Franklin (331)	15.00	7.00	250.00	(2)		
386	2¢ carmine Washington (332)	27.50	10.00	500.00	(2)		
	Issues of 1910-11, Coil Stamps, Perf. 12 Vertically						
387	1¢ grn. Franklin (331), Nov. 1, 1910	40.00	20.00	350.00			
388	2¢ carmine						
	Washington (332), Nov. 1, 1910	400.00	75.00	3,750.00			
389	3¢ dp. vio. Washington,						
	type I (333), Jan. 24, 1911	15,000.00	6,000.00	45,000.00	(2)		

367

370

372

Watermark 190

397

398

399

400

	Issues of 1910-13, Perf. 8½, Horizontally, Wmkd. (190)	Un	U	PB/LP	#	FDC	Q
390	1¢ green Franklin (331), 1910	3.00	3.00	30.00	(2)		
391	2¢ carmine Washington (332), 1910	20.00	4.75	175.00	(2)		
	Perf. 8½ Vertically #394-396: Washington (333)						
392	1¢ green Franklin (331), 1910	12.00	12.00	125.00	(2)		
393	2¢ carmine Washington (332), 1910	24.00	4.50	200.00	(2)		
394	3¢ deep violet, type I, Sept. 18, 1911	32.50	27.50	300.00	(2)		
395	4¢ brown, Apr. 15, 1912	32.50	27.50	300.00	(2)		
396	5¢ blue, Mar. 1913	32.50	27.50	300.00	(2)		
	Issues of 1913, Panama Pacific Exposition Issue, Perf. 12						
397	1¢ Balboa, Jan. 1	11.00	.85	175.00	(6)	*3,250.00*	167,398,463
398	2¢ Locks, Panama Canal, Jan.	12.50	.28	300.00	(6)		251,856,543
399	5¢ Golden Gate, Jan. 1	47.50	6.50	2,250.00	(6)	*4,000.00*	14,544,363
400	10¢ Discovery						
	of San Francisco Bay, Jan. 1	90.00	14.00	3,000.00	(6)	*5,000.00*	8,484,182
400A	10¢ orange (400), Aug.	160.00	10.50	*9,500.00*	(6)		
	Issues of 1914-15, Perf. 10						
401	1¢ green (397), Dec. 1914	16.00	4.00	375.00	(6)		167,398,463
402	2¢ carmine (398), Feb. 1915	52.50	1.00	1,850.00	(6)		251,856,543
403	5¢ blue (399), Feb. 1915	115.00	11.50	4,500.00	(6)		14,544,363
404	10¢ orange (400), July 1915	775.00	42.50	*15,000.00*	(6)		8,484,182

405   406   407

414   415   416   417   418

419   420   421   423

Issues of 1912-14, Perf. 12 #405-413: Washington (333)	Un	U	PB/LP	#
405 1¢ green, Feb. 1912	3.50	.06	115.00	(6)
405b Booklet pane of 6, Feb. 8, 1912	50.00	7.50		
406 2¢ carmine, type I, 1912	3.25	.05	140.00	(6)
406a Booklet pane of 6, Feb. 8, 1912	60.00	17.50		
407 7¢ black, Apr. 1914	60.00	8.00	1,250.00	(6)
Imperf.				
408 1¢ green, Mar. 1912	.90	.50	25.00	(6)
409 2¢ carmine, type I, Mar. 1912	1.00	.50	50.00	(6)
Coil Stamps. Perf. 8½ Horizontally				
410 1¢ green, Mar. 1912	4.00	2.50	35.00	(2)
411 2¢ carmine, type I, Mar. 1912	5.00	2.00	45.00	(2)
Coil Stamps, Perf. 8½ Vertically				
412 1¢ green, Mar. 18, 1912	13.00	3.00	95.00	(2)
413 2¢ carmine, type I, Mar. 1912	22.00	.60	190.00	(2)
Perf. 12 #414-423: Franklin (414)				
414 8¢ Franklin, Feb. 1912	25.00	.85	475.00	(6)
415 9¢ Franklin, Apr. 1914	32.50	9.50	750.00	(6)
416 10¢ Franklin, Jan. 1912	26.00	.25	525.00	(6)
417 12¢ Franklin, Apr. 1914	28.50	3.00	550.00	(6)
418 15¢ Franklin, Feb. 1912	47.50	2.00	750.00	(6)
419 20¢ Franklin, Apr. 1914	110.00	9.00	2,000.00	(6)
420 30¢ Franklin, Apr. 1914	80.00	10.00	1,750.00	(6)
421 50¢ Franklin, Apr. 29, 1914	300.00	10.00	9,000.00	(6)
Wmkd. (191)				
422 50¢ Franklin (421), Feb. 12, 1912	160.00	9.50	5,500.00	(6)
423 $1 Franklin, Feb. 12, 1912	360.00	40.00	12,500.00	(6)

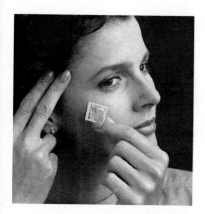

STAMP OUT WRINKLES

Stick stamps on your face? According to skin-care expert Constance Schrader, this is a great way to iron out wrinkles temporarily. Just pull the skin taut and stick on a stamp, causing a healing rush of blood to the affected area. Repeated over time, this procedure is said to smooth away those offending wrinkles.

	Issues of 1914-15, Perf. 10 Wmkd. (190) #424-430: Washington (333)	Un	U	PB/LP	#	FDC	Q
424	1¢ green, Sept. 5, 1914	1.60	.06	45.00	(6)		
424d	Booklet pane of 6, Jan. 6, 1914	3.50	.75				
425	2¢ rose red, type I, Sept. 5, 1914	1.50	.05	30.00	(6)		
425e	Booklet pane of 6, Jan. 6, 1914	12.50	3.00				
426	3¢ deep violet, type I, Sept. 18, 1914	8.50	.90	135.00	(6)		
427	4¢ brown, Sept. 7, 1914	22.00	.28	400.00	(6)		
428	5¢ blue, Sept. 14, 1914	18.50	.28	285.00	(6)		
429	6¢ red orange, Sept. 28, 1914	24.00	.90	350.00	(6)		
430	7¢ black, Sept. 10, 1914	55.00	2.50	850.00	(6)		
	#431-440: Franklin (414)						
431	8¢ pale olive green, Sept. 26, 1914	24.00	1.10	400.00	(6)		
432	9¢ salmon red, Oct. 6, 1914	32.50	5.00	550.00	(6)		
433	10¢ orange yellow, Sept. 9, 1914	30.00	.18	550.00	(6)		
434	11¢ dark green, Aug. 11, 1915	13.50	5.50	200.00	(6)		
435	12¢ claret brown, Sept. 10, 1914	15.00	2.75	250.00	(6)		
437	15¢ gray, Sept. 16, 1914	72.50	4.50	850.00	(6)		
438	20¢ ultramarine, Sept. 19, 1914	140.00	2.50	2,500.00	(6)		
439	30¢ orange red, Sept. 19, 1914	190.00	10.00	3,500.00	(6)		
440	50¢ violet, Dec. 10, 1914	500.00	10.00	11,000.00	(6)		
	Issues of 1914, Coil Stamps, Perf. 10 Horizontally #441-459: Washington (333)						
441	1¢ green, Nov. 14	.55	.80	7.50	(2)		
442	2¢ carmine, type I, July 22	6.00	4.50	57.50	(2)		
	Coil Stamps, Perf. 10 Vertically						
443	1¢ green, May 29	14.00	4.00	115.00	(2)		
444	2¢ carmine, type I, Apr. 25	19.00	1.00	175.00	(2)		
445	3¢ violet, type I, Dec. 18	160.00	75.00	1,100.00	(2)		
446	4¢ brown, Oct. 2	82.50	21.00	650.00	(2)		
447	5¢ blue, July 30	27.50	17.50	225.00	(2)		
	Issues of 1915-16, Coil Stamps, Perf. 10 Horizontally (Rotary Press, Designs 18½-19 x 22½ mm.)						
448	1¢ green, Dec. 12, 1915	4.25	2.25	50.00	(2)		
449	2¢ red, type I, Dec. 5, 1915	1,750.00	190.00	7,500.00	(2)		
450	2¢ carmine, type III, Feb. 1916	7.00	2.25	60.00	(2)		
	Issues of 1914-16, Coil Stamps, Perf. 10 Vertically (Rotary Press, Designs 19½-20 x 22 mm.)						
452	1¢ green, Nov. 11, 1914	7.00	1.40	80.00	(2)		
453	2¢ red, type I, July 3, 1914	72.50	3.25	600.00	(2)		
454	2¢ carmine, type II, June 1915	70.00	7.50	575.00	(2)		
455	2¢ carmine, type III, Dec. 1915	6.50	.75	60.00	(2)		
456	3¢ violet, type I, Feb. 18, 1916	190.00	75.00	1,300.00	(2)		
457	4¢ brown, Feb. 18, 1916	18.00	15.00	165.00	(2)		
458	5¢ blue, Mar. 9, 1916	22.50	15.00	165.00	(2)		
	Issue of 1914, Imperf., Coil						
459	2¢ carmine, type I, June 30	375.00	600.00	2,100.00	(2)		
	Issues of 1915, Perf. 10, Wmkd. (191)						
460	$1 violet black Franklin (423), Feb. 8	600.00	55.00	12,500.00	(6)		
	Perf. 11						
461	2¢ pale carmine red,						
	Washington (333), type I, June 17	75.00	50.00	950.00	(6)		

Privately perforated copies of #409 have been made to resemble #461.

From 1916 to date, all postage stamps except #519 and #832b are on unwatermarked paper.

	Issues of 1916-17, Perf. 10, Unwmkd. #462-469: Washington (333)	Un	U	PB	#	FDC	Q
462	1¢ green, Sept. 27, 1916	5.00	.15	150.00	(6)		
462a	Booklet pane of 6, Oct. 15, 1916	7.50	1.00				
463	2¢ carmine, type I, Sept. 25, 1916	3.25	.10	120.00	(6)		
463a	Booklet pane of 6, Oct. 8, 1916	70.00	20.00				
464	3¢ violet, type I, Nov. 11, 196	47.50	8.00	1,350.00	(6)		
465	4¢ orange brown, Oct. 7, 1916	27.50	1.00	650.00	(6)		
466	5¢ blue, Oct. 17, 1916	47.50	1.00	900.00	(6)		
467	5¢ carmine (error in plate of 2¢),						
	Mar. 7, 1917	475.00	500.00	135.00	(6)		
468	6¢ red orange, Oct. 10, 1916	60.00	5.00	1,150.00	(6)		
469	7¢ black, Oct. 10, 1916	77.50	7.50	1,350.00	(6)		
	#470-478: Franklin (414)						
470	8¢ olive green, Nov. 13, 1916	35.00	3.75	525.00	(6)		
471	9¢ salmon red, Nov. 16, 1916	37.50	9.50	675.00	(6)		
472	10¢ orange yellow, Oct. 17, 1916	70.00	.75	1,350.00	(6)		
473	11¢ dark green, Nov. 16, 1916	20.00	11.00	325.00	(6)		
474	12¢ claret brown, Oct. 10, 1916	32.50	3.50	550.00	(6)		
475	15¢ gray, Nov. 16, 1916	110.00	7.00	2,500.00	(6)		
476	20¢ light ultramarine, Dec. 5, 1916	160.00	7.50	3,500.00	(6)		
477	50¢ light violet, Mar. 2, 1917	900.00	40.00	25,000.00	(6)		
478	$1 violet black, Dec. 22, 1916	600.00	11.00	13,000.00	(6)		
479	$2 dark blue						
	Madison (312), Mar. 22, 1917	325.00	30.00	6,000.00	(6)		
480	$5 light green						
	Marshall (313), Mar. 22, 1917	250.00	32.50	4,500.00	(6)		
	Issues of 1916-17, Imperf., Unwmkd.						
	#481-496: Washington (333)						
481	1¢ green, Nov. 1916	.65	.45	15.00	(6)		
482	2¢ carmine, type I, Dec. 8, 1916	1.00	1.00	25.00	(6)		
482a	2¢ deep rose, type 1a		6,000.00				
483	3¢ violet, type I, Oct. 13, 1917	9.50	6.50	175.00	(6)		
484	3¢ violet, type II, Oct. 13, 1917	7.00	3.00	135.00	(6)		
485	5¢ carmine (error in plate of 2¢),						
	Mar. 1917	13,000		300.00	(6)		
	Issues of 1916-22, Coil Stamps, Perf. 10 Horizontally						
486	1¢ green, Jan. 1918	.60	.20	4.50	(2)		
487	2¢ carmine, type II, Nov. 15, 1916	10.00	2.50	135.00	(2)		
488	2¢ carmine, type III, 1919	1.75	1.35	20.00	(2)		
489	3¢ violet, type I, Oct. 10, 1917	3.75	1.00	37.50	(2)		
	Coil Stamps, Perf. 10 Vertically						
490	1¢ green, Nov. 17, 1916	.40	.15	4.75	(2)		
491	2¢ carmine, type II, Nov. 17, 1916	1,450.00	225.00	7,000.00	(2)		
492	2¢ carmine, type III, 1916	5.75	.15	65.00	(2)		
493	3¢ violet, type I, July 23, 1917	13.50	1.75	140.00	(2)		
494	3¢ violet, type II, Feb. 4, 1918	7.50	.90	75.00	(2)		
495	4¢ orange brown, Apr. 15, 1917	8.00	3.00	85.00	(2)		
496	5¢ blue, Jan. 15, 1919	2.75	.90	30.00	(2)		
497	10¢ orange yellow						
	Franklin (416), Jan. 31, 1922	16.00	7.00	150.00	(2)	2,000.00	

523   **524**

513

	Issues of 1917-19, **Perf. 11** #498-507: Washington (333)	Un	U	PB	#
498	1¢ green, Mar. 1917	.30	.05	17.50	(6)
498e	Booklet pane of 6, Apr. 6, 1917	1.75	.35		
498f	Booklet pane of 30	600.00			
499	2¢ rose, type I, Mar. 1917	.25	.05	14.00	(6)
499e	Booklet pane of 6, Mar. 31, 1917	2.00	.50		
499f	Booklet pane of 30	10,000.00			
500	2¢ deep rose, type Ia, 1917	200.00	85.00	2,250.00	(6)
501	3¢ light violet, type I, Mar. 1917	8.00	.10	175.00	(6)
501b	Booklet pane of 6, Oct. 1917	65.00	15.00		
502	3¢ dark violet, type II, 1917	11.00	.15	210.00	(6)
502b	Booklet pane of 6, Feb. 25, 1918	50.00	10.00		
503	4¢ brown, Mar. 1917	7.50	.12	185.00	(6)
504	5¢ blue, Mar. 1917	6.50	.08	150.00	(6)
505	5¢ rose (error in plate of 2¢),				
	Mar. 23, 1917	350.00	400.00	35.00	(6)
506	6¢ red orange, Mar. 1917	9.50	.20	210.00	(6)
507	7¢ black, Mar. 1917	20.00	.85	325.00	(6)
	Unwmkd., Perf. 11 #508-518: Franklin (414)				
508	8¢ olive bistre, Mar. 1917	8.50	.40	200.00	(6)
509	9¢ salmon red, Mar. 1917	11.00	1.40	190.00	(6)
510	10¢ orange yellow, Mar. 1917	12.50	.10	250.00	(6)
511	11¢ light green, May 1917	6.75	2.00	135.00	(6)
512	12¢ claret brown, May 1917	6.50	.30	150.00	(6)
513	13¢ apple green, Jan. 10, 1919	8.00	4.75	140.00	(6)
514	15¢ gray, May 1917	30.00	.80	675.00	(6)
515	20¢ light ultramarine, May 1917	37.50	.16	750.00	(6)
516	30¢ orange red, May 1917	30.00	.55	600.00	(6)
517	50¢ red violet, May 1917	60.00	.40	1,500.00	(6)
518	$1 violet brown, May 1917	74.00	1.10	1,200.00	(6)
	Issue of 1917, Wmkd. (191)				
519	2¢ carmine				
	Washington (332), Oct. 10	200.00	275.00	2,500.00	(6)
	Privately perforated copies of #344 have been made to resemble #519.				
	520-22 not assigned.				
	Issues of 1918, Aug., Unwmkd.				
523	$2 Franklin	675.00	250.00	18,500.00	(8)
524	$5 Franklin	275.00	20.00	6,000.00	(8)

537 **547** **548** **549** **550**

	Issues of 1918-20, **Perf. 11** #525-535: Washington (333)	Un	U	PB	#	FDC	Q
525	1¢ gray green, Dec. 1918	1.15	.35	30.00	(6)		
526	2¢ carmine, type IV,						
	Mar. 15, 1920	19.00	2.75	275.00	(6)	950.00	
527	2¢ carmine, type V, 1920	10.00	.60	150.00	(6)		
528	2¢ carmine, type Va, 1920	5.25	.15	65.00	(6)		
528A	2¢ carmine, type VI, 1920	32.50	1.00	400.00	(6)		
528B	2¢ carmine, type VII, 1920	12.50	.12	165.00	(6)		
529	3¢ violet, type III, 1918	1.75	.10	70.00	(6)		
530	3¢ purple, type IV, 1918	.50	.06	12.00	(6)		
	Imperf.						
531	1¢ green, Jan. 1920	6.00	7.00	100.00	(6)		
532	2¢ carmine rose, type IV, 1920	30.00	22.50	350.00	(6)		
533	2¢ carmine, type V, 1920	150.00	55.00	2,000.00	(6)		
534	2¢ carmine, type Va, 1920	8.50	6.00	110.00	(6)		
534A	2¢ carmine, type VI, 1920	27.50	17.50	375.00	(6)		
534B	2¢ carmine, type VII, 1920	1,250.00	425.00	12,500.00	(6)		
535	3¢ violet, type IV, 1918	6.00	4.50	70.00	(6)		
	Issues of 1919, Perf. 12½						
536	1¢ gray green Washington (333), Aug.	9.00	11.00	200.00	(6)		
537	3¢ Allied Victory, Mar. 3	6.25	2.75	150.00	(6)	750.00	99,585,200
	#538-546: Washington (333)						
	Perf. 11x10 (Designs 19½-20 x 22-22¼ mm)						
538	1¢ green, June	6.50	6.00	110.00	(4)		
539	2¢ carmine rose, type II	2,500.00	750.00	15,000.00	(4)		
540	2¢ carmine rose, type III, June 14	7.00	6.00	115.00	(4)		
541	3¢ violet, type II, June	22.50	20.00	400.00	(4)		
	Issue of 1920, Perf. 10x11 (Design 19 x 22½-22¾ mm)						
542	1¢ green, May 26	6.50	.65	175.00	(6)	950.00	
	Issue of 1921, Perf. 10 (Design 19 x 22½ mm)						
543	1¢ green	.35	.06	20.00	(4)		
	Issues of 1923, Perf. 11 (Design 19 x 22½ mm)						
544	1¢ green	7,500.00	2,400.00				
	Issues of 1921 (Designs 19½-20 x 22 mm)						
545	1¢ green	95.00	45.00	1,150.00	(4)		
546	2¢ carmine rose, type III	60.00	45.00	875.00	(4)		
	Issues of 1920						
547	$2 carmine and black						
	Franklin (523)	225.00	25.00	6,000.00	(8)		
	Pilgrim Tercentenary Issue, Dec. 21						
548	1¢ The Mayflower	3.25	1.65	55.00	(6)	800.00	137,978,207
549	2¢ Landing of the Pilgrims	5.25	1.25	80.00	(6)	650.00	196,037,327
550	5¢ Signing of the Compact	32.50	10.00	650.00	(6)		11,321,607

551   552   553   554

555   556   557   558   559

560   561   562   563   564

565   566   567   568   569

570   571   572   573

Issues of 1922-26, Perf. 11
(see also #581-91, 594-606, 622-23, 631-42, 692-701, 723)

		Un	U	PB	#	FDC
551	½¢ Nathan Hale, Apr. 4, 1925	.09	.08	7.00	(6)	25.00
552	1¢ Franklin, Jan. 17, 1923	1.10	.05	25.00	(6)	35.00
552a	Booklet pane of 6, Aug. 11, 1923	4.50	.50			
553	1½¢ Harding, May 19, 1925	1.90	.15	40.00	(6)	35.00
554	2¢ Washington, Jan. 15, 1923	1.00	.05	25.00	(6)	45.00
554c	Booklet pane of 6, Feb. 10, 1923	6.00	1.00			
555	3¢ Lincoln, Feb.12, 1923	12.50	.85	210.00	(6)	37.50
556	4¢ M. Washington, Jan. 15, 1923	12.50	.20	225.00	(6)	50.00
557	5¢ T. Roosevelt, Oct. 27, 1922	12.50	.08	250.00	(6)	150.00
558	6¢ Garfield, Nov. 20, 1922	24.00	.75	425.00	(6)	225.00
559	7¢ McKinley, May 1, 1923	5.75	.45	90.00	(6)	125.00
560	8¢ Grant, May 1, 1923	35.00	.35	725.00	(6)	125.00
561	9¢ Jefferson, Jan. 15, 1923	10.00	.90	210.00	(6)	125.00
562	10¢ Monroe, Jan. 15, 1923	14.00	.10	300.00	(6)	140.00
563	11¢ Hayes, Oct. 4, 1922	1.10	.25	35.00	(6)	550.00
564	12¢ Cleveland, Mar. 20, 1923	4.50	.08	90.00	(6)	170.00
565	14¢ American Indian, May 1, 1923	3.25	.65	60.00	(6)	350.00
566	15¢ Statue of Liberty, Nov. 11, 1922	17.50	.06	300.00	(6)	400.00
567	20¢ Golden Gate, May 1, 1923	17.50	.06	300.00	(6)	400.00
568	25¢ Niagara Falls, Nov. 11, 1922	15.00	.38	250.00	(6)	625.00
569	30¢ Buffalo, Mar. 20, 1923	27.50	.30	450.00	(6)	750.00
570	50¢ Arlington Amphitheater, Nov. 11, 1922	50.00	.12	900.00	(6)	1,100.00
571	$1 Lincoln Memorial, Feb. 12, 1923	37.50	.35	500.00	(6)	4,500.00
572	$2 U.S. Capitol, Mar. 20, 1923	85.00	8.00	1,650.00	(6)	10,000.00
573	$5 Head of Freedom, Capitol Dome, Mar. 20, 1923	200.00	12.50	4,000.00	(8)	14,000.00
574 not assigned						

Issues of 1923-25, Imperf.

		Un	U	PB	#	FDC
575	1¢ green Franklin (552), Mar. 20, 1923	6.00	2.75	100.00	(6)	
576	1½¢ yellow brown Harding (553), Apr. 4, 1925	1.25	1.00	30.00	(6)	45.00
577	2¢ carmine Washington (554)	1.40	1.25	30.00	(6)	

For listings of other perforated stamps of issues 551-573 see:

#578 and 579	Perf. 11x10
#581 to 591	Perf. 10
#594 and 595	Perf. 11
#622 and 623	Perf. 11
#632 to 642, 653, 692 to 696	Perf. 11x10½
#697 to 701	Perf. 10½x11

Issues of 1923-26, Perf. 11x10

		Un	U	PB	#	FDC
578	1¢ green Franklin (552)	50.00	47.50	750.00	(4)	
579	2¢ carmine Washington (554)	35.00	35.00	450.00	(4)	
580 not assigned						

A Reminder: Beginning with this edition, catalog values for all stamps listed reflect (as accurately as possible) actual retail values as found in the marketplace.

	Issues of 1923-29, Perf. 10	Un	U	PB/LP	#	FDC	Q
581	1¢ green Franklin (552), Apr. 21, 1923	6.00	.55	125.00	(4)	2,000.00	
582	1½¢ brown Harding (553), Mar. 19, 1925	3.00	.45	45.00	(4)	47.50	
583	2¢ carmine Washington (554), Apr. 14, 1924	1.40	.05	30.00	(4)		
583a	Booklet pane of 6, Aug. 27, 1926	75.00	25.00			1,200.00	
584	3¢ violet Lincoln (555), Aug. 1, 1925	17.50	1.75	250.00	(4)	55.00	
585	4¢ yellow brown						
	M. Washington (556), Mar., 1925	11.00	.30	175.00	(4)	55.00	
586	5¢ blue T. Roosevelt (557), Dec., 1924	11.50	.18	165.00	(4)	60.00	
587	6¢ red orange Garfield (558), Mar., 1925	4.50	.25	70.00	(4)	70.00	
588	7¢ black McKinley (559), May 29, 1926	7.00	4.25	110.00	(4)	72.50	
589	8¢ olive green Grant (560), May 29, 1926	17.50	2.75	250.00	(4)	72.50	
590	9¢ rose Jefferson, (561), May 29, 1926	3.25	1.90	45.00	(4)	77.50	
591	10¢ orange Monroe (562), June 8, 1925	45.00	.15	675.00	(4)	100.00	

592-93 not assigned.

	Perf. 11						
594	1¢ green Franklin (552),						
	design 19¾x22¼mm	10,000.00	3,500.00				
595	2¢ carmine Washington (554),						
	design 19¾x22¼mm	225.00	225.00	1,500.00	(4)		
596	1¢ green Franklin (552),						
	design 19¼x22¾mm	—	13,500.00				

	Coil Stamps, Perf. 10 Vertically						
597	1¢ green Franklin (552), July 18, 1923	.20	.06	2.25	(2)	550.00	
598	1½¢ brown Harding (553), Mar. 19, 1925	.40	.10	5.25	(2)	55.00	
599	2¢ carmine						
	Washington (554), type I, Jan., 1923	.25	.05	2.00	(2)	850.00	
599A	2¢ carmine						
	Washington (554), type II, Mar., 1929	100.00	8.50	800.00	(2)		
600	3¢ violet Lincoln (555), May 10, 1924	4.25	.08	35.00	(2)	77.50	
601	4¢ yellow brown						
	M. Washington (556), Aug. 5, 1923	2.50	.30	27.50	(2)		
602	5¢ dark blue						
	T. Roosevelt (557), Mar. 5, 1924	1.10	.14	10.00	(2)	82.50	
603	10¢ orange Monroe (562), Dec. 1, 1924	2.25	.08	27.50	(2)	100.00	

	Perf. 10 Horizontally						
604	1¢ yellow green						
	Franklin (552), July 19, 1924	.18	.08	3.00	(2)	100.00	
605	1½¢ yellow brown						
	Harding (553), May 9, 1925	.18	.15	2.75	(2)	70.00	
606	2¢ carmine						
	Washington (554), Dec. 31, 1923	.18	.08	2.00	(2)	125.00	

607-09 not assigned.

610   614   615   616

617   618   619

620   621   622   623

	Issue of 1923	Un	U	PB	#	FDC	Q
	Harding Memorial Issue, Perf. 11						
610	2¢ Harding, Sept. 1	.45	.10	30.00	(6)	40.00	1,459,487,085
	Imperf.						
611	2¢ blk. Harding (610), Nov. 15	6.50	4.25	140.00	(6)	100.00	770,000
	Perf. 10						
612	2¢ blk. Harding (610), Sept. 12	11.00	1.50	375.00	(4)	110.00	99,950,300
	Perf. 11						
613	2¢ black Harding (610), design 19¼ x 22¾ mm		13,500.00				
	Issues of 1924, Huguenot-Walloon Tercentary Issue, May 1						
614	1¢ Ship *Nieu Nederland*	2.25	3.00	50.00	(6)	32.50	51,378,023
615	2¢ Walloons' Landing at Fort Orange (Albany)	5.25	1.90	85.00	(6)	37.50	77,753,423
616	5¢ Huguenot Monument to Jan Ribault at Mayport, FL	26.00	11.00	450.00	(6)	70.00	5,659,023
	Issues of 1925, Lexington-Concord Issue, Apr. 4						
617	1¢ Washington at Cambridge	2.50	2.25	50.00	(6)	32.50	15,615,000
618	2¢ "The Birth of Liberty," by Henry Sandham	5.00	3.75	95.00	(6)	37.50	26,596,600
619	5¢ "The Minute Man," by Daniel Chester French	24.00	12.50	400.00	(6)	65.00	5,348,800
	Norse-American Issue, May 18						
620	2¢ Sloop *Restaurationen*	4.00	2.75	225.00	(8)	27.50	9,104,983
621	5¢ Viking Ship	14.00	10.50	750.00	(8)	47.50	1,900,983
	Issues of 1925-26						
622	13¢ Benjamin Harrison, Jan. 11, 1926	11.00	.40	200.00	(6)	35.00	
623	17¢ Woodrow Wilson, Dec. 28, 1925	15.00	.20	250.00	(6)	30.00	

624-626 not assigned.

1926-1929

627

628

629

630

643

644

645

646

647

648

649

650

	Issues of 1926, Perf. 11	Un	U	PB	#	FDC	Q
627	2¢ Independence						
	Sesquicentennial						
	Exposition, May 10	2.25	.35	50.00	(6)	15.00	307,731,900
628	5¢ John Ericsson Memorial,						
	May 29	5.00	2.50	110.00	(6)	22.50	20,280,500
629	2¢ Battle of White Plains, Oct. 18	1.50	1.25	50.00	(6)	6.25	40,639,485
	International Philatelic Exhibition Issue, Oct. 18, Souvenir Sheet, Perf. 11						
630	2¢ Battle of White Plains, sheet of 25						
	with selvage inscription (629)	350.00	300.00			1,400.00	107,398
	Imperf.						
631	1½¢ yellow brown Harding (553),						
	design 18½-19 x 22½ mm, Aug. 27	1.45	1.40	70.00	(4)	35.00	
	Issues of 1926-34, Perf. 11x10½						
632	1¢ green Franklin (552), June 10, 1927	.12	.05	2.00	(4)	55.00	
632a	Booklet pane of 6, Nov. 2, 1927	4.50	.25				
633	1½¢ yellow brown Harding (553),						
	May 17, 1927	1.25	.08	90.00	(4)	55.00	
634	2¢ carmine Washington (554), type I						
	Dec. 10, 1926	.10	.05	1.20	(4)	57.50	
634d	Booklet pane of 6, Feb. 25, 1927	1.75	.15				
634A	2¢ carmine Washington (554), type II						
	Dec. 1928	300.00	10.00	2,100.00	(4)		
635	3¢ violet Lincoln (555), Feb. 3, 1927	.35	.05	7.00	(4)	47.50	
635a	3¢ bright violet Lincoln, Feb. 7, 1934	.25	.05	4.00	(4)	25.00	
636	4¢ yellow brown						
	M. Washington (556), May 17, 1927	1.75	.08	100.00	(4)	55.00	
637	5¢ dark blue T. Roosevelt (557),						
	Mar. 24, 1927	1.65	.05	21.00	(4)	55.00	
638	6¢ red orange						
	Garfield (558), July 27, 1927	1.75	.05	21.00	(4)	65.00	
639	7¢ black						
	McKinley (559), Mar. 24, 1927	1.75	.08	21.00	(4)	67.50	
640	8¢ olive green						
	Grant (560), June 10, 1927	1.75	.05	21.00	(4)	70.00	
641	9¢ orange red Jefferson (561), 1931	1.75	.05	21.00	(4)	85.00	
642	10¢ orange						
	Monroe (562), Feb. 3, 1927	2.75	.05	35.00	(4)	90.00	
	Issues of 1927, Perf. 11						
643	2¢ Vermont Sesquicentennial, Aug. 3	1.00	.75	45.00	(6)	7.00	39,974,900
644	2¢ Burgoyne Campaign, Aug. 3	2.50	1.90	60.00	(6)	17.50	25,628,450
	Issues of 1928						
645	2¢ Valley Forge, May 26	.70	.35	40.00	(6)	6.00	101,330,328
	Perf. 11x10½						
646	2¢ Battle of Monmouth/Molly Pitcher,						
	Oct. 20	.80	.80	40.00	(4)	22.50	9,779,896
	Hawaii Sesquicentennial Issue, Aug. 13						
647	2¢ Washington (554)	3.00	3.25	150.00	(4)	17.50	5,519,897
648	5¢ T. Roosevelt (557)	10.00	10.00	300.00	(4)	32.50	1,459,897
	Aeronautics Conference Issue, Dec. 12, Perf. 11						
649	2¢ Wright Airplane	.70	.75	17.50	(6)	12.50	51,342,273
650	5¢ Globe and Airplane	4.50	3.00	90.00	(6)	17.50	10,319,700

	Issues of 1929, Perf. 11	Un	U	PB/LP	#	FDC	Q
651	2¢ George Rogers Clark, Feb. 25	.45	.35	16.00	(6)	10.00	16,684,674
652 not assigned.							
	Perf. 11x10½						
653	½¢ olive brn. Nathan Hale (551), May 25	.05	.05	1.00	(4)	30.00	
	Electric Light's Golden Jubilee Issue, June 5, Perf. 11						
654	2¢ Thomas Edison's First Lamp	.50	.50	35.00	(6)	15.00	31,679,200
	Perf. 11x10½						
655	2¢ carmine rose (654), June 11	.45	.15	55.00	(4)	90.00	210,119,474
	Coil Stamp, Perf. 10 Vertically						
656	2¢ carmine rose (654), June 11	9.50	1.25	90.00		100.00	133,530,000
	Perf. 11						
657	2¢ Sullivan Expedition, June 17	.60	.50	35.00	(6)	5.00	51,451,880
	658-668 Overprinted "Kans.", May 1, Perf. 11x10½						
658	1¢ Franklin	1.40	1.25	30.00	(4)	30.00	13,390,000
659	1½¢ brown Harding (553)	1.90	1.75	45.00	(4)	27.50	8,240,000
660	2¢ carmine Washington (554)	2.50	.70	40.00	(4)	27.50	87,410,000
661	3¢ violet Lincoln (555)	11.00	9.00	175.00	(4)	30.00	2,540,000
662	4¢ yellow brown						
	M. Washington (556)	11.00	5.50	175.00	(4)	32.50	2,290,000
663	5¢ deep blue T. Roosevelt (557)	8.00	6.00	150.00	(4)	35.00	2,700,000
664	6¢ red orange Garfield (558)	17.50	11.50	400.00	(4)	42.50	1,450,000
665	7¢ black McKinley (559)	16.00	17.00	400.00	(4)	42.50	1,320,000
666	8¢ olive green Grant (560)	55.00	45.00	800.00	(4)	80.00	1,530,000
667	9¢ light rose Jefferson (561)	8.00	7.00	175.00	(4)	72.50	1,130,000
668	10¢ orange yel. Monroe (562)	14.00	7.50	325.00	(4)	85.00	2,860,000
	669-679 Overprinted "Nebr.", May 1						
669	1¢ Franklin	2.00	1.40	30.00	(4)	27.50	8,220,000
670	1½¢ brown Harding (553)	1.65	1.50	45.00	(4)	25.00	8,990,000
671	2¢ carmine Washington (554)	1.65	.70	30.00	(4)	25.00	73,220,000
672	3¢ violet Lincoln (555)	7.00	6.50	150.00	(4)	32.50	2,110,000
673	4¢ yellow brown						
	M. Washington (556)	12.50	9.00	200.00	(4)	37.50	1,600,000
674	5¢ deep blue T. Roosevelt (557)	10.00	9.00	210.00	(4)	37.50	1,860,000
675	6¢ red orange Garfield (558)	24.00	14.00	500.00	(4)	55.00	980,000
676	7¢ black McKinley (559)	13.00	11.00	275.00	(4)	57.50	850,000
677	8¢ olive green Grant (560)	17.00	15.00	375.00	(4)	60.00	1,480,000
678	9¢ light rose Jefferson (561)	22.50	17.00	400.00	(4)	62.50	530,000
679	10¢ orange yel. Monroe (562)	70.00	14.00	900.00	(4)	70.00	1,890,000
	Warning: Excellent forgeries of the Kansas and Nebraska overprints exist.						
	Perf. 11						
680	2¢ Battle of Fallen Timbers, Sept. 14	.60	.65	35.00	(6)	5.00	29,338,274
681	2¢ Ohio River Canalization, Oct. 19	.45	.50	27.50	(6)	4.50	32,680,900
	Issues of 1930						
682	2¢ Massachusetts Bay Colony, Apr. 8	.40	.38	40.00	(6)	5.25	74,000,774
683	2¢ Carolina-Charleston, Apr. 10	.85	.85	65.00	(6)	5.50	25,215,574
	Perf. 11x10½						
684	1½¢ Warren G. Harding, Dec. 1	.18	.05	1.50	(4)	6.25	
685	4¢ William H. Taft, June 4	.55	.06	10.00	(4)	10.00	
	Coil Stamps, Perf. 10 Vertically						
686	1½¢ brown Harding (684), Dec. 1	1.25	.07	7.50	(2)	7.50	
687	4¢ brown Taft (685), Sept. 18	2.25	.50	15.00	(2)	30.00	

651

654

657

658

669

680

681

682

683

684

685

688   689   690   702   703

704   705   706   707   708   709

710   711   712   713   714   715

	1930 continued, Perf. 11	Un	U	PB	#	FDC	Q
688	2¢ Battle of Braddock's Field,						
	July 9	.65	.65	55.00	(6)	6.00	25,609,470
689	2¢ General von Steuben, Sept. 17	.38	.40	35.00	(6)	6.00	66,487,000
	Issues of 1931						
690	2¢ General Pulaski, Jan. 16	.16	.10	17.50	(6)	5.00	96,559,400
691 not assigned							
	Perf. 11x10½						
692	11¢ light blue Hayes (563), Sept. 4	1.65	.10	19.00	(4)	110.00	
693	12¢ bright violet						
	Cleveland (564), Aug. 25	3.25	.06	35.00	(4)	110.00	
694	13¢ yellow green						
	Harrison (622), Sept. 4	1.40	.10	18.00	(4)	110.00	
695	14¢ dark blue						
	American Indian (565), Sept. 8	2.00	.22	25.00	(4)	110.00	
696	15¢ gray						
	Statue of Liberty (566), Aug. 27	5.75	.06	60.00	(4)	150.00	
	Perf. 10½x11						
697	17¢ black Wilson (623), July 25	3.25	.14	30.00	(4)	350.00	
698	20¢ carmine rose						
	Golden Gate (567), Sept. 8	7.00	.05	65.00	(4)	185.00	
699	25¢ blue green						
	Niagara Falls (568), July 25	6.75	.08	62.50	(4)	350.00	
700	30¢ brown Buffalo (569), Sept. 8	10.50	.07	100.00	(4)	300.00	
701	50¢ lilac Arlington						
	Amphitheater (570), Sept.4	30.00	.07	300.00	(4)	450.00	
	Perf. 11						
702	2¢ Red Cross, May 21	.08	.08	2.25	(4)	4.00	99,074,600
703	2¢ Yorktown, Oct. 19	.24	.20	3.50	(4)	5.00	25,006,400
	Issues of 1932, Washington Bicentennial Issue, Jan., 1, Perf. 11x10½						
704	½¢ Portrait by Charles W. Peale	.09	.08	4.00	(4)	5.00	87,969,700
705	1¢ Bust by Jean Antoine Houdon	.10	.05	5.00	(4)	5.50	1,265,555,100
706	1½¢ Portrait by Charles W. Peale	.32	.08	22.50	(4)	5.50	304,926,800
707	2¢ Portrait by Gilbert Stuart	.10	.05	2.00	(4)	5.50	4,222,198,300
708	3¢ Portrait by Charles W. Peale	.40	.06	16.00	(4)	5.75	456,198,500
709	4¢ Portrait by Charles P. Polk	.22	.06	5.00	(4)	5.75	151,201,300
710	5¢ Portrait by Charles W. Peale	1.40	.10	24.00	(4)	6.00	170,565,100
711	6¢ Portrait by John Trumbull	2.75	.06	75.00	(4)	6.75	111,739,400
712	7¢ Portrait by John Trumbull	.22	.10	6.00	(4)	6.75	83,257,400
713	8¢ Portrait						
	by Charles B.J.F. Saint Memin	2.25	.50	70.00	(4)	6.75	96,506,100
714	9¢ Portrait by W. Williams	2.00	.15	45.00	(4)	8.75	75,709,200
715	10¢ Portrait by Gilbert Stuart	8.50	.10	150.00	(4)	12.00	147,216,000

	1932 continued	Un	U	PB/LP	#	FDC	Q
	Olympic Winter Games Issue, Jan. 25, Perf. 11						
716	2¢ Ski Jumper	.35	.16	15.00	(6)	7.50	51,102,800
	Perf. 11x10½						
717	2¢ Arbor Day, Apr. 22	.10	.08	10.00	(4)	5.00	100,869,300
	Olympic Summer Games Issue, June 15, Perf. 11x10½						
718	3¢ Runner at Starting Mark	1.10	.08	20.00	(4)	7.50	168,885,300
719	5¢ Myron's Discobolus	1.90	.20	35.00	(4)	9.50	52,376,100
720	3¢ Washington, June 16	.12	.05	1.50	(4)	10.00	
720b	Booklet pane of 6, July 25	22.50	5.00			100.00	
	Coil Stamps, Perf. 10 Vertically						
721	3¢ deep violet (720), June 24	2.25	.08	11.00	(2)	.20.00	
	Perf. 10 Horizontally						
722	3¢ deep violet (720), Oct. 12	1.00	.30	9.00	(2)	20.00	
	Perf. 10 Vertically						
723	6¢ deep orange						
	Garfield (558), Aug. 18	7.50	.25	70.00	(2)	20.00	
	Perf. 11						
724	3¢ William Penn, Oct. 24	.22	.25	16.00	(6)	3.25	49,949,000
725	3¢ Daniel Webster, Oct. 24	.28	.24	30.00	(6)	3.25	49,538,500
	Issues of 1933						
726	3¢ Georgia Settlement, Feb. 12	.20	.18	17.50	(6)	3.25	61,719,200
	Perf. 10½x11						
727	3¢ Peace of 1783, Apr. 19	.09	.08	6.50	(4)	3.50	73,382,400
	Century of Progress Issue, May 25						
728	1¢ Restoration of Fort Dearborn	.10	.06	2.50	(4)	3.00	348,266,800
729	3¢ Federal Building at Chicago	.10	.05	3.50	(4)	3.00	480,239,300
	American Philatelic Society Issue, Souvenir Sheets, Aug. 25, Without Gum, Imperf.						
730	1¢ sheet of 25 (728)	24.00	24.00			120.00	456,704
730a	Single stamp from sheet	.65	.35			3.25	11,417,600
731	3¢ sheet of 25 (729)	22.50	22.50			120.00	441,172
731a	Single stamp from sheet	.50	.35			3.25	11,029,300

Olympic Station
Feb. 13, 1988
Anchorage, AK 99510

HISTORY OF '92 OLYMPICS HAS BEGUN
It's not too early to start collecting the postal history of the 1992 Olympic Games. Prior to their selection as respective hosts for the next winter and summer games, Albertville, France and Barcelona, Spain each issued postal publicity. Albertville used a cancellation slogan in 1985 and early 1986, while Barcelona issued a special publicity corner card. To obtain information on collecting 1992 Olympics postal history, write Comite Organisateur, Jeux Olympiques d'hiver 1992, 73200 Mairie d'Albertville, France; and Barcelona '92, Oficina Olimpica, C62 Nr. 420, 08004 Barcelona, Spain.

716   **717**   **718**   **719**   **720**

724   **725**   **726**

727   **728**   **729**

730

731

732

734

733

735

736

737

739

741

742

740

743

745

744

746

748

747

749

	1933 continued, Perf. 10½x11	Un	U	PB	#	FDC	Q
732	3¢ NRA, Aug. 15	.10	.05	1.75	(4)	3.25	1,978,707,300
	Perf. 11						
733	3¢ Byrd Antarctic Expedition II,						
	Oct. 9	.40	.48	25.00	(6)	6.00	5,735,944
734	5¢ Kosciuszko, Oct. 13	.40	.22	45.00	(6)	5.50	45,137,700
	Issues of 1934						
	National Stamp Exhibition Issue, Souvenir Sheet, Feb. 10, Without Gum, Imperf.						
735	3¢ sheet of 6 (733)	15.00	12.50			55.00	811,404
735a	Single stamp from sheet	2.00	2.00			6.00	4,868,424
	Perf. 11						
736	3¢ Maryland Tercentary, Mar. 23	.12	.08	12.50	(6)	1.60	46,258,300
	Mothers of America Issue, May 2, Perf. 11x10½						
737	3¢ Portrait of his Mother, by						
	James A. McNeill Whistler	.09	.06	1.75	(4)	1.60	193,239,100
	Perf. 11						
738	3¢ deep violet (737)	.12	.10	7.25	(6)	1.60	15,432,200
739	3¢ Wisconsin Tercentary, July 7	.12	.10	7.00	(6)	1.60	64,525,400
	National Parks Issue						
740	1¢ El Capitan, Yosemite (California),						
	July 16	.07	.06	1.50	(6)	3.25	84,896,350
741	2¢ Grand Canyon (Arizona), July 24	.09	.06	2.00	(6)	3.25	74,400,200
742	3¢ Mirror Lake, Mt. Rainier						
	(Washington), Aug. 3	.10	.06	3.00	(6)	3.50	95,089,000
743	4¢ Cliff Palace, Mesa Verde						
	(Colorado), Sept. 25	.35	.50	11.00	(6)	4.25	19,178,650
744	5¢ Old Faithful, Yellowstone						
	(Wyoming), July 30	.60	.90	16.00	(6)	4.25	30,980,100
745	6¢ Crater Lake (Oregon), Sept. 5	1.00	.75	30.00	(6)	5.00	16,923,350
746	7¢ Great Head, Acadia Park						
	(Maine), Oct. 2	.55	.65	18.00	(6)	5.00	15,988,250
747	8¢ Great White Throne,						
	Zion Park (Utah), Sept. 18	1.40	1.65	30.00	(6)	5.25	15,288,700
748	9¢ Mt. Rockwell and Two Medicine						
	Lake, Glacier National Park						
	(Montana), Aug. 27	1.50	.55	30.00	(6)	5.50	17,472,600
749	10¢ Great Smoky Mountains						
	(North Carolina), Oct. 8	2.75	.90	50.00	(6)	11.00	18,874,300

A Reminder: Beginning with this edition, catalog values for all stamps listed reflect (as accurately as possible) actual retail values as found in the marketplace.

	1934 continued	Un	U	PB/LP	#	FDC	Q
	American Philatelic Society Issue, Souvenir Sheet, Imperf.						
750	3¢ sheet of 6 (742), Aug. 28	30.00	27.50			55.00	511,391
750a	Single stamp from sheet	3.50	3.50			6.25	3,068,346
	Trans-Mississippi Philatelic Exposition Issue, Souvenir Sheet						
751	1¢ sheet of 6 (740), Oct. 10	10.00	10.00			40.00	793,551
751a	Single stamp from sheet	1.40	1.40			4.50	4,761,306
	Issues of 1935, Special Printing (#752 to 771 inclusive), March 15, Without Gum, Perf. 10½x11						
752	3¢ violet Peace of 1783 (727) Mar. 15	.14	.08	16.00	(4)	10.00	3,274,556
	Perf. 11						
753	3¢ blue						
	Byrd Antarctic Expedition II (733)	.40	.40	25.00	(6)	12.00	2,040,760
	Imperf.						
754	3¢ deep violet						
	Portrait of Whistler's Mother (737)	.50	.50	30.00	(6)	12.00	2,389,288
755	3¢ deep violet						
	Wisconsin Tercentary (739)	.50	.50	30.00	(6)	12.00	2,294,948
756	1¢ green Yosemite (740)	.20	.20	5.50	(6)	12.00	3,217,636
757	2¢ red Grand Canyon (741)	.22	.22	6.50	(6)	12.00	2,746,640
758	3¢ deep violet Mt. Rainier (742)	.45	.40	17.50	(6)	13.00	2,168,088
759	4¢ brown Mesa Verde (743)	.90	.90	24.00	(6)	13.00	1,822,684
760	5¢ blue Yellowstone (744)	1.40	1.25	30.00	(6)	13.00	1,724,576
761	6¢ dark blue Crater Lake (745)	2.25	2.00	47.50	(6)	13.00	1,647,696
762	7¢ black Acadia (746)	1.40	1.25	40.00	(6)	13.00	1,682,948
763	8¢ sage green Zion (747)	1.50	1.40	50.00	(6)	15.00	1,638,644
764	9¢ red orange Glacier (748)	1.75	1.50	55.00	(6)	15.00	1,625,224
765	10¢ gray black Smoky Mts. (749)	3.50	3.00	62.50	(6)	15.00	1,644,900
766	1¢ yellow green (728), pane of 25	24.00	24.00				98,712
766a	Single stamp from pane	.65	.35			11.00	2,467,800
767	3¢ violet (729), pane of 25	22.50	22.50				85,914
767a	Single stamp from pane	.50	.35			11.00	2,147,850
768	3¢ dark blue (733), pane of 6	15.00	12.50				267,200
768a	Single stamp from pane	2.00	2.00			13.00	1,603,200
769	1¢ green (740), pane of 6	10.00	10.00				279,960
769a	Single stamp from pane	1.40	1.40			8.00	1,679,760
770	3¢ deep violet (742), pane of 6	30.00	27.50				215,920
770a	Single stamp from pane	3.50	3.50			10.00	1,295,520
771	16¢ dark blue Great Seal of U.S.	2.00	2.00	65.00	(6)	25.00	1,370,560
	For perforate variety, see #CE2.						

UNDER AUTHORITY OF
JAMES A. FARLEY, POSTMASTER GENERAL

ATLANTIC CITY, NEW JERSEY, AUGUST 1934.
PLATE NUMBER 21303

UNDER AUTHORITY OF
JAMES A. FARLEY, POSTMASTER GENERAL

OMAHA, NEBRASKA, OCTOBER, 1934.
PLATE NUMBER 21341

772

773

774

775

776

777

778

782

783

784

	1935 continued, Perf. 11x10½	Un	U	PB	#	FDC	Q
772	3¢ Connecticut Settlement, Apr. 26	.10	.06	2.00	(4)	8.00	70,726,800
773	3¢ California Pacific						
	International Exposition, May 29	.09	.06	1.80	(4)	8.00	100,839,600
	Perf. 11						
774	3¢ Boulder Dam, Sept. 30	.09	.06	2.50	(6)	10.00	73,610,650
	Perf. 11x10½						
775	3¢ Michigan Statehood, Nov. 1	.09	.06	1.80	(4)	8.00	75,823,900
	Issues of 1936						
776	3¢ Republic of Texas Independence,						
	Mar. 2	.09	.06	1.80	(4)	12.50	124,324,500
	Perf. 10½x11						
777	3¢ Rhode Island Settlement, May 4	.10	.06	1.80	(4)	8.00	67,127,650
	Third International Philatelic Exhibition Issue, Souvenir Sheet, May 9, Imperf.						
778	Sheet of 4 different stamps						
	(772, 773, 775 and 776)	1.75	1.75			13.00	2,809,039
779-81 not assigned							
	Perf. 11x10½						
782	3¢ Arkansas Statehood, June 15	.09	.06	1.80	(4)	8.00	72,992,650
783	3¢ Oregon Territory, July 14	.09	.06	1.80	(4)	8.50	74,407,450
784	3¢ Susan B. Anthony, Aug. 26	.09	.05	.75	(4)	17.50	269,522,200

SAN DIEGO HOME TO PACIFIC CELEBRATION *In 1935 and 1936, San Diego hosted the California Pacific International Exposition (#773), a celebration of the Pacific Ocean and its bordering countries. Four hundred years earlier, in 1535, Hernando Cortes attempted to establish a Spanish colony on Baja at La Paz, Mexico. Soon thereafter, in 1542, Juan Rodriguez Cabrillo, a Portuguese explorer in the service of Spain, discovered the magnificent San Diego Bay.*

	Issues of 1936-37	Un	U	PB	#	FDC	Q
	Army Issue, Perf. 11x10½						
785	1¢ George Washington,						
	Nathanael Green and Mount Vernon,						
	Dec. 15, 1936	.08	.06	1.00	(4)	5.00	105,196,150
786	2¢ Andrew Jackson, Winfield Scott						
	and The Hermitage, Jan. 15, 1937	.08	.06	1.10	(4)	5.00	93,848,500
787	3¢ Generals Sherman, Grant						
	and Sheridan, Feb. 18, 1937	.12	.06	1.50	(4)	5.00	87,741,150
788	4¢ Generals Robert E. Lee,						
	"Stonewall" Jackson						
	and Stratford Hall, Mar. 23, 1937	.30	.12	12.00	(4)	5.50	35,794,150
789	5¢ U.S. Military Academy						
	at West Point, May 26, 1937	.60	.12	13.00	(4)	5.50	36,839,250
	Navy Issue						
790	1¢ John Paul Jones, John Barry,						
	Bon Homme Richard and *Lexington*,						
	Dec. 15, 1936	.08	.06	1.00	(4)	5.00	104,773,450
791	2¢ Stephen Decatur,						
	Thomas Macdonough						
	and *Saratoga*, Jan. 15, 1937	.09	.06	1.10	(4)	5.00	92,054,550
792	3¢ David G. Farragut						
	and David D. Porter, *Hartford*						
	and *Powhatan*, Feb. 18, 1937	.14	.06	1.50	(4)	5.00	93,291,650
793	4¢ Admirals William T. Sampson,						
	George Dewey and						
	Winfield S. Schley, Mar. 23, 1937	.32	.12	12.00	(4)	5.50	34,552,950
794	5¢ Seal of U.S. Naval Academy						
	and Naval Cadets, May 26, 1937	.60	.12	13.00	(4)	5.50	36,819,050
	Issues of 1937						
795	3¢ Northwest Territory Ordinance,						
	July 13	.10	.06	1.75	(4)	6.00	84,825,250
	Perf. 11						
796	5¢ Virginia Dare, Aug. 18	.20	.28	10.00	(6)	7.00	25,040,400
	Society of Philatelic Americans Issue, Souvenir Sheet, Aug. 26, Imperf.						
797	10¢ blue green (749)	.60	.40			6.00	5,277,445
	Perf. 11x10½						
798	3¢ Constitution Sesquicentennial,						
	Sept. 17	.12	.07	1.65	(4)	6.50	99,882,300
	Territorial Issues, Perf. 10½x11						
799	3¢ Hawaii, Oct. 18	.10	.07	1.75	(4)	7.00	78,454,450
	Perf. 11x10½						
800	3¢ Alaska, Nov. 12	.10	.07	1.75	(4)	7.00	77,004,200
801	3¢ Puerto Rico, Nov. 25	.10	.07	1.75	(4)	7.00	81,292,450
802	3¢ Virgin Islands, Dec. 15	.10	.07	1.75	(4)	7.00	76,474,550

785

786

787

788

789

790

791

792

793

794

795

796

798

799

800

801

802

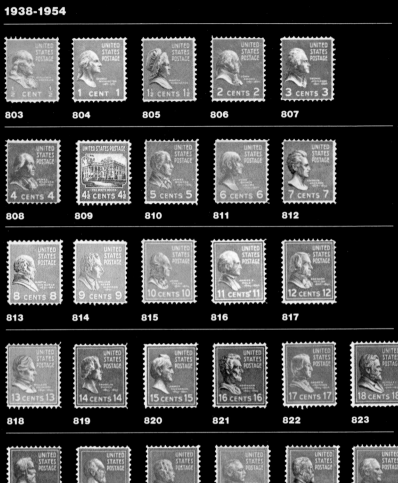

803   804   805   806   807

808   809   810   811   812

813   814   815   816   817

818   819   820   821   822   823

824   825   826   827   828   829

830   831   832   833   834

	Issues of 1938-54	Un	U	PB	#	FDC	Q
	Presidential Issue, Perf. 11x10½ (#804b, 806b, 807a issued in 1939, 832b in 1951, 832c in 1954; rest in 1938) (see also #839-851)						
803	½¢ Benjamin Franklin, May 19	.05	.05	.40	(4)	1.50	
804	1¢ George Washington, Apr. 25	.05	.05	.25	(4)	2.25	
804b	Booklet pane of 6, Jan. 27, 1939	1.50	.20			20.00	
805	1½¢ Martha Washington, May 5	.06	.05	.30	(4)	2.25	
806	2¢ John Adams, June 3	.07	.05	.40	(4)	2.25	
806b	Booklet pane of 6, Jan. 27, 1939	3.25	.50			20.00	
807	3¢ Thomas Jefferson, June 16	.07	.05	.50	(4)	2.25	
807a	Booklet pane of 6, Jan. 27, 1939	6.50	.50			24.00	
808	4¢ James Madison, July 1	.80	.05	5.00	(4)	2.25	
809	4½¢ White House, July 11	.14	.06	1.60	(4)	2.75	
810	5¢ James Monroe, July 21	.22	.05	2.00	(4)	2.50	
811	6¢ John Q. Adams, July 28	.25	.05	2.25	(4)	2.50	
812	7¢ Andrew Jackson, Aug. 4	.28	.05	2.50	(4)	2.75	
813	8¢ Martin Van Buren, Aug. 11	.30	.05	3.25	(4)	2.75	
814	9¢ William H. Harrison, Aug. 18	.38	.05	3.50	(4)	3.00	
815	10¢ John Tyler, Sept. 2	.28	.05	2.50	(4)	3.00	
816	11¢ James K. Polk, Sept. 8	.65	.08	6.00	(4)	3.00	
817	12¢ Zachary Taylor, Sept. 14	1.10	.06	9.50	(4)	3.25	
818	13¢ Millard Fillmore, Sept. 22	1.25	.08	10.00	(4)	3.25	
819	14¢ Franklin Pierce, Oct. 6	.90	.08	8.75	(4)	3.50	
820	15¢ James Buchanan, Oct. 13	.50	.05	3.75	(4)	3.50	
821	16¢ Abraham Lincoln, Oct. 20	.90	.25	8.75	(4)	3.75	
822	17¢ Andrew Johnson, Oct. 27	.85	.12	7.50	(4)	4.00	
823	18¢ Ulysses S. Grant, Nov. 3	1.50	.08	14.00	(4)	4.50	
824	19¢ Rutherford B. Hayes, Nov. 10	1.25	.35	10.00	(4)	4.50	
825	20¢ James A. Garfield, Nov. 10	.70	.05	6.00	(4)	4.75	
826	21¢ Chester A. Arthur, Nov. 22	1.50	.10	12.00	(4)	5.25	
827	22¢ Grover Cleveland, Nov. 22	1.25	.40	12.50	(4)	5.50	
828	24¢ Benjamin Harrison, Dec. 2	3.75	.18	30.00	(4)	5.50	
829	25¢ William McKinley, Dec. 2	.80	.05	5.00	(4)	6.75	
830	30¢ Theodore Roosevelt, Dec. 8	4.75	.05	37.50	(4)	10.00	
831	50¢ William Howard Taft, Dec. 8	6.50	.06	55.00	(4)	20.00	
	Perf. 11						
832	$1 Woodrow Wilson, Aug. 29	8.25	.10	62.50	(4)	60.00	
	Wmkd. USIR						
832b	purple and black, 1951	250.00	50.00	1,850	(4)		
	Unwmkd.						
832c	red violet and black,						
	Aug. 31, 1954	6.75	.15	47.50	(4)	30.00	
833	$2 Warren G. Harding, Sept. 29	21.00	3.75	165.00	(4)	125.00	
834	$5 Calvin Coolidge, Nov. 17	105.00	3.50	625.00	(4)	190.00	

This series was in use for approximately 16 years when the Liberty Series began replacing it. Various shades of these stamps are in existence because of numerous reprintings.

	1938 continued, Perf. 11x10½	Un	U	PB	#	FDC	Q
835	3¢ Constitution Ratification,						
	June 21	.16	.07	5.50	(4)	6.50	73,043,650
	Perf. 11						
836	3¢ Swedish-Finnish Sesquicentennial,						
	June 27	.12	.08	4.50	(6)	6.00	58,564,368
	Perf. 11x10½						
837	3¢ Northwest Territory Sesquicentennial,						
	July 15	.14	.08	12.50	(4)	6.00	65,939,500
838	3¢ Iowa Territorial Centennial,						
	Aug. 24	.12	.08	7.00	(4)	6.00	47,064,300
	Issues of 1939, Coil Stamps, Jan. 20, Perf. 10 Vertically						
839	1¢ green Washington (804)	.20	.06	1.25	(2)	7.00	
840	1½¢ bistre brown						
	M. Washington (805)	.24	.06	1.30	(2)	7.00	
841	2¢ rose carmine Adams (806)	.24	.05	1.75	(2)	7.00	
842	3¢ deep violet Jefferson (807)	.42	.05	2.50	(2)	8.00	
843	4¢ red violet Madison (808)	6.75	.35	35.00	(2)	10.00	
844	4½¢ dark gray White House (809)	.42	.35	4.00	(2)	10.00	
845	5¢ bright blue Monroe (810)	4.75	.30	30.00	(2)	11.00	
846	6¢ red orange J.Q. Adams (811)	1.10	.15	8.75	(2)	16.00	
847	10¢ brown red Tyler (815)	11.00	.40	55.00	(2)	22.00	
	Jan. 27, Perf. 10 Horizontally						
848	1¢ green Washington (804)	.55	.12	3.75	(2)	7.00	
849	1½¢ bistre brown						
	M. Washington (805)	1.10	.30	4.75	(2)	9.00	
850	2¢ rose carmine Adams (806)	2.50	.40	9.00	(2)	11.00	
851	3¢ deep violet Jefferson (807)	2.25	.35	7.50	(2)	13.50	
	Perf. 10½x11						
852	3¢ Golden Gate Exposition, Feb. 18	.10	.06	1.75	(4)	5.00	114,439,600
853	3¢ New York World's Fair, Apr. 1	.10	.06	2.00	(4)	8.00	101,699,550
	Perf. 11						
854	3¢ Washington's Inauguration,						
	Apr. 30	.25	.10	4.25	(6)	5.00	72,764,550
	Perf. 11x10½						
855	3¢ Baseball, June 12	.32	.08	4.50	(4)	25.00	81,269,600
	Perf. 11						
856	3¢ Panama Canal, Aug. 15	.18	.08	5.25	(6)	5.00	67,813,350
	Perf. 10½x11						
857	3¢ Printing, Sept. 25	.09	.08	1.65	(4)	5.00	71,394,750
	Perf. 11x10½						
858	3¢ 50th Anniversary of Statehood						
	(Montana, North Dakota, South						
	Dakota, Washington), Nov. 2	.09	.08	1.65	(4)	5.00	66,835,000

835

836

837

838

852

853

854

856

857

858

859 860 861 862 863

864 865 866 867 868

869 870 871 872 873

874 875 876 877 878

879 880 881 882 883

884 885 886 887 888

889 890 891 892 893

Issues of 1940	Un	U	PB	#	FDC	Q
Famous Americans Issue, Perf. 10½x11						
Authors						
859	1¢ Washington Irving, Jan. 29	.07	.06	1.25	(4)	1.90	56,348,320
860	2¢ James Fenimore Cooper, Jan. 29	.08	.08	1.25	(4)	1.90	53,177,110
861	3¢ Ralph Waldo Emerson, Feb. 5	.10	.06	2.00	(4)	1.90	53,260,270
862	5¢ Louisa May Alcott, Feb. 5	.28	.20	11.00	(4)	4.50	22,104,950
863	10¢ Samuel L. Clemens						
	(Mark Twain), Feb. 13	1.60	1.35	50.00	(4)	7.50	13,201,270
Poets						
864	1¢ Henry W. Longfellow, Feb. 16	.10	.08	2.25	(4)	1.90	51,603,580
865	2¢ John Greenleaf Whittier, Feb. 16	.10	.08	2.00	(4)	1.90	52,100,510
866	3¢ James Russell Lowell, Feb. 20	.14	.06	3.50	(4)	1.90	51,666,580
867	5¢ Walt Whitman, Feb. 20	.32	.18	11.00	(4)	4.00	22,207,780
868	10¢ James Whitcomb Riley, Feb. 24	1.75	1.40	45.00	(4)	7.50	11,835,530
Educators						
869	1¢ Horace Mann, Mar. 14	.12	.08	2.50	(4)	1.90	52,471,160
870	2¢ Mark Hopkins, Mar. 14	.09	.06	1.40	(4)	1.90	52,366,440
871	3¢ Charles W. Eliot, Mar. 28	.15	.06	3.25	(4)	1.90	51,636,270
872	5¢ Frances E. Willard, Mar. 28	.38	.25	14.00	(4)	4.00	20,729,030
873	10¢ Booker T. Washington, Apr. 7	1.25	1.25	32.50	(4)	7.50	14,125,580
Scientists						
874	1¢ John James Audubon, Apr. 8	.08	.06	1.00	(4)	1.90	59,409,000
875	2¢ Dr. Crawford W. Long, Apr. 8	.08	.06	1.00	(4)	1.90	57,888,600
876	3¢ Luther Burbank, Apr. 17	.10	.06	1.75	(4)	2.75	58,273,180
877	5¢ Dr. Walter Reed, Apr. 17	.25	.15	9.00	(4)	4.00	23,779,000
878	10¢ Jane Addams, Apr. 26	1.05	.95	32.50	(4)	7.50	15,112,580
Composers						
879	1¢ Stephen Collins Foster, May 3	.07	.06	1.50	(4)	1.90	57,322,790
880	2¢ John Philip Sousa, May 3	.09	.06	1.25	(4)	1.90	58,281,580
881	3¢ Victor Herbert, May 13	.10	.06	1.75	(4)	1.90	56,398,790
882	5¢ Edward A. MacDowell, May 13	.35	.22	12.50	(4)	4.00	21,147,000
883	10¢ Ethelbert Nevin, June 10	3.75	1.35	50.00	(4)	7.00	13,328,000
Artists						
884	1¢ Gilbert Charles Stuart, Sept. 5	.08	.06	1.25	(4)	1.90	54,389,510
885	2¢ James A. McNeill Whistler, Sept. 5	.08	.06	1.10	(4)	1.90	53,636,580
886	3¢ Augustus Saint-Gaudens, Sept. 16	.10	.06	1.25	(4)	1.90	55,313,230
887	5¢ Daniel Chester French, Sept. 16	.45	.22	11.50	(4)	3.50	21,720,580
888	10¢ Frederic Remington, Sept. 30	1.65	1.40	35.00	(4)	7.00	13,600,580
Inventors						
889	1¢ Eli Whitney, Oct. 7	.12	.08	2.50	(4)	1.90	47,599,580
890	2¢ Samuel F.B. Morse, Oct. 7	.12	.06	1.30	(4)	1.90	53,766,510
891	3¢ Cyrus Hall McCormick, Oct. 14	.25	.06	2.50	(4)	1.90	54,193,580
892	5¢ Elias Howe, Oct. 14	1.00	.32	20.00	(4)	4.50	20,264,580
893	10¢ Alexander Graham Bell, Oct. 28	11.00	2.25	100.00	(4)	12.50	13,726,580

A Reminder: Beginning with this edition, catalog values for all stamps listed reflect (as accurately as possible) actual retail values as found in the marketplace.

	1940 continued, Perf. 11x10½	Un	U	PB	#	FDC	Q
894	3¢ Pony Express, Apr. 3	.22	.10	5.50	(4)	6.00	46,497,400
	Perf. 10½x11						
895	3¢ Pan American Union, Apr. 14		.09	5.00	(4)	4.50	47,700,000
	Perf. 11x10½						
896	3¢ Idaho Statehood, July 3	.14	.08	3.00	(4)	4.50	50,618,150
	Perf. 10½x11						
897	3¢ Wyoming Statehood, July 10	.14	.08	2.75	(4)	4.50	50,034,400
	Perf. 11x10½						
898	3¢ Coronado Expedition, Sept. 7	.14	.08	2.75	(4)	4.50	60,943,700
	National Defense Issue, Oct. 16						
899	1¢ Statue of Liberty	.05	.05	.70	(4)	4.25	
900	2¢ 90mm Anti-aircraft Gun	.06	.05	.70	(4)	4.25	
901	3¢ Torch of Enlightenment	.09	.05	1.40	(4)	4.25	
	Perf. 10½x11						
902	3¢ Thirteenth Amendment, Oct. 20	.16	.10	5.00	(4)	5.00	44,389,550
	Issue of 1941, Perf. 11x10½						
903	3¢ Vermont Statehood, Mar. 4	.14	.08	2.50	(4)	4.50	54,574,550
	Issues of 1942						
904	3¢ Kentucky Statehood, June 1	.10	.09	1.75	(4)	4.00	63,558,400
905	3¢ Win the War, July 4	.08	.05	.50	(4)	3.75	
906	5¢ Chinese Resistance, July 7	.18	.16	16.00	(4)	5.75	21,272,800
	Issues of 1943						
907	2¢ Allied Nations, Jan. 14	.08	.05	.40	(4)	3.50	1,671,564,200
908	1¢ Four Freedoms, Feb. 12	.08	.05	.90	(4)	3.50	1,227,334,200

PAN AMERICAN UNION SPARKED COOPERATION

From 1910 through 1970 the Pan American Union (#895) was the name of the permanent body of the Organization of American States, an association of North, South and Central American countries. The spirit of cooperation fostered by the Pan American Union led to the establishment of the Pan American Postal Union and the building of the Pan American Highway linking the United States with Mexico as well as Central and South America.

894

895

896

897

898

899

900

901

902

903

904

905

906

907

908

909

910

911

912

913

914

915

916

917

918

919

920

921

922

923

924

925

926

	Issue of 1943-44, Overrun Countries Issue, Perf. 12	Un	U	PB	#	FDC	Q
909	5¢ Poland, June 22	.18	.12	8.75*	(4)	6.00	19,999,646
910	5¢ Czechoslovakia, July 12	.18	.09	4.25*	(4)	5.00	19,999,646
911	5¢ Norway, July 27	.14	.07	2.25*	(4)	4.00	19,999,646
912	5¢ Luxembourg, Aug. 10	.14	.07	2.00*	(4)	4.00	19,999,646
913	5¢ Netherlands, Aug. 24	.14	.07	2.00*	(4)	4.00	19,999,646
914	5¢ Belgium, Sept. 14	.14	.07	2.00*	(4)	4.00	19,999,646
915	5¢ France, Sept. 28	.14	.07	2.00*	(4)	4.00	19,999,646
916	5¢ Greece, Oct. 12	.38	.25	20.00*	(4)	4.00	14,999,646
917	5¢ Yugoslavia, Oct. 26	.28	.15	7.50*	(4)	4.00	14,999,646
918	5¢ Albania, Nov. 9	.18	.15	9.00*	(4)	4.00	14,999,646
919	5¢ Austria, Nov. 23	.18	.15	5.50*	(4)	4.00	14,999,646
920	5¢ Denmark, Dec. 7	.18	.15	7.50*	(4)	4.00	14,999,646
921	5¢ Korea, Nov. 2, 1944	.15	.12	7.00*	(4)	5.00	14,999,646
	*Instead of plate numbers, the selvage is inscribed with the name of the country.						
	Issues of 1944, Perf. 11x10½						
922	3¢ Transcontinental Railroad, May 10	.15	.05	2.50	(4)	6.00	61,303,000
923	3¢ Steamship, May 22	.09	.05	2.50	(4)	4.00	61,001,450
924	3¢ Telegraph, May 24	.08	.05	1.60	(4)	3.50	60,605,000
925	3¢ Philippines, Sept. 27	.08	.05	2.00	(4)	3.50	50,129,350
926	3¢ Motion Pictures, Oct. 31	.08	.05	1.50	(4)	3.50	53,479,400

FRANCE REMAINS FREE *Although subdued by the German Occupation during World War II (#915), the tradition of French independence has never waned. In 1989, France celebrates the 200-year anniversary of the French Revolution, which overthrew its monarchy and established a republican form of government. The U.S. Postal Service observed the occasion by issuing a new 45-cent airmail stamp on July 14, 1989.*

	Issues of 1945, Perf. 11x10½	Un	U	PB	#	FDC	Q
927	3¢ Florida Statehood, Mar. 3	.08	.05	1.00	(4)	3.50	61,617,350
928	5¢ United Nations Conference,						
	Apr. 25	.08	.05	.70	(4)	3.50	75,500,000
	Perf. 10½x11						
929	3¢ Iwo Jima (Marines), July 11	.08	.05	.50	(4)	5.25	137,321,000
	Issues of 1945-46, Franklin D. Roosevelt Issue, Perf. 11x10½						
930	1¢ Roosevelt and Hyde Park						
	Residence, July 26, 1945	.05	.05	.30	(4)	2.50	128,140,000
931	2¢ Roosevelt and "The Little						
	White House" at Warm Springs, Ga.,						
	Aug. 24, 1945	.06	.05	.40	(4)	2.50	67,255,000
932	3¢ Roosevelt and White House,						
	June 27, 1945	.06	.05	.55	(4)	2.50	133,870,000
933	5¢ Roosevelt, Map of Western						
	Hemisphere and Four Freedoms,						
	Jan. 30, 1946	.09	.05	.65	(4)	3.00	76,455,400
934	3¢ Army, Sept. 28	.06	.05	.50	(4)	3.50	128,357,750
935	3¢ Navy, Oct. 27	.06	.05	.50	(4)	3.50	135,863,000
936	3¢ Coast Guard, Nov. 10	.06	.05	.50	(4)	3.50	111,616,700
937	3¢ Alfred E. Smith, Nov. 26	.06	.05	.50	(4)	2.50	308,587,700
938	3¢ Texas Statehood, Dec. 29	.06	.05	.50	(4)	3.50	170,640,000
	Issues of 1946						
939	3¢ Merchant Marine, Feb. 26	.06	.05	.50	(4)	2.50	135,927,000
940	3¢ Veterans of World War II, May 9	.06	.05	.55	(4)	2.50	260,339,100
941	3¢ Tennessee Statehood, June 1	.06	.05	.50	(4)	2.50	132,274,500
942	3¢ Iowa Statehood, Aug. 3	.06	.05	.50	(4)	2.50	132,430,000
943	3¢ Smithsonian Institution, Aug. 10	.06	.05	.50	(4)	2.50	139,209,500
944	3¢ Kearny Expedition, Oct. 16	.06	.05	.50	(4)	2.50	114,684,450
	Issues of 1947, Perf. 10½x11						
945	3¢ Thomas A. Edison, Feb. 11	.06	.05	.50	(4)	2.50	156,540,510
	Perf. 11x10½						
946	3¢ Joseph Pulitzer, Apr. 10	.06	.05	.50	(4)	2.50	120,452,600
947	3¢ Postage Stamps Centenary, May 17	.06	.05	.50	(4)	2.50	127,104,300

FLORIDA CENTENNIAL
1845 1945
3¢ UNITED STATES POSTAGE

27

"TOWARD
UNITED NATIONS
APRIL 25, 1945"
FRANKLIN D. ROOSEVELT
5¢ UNITED STATES POSTAGE

928

UNITED STATES POSTAGE
3¢
IWO JIMA

929

U.S. Postage
1842 1945 HYDE PARK
1¢ ROOSEVELT

30

U.S. POSTAGE
1882 1945 THE WHITE HOUSE
2¢ ROOSEVELT

931

UNITED STATES POSTAGE
1882 1945
3¢ ROOSEVELT

932

UNITED STATES POSTAGE
FREEDOM
OF SPEECH
AND RELIGION
FROM WANT
AND FEAR
1882 1945 ROOSEVELT
5¢

33

U.S. ARMY
3¢ 3¢

934

3¢ UNITED STATES POSTAGE U.S. NAVY

935

UNITED STATES POSTAGE
3
1790 U.S. COAST GUARD 1945

936

ALFRED E. SMITH
1873 1944
U.S. POSTAGE 3¢

937

TEXAS 3¢
STATEHOOD
1845 1945
UNITED STATES POSTAGE

938

U.S. MERCHANT MARINE

939

UNITED STATES POSTAGE
3¢ HONORING THOSE WHO HAVE SERVED 3¢

940

U.S. POSTAGE
3¢ 3¢
TENNESSEE – VOLUNTEER STATE
150TH ANNIVERSARY OF STATEHOOD

941

1846 – IOWA STATEHOOD CENTENNIAL – 1946
UNITED STATES POSTAGE 3¢

942

FOR THE INC
KNOW
3¢ UNITE

943

STEPHEN WATTS
KEARNY
EXPEDITION
U.S. POSTAGE
1846 ENTRY INTO SANTA FE 1946 3¢

940

UNITED STATES POSTAGE
3¢

"OUR REPUBLIC
AND ITS PRESS
WILL RISE OR FALL
TOGETHER"
JOSEPH PULITZER
3¢ UNITED STATES POSTAGE

3¢
U.S. POST

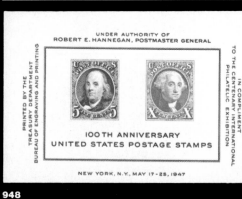

948

949

950

951

952

953

954

955

956

957

958

959

960

961

962

963

964

965

966

967

	1947 continued, Imperf.	Un	U	PB	#	FDC	Q
	Centenary International Philatelic Exhibition Issue, Souvenir Sheet, May 19						
948	Souvenir sheet of 2	.65	.45			3.00	10,299,600
948a	5¢ single stamp from sheet	.25	.25				
948b	10¢ single stamp from sheet	.30	.30				
	Perf. 11x10½						
949	3¢ Doctors, June 9	.06	.05	.50	(4)	1.50	132,902,000
950	3¢ Utah Settlement, July 24	.06	.05	.50	(4)	1.50	131,968,000
951	3¢ U.S. Frigate Constitution, Oct. 21	.06	.05	.50	(4)	1.50	131,488,000
	Perf. 10½x11						
952	3¢ Everglades National Park, Dec. 5	.06	.05	.50	(4)	1.50	122,362,000
	Issues of 1948, Perf. 10½x11						
953	3¢ Dr. George Washington Carver,						
	Jan. 5	.06	.05	.50	(4)	1.50	121,548,000
	Perf. 11x10½						
954	3¢ California Gold, Jan. 24	.06	.05	.50	(4)	1.50	131,109,500
955	3¢ Mississippi Territory, Apr. 7	.06	.05	.50	(4)	1.50	122,650,500
956	3¢ Four Chaplains, May 28	.06	.05	.50	(4)	1.50	121,953,500
957	3¢ Wisconsin Statehood, May 29	.06	.05	.50	(4)	1.50	115,250,000
958	5¢ Swedish Pioneer, June 4	.09	.05	.90	(4)	1.50	64,198,500
959	3¢ Progress of Women, July 19	.06	.05	.50	(4)	1.50	117,642,500
	Perf. 10½x11						
960	3¢ William Allen White, July 31	.06	.06	.60	(4)	1.50	77,649,600
	Perf. 11x10½						
961	3¢ U.S.-Canada Friendship, Aug. 2	.06	.05	.50	(4)	1.50	113,474,500
962	3¢ Francis Scott Key, Aug. 9	.06	.05	.50	(4)	1.50	120,868,500
963	3¢ Salute to Youth, Aug. 11	.06	.06	.50	(4)	1.50	77,800,500
964	3¢ Oregon Territory, Aug. 14	.06	.05	.50	(4)	1.50	52,214,000
	Perf. 10½x11						
965	3¢ Harlan F. Stone, Aug. 25	.09	.08	1.00	(4)	1.50	53,958,100
966	3¢ Palomar Mountain Observatory,						
	Aug. 30	.09	.05	1.75	(4)	1.50	61,120,010
	Perf. 11x10½						
967	3¢ Clara Barton, Sept. 7	.06	.05	.50	(4)	1.25	57,823,000

		Un	U	PB	#	FDC	Q
	1948 continued, Perf. 11x10½						
968	3¢ Poultry Industry, Sept. 9	.06	.05	.60	(4)	1.25	52,975,000
	Perf. 10½x11						
969	3¢ Gold Star Mothers, Sept. 21	.06	.05	.60	(4)	1.50	77,149,000
	Perf. 11x10½						
970	3¢ Fort Kearny, Sept. 22	.06	.05	.60	(4)	1.50	58,332,000
971	3¢ Volunteer Firemen, Oct. 4	.06	.05	.60	(4)	1.50	56,228,000
972	3¢ Indian Centennial, Oct. 15	.06	.05	.60	(4)	1.25	57,832,000
973	3¢ Rough Riders, Oct. 27	.06	.05	.65	(4)	1.25	53,875,000
974	3¢ Juliette Gordon Low, Oct. 29	.06	.05	.60	(4)	1.25	63,834,000
	Perf. 10½x11						
975	3¢ Will Rogers, Nov. 4	.06	.05	.80	(4)	1.25	67,162,200
976	3¢ Fort Bliss, Nov. 5	.09	.05	1.75	(4)	1.25	64,561,000
	Perf. 11x10½						
977	3¢ Moina Michael, Nov. 9	.06	.05	.60	(4)	1.25	64,079,500
978	3¢ Gettysburg Address, Nov. 19	.06	.05	.60	(4)	1.25	63,388,000
	Perf. 10½x11						
979	3¢ American Turners, Nov. 20	.06	.05	.60	(4)	1.25	62,285,000
980	3¢ Joel Chandler Harris, Dec. 9	.06	.05	.85	(4)	1.25	57,492,610
	Issues of 1949, Perf. 11x10½						
981	3¢ Minnesota Territory, Mar. 3	.06	.05	.50	(4)	1.25	99,190,000
982	3¢ Washington and Lee University,						
	Apr. 12	.06	.05	.50	(4)	1.25	104,790,000
983	3¢ Puerto Rico Election, Apr. 27	.06	.05	.50	(4)	1.25	108,805,000
984	3¢ Annapolis Tercentary, May 23	.06	.05	.50	(4)	1.25	107,340,000
985	3¢ Grand Army of the Republic,						
	Aug. 29	.06	.05	.50	(4)	1.25	117,020,000
	Perf. 10½x11						
986	3¢ Edgar Allan Poe, Oct. 7	.06	.05	.60	(4)	1.25	122,633,000
	Issues of 1950, Perf. 11x10½						
987	3¢ American Bankers Association,						
	Jan. 3	.06	.05	.50	(4)	1.25	130,960,000
	Perf. 10½x11						
988	3¢ Samuel Gompers, Jan. 27	.06	.05	.50	(4)	1.25	128,478,000

968

969

970

971

972

973

974

975

976

977

978

979

980

981

982

983

984

985

986

987

988

989

990

991

992

993

994

995

996

997

998

999

1000

1001

1002

1003

1004

	1950 continued,	Un	U	PB	#	FDC	Q
	National Capital Sesquicentennial Issue, Perf. 10½x11, Perf. 11x10½						
989	3¢ Statue of Freedom						
	on Capitol Dome, Apr. 20	.06	.05	.50	(4)	1.25	132,090,000
990	3¢ Executive Mansion, June 12	.06	.05	.50	(4)	1.25	130,050,000
991	3¢ Supreme Court, Aug. 2	.06	.05	.50	(4)	1.25	131,350,000
992	3¢ U.S. Capitol, Nov. 22	.06	.05	.50	(4)	1.25	129,980,000
	Perf. 11x10½						
993	3¢ Railroad Engineers, Apr. 29	.06	.05	.50	(4)	1.25	122,315,000
994	3¢ Kansas City, MO, June 3	.06	.05	.50	(4)	1.25	122,170,000
995	3¢ Boy Scouts, June 30	.06	.06	.55	(4)	2.00	131,635,000
996	3¢ Indiana Territory, July 4	.06	.05	.50	(4)	1.25	121,860,000
997	3¢ California Statehood, Sept. 9	.06	.05	.50	(4)	1.25	121,120,000
	Issues of 1951						
998	3¢ United Confederate Veterans, May 30	.06	.05	.50	(4)	1.25	119,120,000
999	3¢ Nevada Settlement, July 14	.06	.05	.50	(4)	1.25	112,125,000
1000	3¢ Landing of Cadillac, July 24	.06	.05	.50	(4)	1.25	114,140,000
1001	3¢ Colorado Statehood, Aug. 1	.06	.05	.50	(4)	1.25	114,490,000
1002	3¢ American Chemical Society, Sept. 4	.06	.05	.50	(4)	1.25	117,200,000
1003	3¢ Battle of Brooklyn, Dec. 10	.07	.05	.50	(4)	1.25	116,130,000
	Issues of 1952						
1004	3¢ Betsy Ross, Jan. 2	.07	.05	.50	(4)	1.25	116,175,000

DETROIT FOUNDER'S NAME NOW HOUSEHOLD WORD
Leading a group of French settlers, Antoine de la Mothe Cadillac founded Detroit in 1701. Upon landing, the colonists built Fort Pontchartrain on the north bank of the Detroit River. While Cadillac (#1000) perhaps dreamed of glory, he is unlikely to have envisioned anything like the luxury car that today bears his name.

	1952 continued, Perf. 11x10½	Un	U	PB	#	FDC	Q
1005	3¢ 4-H Club, Jan. 15	.06	.05	.50	(4)	1.25	115,945,000
1006	3¢ B&O Railroad, Feb. 28	.07	.05	.55	(4)	1.50	112,540,000
1007	3¢ American Automobile						
	Association, Mar. 4	.06	.05	.50	(4)	.85	117,415,000
1008	3¢ NATO, Apr. 4	.06	.05	.50	(4)	.85	2,899,580,000
1009	3¢ Grand Coulee Dam, May 15	.06	.05	.50	(4)	.85	114,540,000
1010	3¢ Arrival of Lafayette, June 13	.06	.05	.50	(4)	.85	113,135,000
	Perf. 10½x11						
1011	3¢ Mt. Rushmore Memorial, Aug. 11	.06	.05	.60	(4)	.85	116,255,000
	Perf. 11x10½						
1012	3¢ Engineering, Sept. 6	.06	.05	.50	(4)	.85	113,860,000
1013	3¢ Service Women, Sept. 11	.06	.05	.50	(4)	.85	124,260,000
1014	3¢ Gutenberg Bible, Sept. 30	.06	.05	.50	(4)	.85	115,735,000
1015	3¢ Newspaper Boys, Oct. 4	.06	.05	.50	(4)	.85	115,430,000
1016	3¢ International Red Cross, Nov. 21	.06	.05	.50	(4)	.85	136,220,000
	Issues of 1953						
1017	3¢ National Guard, Feb. 23	.06	.05	.50	(4)	.85	114,894,000
1018	3¢ Ohio Statehood, Mar. 2	.06	.05	.60	(4)	.85	118,706,000
1019	3¢ Washington Territory, Mar. 2	.06	.05	.50	(4)	.85	114,190,000
1020	3¢ Louisiana Purchase, Apr. 30	.06	.05	.50	(4)	.85	113,990,000
1021	5¢ Opening of Japan, July 14	.09	.05	1.40	(4)	.85	89,289,600
1022	3¢ American Bar Association, Aug. 24	.06	.05	.50	(4)	.85	114,865,000
1023	3¢ Sagamore Hill, Sept. 14	.06	.05	.50	(4)	1.00	115,780,000

"LIBERTY UNDER LAW"

The American Bar Association (ABA) accredits law schools and actively seeks to promote justice and the upholding of legal ethics. The world's largest voluntary professional association, its 350,000 members are lawyers, justices, law students and teachers in the United States and its possessions. The ABA was established in 1878 and is headquartered in Chicago (#1022).

A Reminder: Beginning with this edition, catalog values for all stamps listed reflect (as accurately as possible) actual retail values as found in the marketplace.

1005

1006

1007

1008

1009

1010

1011

1012

1013

1014

1015

1016

1017

1018

1019

1020

1021

1022

1023

1024

1025

1026

1027

1028

1029

1030

1031

1031A

1032

1033

1034

1035

1036

1037

1038

1039

1040

1041

1042

1042A

1043

1044

1044A

1045

1046

1047

1048

1049

1050

1051

1052

1053

	1953 continued, Perf. 11x10½	Un	U	PB	#	FDC	Q
1024	3¢ Future Farmers, Oct. 13	.06	.05	.50	(4)	.85	115,244,600
1025	3¢ Trucking Industry, Oct. 27	.06	.05	.50	(4)	.85	123,709,600
1026	3¢ General George S. Patton, Nov. 11	.07	.05	.60	(4)	.85	114,798,600
1027	3¢ New York City, Nov. 20	.06	.05	.60	(4)	.85	115,759,600
1028	3¢ Gadsden Purchase, Dec. 30	.07	.05	.50	(4)	.85	116,134,600
	Issue of 1954						
1029	3¢ Columbia University, Jan. 4	.06	.05	.50	(4)	.85	118,540,000
	Liberty Issue, 1954-61, Perf. 11x10½, 10½x11						
1030	½¢ Franklin, Oct. 20, 1954	.05	.05	.30	(4)	.85	
1031	1¢ Washington, Aug. 26, 1954	.05	.05	.25	(4)	.85	
1031A	1¼¢ Palace of the Governors,						
	Santa Fe, June 17, 1960	.05	.05	1.00	(4)	.85	
1032	1½¢ Mt. Vernon, Feb. 22, 1956	.07	.05	5.00	(4)	.60	
1033	2¢ Jefferson, Sept. 15, 1954	.05	.05	.25	(4)	.60	
1034	2½¢ Bunker Hill Monument and						
	Massachusetts Flag, June 17, 1959	.06	.05	1.25	(4)	.60	
1035	3¢ Statue of Liberty, June 24, 1954	.06	.05	.40	(4)	.60	
1035a	Booklet pane of 6, June 30, 1954	3.00	.50	6.00			
1036	4¢ Lincoln, Nov. 19, 1954	.07	.05	.50	(4)	.60	
1036a	Booklet pane of 6, July 31, 1958	2.25	.50	5.00			
1037	4½¢ The Hermitage, Mar. 16, 1959	.08	.05	1.00	(4)	.60	
1038	5¢ James Monroe, Dec. 2, 1954	.10	.05	.75	(4)	.60	
1039	6¢ T. Roosevelt, Nov. 18, 1955	.25	.05	2.00	(4)	.65	
1040	7¢ Wilson, Jan. 10, 1956	.20	.05	1.50	(4)	.70	
	Perf. 11						
1041	8¢ Statue of Liberty, Apr. 9, 1954	.24	.06	5.00	(4)	.80	
1042	8¢ Statue of Liberty,						
	redrawn, Mar. 22, 1958	.25	.05	1.75	(4)	.60	
	Perf. 11x10½, 10½x11						
1042A	8¢ Gen. John J. Pershing,						
	Nov. 17, 1961	.22	.05	1.50	(4)	.60	
1043	9¢ The Alamo, June 14, 1956	.28	.05	2.25	(4)	1.50	
1044	10¢ Independence Hall, July 4, 1956	.22	.05	1.65	(4)	.90	
	Perf. 11						
1044A	11¢ Statue of Liberty, June 15, 1961	.30	.06	2.00	(4)	.90	
	Perf. 11x10½, 10½x11						
1045	12¢ Benjamin Harrison, June 6, 1959	.32	.05	2.75	(4)	.90	
1046	15¢ John Jay, Dec. 12, 1958	.95	.05	5.25	(4)	1.00	
1047	20¢ Monticello, Apr. 13, 1956	.50	.05	3.75	(4)	1.20	
1048	25¢ Paul Revere, April 18, 1958	1.50	.05	11.50	(4)	1.30	
1049	30¢ Robert E. Lee, Sept. 21, 1955	1.20	.05	7.50	(4)	1.50	
1050	40¢ John Marshall, Sept. 24, 1955	1.90	.06	12.50	(4)	1.75	
1051	50¢ Susan B. Anthony, Aug. 25, 1955	1.75	.05	14.00	(4)	6.00	
1052	$1 Patrick Henry, Oct. 7, 1955	5.75	.06	50.00	(4)	13.00	
	Perf. 11						
1053	$5 Alexander Hamilton, Mar. 19, 1956	75.00	6.75	425.00	(4)	75.00	

	Issues of 1954-65, Coil Stamps, Perf. 10 Vertically	Un	U	PB/LP	#	FDC	Q
1054	1¢ dark green Washington						
	(1031), Oct. 8, 1954	.18	.12	1.25	(2)	.75	
	Perf. 10 Horizontally						
1054A	1¼¢ turquoise, Palace of the						
	Governors (1031A), June 17, 1960	.18	.12	3.50	(2)	1.00	
	Perf. 10 Vertically						
1055	2¢ rose carmine						
	Jefferson (1033), Oct. 22, 1954	.08	.05	.60	(2)	.75	
1056	2½¢ gray blue, Bunker Hill Monument,						
	Mass. Flag (1034), Sept. 9, 1959	.38	.25	6.50	(2)	1.20	
1057	3¢ deep violet Statue of Liberty						
	(1035), July 20, 1954	.10	.05	.80	(2)	.75	
1058	4¢ red violet Lincoln (1036),						
	July 31, 1958	.12	.05	1.00	(2)	.75	
	Perf. 10 Horizontally						
1059	4½¢ bl. grn. Hermitage (1037),						
	May 1, 1959	1.75	1.20	20.00	(2)	1.75	
	Perf. 10 Vertically						
1059A	25¢ grn. Revere (1048), Feb. 25, 1965	.50	.30	3.00	(2)	1.20	
	Issues of 1954, Perf. 11x10½						
1060	3¢ Nebraska Territory, May 7	.06	.05	.50	(4)	.75	115,810,000
1061	3¢ Kansas Territory, May 31	.06	.05	.50	(4)	.75	113,603,700
	Perf. 10½x11						
1062	3¢ George Eastman, July 12	.06	.05	.50	(4)	.75	128,002,000
	Perf. 11x10½						
1063	3¢ Lewis and Clark Expedition, July 28	.06	.05	.50	(4)	.75	116,078,150
	Issues of 1955, Perf. 10½x11						
1064	3¢ Pennsylvania Academy						
	of the Fine Arts, Jan. 15	.06	.05	.50	(4)	.75	116,139,800
	Perf. 11x10½						
1065	3¢ Land-Grant Colleges, Feb. 12	.06	.05	.50	(4)	.75	120,484,800
1066	8¢ Rotary International, Feb. 23	.15	.05	1.25	(4)	.90	53,854,750
1067	3¢ Armed Forces Reserve, May 21	.06	.05	.50	(4)	.75	176,075,000
	Perf. 10½x11						
1068	3¢ New Hampshire, June 21	.06	.05	.50	(4)	.75	125,944,400
	Perf. 11x10½						
1069	3¢ Soo Locks, June 28	.06	.05	.50	(4)	.75	122,284,600
1070	3¢ Atoms for Peace, July 28	.08	.05	.65	(4)	.75	133,638,850
1071	3¢ Fort Ticonderoga, Sept. 18	.06	.05	.50	(4)	.75	118,664,600
	Perf. 10½x11						
1072	3¢ Andrew W. Mellon, Dec. 20	.06	.05	.50	(4)	.75	112,434,000
	Issues of 1956						
1073	3¢ Benjamin Franklin, Jan. 17	.06	.05	.50	(4)	.75	129,384,550
	Perf. 11x10½						
1074	3¢ Booker T. Washington, Apr. 5	.06	.05	.50	(4)	.75	121,184,600

1060

1061

1062

1063

1065

1064

1066

1067

1068

1069

1070

1071

1072

1074

1073

1075

1076

1077

1078

1079

1080

1081

1082

1083

1084

1085

1086

1087

1088

1089

1090

	1956 continued	Un	U	PB	#	FDC	Q
	Fifth International Philatelic Exhibition Issues, Souvenir Sheet, Apr. 28, Imperf.						
1075	Sheet of 2 stamps (1035, 1041),						
	Apr. 28	2.25	2.00			6.50	2,900,731
1075a	3¢ (1035), single stamp from sheet	.90	.80				
1075b	8¢ (1041), single stamp from sheet	1.25	1.00				
	Apr. 30, Perf. 11x10½						
1076	3¢ New York Coliseum						
	and Columbus Monument	.06	.05	.50	(4)	.75	119,784,200
	Wildlife Conservation Issue						
1077	3¢ Wild Turkey, May 5	.06	.05	.65	(4)	1.10	123,159,400
1078	3¢ Pronghorn Antelope, June 22	.06	.05	.65	(4)	1.10	123,138,800
1079	3¢ King Salmon, Nov. 9	.06	.05	.65	(4)	1.10	109,275,000
	Perf. 10½x11						
1080	3¢ Pure Food and Drug Laws, June 27	.06	.05	.50	(4)	.80	112,932,200
	Perf. 11x10½						
1081	3¢ Wheatland, Aug. 5	.06	.05	.50	(4)	.80	125,475,000
	Perf. 10½x11						
1082	3¢ Labor Day, Sept. 3	.06	.05	.50	(4)	.80	117,855,000
	Perf. 11x10½						
1083	3¢ Nassau Hall, Sept. 22	.06	.05	.50	(4)	.80	122,100,000
	Perf. 10½x11						
1084	3¢ Devils Tower, Sept. 24	.06	.05	.50	(4)	.80	118,180,000
	Perf. 11x10½						
1085	3¢ Children's Stamp, Dec. 15	.06	.05	.50	(4)	.80	100,975,000
	Issues of 1957						
1086	3¢ Alexander Hamilton, Jan. 11	.06	.05	.50	(4)	.80	115,299,450
	Perf. 10½x11						
1087	3¢ Polio, Jan. 15	.06	.05	.50	(4)	.80	186,949,627
	Perf. 11x10½						
1088	3¢ Coast and Geodetic Survey, Feb. 11	.06	.05	.50	(4)	.80	115,235,000
1089	3¢ American Institute						
	of Architects, Feb. 23	.06	.05	.50	(4)	.80	106,647,500
	Perf. 10½x11						
1090	3¢ Steel Industry, May 22	.06	.05	.50	(4)	.80	112,010,000

	1957 continued, Perf. 11x10½	Un	U	PB	#	FDC	Q
1091	3¢ International Naval Review-						
	Jamestown Festival, June 10	.06	.05	.50	(4)	.80	118,470,000
1092	3¢ Oklahoma Statehood, June 14	.06	.05	.55	(4)	.80	102,230,000
1093	3¢ School Teachers, July 1	.06	.05	.50	(4)	.80	102,410,000
	Perf. 11						
1094	4¢ Flag, July 4	.07	.05	.60	(4)	.80	84,054,400
	Perf. 10½x11						
1095	3¢ Shipbuilding, Aug. 15	.06	.05	.70	(4)	.80	126,266,000
	Champion of Liberty Issue, Ramon Magsaysay, Aug. 31, Perf. 11						
1096	8¢ Bust of Magsaysay on Medal	.15	.08	1.25	(4)	.80	39,489,600
	Perf. 10½x11						
1097	3¢ Lafayette, Sept. 6	.06	.05	.50	(4)	.80	122,990,000
	Perf. 11						
1098	3¢ Wildlife Conservation, Nov. 22	.06	.05	.55	(4)	1.00	174,372,800
	Perf. 10½x11						
1099	3¢ Religious Freedom, Dec. 27	.06	.05	.50	(4)	.80	114,365,000
	Issues of 1958						
1100	3¢ Gardening-Horticulture, Mar. 15	.06	.05	.50	(4)	.80	122,765,200
1101-03 not assigned							
	Perf. 11x10½						
1104	3¢ Brussels Universal and						
	International Exhibition, Apr. 17	.06	.05	.50	(4)	.80	113,660,200
1105	3¢ James Monroe, Apr. 28	.06	.05	.55	(4)	.80	120,196,580
1106	3¢ Minnesota Statehood, May 11	.06	.05	.50	(4)	.80	120,805,200
	Perf. 11						
1107	3¢ International Geophysical Year,						
	May 31	.06	.05	.60	(4)	.80	125,815,200
	Perf. 11x10½						
1108	3¢ Gunston Hall, June 12	.06	.05	.50	(4)	.80	108,415,200
	Perf. 10½x11						
1109	3¢ Mackinac Bridge, June 25	.06	.05	.50	(4)	.80	107,195,200
	Champion of Liberty Issue, Simon Bolivar, July 24						
1110	4¢ Bust of Bolivar on Medal	.07	.05	.60	(4)	.80	115,745,280
	Perf. 11						
1111	8¢ Bust of Bolivar on Medal	.15	.08	3.00	(4)	.80	39,743,640
	Perf. 11x10½						
1112	4¢ Atlantic Cable, Aug. 15	.08	.05	.50	(4)	.80	114,570,200

1091

1092

1093

1094

1095

1096

1097

1098

1099

1100

1104

1105

1106

1107

1108

1109

1110

1111

1112

1113

1114

1115

1116

1117

1118

1119

1120

1121

1122

1123

1124

1125

1126

1127

1128

1129

1130

1131

	1958 continued	Un	U	PB	#	FDC	Q
	Lincoln Sesquicentennial Issue, 1958-59, Perf. 10½x11, 11x10½						
1113	1¢ Portrait by George Healy,						
	Feb. 12, 1959	.05	.05	.30	(4)	.80	120,400,200
1114	3¢ Sculptured Head						
	by Gutzon Borglum, Feb. 27, 1959	.06	.05	.50	(4)	.80	91,160,200
1115	4¢ Lincoln and Stephen Douglas						
	Debating, by Joseph Boggs Beale,						
	Aug. 27, 1958	.08	.05	.50	(4)	.80	114,860,200
1116	4¢ Statue in Lincoln Memorial						
	by Daniel Chester French,						
	May 30, 1959	.08	.05	.55	(4)	.80	126,500,000
	Issues of 1958, Champion of Liberty Issue, Lajos Kossuth, Sept. 19, Perf. 10½x11						
1117	4¢ Bust of Kossuth on Medal	.08	.05	.55	(4)	.80	120,561,280
	Perf. 11						
1118	8¢ Bust of Kossuth on Medal	.16	.08	2.75	(4)	.80	44,064,576
	Perf. 10½x11						
1119	4¢ Freedom of the Press, Sept. 22	.08	.05	.50	(4)	.80	118,390,200
	Perf. 11x10½						
1120	4¢ Overland Mail, Oct. 10	.08	.05	.50	(4)	.80	125,770,200
	Perf. 10½x11						
1121	4¢ Noah Webster, Oct. 16	.08	.05	.50	(4)	.80	114,114,280
	Perf. 11						
1122	4¢ Forest Conservation, Oct. 27	.08	.05	.55	(4)	.80	156,600,200
	Perf. 11x10½						
1123	4¢ Fort Duquesne, Nov. 25	.08	.05	.50	(4)	.80	124,200,200
	Issues of 1959						
1124	4¢ Oregon Statehood, Feb. 14	.08	.05	.50	(4)	.80	120,740,200
	Champion of Liberty Issue, José de San Martin, Feb. 25, Perf. 10½x11						
1125	4¢ Bust of San Martin on Medal	.08	.05	.55	(4)	.80	133,623,280
	Perf. 11						
1126	8¢ Bust of San Martin on Medal	.16	.08	1.50	(4)	.80	45,569,088
	Perf. 10½x11						
1127	4¢ NATO, Apr. 1	.08	.05	.50	(4)	.80	122,493,280
	Perf. 11x10½						
1128	4¢ Arctic Explorations, Apr. 6	.08	.05	.65	(4)	.80	131,260,200
1129	8¢ World Peace						
	Through World Trade, Apr. 20	.15	.12	1.00	(4)	.80	47,125,200
1130	4¢ Silver Centennial, June 8	.08	.05	.50	(4)	.80	123,105,000
	Perf. 11						
1131	4¢ St. Lawrence Seaway, June 26	.08	.05	.50	(4)	.80	126,105,050

A Reminder: Beginning with this edition, catalog values for all stamps listed reflect (as accurately as possible) actual retail values as found in the marketplace.

	1959 continued, Perf. 11	Un	U	PB	#	FDC	Q
1132	4¢ 49-Star Flag, July 4	.08	.05	.50	(4)	.80	209,170,000
1133	4¢ Soil Conservation, Aug. 26	.08	.05	.65	(4)	.80	120,835,000
1134	4¢ Petroleum Industry, Aug. 27	.08	.05	.50	(4)	.80	115,715,000
	Perf. 11x10½						
1135	4¢ Dental Health, Sept. 14	.08	.05	.50	(4)	.80	118,445,000
	Champion of Liberty Issue, Ernst Reuter, Sept. 29, Perf. 10½x11						
1136	4¢ Bust of Reuter on Medal	.08	.05	.55	(4)	.80	111,685,000
	Perf. 11						
1137	8¢ Bust of Reuter on Medal	.16	.08	1.50	(4)	.80	43,099,200
	Perf. 10½x11						
1138	4¢ Dr. Ephraim McDowell, Dec. 3	.08	.05	.50	(4)	.80	115,444,000
	Issues of 1960-61, American Credo Issue, Perf. 11						
1139	4¢ Quotation from Washington's						
	Farewell Address, Jan. 20, 1960	.08	.05	.70	(4)	1.25	126,470,000
1140	4¢ Benjamin Franklin Quotation,						
	Mar. 31, 1960	.08	.05	.70	(4)	1.00	124,560,000
1141	4¢ Thomas Jefferson Quotation,						
	May 18, 1960	.09	.05	.75	(4)	1.00	115,455,000
1142	4¢ Francis Scott Key Quotation,						
	Sept. 14, 1960	.10	.05	.75	(4)	1.25	122,060,000
1143	4¢ Abraham Lincoln Quotation,						
	Nov. 19, 1960	.10	.05	.80	(4)	1.25	120,540,000
1144	4¢ Patrick Henry Quotation,						
	Jan. 11, 1961	.12	.05	.80	(4)	1.25	113,075,000
	Issues of 1960						
1145	4¢ Boy Scouts, Feb. 8	.08	.05	.50	(4)	1.25	139,325,000
	Olympic Winter Games Issue, Feb. 18, Perf. 10½x11						
1146	4¢ Olympic Rings and Snowflake	.08	.05	.50	(4)	.80	124,445,000
	Champion of Liberty Issue, Thomas G. Masaryk, Mar. 7						
1147	4¢ Bust of Masaryk on Medal	.08	.05	.55	(4)	.80	113,792,000
	Perf. 11						
1148	8¢ Bust of Masaryk on Medal	.16	.08	1.50	(4)	.80	44,215,200
	Perf. 11x10½						
1149	4¢ World Refugee Year, Apr. 7	.08	.05	.50	(4)	.80	113,195,000
	Perf. 11						
1150	4¢ Water Conservation, Apr. 18	.08	.05	.55	(4)	.80	121,805,000
	Perf. 10½x11						
1151	4¢ SEATO, May 31	.08	.05	.50	(4)	.80	115,353,000

1132

1133

1134

1135

1136

1137

1138

1139

1140

1141

1142

1143

1144

1145

1146

1147

1148

1149

1150

1151

127

1152

1153

1154

1155

1156

1157

1158

1159

1160

1161

1162

1163

1164

1165

1166

1167

1168

1169

1170

1171

1172

1173

	1960 continued, Perf. 11x10½	Un	U	PB	#	FDC	Q
1152	4¢ American Woman, June 2	.08	.05	.50	(4)	.80	111,080,000
	Perf. 11						
1153	4¢ 50-Star Flag, July 4	.08	.05	.50	(4)	.80	153,025,000
	Perf. 11x10½						
1154	4¢ Pony Express, July 19	.08	.05	.50	(4)	.80	119,665,000
	Perf. 10½x11						
1155	4¢ Employ the Handicapped, Aug. 28	.08	.05	.50	(4)	.80	117,855,000
1156	4¢ World Forestry Congress, Aug. 29	.08	.05	.50	(4)	.80	118,185,000
	Perf. 11						
1157	4¢ Mexican Independence, Sept. 16	.08	.05	.50	(4)	.80	112,260,000
1158	4¢ U.S.-Japan Treaty, Sept. 28	.08	.05	.50	(4)	.80	125,010,000
	Champion of Liberty Issue, Ignacy Jan Paderewski, Oct. 8, Perf. 10½x11						
1159	4¢ Bust of Paderewski on Medal	.08	.05	.50	(4)	.80	119,798,000
	Perf. 11						
1160	8¢ Bust of Paderewski on Medal	.16	.08	1.50	(4)	.80	42,696,000
	Perf. 10½x11						
1161	4¢ Sen. Robert A. Taft Memorial, Oct. 10	.08	.05	.50	(4)	.80	106,610,000
	Perf. 11x10½						
1162	4¢ Wheels of Freedom, Oct. 15	.08	.05	.50	(4)	.80	109,695,000
	Perf. 11						
1163	4¢ Boys' Club of America, Oct. 18	.08	.05	.50	(4)	.80	123,690,000
1164	4¢ First Automated Post Office, Oct. 20	.08	.05	.50	(4)	.80	123,970,000
	Champion of Liberty Issue, Gustaf Mannerheim, Oct. 26, Perf. 10½x11						
1165	4¢ Bust of Mannerheim on Medal	.08	.05	.50	(4)	.80	124,796,000
	Perf. 11						
1166	8¢ Bust of Mannerheim on Medal	.16	.08	1.50	(4)	.80	42,076,800
1167	4¢ Camp Fire Girls, Nov. 1	.08	.05	.50	(4)	.80	116,210,000
	Champion of Liberty Issue, Giusseppe Garibaldi, Nov. 2, Perf. 10½x11						
1168	4¢ Bust of Garibaldi on Medal	.08	.05	.50	(4)	.80	126,252,000
	Perf. 11						
1169	8¢ Bust of Garibaldi on Medal	.16	.08	1.50	(4)	.80	42,746,400
	Perf. 10½x11						
1170	4¢ Sen. Walter F. George Memorial, Nov. 5	.08	.05	.50	(4)	.80	124,117,000
1171	4¢ Andrew Carnegie, Nov. 25	.08	.05	.50	(4)	.80	119,840,000
1172	4¢ John Foster Dulles Memorial, Dec. 6	.08	.05	.50	(4)	.80	117,187,000
	Perf. 11x10½						
1173	4¢ Echo 1-Communications for Peace, Dec. 15	.25	.08	1.50	(4)	2.00	124,390,000

	Issues of 1961	Un	U	PB	#	FDC	Q
	Champion of Liberty Issue, Mahatma Gandhi, Jan. 26, Perf. 10½x11						
1174	4¢ Bust of Gandhi on Medal	.08	.05	.50	(4)	.80	112,966,000
	Perf. 11						
1175	8¢ Bust of Gandhi on Medal	.16	.08	1.65	(4)	.80	41,644,200
1176	4¢ Range Conservation, Feb. 2	.08	.05	.55	(4)	.75	110,850,000
	Perf. 10½x11						
1177	4¢ Horace Greeley, Feb. 3	.08	.05	.50	(4)	.75	98,616,000
	Issues of 1961-65, Civil War Centennial Issue, Perf. 11x10½						
1178	4¢ Fort Sumter, Apr. 12, 1961	.12	.05	1.00	(4)	1.75	101,125,000
1179	4¢ Shiloh, Apr. 7, 1962	.10	.05	1.00	(4)	1.75	124,865,000
	Perf. 11						
1180	5¢ Gettysburg, July 1, 1963	.10	.05	1.00	(4)	1.75	79,905,000
1181	5¢ Wilderness, May 5, 1964	.10	.05	.80	(4)	1.75	125,410,000
1182	5¢ Appomattox, Apr. 9, 1965	.12	.05	1.50	(4)	1.75	112,845,000
	Issues of 1961						
1183	4¢ Kansas Statehood, May 10	.08	.05	.55	(4)	.75	106,210,000
	Perf. 11x10½						
1184	4¢ Sen. George W. Norris, July 11	.08	.05	.50	(4)	.75	110,810,000
1185	4¢ Naval Aviation, Aug. 20	.08	.05	.50	(4)	.90	116,995,000
	Perf. 10½x11						
1186	4¢ Workmen's Compensation, Sept. 4	.08	.05	.50	(4)	.75	121,015,000
	Perf. 11						
1187	4¢ Frederic Remington, Oct. 4	.08	.05	.60	(4)	.75	111,600,000
	Perf. 10½x11						
1188	4¢ Republic of China, Oct. 10	.08	.05	.50	(4)	.75	110,620,000
1189	4¢ Naismith-Basketball, Nov. 6	.08	.05	.55	(4)	1.50	109,110,000
	Perf. 11						
1190	4¢ Nursing, Dec. 28	.08	.05	.55	(4)	.75	145,350,000
	Issues of 1962						
1191	4¢ New Mexico Statehood, Jan. 6	.08	.05	.50	(4)	.75	112,870,000

174   **1175**   **1176**   **1177**

178   **1179**   **1180**

181   **1182**   **1183**

184   **1185**   **1186**   **1187**

188   **1189**   **1190**   **1191**

1192

1193

1194

1195

1196

1197

1198

1199

1200

1201

1202

1203

1204

1205

1206

1207

1208

1962 continued, Perf. 11	Un	U	PB/LP	#	FDC	Q
1192 4¢ Arizona Statehood, Feb. 14	.08	.05	.55	(4)	.75	121,820,000
1193 4¢ Project Mercury, Feb. 20	.08	.05	.55	(4)	2.00	289,240,000
1194 4¢ Malaria Eradication, Mar. 30	.08	.05	.50	(4)	.75	120,155,000
Perf. 10½x11						
1195 4¢ Charles Evans Hughes, Apr. 11	.08	.05	.50	(4)	.75	124,595,000
Perf. 11						
1196 4¢ Seattle World's Fair, Apr. 25	.08	.05	.55	(4)	.75	147,310,000
1197 4¢ Louisiana Statehood, Apr. 30	.08	.05	.50	(4)	.75	118,690,000
Perf. 11x10½						
1198 4¢ Homestead Act, May 20	.08	.05	.50	(4)	.75	122,730,000
1199 4¢ Girl Scouts, July 24	.08	.05	.50	(4)	1.00	126,515,000
1200 4¢ Sen. Brien McMahon, July 28	.08	.05	.55	(4)	.75	130,960,000
1201 4¢ Apprenticeship, Aug. 31	.08	.05	.50	(4)	.75	120,055,000
Perf. 11						
1202 4¢ Sam Rayburn, Sept. 16	.08	.05	.50	(4)	.75	120,715,000
1203 4¢ Dag Hammarskjold, Oct. 23	.08	.05	.60	(4)	.75	121,440,000
1204 4¢ Dag Hammarskjold, Special						
Printing black, brown and yellow						
(yellow inverted), Nov. 16	.09	.06	2.75	(4)	6.00	40,270,000
Christmas Issue, Nov. 1						
1205 4¢ Wreath and Candles	.08	.05	.50	(4)	.75	861,970,000
1206 4¢ Higher Education, Nov. 14	.08	.05	.50	(4)	.75	120,035,000
1207 4¢ Winslow Homer, Dec. 15	.08	.05	.60	(4)	.75	117,870,000
Issue of 1963						
1208 5¢ Flag over White House, Jan. 9	.10	.05	.60	(4)	.75	
Issues of 1962-63, Perf. 11x10½						
1209 1¢ Andrew Jackson, Mar. 22, 1963	.05	.05	.25	(4)	.75	
1210-12 not assigned						
1213 5¢ George Washington, Nov. 23, 1962	.12	.05	.55	(4)	.75	
1213a Booklet pane of 5 + label,						
Nov. 23, 1962	2.25	.75			5.00	
1214-24 not assigned						
Coil Stamps, Perf. 10 Vertically						
1225 1¢ green Jackson (1209),						
May 31, 1963	.12	.05	.85	(2)	.75	
1226-28 not assigned						
1229 5¢ dark blue gray Washington (1213),						
Nov. 23, 1962	1.25	.05	4.75	(2)	.75	
Issues of 1963, Perf. 11						
1230 5¢ Carolina Charter, Apr. 6	.10	.05	.60	(4)	.75	129,945,000

ROSS'S KEY UNLOCKED MALARIA MYSTERY

In 1902, English scientist Sir Ronald Ross received a Nobel Prize for research on the transmission of malaria. Ross discovered that the Anopheles *mosquito infects victims of its sting with a disease-causing parasite. This knowledge is crucial to the World Health Organization, whose goal is to eliminate malaria (#1194) once and for all.*

	1963 continued, Perf. 11	Un	U	PB/LP	#	FDC	Q
1231	5¢ Food for Peace-						
	Freedom from Hunger, June 4	.10	.05	.60	(4)	.75	135,620,000
1232	5¢ West Virginia Statehood, June 20	.10	.05	.60	(4)	.75	137,540,000
1233	5¢ Emancipation Proclamation, Aug. 16	.10	.05	.60	(4)	.75	132,435,000
1234	5¢ Alliance for Progress, Aug. 17	.10	.05	.60	(4)	.75	135,520,000
	Perf. 10½x11						
1235	5¢ Cordell Hull, Oct. 5	.10	.05	.60	(4)	.75	131,420,000
	Perf. 11x10½						
1236	5¢ Eleanor Roosevelt, Oct. 11	.10	.05	.60	(4)	.75	133,170,000
	Perf. 11						
1237	5¢ The Sciences, Oct. 14	.10	.05	.60	(4)	.75	130,195,000
1238	5¢ City Mail Delivery, Oct. 26	.10	.05	.60	(4)	.75	128,450,000
1239	5¢ International Red Cross, Oct. 29	.10	.05	.60	(4)	.75	118,665,000
	Christmas Issue, Nov. 1						
1240	5¢ National Christmas Tree						
	and White House	.10	.05	.60	(4)	.75	1,291,250,000
1241	5¢ John James Audubon, Dec. 7,						
	(see also #C71)	.10	.05	.60	(4)	.75	175,175,000
	Issues of 1964, Perf. 10½x11						
1242	5¢ Sam Houston, Jan. 10	.10	.05	.60	(4)	.75	125,995,000
	Perf. 11						
1243	5¢ Charles M. Russell, Mar. 19	.10	.05	.75	(4)	.75	128,925,000
	Perf. 11x10½						
1244	5¢ New York World's Fair, Apr. 22	.10	.05	.60	(4)	.75	145,700,000
	Perf. 11						
1245	5¢ John Muir, Apr. 29	.10	.05	.60	(4)	.75	120,310,000
	Perf. 11x10½						
1246	5¢ President John Fitzgerald Kennedy						
	Memorial, May 29	.10	.05	.60	(4)	.75	511,750,000
	Perf. 10½x11						
1247	5¢ New Jersey Settlement, June 15	.10	.05	.60	(4)	.75	123,845,000

1231

1232

1233

1234

1235

1236

1237

1238

1239

1240

1241

1242

1243

1244

1245

1246

1247

1248

1249

1250

1251

1252

1253

1254 1255 1257b
1256 1257

1258

1259

1260

1261

1262

1263

1264

1265

1266

1267

1268

	1964 continued, Perf. 11	Un	U	PB/LP	#	FDC	Q
1248	5¢ Nevada Statehood, July 22	.10	.05	.60	(4)	.75	122,825,000
1249	5¢ Register and Vote, Aug. 1	.10	.05	.60	(4)	.75	453,090,000
	Perf. 10½x11						
1250	5¢ Shakespeare, Aug. 14	.10	.05	.60	(4)	.75	123,245,000
1251	5¢ Doctors Mayo, Sept. 11	.10	.05	.60	(4)	.75	123,355,000
	Perf. 11						
1252	5¢ American Music, Oct. 15	.10	.05	.60	(4)	.75	126,970,000
1253	5¢ Homemakers, Oct. 26	.10	.05	.60	(4)	.75	121,250,000
	Christmas Issue, Nov. 9						
1254	5¢ Holly	.35	.05	3.00	(4)	.75	351,940,000
1255	5¢ Mistletoe	.35	.05	3.00	(4)	.75	351,940,000
1256	5¢ Poinsettia	.35	.05	3.00	(4)	.75	351,940,000
1257	5¢ Sprig of Conifer	.35	.05	3.00	(4)	.75	351,940,000
1257b	Block of four, #1254-1257	1.40	.75			3.00	
	Perf. 10½x11						
1258	5¢ Verrazano-Narrows Bridge,						
	Nov. 21	.10	.05	.60	(4)	.75	120,005,000
	Perf. 11						
1259	5¢ Fine Arts, Dec. 2	.10	.05	.60	(4)	.75	125,800,000
	Perf. 10½x11						
1260	5¢ Amateur Radio, Dec. 15	.10	.05	.60	(4)	.75	122,230,000
	Issues of 1965, Perf. 11						
1261	5¢ Battle of New Orleans, Jan. 8	.10	.05	.60	(4)	.75	115,695,000
1262	5¢ Physical Fitness-Sokols, Feb. 15	.10	.05	.60	(4)	.75	115,095,000
1263	5¢ Crusade Against Cancer, Apr. 1	.10	.05	.60	(4)	.75	119,560,000
	Perf. 10½x11						
1264	5¢ Winston Churchill Memorial, May 13	.10	.05	.60	(4)	.75	125,180,000
	Perf. 11						
1265	5¢ Magna Carta, June 15	.10	.05	.60	(4)	.75	120,135,000
1266	5¢ Inernational Cooperation Year-						
	United Nations, June 26	.10	.05	.60	(4)	.75	115,405,000
1267	5¢ Salvation Army, July 2	.10	.05	.60	(4)	.75	115,855,000
	Perf. 10½x11						
1268	5¢ Dante, July 17	.10	.05	.60	(4)	.75	115,340,000

A Reminder: Beginning with this edition, catalog values for all stamps listed reflect (as accurately as possible) actual retail values as found in the marketplace.

	1965 continued, Perf. 10½x11	Un	U	PB/LP	#	FDC	Q
1269	5¢ President Herbert Hoover Memorial,						
	Aug. 10	.10	.05	.60	(4)	.75	114,840,000
	Perf. 11						
1270	5¢ Robert Fulton, Aug. 19	.10	.05	.60	(4)	.75	116,140,000
1271	5¢ Florida Settlement, Aug. 28	.10	.05	.65	(4)	.75	116,900,000
1272	5¢ Traffic Safety, Sept. 3	.10	.05	.65	(4)	.75	114,085,000
1273	5¢ John Singleton Copley, Sept. 17	.10	.05	.75	(4)	.75	114,880,000
1274	11¢ International						
	Telecommunication Union, Oct. 6	.32	.16	10.00	(4)	.75	26,995,000
1275	5¢ Adlai E. Stevenson, Oct. 23	.10	.05	.60	(4)	.75	128,495,000
	Christmas Issue, Nov. 2						
1276	5¢ Angel with Trumpet						
	(1840 Weathervane)	.10	.05	.60	(4)	.75	1,139,930,000
1277 not assigned							
	Issues of 1965-78, Prominent Americans Issue, Perf. 11x10½, 10½x11						
1278	1¢ Jefferson, Jan. 12, 1968	.05	.05	.25	(4)	.60	
1278a	Booklet pane of 8, Jan. 12, 1968	1.00	.25			2.50	
1278b	Booklet pane of 4 + 2 labels, May 10, 1971	.75	.20			15.00	
1279	1¼¢ Albert Gallatin, Jan. 30, 1967	.08	.05	25.00	(4)	.60	
1280	2¢ Frank Lloyd Wright, June 8, 1966	.05	.05	.30	(4)	.60	
1280a	Booklet pane of 5+ label, Jan. 8, 1968	1.20	.40			2.50	
1280c	Booklet pane of 6, May 7, 1971	1.00	.35			15.00	
1281	3¢ Francis Parkman, Sept. 16, 1967	.06	.05	.30	(4)	.60	
1282	4¢ Lincoln, Nov. 19, 1965	.08	.05	.40	(4)	.60	
1283	5¢ Washington, Feb. 22, 1966	.10	.05	.50	(4)	.60	
1283B	5¢ redrawn, Nov. 17, 1967	.10	.05	.70	(4)	.45	
1284	6¢ Roosevelt, Jan. 29, 1966	.18	.05	.90	(4)	.45	
1284b	Booklet pane of 8, Dec. 28, 1967	1.50	.50			3.50	
1284c	Booklet pane of 5+ label, Jan. 9, 1968	1.25	.50			110.00	
1285	8¢ Albert Einstein, Mar. 14, 1966	.20	.05	1.50	(4)	.50	
1286	10¢ Jackson, Mar. 14, 1967	.22	.05	2.00	(4)	.60	
1286A	12¢ Henry Ford, July 30, 1968	.28	.05	1.75	(4)	.50	
1287	13¢ Kennedy, May 29, 1967	.24	.05	1.65	(4)	.65	
1288	15¢ Oliver Wendell Holmes, Mar. 8, 1968	.30	.06	1.50	(4)	.60	
	Perf. 10						
1288B	15¢ dark rose claret Holmes (1288),						
	Single from booklet	.30	.05			.65	
1288Bc	Booklet pane of 8, June 14, 1978	2.40	1.25			4.00	
	Perf. 11x10½, 10½x11						
1289	20¢ George C. Marshall, Oct. 24, 1967	.42	.06	3.00	(4)	.80	
1290	25¢ Frederick Douglass, Feb. 14, 1967	.55	.05	3.50	(4)	1.00	
1291	30¢ John Dewey, Oct. 21, 1968	.65	.08	3.75	(4)	1.20	
1292	40¢ Thomas Paine, Jan. 29, 1968	1.10	.10	5.50	(4)	1.60	
1293	50¢ Lucy Stone, Aug. 13, 1968	1.00	.05	5.00	(4)	3.25	
1294	$1 Eugene O'Neill, Oct. 16, 1967	2.50	.08	12.00	(4)	7.50	
1295	$5 John Bassett Moore, Dec. 3, 1966	12.50	2.00	62.50	(4)	60.00	

1269

1270

1271

1272

1273

1274

1275

1276

1278

1279

1280

1281

1282

1283

1283B

1284

1285

1286

1286A

1287

1288

1289

1290

1291

1292

1293

1294

1295

1305

1306

1307

1308

1309

1310

1312

1313

1311

1314

1315

1316

1317

1318

1319

	Issues of 1966-81, Coil Stamps, Perf. 10 Horizontally	Un	U	PB/LP	#	FDC	Q
1297	3¢ violet Parkman (1281), Nov. 4, 1975	.08	.05	.60	(2)	.75	
1298	6¢ gray brown Roosevelt (1284),						
	Dec. 28, 1967	.15	.05	2.00	(2)	.75	
	Perf. 10 Vertically						
1299	1¢ green Jefferson (1278), Jan. 12, 1968	.07	.05	.35	(2)	.75	
1300-02	not assigned.						
1303	4¢ black Lincoln (1282), May 28, 1966	.14	.05	2.25	(2)	.75	
1304	5¢ blue Washington (1283),						
	Sept. 8, 1966	.12	.05	.90	(2)	.75	
1304C	5¢ redrawn (1283B), 1981	.12	.05	.75	(2)		
1305	6¢ Roosevelt, Feb. 28, 1968	.15	.05	1.25	(2)	.75	
1305E	15¢ rose claret						
	Holmes (1288), June 14, 1978	.25	.05	1.65	(2)	.75	
1305C	$1 dull purple Eugene O'Neill (1294),						
	Jan. 12, 1973	1.50	.20	6.00	(2)	3.00	
	Issues of 1966, Perf. 11						
1306	5¢ Migratory Bird Treaty, Mar. 16	.10	.05	.75	(4)	.75	116,835,000
1307	Humane Treatment of Animals, Apr. 9	.10	.05	.65	(4)	.75	117,470,000
1308	5¢ Indiana Statehood, Apr. 16	.10	.05	.60	(4)	.75	123,770,000
1309	5¢ American Circus, May 2	.10	.05	.75	(4)	.75	131,270,000
	Sixth International Philatelic Exhibition Issue, May 21						
1310	5¢ Stamped Cover	.10	.05	.75	(4)	.75	122,285,000
	Souvenir Sheet, May 23, Imperf.						
1311	5¢ Stamped Cover (1310) and						
	Washington, D.C., Scene	.15	.12			.75	14,680,000
	Perf. 11						
1312	5¢ Bill of Rights, July 1	.10	.05	.75	(4)	.75	114,160,000
	Perf. 10½x11						
1313	5¢ Poland's Millennium, July 30	.10	.05	.75	(4)	.75	128,475,000
	Perf. 11						
1314	5¢ National Park Service, Aug. 25	.10	.05	.75	(4)	.75	119,535,000
1315	5¢ Marine Corps Reserve, Aug. 29	.10	.05	.75	(4)	.75	125,110,000
1316	5¢ General Federation						
	of Women's Clubs, Sept. 12	.10	.05	.75	(4)	.75	114,853,200
	American Folklore Issue, Johnny Appleseed, Sept. 24						
1317	5¢ Appleseed Carrying Shovel						
	and Seed Sack, Apple in Background	.10	.05	.75	(4)	.75	124,290,000
1318	5¢ Beautification of America, Oct. 5	.10	.05	.80	(4)	.75	128,460,000
1319	5¢ Great River Road, Oct. 21	.10	.05	.75	(4)	.75	127,585,000

	1966 continued, Perf. 11	Un	U	PB	#	FDC	Q
1320	5¢ Savings Bond-Servicemen, Oct. 26	.10	.05	.75	(4)	.75	115,875,000
	Christmas Issue, Nov. 1						
1321	5¢ Madonna and Child,						
	by Hans Memling	.10	.05	.75	(4)	.75	1,173,547,000
1322	5¢ Mary Cassatt, Nov. 17	.12	.05	1.25	(4)	.75	114,015,000
	Issues of 1967						
1323	5¢ National Grange, Apr. 17	.10	.05	.80	(4)	.75	121,105,000
1324	5¢ Canada, May 25	.10	.05	.75	(4)	.75	132,045,000
1325	5¢ Erie Canal, July 4	.10	.05	.75	(4)	.75	118,780,000
1326	5¢ Search for Peace-						
	Lions International, July 5	.10	.05	.75	(4)	.75	121,985,000
1327	5¢ Henry David Thoreau, July 12	.10	.05	.75	(4)	.75	111,850,000
1328	5¢ Nebraska Statehood, July, 29	.10	.05	.75	(4)	.75	117,225,000
1329	5¢ Voice of America, Aug. 1	.10	.05	.75	(4)	.75	111,515,000
	American Folklore Issue, Davy Crockett, Aug. 17						
1330	5¢ Davy Crockett with Rifle,						
	and Scrub Pine	.10	.05	.80	(4)	.75	114,270,000
	Accomplishments in Space Issue, Sept. 29						
1331	5¢ Space-Walking Astronaut	.65	.15	7.00	(4)	3.00	60,432,500
1331a	Attached pair, #1331-1332	1.50	1.25			8.00	
1332	5¢ Gemini 4 Capsule and Earth	.65	.15	7.00	(4)	3.00	60,432,500
1333	5¢ Urban Planning, Oct. 2	.10	.05	.80	(4)	.75	110,675,000
1334	5¢ Finland Independence, Oct. 6	.10	.05	.80	(4)	.75	110,670,000
	Perf. 12						
1335	5¢ Thomas Eakins, Nov. 2	.10	.05	.90	(4)	.75	113,825,000
	Christmas Issue, Nov. 6, Perf. 11						
1336	5¢ Madonna and Child,						
	by Hans Memling	.10	.05	.60	(4)	.75	1,208,700,000
1337	5¢ Mississippi Statehood, Dec. 11	.10	.05	.75	(4)	.75	113,330,000
	Issues of 1968-1971						
1338	6¢ Flag over White House						
	design 19 x 22 mm, Jan. 24, 1968	.12	.05	.60	(4)	.75	
	Perf. 11x10½						
1338D	6¢ dark blue, red and green (1338),						
	design 18¼ x 21 mm, Aug. 7, 1970	.16	.05	4.25	(20)	.75	
1338F	8¢ multicolored (1338),						
	May 10, 1971	.18	.05	4.25	(20)	.75	
	Coil Stamps, Perf. 10 Vertically						
1338A	6¢ dark blue, red and green (1338),						
	May 30, 1969	.14	.05			.75	
1338G	8¢ multicolored (1338),						
	May 10, 1971	.18	.05			.75	

1320

1321

1322

1323

1324

1325

1326

1327

1328

1329

1330

1331   1332   1331a

1333

1334

1968

1339

1340

1341

1342

1343

1344

1345

1346

1347

1348

1349

1350

1351

1352

1353

1354

1355

1356

1357

1358

	Issues of 1968, Perf. 11	Un	U	PB	#	FDC	Q
1339	6¢ Illinois Statehood, Feb. 12	.12	.05	.90	(4)	.75	141,350,000
1340	6¢ HemisFair '68, Mar. 30	.12	.05	.90	(4)	.75	144,345,000
1341	$1 Airlift, Apr. 4	2.75	1.25	20.00	(4)	6.50	
1342	6¢ Support Our Youth-Elks, May 1	.12	.05	.90	(4)	.75	147,120,000
1343	6¢ Law and Order, May 17	.12	.05	.90	(4)	.75	130,125,000
1344	6¢ Register and Vote, June 27	.12	.05	.90	(4)	.75	158,700,000
	Historic Flag Issue, July 4						
1345	6¢ Fort Moultrie Flag, 1776	.50	.25			4.00	23,153,000
1346	6¢ U.S. Flag, 1795-1818						
	(Ft. McHenry Flag)	.35	.25			4.00	23,153,000
1347	6¢ Washington's Cruisers Flag, 1775	.30	.25			4.00	23,153,000
1348	6¢ Bennington Flag, 1777	.30	.25			4.00	23,153,000
1349	6¢ Rhode Island Flag, 1775	.30	.25			4.00	23,153,000
1350	6¢ First Stars and Stripes, 1777	.30	.25			4.00	23,153,000
1351	6¢ Bunker Hill Flag, 1775	.30	.25			4.00	23,153,000
1352	6¢ Grand Union Flag, 1776	.30	.25			4.00	23,153,000
1353	6¢ Philadelphia Light Horse Flag, 1775	.30	.25			4.00	23,153,000
1354	6¢ First Navy Jack, 1775	.30	.25			4.00	23,153,000
	Plate Block, #1345-1354			12.00	(20)		
1354a	#1345-1354 printed se-tenant in						
	vertical rows of 10	3.25	3.00			12.00	
	Perf. 12						
1355	6¢ Walt Disney, Sept. 11	.14	.05	1.25	(4)	1.00	153,015,000
	Perf. 11						
1356	6¢ Father Marquette, Sept. 20	.12	.05	.90	(4)	.75	132,560,000
	American Folklore Issue, Daniel Boone, Sept. 26						
1357	6¢ Pennsylvania Rifle, Powder Horn,						
	Tomahawk, Pipe and Knife	.12	.05	.90	(4)	.75	130,385,000
1358	6¢ Arkansas River Navigation, Oct. 1	.12	.05	.90	(4)	.75	132,265,000

	1968 continued, Perf. 11	Un	U	PB	#	FDC	Q
1359	6¢ Leif Erikson, Oct. 9	.12	.05	.90	(4)	.75	128,710,000
	Perf. 11x10½						
1360	6¢ Cherokee Strip, Oct. 15	.12	.05	.90	(4)	.75	124,775,000
	Perf. 11						
1361	6¢ John Trumbull, Oct. 18	.12	.05	1.00	(4)	.75	128,295,000
1362	6¢ Waterfowl Conservation, Oct. 24	.14	.05	1.25	(4)	.75	142,245,000
	Christmas Issue, Nov. 1						
1363	6¢ Angel Gabriel,						
	from "The Annunciation," by Jan van Eyck	.12	.05	2.75	(10)	.75	1,410,580,000
1364	6¢ American Indian, Nov. 4	.14	.05	1.25	(4)	.75	125,100,000
	Issues of 1969, Beautification of America Issue, Jan. 16						
1365	6¢ Capitol, Azaleas and Tulips	.48	.15	5.00	(4)	2.00	48,142,500
1366	6¢ Washington Monument,						
	Potomac River and Daffodils	.48	.15	5.00	(4)	2.00	48,142,500
1367	6¢ Poppies and Lupines						
	along Highway	.48	.15	5.00	(4)	2.00	48,142,500
1368	6¢ Blooming Crabapples						
	Lining Avenue	.48	.15	5.00	(4)	2.00	48,142,500
1368a	Block of four, #1365-1368	2.00	1.25			5.00	
1369	6¢ American Legion, Mar. 15	.12	.05	.90	(4)	.75	148,770,000
	American Folklore Issue, Grandma Moses, May 1						
1370	6¢ "July Fourth," by Grandma Moses	.12	.05	1.00	(4)	.75	139,475,000
1371	6¢ Apollo 8, May 5	.14	.06	1.25	(4)	2.00	187,165,000
1372	6¢ W.C. Handy, May 17	.12	.05	.90	(4)	.75	125,555,000
1373	6¢ California Settlement, July 16	.12	.05	.90	(4)	.75	144,425,000
1374	6¢ John Wesley Powell, Aug. 1	.12	.05	.90	(4)	.75	135,875,000
1375	6¢ Alabama Statehood, Aug. 2	.12	.05	.90	(4)	.75	151,110,000

TRAVELS IN SPACE
The U.S. Apollo 8 space mission (#1371) was the first to place humans in orbit around the moon. Astronauts James A. Lovell, Jr., William A. Anders and Frank Borman (left to right) orbited the moon 10 times from December 21 to December 27, 1968. Don't miss the four new fall '89 U.S. stamp issues featuring methods of space travel.

1359

1360

1361

1362

1363

1364

1365   **1366**   **1368a**
1367   **1368**

1369

1370

1371

1372

1373

1374

1375

147

1376
1378

1377
1379

1379a

1380

1381

1382

1383

1384

1384a

1385

1386

AMERICAN BALD EAGLE

AFRICAN ELEPHANT HERD

1391

HAIDA CEREMONIAL CANOE

THE AGE OF REPTILES

1387
1389

1388
1390

1390a

1392

	1969 continued	Un	U	PB	#	FDC	Q
	Botanical Congress Issue, Aug. 23, Perf. 11						
1376	6¢ Douglas Fir (Northwest)	1.10	.15	8.50	(4)	2.00	39,798,750
1377	6¢ Lady's Slipper (Northeast)	1.10	.15	8.50	(4)	2.00	39,798,750
1378	6¢ Ocotillo (Southwest)	1.10	.15	8.50	(4)	2.00	39,798,750
1379	6¢ Franklinia (Southeast)	1.10	.15	8.50	(4)	2.00	39,798,750
1379a	Block of four, #1376-1379	5.50	5.00			7.00	
	Perf. 10½x11						
1380	6¢ Dartmouth College Case, Sept. 22	.18	.05	1.00	(4)	.75	129,540,000
	Perf. 11						
1381	6¢ Professional Baseball, Sept. 24	.25	.05	1.75	(4)	1.50	130,925,000
1382	6¢ College Football, Sept. 26	.20	.05	1.25	(4)	1.50	139,055,000
1383	6¢ Dwight D. Eisenhower, Oct. 14	.12	.05	.90	(4)	.75	150,611,200
	Christmas Issue, Nov. 3, Perf. 11x10½						
1384	6¢ Winter Sunday in Norway, Maine	.12	.05	2.00	(10)	.75	1,709,795,000
1384a	Precanceled	.60	.06				
	Issued on an experimental basis in four cities whose names appear on the stamps: Atlanta, GA; Baltimore, MD; Memphis, TN; and New Haven, CT.						
1385	6¢ Hope for the Crippled, Nov. 20	.12	.05	.90	(4)	.75	127,545,000
1386	6¢ William M. Harnett, Dec. 3	.12	.05	1.00	(4)	.75	145,788,800
	Issues of 1970, Natural History Issue, May 6, Perf. 11						
1387	6¢ American Bald Eagle	.12	.12	1.25	(4)	2.00	50,448,550
1388	6¢ African Elephant Herd	.12	.12	1.25	(4)	2.00	50,448,550
1389	6¢ Tlingit Chief						
	in Haida Ceremonial Canoe	.12	.12	1.25	(4)	2.00	50,448,550
1390	6¢ Brontosaurus, Stegosaurus						
	and Allosaurus from Jurassic Period	.12	.12	1.25	(4)	2.00	50,448,550
1390a	Block of four, #1387-1390	.50	.50			3.00	
1391	6¢ Maine Statehood, July 9	.12	.05	1.00	(4)	.75	171,850,000
	Perf. 11x10½						
1392	6¢ Wildlife Conservation, July 20	.12	.05	1.00	(4)	1.00	142,205,000

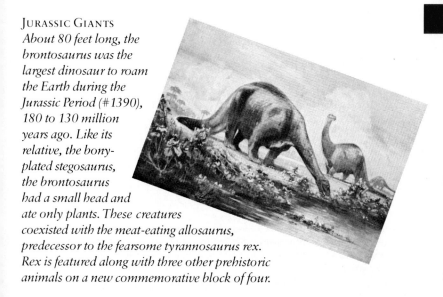

JURASSIC GIANTS
About 80 feet long, the brontosaurus was the largest dinosaur to roam the Earth during the Jurassic Period (#1390), 180 to 130 million years ago. Like its relative, the bony-plated stegosaurus, the brontosaurus had a small head and ate only plants. These creatures coexisted with the meat-eating allosaurus, predecessor to the fearsome tyrannosaurus rex. Rex is featured along with three other prehistoric animals on a new commemorative block of four.

	Issues of 1970-74, Perf. 11x10½	Un	U	PB/LP	#	FDC	Q
1393	6¢ Eisenhower, Aug. 6, 1970	.12	.05	.60	(4)	.75	
1393a	Booklet pane of 8	1.25	.50			3.75	
1393b	Booklet pane of 5 + label	1.20	.35			2.00	
	Perf. 11x10½						
1393D	7¢ Franklin, Oct. 20, 1972	.14	.05	1.00	(4)	.75	
	Perf. 11						
1394	8¢ Eisenhower, May 10, 1971	.16	.05	1.00	(4)	.75	
	Perf. 11x10½						
1395	8¢ deep claret,Eisenhower (1394),						
	Single from booklet	.16	.05			.75	
1395a	Booklet pane of 8, May 10, 1971	2.00	1.25			3.50	
1395b	Booklet pane of 6, May 10, 1971	1.25	.75			3.00	
1395c	Booklet pane of 4 + 2 labels,						
	Jan. 28, 1972	1.50	.50			2.25	
1395d	Booklet pane of 7 + label, Jan. 28, 1972	1.75	1.00			2.50	
1396	8¢ U.S. Postal Service, July 1, 1971	.15	.05	3.50	(12)	.75	
1397	14¢ Fiorello H. LaGuardia, Apr. 24, 1972	.25	.05	1.75	(4)	.85	
1398	16¢ Ernie Pyle, May 7, 1971	.30	.05	1.75	(4)	.75	
1399	18¢ Dr. Elizabeth Blackwell,						
	Jan. 23, 1974	.32	.06	2.10	(4)	1.25	
1400	21¢ Amadeo P. Giannini,						
	June 27, 1973	.35	.06	2.25	(4)	1.00	
	Coil Stamps, Perf. 10 Vertically						
1401	6¢ dark blue gray						
	Eisenhower (1393), Aug. 6, 1970	.14	.05	1.00	(2)	.75	
1402	8¢ deep claret						
	Eisenhower (1394), May 10, 1971	.18	.05	1.00	(2)	.75	
1403-04 not assigned.							
	Issues of 1970, Perf. 11						
1405	6¢ Edgar Lee Masters, Aug. 22	.12	.05	.90	(4)	.75	137,660,000
1406	6¢ Woman Suffrage, Aug. 26	.12	.05	.90	(4)	.75	135,125,000
1407	6¢ South Carolina Settlement, Sept. 12	.12	.05	.90	(4)	.75	135,895,000
1408	6¢ Stone Mountain Memorial, Sept. 19	.12	.05	.90	(4)	.75	132,675,000
1409	6¢ Fort Snelling, Oct. 17	.12	.05	.90	(4)	.75	134,795,000
	Anti-Pollution Issue, Oct. 28, Perf. 11x10½						
1410	6¢ Save Our Soil-Globe						
	and Wheat Field	.22	.13	4.50	(10)	1.40	40,400,000
1411	6¢ Save Our Cities-Globe						
	and City Playground	.22	.13	4.50	(10)	1.40	40,400,000
1412	6¢ Save Our Water-Globe						
	and Bluegill Fish	.22	.13			1.40	40,400,000
1413	6¢ Save Our Air-Globe						
	and Seagull	.22	.13			1.40	40,400,000
1413a	Block of four, #1410-1413	1.00	1.00			4.25	

A Reminder: Beginning with this edition, catalog values for all stamps listed reflect (as accurately as possible) actual retail values as found in the marketplace.

1393

1393D

1394

1396

1397

1398

1399

1400

1405

1406

1407

1408

1409

Christmas 6¹⁄ₜₛ

414   1414a

1415   1416   1418

1417   1418

419

1420   1421   1422   1421a   1423

424

1425   1426

	1970 continued	Un	U	PB	#	FDC	Q
	Christmas Issue, Nov. 5, Perf. 10½x11						
1414	6¢ Nativity, by Lorenzo Lotto	.12	.05	1.75	(8)	1.40	638,730,000
1414a	Precanceled	.25	.08				358,245,000
	#1414a-1418a were furnished to 68 cities. Unused prices are for copies with gum and used prices are for copies with or without gum but with an additional cancellation.						
	Perf. 11x10½						
1415	6¢ Tin and Cast Iron Locomotive	.40	.10	7.75	(8)	1.40	122,313,750
1415a	Precanceled	1.00	.15				109,912,500
1416	6¢ Toy Horse on Wheels	.40	.10	7.75	(8)	1.40	122,313,750
1416a	Precanceled	1.00	.15				109,912,500
1417	6¢ Mechanical Tricycle	.40	.10			1.40	122,313,750
1417a	Precanceled	1.00	.15				109,912,500
1418	6¢ Doll Carriage	.40	.10			1.40	122,313,750
1418a	Precanceled	1.00	.15				109,912,500
1418b	Block of 4, #1415-1418	1.75	1.25			3.50	
1418c	Block of 4, #1415a-1418a	4.00	2.50				
	Perf. 11						
1419	6¢ United Nations, Nov. 20	.12	.05	.90	(4)	.75	127,610,000
1420	6¢ Landing of the Pilgrims, Nov. 21	.12	.05	1.00	(4)	.75	129,785,000
	Disabled American Veterans and Servicemen Issue, Nov. 24						
1421	6¢ Disabled American Veterans Emblem	.15	.06	1.75	(4)	.75	67,190,000
1421a	Attached pair, #1421-1422	.30	.30			1.20	
1422	6¢ U.S. Servicemen	.15	.06	1.75	(4)	.75	67,190,000
	Issues of 1971						
1423	6¢ American Wool Industry, Jan. 19	.12	.05	.90	(4)	.75	136,305,000
1424	6¢ Gen. Douglas MacArthur, Jan. 26	.12	.05	.90	(4)	.75	134,840,000
1425	6¢ Blood Donor, Mar. 12	.12	.05	.90	(4)	.75	130,975,000
	Perf. 11x10½						
1426	8¢ Missouri Statehood, May 8	.15	.05	2.75	(12)	.75	161,235,000
	Wildlife Conservation Issue, June 12, Perf. 11						
1427	8¢ Trout	.14	.08	1.25	(4)	1.75	43,920,000
1428	8¢ Alligator	.14	.08	1.25	(4)	1.75	43,920,000
1429	8¢ Polar Bear and Cubs	.14	.08	1.25	(4)	1.75	43,920,000
1430	8¢ California Condor	.14	.08	1.25	(4)	1.75	43,920,000
1430a	Block of four #1427-1430	.60	.60			3.00	

	1971 continued, Perf. 11	Un	U	PB	#	FDC	Q
1431	8¢ Antarctic Treaty, June 23	.15	.05	1.25	(4)	.75	138,700,000
	American Bicentennial Issue, American Revolution, July 4						
1432	8¢ Bicentennial Commission Emblem	.15	.05	1.75	(4)	.75	138,165,000
1433	8¢ John Sloan, Aug. 2	.15	.05	1.25	(4)	.75	152,125,000
	Space Achievement Decade Issue, Aug. 2						
1434	8¢ Earth, Sun and Landing Craft on Moon	.15	.10	1.40	(4)		88,147,500
1434a	Attached pair, #1434-1435	.30	.25			1.75	
1435	8¢ Lunar Rover and Astronauts	.15	.10	1.40	(4)		88,147,500
1436	8¢ Emily Dickinson, Aug. 28	.15	.05	1.25	(4)	.75	142,845,000
1437	8¢ San Juan, Puerto Rico, Sept. 12	.15	.05	1.25	(4)	.75	148,755,000
	Perf. 10½x11						
1438	8¢ Prevent Drug Abuse, Oct. 4	.15	.05	1.50	(6)	.75	139,080,000
1439	8¢ CARE, Oct. 27	.15	.05	1.75	(8)	.75	130,755,000
	Historic Preservation Issue, Oct. 29, Perf. 11						
1440	8¢ Decatur House,						
	Washington, D.C.	.16	.12	1.25	(4)	1.50	42,552,000
1441	8¢ Whaling Ship						
	Charles W. Morgan, Mystic,						
	Connecticut	.16	.12	1.25	(4)	1.50	42,552,000
1442	8¢ Cable Car, San Francisco	.16	.12	1.25	(4)	1.50	42,552,000
1443	8¢ San Xavier del Bac Mission,						
	Tucson, Arizona	.16	.12	1.25	(4)	1.50	42,552,000
1443a	Block of four, #1440-1443	.75	.75			3.00	
	Christmas Issue, Nov. 10, Perf. 10½x11						
1444	8¢ Adoration of the Shepherds,						
	by Giorgione	.15	.05	2.50	(12)	.75	1,074,350,000
1445	8¢ Partridge in a Pear Tree	.15	.05	2.50	(12)	.75	979,540,000
	Issues of 1972, Perf. 11						
1446	8¢ Sidney Lanier, Feb. 3	.15	.05	.90	(4)	.75	137,355,000
	Perf. 10½x11						
1447	8¢ Peace Corps., Feb. 11	.15	.05	1.30	(6)	.75	150,400,000

1431

1432

1433

1434

1435   1434a

1436

1437

1438

1439

HISTORIC PRESERVATION   HISTORIC PRESERVATION

HISTORIC PRESERVATION   HISTORIC PRESERVATION

1440   1441   1443a

1442   1443

1444

1445

1446

1447

1972

1452

1451a

1448   1449

1450   1451

1453

1454

1455

1456   1457   1459a

1458   1459

1460

1461

1462

1463

1464   1465   1467a

1466   1467

	1972 continued	Un	U	PB	#	FDC	Q
	National Parks Centennial Issue, Cape Hatteras, Apr. 5, Perf. 11 (See also #C84)						
1448	2¢ Hull of Ship	.05	.05	1.00	(4)		172,730,000
1449	2¢ Cape Hatteras Lighthouse	.05	.05	1.00	(4)		172,730,000
1450	2¢ Laughing Gulls on Driftwood	.05	.05	1.00	(4)		172,730,000
1451	2¢ Laughing Gulls and Dune	.05	.05	1.00	(4)		172,730,000
1451a	Block of four, #1448-1451	.25	.20			1.25	
	Wolf Trap Farm, June 26						
1452	6¢ Performance at Shouse Pavilion	.12	.08	1.00	(4)	.75	104,090,000
	Yellowstone, Mar. 1						
1453	8¢ Old Faithful, Yellowstone	.16	.05	1.00	(4)	.75	164,096,000
	Mount McKinley, July 28						
1454	15¢ View of Mount McKinley in Alaska	.30	.18	1.75	(4)	.75	53,920,000
	Note: Beginning with this National Parks Centennial issue, the USPS began to offer stamp collectors first day cancellations affixed to 8" x 10½" souvenir pages. The pages are similar to the stamp announcements that have appeared on Post Office bulletin boards beginning with Scott #1132.						
1455	8¢ Family Planning, Mar. 18	.15	.05	1.00	(4)	.75	153,025,000
	American Bicentennial Issue, Colonial American Craftsmen, July 4, Perf. 11x10½						
1456	8¢ Glassblower	.30	.08	1.25	(4)	1.00	50,472,500
1457	8¢ Silversmith	.30	.08	1.25	(4)	1.00	50,472,500
1458	8¢ Wigmaker	.30	.08	1.25	(4)	1.00	50,472,500
1459	8¢ Hatter	.30	.08	1.25	(4)	1.00	50,472,500
1459a	Block of four, #1456-1459	1.25	1.25			2.50	
	Olympic Games Issue, Aug. 17 (See also #C85)						
1460	6¢ Bicycling and Olympic Rings	.16	.12	2.00	(10)	.75	67,335,000
1461	8¢ Bobsledding and Olympic Rings	.16	.05	2.00	(10)	.85	179,675,000
1462	15¢ Running and Olympic Rings	.35	.18	4.50	(10)	1.00	46,340,000
1463	8¢ Parent Teachers Association, Sept. 15	.16	.05	.90	(4)	.75	180,155,000
	Wildlife Conservation Issue, Sept. 20, Perf. 11						
1464	8¢ Fur Seals	.16	.08	1.25	(4)	2.00	49,591,200
1465	8¢ Cardinal	.16	.08	1.25	(4)	2.00	49,591,200
1466	8¢ Brown Pelican	.16	.08	1.25	(4)	2.00	49,591,200
1467	8¢ Bighorn Sheep	.16	.08	1.25	(4)	2.00	49,591,200
1467a	Block of 4, #1464-1467	.65	.60			3.00	
	Note: With this Wildlife Conservation issue the USPS introduced the "American Commemorative Series" Stamp Panels. Each panel contains a block of four mint stamps with text and background illustrations.						

1972 continued, Perf. 11x10½	Un	U	PB	#	FDC	Q
1468 8¢ Mail Order Business, Sept. 27	.15	.05	2.75	(12)	.75	185,490,000
Perf. 10½x11						
1469 8¢ Osteopathic Medicine, Oct. 9	.15	.05	1.25	(6)	.75	162,335,000
American Folklore Issue, Tom Sawyer, Oct. 13, Perf. 11						
1470 8¢ Tom Sawyer Whitewashing a Fence,						
by Norman Rockwell	.15	.05	1.00	(4)	.75	162,789,950
Christmas Issue, Nov. 9, Perf. 10½x11						
1471 8¢ Angels from "Mary, Queen						
of Heaven," by the Master						
of the St. Lucy Legend	.15	.05	2.75	(12)	.75	1,003,475,000
1472 8¢ Santa Claus	.15	.05	2.75	(12)	.75	1,017,025,000
Perf. 11						
1473 8¢ Pharmacy, Nov. 10	.15	.05	1.00	(4)	.75	165,895,000
1474 8¢ Stamp Collecting, Nov. 17	.15	.05	1.00	(4)	.75	166,508,000
Issues of 1973, Perf. 11x10½						
1475 8¢ Love, Jan. 26	.15	.05	1.35	(6)	.75	320,055,000
American Bicentennial Issues, Communications in Colonial Times, Perf. 11						
1476 8¢ Printer and Patriots						
Examining Pamphlet, Feb. 16	.15	.05	1.10	(4)	.75	166,005,000
1477 8¢ Posting a Broadside, Apr. 13	.15	.05	1.10	(4)	.75	163,050,000
1478 8¢ Post Rider, June 22	.15	.05	1.10	(4)	.75	159,005,000
1479 8¢ Drummer, Sept. 28	.15	.05	1.10	(4)	.75	147,295,000
Boston Tea Party, July 4						
1480 8¢ British Merchantman	.15	.10	1.20	(4)	1.75	49,068,750
1481 8¢ British Three-Master	.15	.10	1.20	(4)	1.75	49,068,750
1482 8¢ Boats and Ship's Hull	.15	.10	1.20	(4)	1.75	49,068,750
1483 8¢ Boat and Dock	.15	.10	1.20	(4)	1.75	49,068,750
1483a Block of four, #1480-1483	.60	.45			3.75	

CHERRY PHOSPHATES AND COD LIVER OIL

Originally places where medicinal drugs were prepared and sold, pharmacies (#1473)—or drugstores—in the United States now sell many products in addition to drugs. For years the drugstore soda fountain has been an American tradition, liberally dispensing ice cream sodas, sundaes and flavored drinks.

100th Anniversary of Mail Order

1468

1469

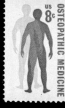

Tom Sawyer

United States 8c

1470

Christmas

1471

Twas the Night before Christmas

U.S. POSTAGE 8c

1472

PHARMACY

UNITED STATES POSTAGE 8c

1473

Stamp Collecting U.S. 8c

1474

1475

Rise of the Spirit of Independence

1476

Rise of the Spirit of Independence

1477

Rise of the Spirit of Independence

1478

Rise of the Spirit of Independence

1479

THE BOSTON TEA PARTY 8c U.S.   U.S. 8c THE BOSTON TEA PARTY

THE BOSTON TEA PARTY 8c U.S.   U.S. 8c THE BOSTON TEA PARTY

1480   1481   1483a
1482   1483

1484

1485

1486

1487

1488

Nearly 27 billion U.S. stamps are sold yearly to carry your letters to every corner of the world.

Mail is picked up from nearly a third of a million local collection boxes, as well as your mailbox.

More than 87 billion letters and packages are handled yearly—almost 300 million every delivery day.

The People in your Postal Service handle and deliver more than 500 million packages yearly.

Thousands of machines, buildings, and vehicles must be operated and maintained to keep your mail moving.

People Serving You

1489   **1490**   **1491**   **1492**   **1493**

The skill of sorting mail manually is still vital to delivery of your mail.

Employees use modern, high-speed equipment to sort and process huge volumes of mail in central locations.

Thirteen billion pounds of mail are handled yearly by postal employees as they speed your letters and packages.

Our customers include 54 million urban and 12 million rural families, plus 9 million businesses.

Employees cover 4 million miles each delivery day to bring mail to your home or business.

People Serving You

1498a

1494   **1495**   **1496**   **1497**   **1498**

	1973 continued	Un	U	PB	#	FDC	Q
	American Arts Issue, Perf. 11						
1484	8¢ George Gershwin and Scene						
	from "Porgy and Bess," Feb. 28	.15	.05	2.75	(12)	.75	139,152,000
1485	8¢ Robinson Jeffers, Man and Children						
	of Carmel with Burro, Aug. 13	.15	.05	2.75	(12)	.75	128,048,000
1486	8¢ Henry Ossawa Tanner,						
	Palette and Rainbow, Sept. 10	.15	.05	2.75	(12)	.75	146,008,000
1487	8¢ Willa Cather, Pioneer Family						
	and Covered Wagon, Sept. 20	.15	.05	2.75	(12)	.75	139,608,000
1488	8¢ Nicolaus Copernicus, Apr. 23	.15	.05	1.00	(4)	.75	159,475,000
	Postal Service Employees Issue, Apr. 30, Perf. 10½x11						
1489	8¢ Stamp Counter	.15	.10			1.10	48,602,000
1490	8¢ Mail Collection	.15	.10			1.10	48,602,000
1491	8¢ Letter-Facing on Conveyor	.15	.10			1.10	48,602,000
1492	8¢ Parcel Post Sorting	.15	.10			1.10	48,602,000
1493	8¢ Mail Canceling	.15	.10			1.10	48,602,000
1494	8¢ Manual Letter Routing	.15	.10			1.10	48,602,000
1495	8¢ Electronic Letter Routing	.15	.10			1.10	48,602,000
1496	8¢ Loading Mail on Truck	.15	.10			1.10	48,602,000
1497	8¢ Carrier Delivering Mail	.15	.10			1.10	48,602,000
1498	8¢ Rural Mail Delivery	.15	.10			1.10	48,602,000
1498a	Strip of 10, #1489-1498	1.50	1.00	4.50	(20)	6.00	

#1489-98 were the first United States stamps to have printing on the back. (See also #1559-62)

ROBINSON JEFFERS, AMERICAN POET
*Born in Pittsburgh in 1887, poet
Robinson Jeffers (#1485) spent most
of his life on the northern coast of
California. Much of his poetry was
inspired by the grandeur of his
natural surroundings.* Roan
Stallion, *written in 1925, is one
of Jeffers' best-known poems.*

	1973 continued, Perf. 11	Un	U	PB/LP	#	FDC	Q
1499	8¢ Harry S. Truman, May 8	.15	.05	.90	(4)	.75	157,052,800
	Progress in Electronics Issue, July 10 (See also #C86)						
1500	6¢ Marconi's Spark Coil and Gap	.12	.10	1.00	(4)	.75	53,005,000
1501	8¢ Transistors						
	and Printed Circuit Board	.15	.05	1.00	(4)	.75	159,775,000
1502	15¢ Microphone, Speaker,						
	Vacuum Tube, TV Camera Tube	.28	.15	3.00	(4)	.80	39,005,000
1503	8¢ Lyndon B. Johnson, Aug. 27	.15	.05	2.50	(12)	.75	152,624,000
	Issues of 1973-74, Rural America Issue						
1504	8¢ Angus and Longhorn Cattle,						
	by F.C. Murphy, Oct. 5, 1973	.15	.05	1.00	(4)	.75	145,840,000
1505	10¢ Chautauqua Tent and Buggies,						
	Aug. 6, 1974	.18	.05	1.10	(4)	.75	151,335,000
1506	10¢ Wheat Fields and Train,						
	Aug. 16, 1974	.28	.05	1.10	(4)	.75	141,085,000
	Issue of 1973, Christmas Issue, Nov. 7, Perf. 10½x11						
1507	8¢ Small Cowper Madonna,						
	by Raphael	.15	.05	2.10	(12)	.75	885,160,000
1508	8¢ Christmas Tree in Needlepoint	.15	.05	2.10	(12)	.75	939,835,000
	Issues of 1973-74 continued, Perf. 11x10½						
1509	10¢ 50-Star and 13-Star Flags,						
	Dec. 8, 1973	.18	.05	5.50	(20)	.75	
1510	10¢ Jefferson Memorial,						
	Dec. 14, 1973	.18	.05	1.00	(4)	.75	
1510b	Booklet pane of 5 + label,						
	Dec. 14, 1973	1.50	.30			2.75	
1510c	Booklet pane of 8, Dec. 14, 1973	1.60	.30			3.00	
1510d	Booklet pane of 6, Aug. 5, 1974	3.50	.30			3.00	
1511	10¢ ZIP Code, Jan. 4, 1974	.18	.05	2.25	(8)	.75	
1512-1517 not assigned.							
	Coil Stamps, Perf. 10 Vertically						
1518	6.3¢ Liberty Bell, Oct. 1, 1974	.12	.07	.35	(2)	.75	
1519	10¢ red and blue Flags (1509),						
	Dec. 8, 1973	.18	.05			.75	
1520	10¢ blue Jefferson Memorial						
	(1510), Dec. 14, 1973	.18	.05	.50	(2)	.75	
1521-24 not assigned.							
	Issues of 1974, Perf. 11						
1525	10¢ Veterans of Foreign Wars, Mar. 11	.18	.05	1.25	(4)	.75	149,930,000
	Perf. 10½x11						
1526	10¢ Robert Frost, Mar. 26	.18	.05	1.00	(4)	.75	145,235,000
	Perf. 11						
1527	10¢ Expo '74 World's Fair, Apr. 18	.18	.05	2.60	(12)	.75	135,052,000

A Reminder: Beginning with this edition, catalog values for all stamps listed reflect (as accurately as possible) actual retail values as found in the marketplace.

1499

1500

1501

1502

1503

1504

1505

1506

1507

1508

1509

1510

1511

1518

1525

1526

1527

1528 **1529**

1530 **1531** **1532** **1533** **1537a**

1534 **1535** **1536** **1537**

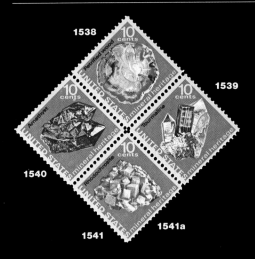

1538

1539

1540

1541 **1541a**

1542

1974 continued, Perf. 11x10½		Un	U	PB/LP	#	FDC	Q
1528	10¢ Horse Racing, May 4	.18	.05	2.60	(12)	.75	156,750,000
	Perf. 11						
1529	10¢ Skylab I, May 14	.18	.05	1.00	(4)	1.25	164,670,000
	Universal Postal Union Issue, June 6, Perf. 11						
1530	10¢ Michelangelo,						
	from "School of Athens," by Raphael	.20	.15	4.00	(16)	1.10	23,769,600
1531	10¢ "Five Feminine Virtues,"						
	by Hokusai	.20	.15			1.10	23,769,600
1532	10¢ "Old Scraps,"						
	by John Fredrick Peto	.20	.15			1.10	23,769,600
1533	10¢ "The Lovely Reader,"						
	by Jean Etienne Liotard	.20	.15	4.00	(16)	1.10	23,769,600
1534	10¢ "Lady Writing Letter,"						
	by Gerard Terborch	.20	.15	4.00	(16)	1.10	23,769,600
1535	10¢ Inkwell and Quill,						
	from "Boy with a Top,"						
	by Jean-Baptiste Simeon Chardin	.20	.15			1.10	23,769,600
1536	10¢ Mrs. John Douglas,						
	by Thomas Gainsborough	.20	.15			1.10	23,769,600
1537	10¢ Don Antonio Noriega,						
	by Francisco de Goya	.20	.15	4.00	(16)	1.10	23,769,600
1537a	Block or strip of 8, #1530-37	1.60	1.50			4.25	
	Mineral Heritage Issue, June 13						
1538	10¢ Petrified Wood	.18	.10	1.35	(4)	1.50	41,803,200
1539	10¢ Tourmaline	.18	.10	1.35	(4)	1.50	41,803,200
1540	10¢ Amethyst	.18	.10	1.35	(4)	1.50	41,803,200
1541	10¢ Rhodochrosite	.18	.10	1.35	(4)	1.50	41,803,200
1541a	Block of 4, #1538-1541	.75	.75			3.00	
1542	10¢ First Kentucky Settlement-						
	Fort Harrod, June 15	.20	.05	1.10	(4)	.75	156,265,000

	1974 continued	Un	U	PB	#	FDC	Q
	American Bicentennial Issue, First Continental Congress, July 4, Perf. 11						
1543	10¢ Carpenters' Hall	.20	.10	1.20	(4)	.90	48,896,250
1544	10¢ "We ask but for Peace,						
	Liberty and Safety"	.20	.10	1.20	(4)	.90	48,896,250
1545	10¢ "Deriving their Just Powers						
	from the Consent of the Governed"	.20	.10	1.20	(4)	.90	48,896,250
1546	10¢ Independence Hall	.20	.10	1.20	(4)	.90	48,896,250
1546a	Block of 4, #1543-1546	1.00	.80			2.75	
1547	10¢ Energy Conservation, Sept. 22	.18	.05	1.00	(4)	.75	148,850,000
	American Folklore Issue, The Legend of Sleepy Hollow, Oct. 10						
1548	10¢ Headless Horseman						
	and Ichabod Crane	.18	.05	1.00	(4)	.75	157,270,000
1549	10¢ Retarded Children, Oct. 12	.18	.05	1.00	(4)	.75	150,245,000
	Christmas Issue						
1550	10¢ Angel from Pérussis Altarpiece,						
	Oct. 23	.18	.05	2.25	(10)	.75	835,180,000
1551	10¢ "The Road-Winter,"						
	by Currier and Ives, Oct. 23	.18	.05	2.60	(12)	.75	882,520,000
	Precanceled Self-Adhesive, Imperf.						
1552	10¢ Dove Weather Vane						
	atop Mount Vernon, Nov. 15	.18	.08	5.50	(20)	.75	213,155,000
	Issues of 1975, American Arts Issue, Perf. 10½x11						
1553	10¢ Benjamin West,						
	Self-Portrait, Feb. 10	.18	.05	2.50	(10)	.75	156,995,000
	Perf. 11						
1554	10¢ Paul Laurence Dunbar						
	and Lamp, May 1	.18	.05	2.50	(10)	.75	146,365,000
1555	10¢ D.W. Griffith						
	and Motion-Picture Camera, May 27	.18	.05	1.00	(4)	.75	148,805,000
	Space Issues						
1556	10¢ Pioneer 10 Passing Jupiter,						
	Feb. 28	.18	.05	1.00	(4)	1.25	173,685,000
1557	10¢ Mariner 10, Venus						
	and Mercury, Apr. 4	.18	.05	1.00	(4)	1.25	158,600,000
1558	10¢ Collective Bargaining, Mar. 13	.18	.05	1.80	(8)	.75	153,355,000

RETARDED CHILDREN CAN BE HELPED

Retardation has many causes, ranging from an extra chromosome to physical injury and poor nutrition. Retarded children (#1549) are most likely to reach their potential by remaining within the family environment. Many grow to become good employees and responsible members of society.

1548

1547

1543

1545

1544

1546

1546a

1551

1552

1549

1550

1555

1553

1554

1556

1557

1558

Sybil Ludington *Youthful Heroine*

Salem Poor *Gallant Soldier*

Haym Salomon *Financial Hero*

YOUTHFUL HEROINE

On the dark night of April 26, 1777, 16-year-old Sybil Ludington rode her horse "Star" alone through the Connecticut countryside rallying her father's militia to repel a raid by the British on Danbury.

GALLANT SOLDIER

The conspicuously courageous actions of black foot soldier Salem Poor at the Battle of Bunker Hill on June 17, 1775, earned him citations for his bravery and leadership ability.

FINANCIAL HERO

Businessman and broker Haym Salomon was responsible for raising most of the money needed to finance the American Revolution and later to save the new nation from collapse.

1559

1560

1561

Peter Francisco *Fighter Extraordinary*

Lexington & Concord 1775 by Sandham

US Bicentennial 10cents

Bunker Hill 1775 by Trumbull

US Bicentennial 10c

FIGHTER EXTRAORDINARY

Peter Francisco's strength and bravery made him a legend around campfires. He fought with distinction at Brandywine, Yorktown and Guilford Court House.

1563

1564

1562

CONTINENTAL ARMY

CONTINENTAL NAVY

CONTINENTAL MARINES

AMERICAN MILITIA

APOLLO SOYUZ 1975

APOLLO SOYUZ SPACE TEST PROJECT

US 10c

UNITED STATES · 1975

1569

1569a

1570

1565

1566   **1568a**

1567

1568

	1975 continued	Un	U	PB/LP	#	FDC	Q
	American Bicentennial Issues, Contributors to the Cause, Mar. 25, Perf. 11x10½						
1559	8¢ Sybil Ludington Riding Horse	.16	.13	2.00	(10)	.75	63,205,000
1560	10¢ Salem Poor Carrying Musket	.18	.05	2.50	(10)	.75	157,865,000
1561	10¢ Haym Salomon						
	Figuring Accounts	.18	.05	2.50	(10)	.75	166,810,000
1562	18¢ Peter Francisco						
	Shouldering Cannon	.32	.20	5.00	(10)	.75	44,825,000
	Battle of Lexington & Concord, Apr. 19, Perf. 11						
1563	10¢ "Birth of Liberty,"						
	by Henry Sandham	.20	.05	2.60	(12)	.75	144,028,000
	Battle of Bunker Hill, June 17						
1564	10¢ "Battle of Bunker Hill,"						
	by John Trumbull	.20	.05	2.60	(12)	.75	139,928,000
	Military Uniforms, July 4						
1565	10¢ Soldier with Flintlock Musket,						
	Uniform Button	.18	.08	3.50	(12)	.90	44,963,750
1566	10¢ Sailor with Grappling Hook,						
	First Navy Jack, 1775	.18	.08			.90	44,963,750
1567	10¢ Marine with Musket,						
	Full-Rigged Ship	.18	.08	3.50	(12)	.90	44,963,750
1568	10¢ Militiaman with Musket						
	and Powder Horn	.18	.08			.90	44,963,750
1568a	Block of 4, #1565-1568	.75	.75			2.40	
	Apollo Soyuz Space Issue, July 15						
1569	10¢ Apollo and Soyuz						
	after Docking, and Earth	.18	.10	2.60	(12)	1.25	80,931,600
1569a	Attached pair, #1569-1570	.36	.25			3.00	
1570	10¢ Spacecraft before Docking,						
	Earth and Project Emblem	.18	.10			1.25	80,931,600

	1975 continued, Perf. 11x10½	Un	U	PB	#	FDC	Q
1571	10¢ International Women's Year,						
	Aug. 26	.18	.05	1.40	(6)	.75	145,640,000
	Postal Service Bicentennial Issue, Sept. 3						
1572	10¢ Stagecoach and Trailer Truck	.18	.08	2.60	(12)	.75	42,163,750
1573	10¢ Old and New Locomotives	.18	.08	2.60	(12)	.75	42,163,750
1574	10¢ Early Mail Plane and Jet	.18	.08			.75	42,163,750
1575	10¢ Satellite						
	for Transmission of Mailgrams	.18	.08			.75	42,163,750
1575a	Block of 4, #1572-1575	.80	.75			2.40	
	Perf. 11						
1576	10¢ World Peace						
	Through Law, Sept. 29	.18	.05	1.00	(4)	.75	146,615,000
	Banking and Commerce Issue, Oct. 6						
1577	10¢ Engine Turning, Indian Head						
	Penny and Morgan Silver Dollar	.18	.08	1.00	(4)	.75	73,098,000
1577a	Attached pair, #1577-1578	.36	.20			1.00	
1578	10¢ Seated Liberty Quarter,						
	$20 Gold Piece (Double Eagle)						
	and Engine Turning	.18	.08	1.00	(4)	.75	73,098,000
	Christmas Issue, Oct. 14, Perf. 11						
1579	(10¢) Madonna and Child,						
	by Domenico Ghirlandaio	.18	.05	2.60	(12)	.75	739,430,000
1580	(10¢) Christmas Card,						
	by Louis Prang, 1878	.18	.05	2.60	(12)	.75	878,690,000
	Issues of 1975-81, Americana Issue, Perf. 11x10½ (Designs 18½ x 22½ mm; #1590-90a, 17½ x 20 mm)						
1581	1¢ Inkwell & Quill, Dec. 8, 1977	.05	.05	.25	(4)	.60	
1582	2¢ Speaker's Stand, Dec. 8, 1977	.05	.05	.25	(4)	.60	
	1583, 1586-89, 1600-02, 1607, 1609 not assigned.						
1584	3¢ Early Ballot Box, Dec. 8, 1977	.06	.05	.30	(4)	.60	
1585	4¢ Books, Bookmark, Eyeglasses, Dec. 8, 1977	.08	.05	.40	(4)	.60	
1590	9¢ Capitol Dome (1591),						
	Single from booklet (#1623a)	.75	.20			1.00	
	Perf. 10						
1590a	Single (1591) from booklet (1623b)	17.50	10.00				
	Perf. 11x10½						
1591	9¢ Capitol Dome, Nov. 24, 1975	.16	.05	.90	(4)	.60	
1592	10¢ Contemplation of Justice, Nov. 17, 1977	.18	.05	1.00	(4)	.60	
1593	11¢ Printing Press, Nov. 13, 1975	.20	.05	1.10	(4)	.60	
1594	12¢ Torch, Apr. 8, 1981	.22	.05	1.20	(4)	.60	
1595	13¢ Liberty Bell						
	Single from booklet	.26	.05			.60	
1595a	Booklet pane of 6, Oct. 31, 1975	1.60	.50			2.00	
1595b	Booklet pane of 7 + label	1.80	.50			2.75	
1595c	Booklet pane of 8	2.10	.50			2.50	
1595d	Booklet pane of 5 + label, Apr. 2, 1976	1.30	.50			2.25	
	Perf. 11						
1596	13¢ Eagle and Shield, Dec. 1, 1975	.24	.05	3.40	(12)	.60	
1597	15¢ Fort McHenry Flag, June 30, 1978	.28	.05	2.10	(6)	.65	
	Perf. 11x10½						
1598	15¢ Fort McHenry Flag (1597),						
	Single from booklet	.28	.05			.65	
1598a	Booklet pane of 8, June 30, 1978	3.25	.60				

1571

1572   **1573**   **1575a**

1574   **1575**

1576   **1577**   **1578**   **1577a**

1579   **1580**

1581   **1582**

1584   **1585**

1591   **1592**   **1596**

1593   **1594**   **1597**

1595   **1595a**

1975-1979

1599

1603

1604

1605

1606

1608

1610

1611

1612

1613

1614

1615

1615c

1622

1623a

1629   1630   1631   1631a

1632

	Issues of 1975-79 continued	Un	U	PB/LP	#	FDC	Q
	Americana Issue, Perf. 11x10½						
1599	16¢ Head of Liberty, Mar. 31, 1978	.32	.05	2.25	(4)	.65	
1603	24¢ Old North Church, Nov. 14, 1975	.50	.09	3.00	(4)	.75	
1604	28¢ Fort Nisqually, Aug. 11, 1978	.55	.08	3.75	(4)	1.20	
1605	29¢ Sandy Hook Lighthouse, Apr. 14, 1978	.55	.08	3.75	(4)	1.10	
1606	30¢ One-Room Schoolhouse, Aug. 27, 1979	.55	.08	4.00	(4)	1.10	
1608	50¢ Whale Oil Lamp, Sept. 11, 1979	.85	.15	5.00	(4)	1.50	
1610	$1 Candle and Rushlight Holder,						
	July 2, 1979	1.75	.15	10.00	(4)	3.00	
1611	$2 Kerosene Table Lamp, Nov. 16, 1978	3.75	.35	22.50	(4)	5.00	
1612	$5 Railroad Lantern, Aug. 23, 1979	9.00	1.65	50.00	(4)	10.00	
	#1590 is on white paper. #1591 is on gray paper. For additional Americana Series, see #1613-19, 1623a-23e, 1625, 1811, 1813 and 1816.						
	Coil Stamps, Perf. 10 Vertically						
1613	3.1¢ Guitar, Oct. 25, 1979	.09	.05	1.75	(2)	.60	
1614	7.7¢ Saxhorns, Nov. 20, 1976	.16	.08	1.00	(2)	.60	
1615	7.9¢ Drum, Apr. 23, 1976	.18	.08	1.10	(2)	.60	
1615C	8.4¢ Piano, July 13, 1978	.18	.08	2.00	(2)	.60	
1616	9¢ slate green Capitol Dome (1591),						
	Mar. 5, 1976	.20	.05	.90	(2)	.60	
1617	10¢ purple Contemplation						
	of Justice (1592), Nov. 4, 1977	.20	.05	1.25	(2)	.60	
1618	13¢ brown						
	Liberty Bell (1595), Nov. 25, 1975	.24	.05	1.00	(2)	.65	
1618C	15¢ Ft. McHenry Flag (1597), June 30, 1978	.25	.05			.65	
1619	16¢ blue						
	Head of Liberty (1599), Mar. 31, 1978	.32	.05	1.50	(2)	.60	
1620-21, 1624 not assigned.							
	Perf. 11x10½						
1622	13¢ Flag over Independence Hall,						
	Nov. 15, 1975	.24	.05	5.50	(20)	.65	
1623	13¢ Flag over Capitol,						
	Single from booklet (1623a)	.24	.05			1.00	
1623a	Booklet pane of 8,						
	(1 #1590 and 7 #1623), Mar. 11, 1977	2.50	.60				
	Perf. 10						
1623b	13¢ Single from booklet	1.50	1.00				
1623c	Booklet pane of 8,						
	(1 #1590 and 7 #1623b)	30.00					
	#1623, 1623b issued only in booklets						
	Perf. 11x10½						
1623d	Attached pair, #1590 and #1623	1.50					
	Perf. 10						
1623e	Attached pair, #1590a and #1623b	22.50					
	Coil Stamp, Perf. 10 Vertically						
1625	13¢ Flag over Independence Hall						
	(1622), Nov. 15, 1975	.26	.05			.65	
	Issues of 1976, American Bicentennial Issues, The Spirit of '76, Jan. 1, Perf. 11						
1629	13¢ Drummer Boy	.24	.08			.65	72,822,000
1630	13¢ Old Drummer	.24	.08			.65	72,822,000
1631	13¢ Fifer	.24	.08			.65	72,822,000
1631a	Strip of 3, #1629-1631	.75	.60	3.40	(12)	1.75	
1632	13¢ Interphil 76, Jan. 17	.26	.05	1.30	(4)	.65	157,825,000

1976 continued		Un	U	FDC	Q
American Bicentennial Issue continued, State Flags, Feb. 23, Perf. 11					
1633	13¢ Delaware	.30	.25	1.75	8,720,100
1634	13¢ Pennsylvania	.30	.25	1.75	8,720,100
1635	13¢ New Jersey	.30	.25	1.75	8,720,100
1636	13¢ Georgia	.30	.25	1.75	8,720,100
1637	13¢ Connecticut	.30	.25	1.75	8,720,100
1638	13¢ Massachusetts	.30	.25	1.75	8,720,100
1639	13¢ Maryland	.30	.25	1.75	8,720,100
1640	13¢ South Carolina	.30	.25	1.75	8,720,100
1641	13¢ New Hampshire	.30	.25	1.75	8,720,100
1642	13¢ Virginia	.30	.25	1.75	8,720,100
1643	13¢ New York	.30	.25	1.75	8,720,100
1644	13¢ North Carolina	.30	.25	1.75	8,720,100
1645	13¢ Rhode Island	.30	.25	1.75	8,720,100
1646	13¢ Vermont	.30	.25	1.75	8,720,100
1647	13¢ Kentucky	.30	.25	1.75	8,720,100
1648	13¢ Tennessee	.30	.25	1.75	8,720,100
1649	13¢ Ohio	.30	.25	1.75	8,720,100
1650	13¢ Louisiana	.30	.25	1.75	8,720,100
1651	13¢ Indiana	.30	.25	1.75	8,720,100
1652	13¢ Mississippi	.30	.25	1.75	8,720,100
1653	13¢ Illinois	.30	.25	1.75	8,720,100

NORTH CAROLINA 12TH STATE TO JOIN UNION

On November 21, 1789, North Carolina (#1644) became the 12th state to ratify the U.S. Constitution. Two years later the state chose Raleigh for its capital. A new stamp celebrates the 1989 bicentennial.

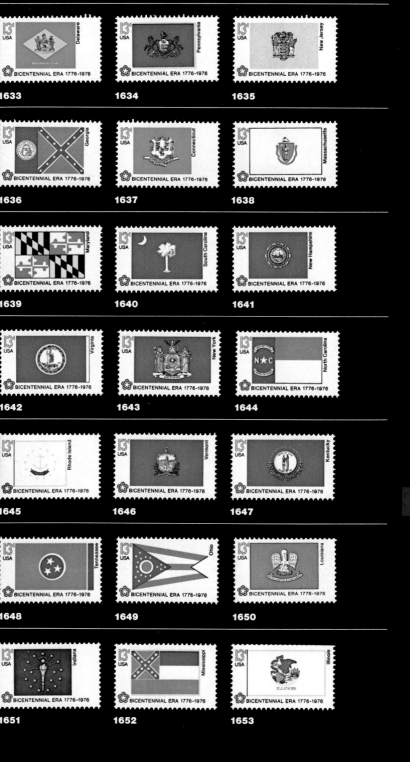

1633   1634   1635

1636   1637   1638

1639   1640   1641

1642   1643   1644

1645   1646   1647

1648   1649   1650

1651   1652   1653

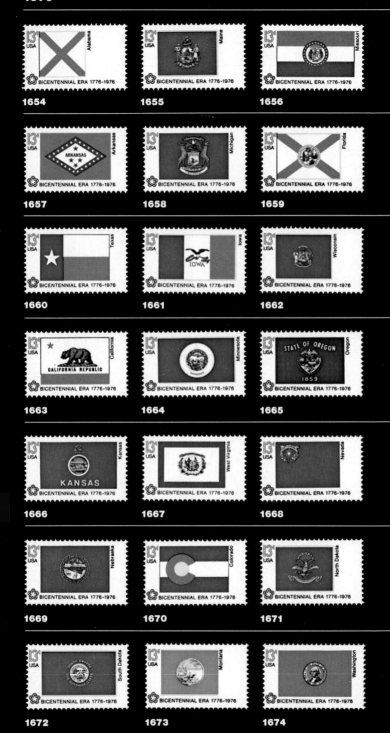

	1976 continued	Un	U		FDC	Q
	American Bicentennial Issue continued, State Flags, Feb. 23, Perf. 11					
1654	13¢ Alabama	.30	.25		1.75	8,720,100
1655	13¢ Maine	.30	.25		1.75	8,720,100
1656	13¢ Missouri	.30	.25		1.75	8,720,100
1657	13¢ Arkansas	.30	.25		1.75	8,720,100
1658	13¢ Michigan	.30	.25		1.75	8,720,100
1659	13¢ Florida	.30	.25		1.75	8,720,100
1660	13¢ Texas	.30	.25		1.75	8,720,100
1661	13¢ Iowa	.30	.25		1.75	8,720,100
1662	13¢ Wisconsin	.30	.25		1.75	8,720,100
1663	13¢ California	.30	.25		1.75	8,720,100
1664	13¢ Minnesota	.30	.25		1.75	8,720,100
1665	13¢ Oregon	.30	.25		1.75	8,720,100
1666	13¢ Kansas	.30	.25		1.75	8,720,100
1667	13¢ West Virginia	.30	.25		1.75	8,720,100
1668	13¢ Nevada	.30	.25		1.75	8,720,100
1669	13¢ Nebraska	.30	.25		1.75	8,720,100
1670	13¢ Colorado	.30	.25		1.75	8,720,100
1671	13¢ North Dakota	.30	.25		1.75	8,720,100
1672	13¢ South Dakota	.30	.25		1.75	8,720,100
1673	13¢ Montana	.30	.25		1.75	8,720,100
1674	13¢ Washington	.30	.25		1.75	8,720,100

Scenic Washington: "The Evergreen State"

ONE HUNDRED YEARS OF STATEHOOD
The only state named for a U.S. president, Washington (#1674) entered the Union as the 42nd state on November 11, 1889. A new U.S. stamp issued in 1989 observes the Washington state centennial.

	1976 continued	Un	U	PB	#	FDC	Q
	American Bicentennial Issue continued, State Flags, Feb. 23, Perf. 11						
1675	13¢ Idaho	.30	.25			1.75	8,720,100
1676	13¢ Wyoming	.30	.25			1.75	8,720,100
1677	13¢ Utah	.30	.25			1.75	8,720,100
1678	13¢ Oklahoma	.30	.25			1.75	8,720,100
1679	13¢ New Mexico	.30	.25			1.75	8,720,100
1680	13¢ Arizona	.30	.25			1.75	8,720,100
1681	13¢ Alaska	.30	.25			1.75	8,720,100
1682	13¢ Hawaii	.30	.25			1.75	8,720,100
1682a	Pane of 50, #1633-1682	15.00		25.00	(50)	32.50	
1683	13¢ Telephone Centennial, Mar. 10	.24	.05	1.30	(4)	.65	158,915,000
1684	13¢ Commercial Aviation, Mar. 19	.24	.05.	2.90	(10)	.65	156,960,000
1685	13¢ Chemistry, Apr. 6	.24	.05	3.40	(12)	.65	158,470,000

A Reminder: Beginning with this edition, catalog values for all stamps listed reflect (as accurately as possible) actual retail values as found in the marketplace.

1675

1676

1677

1678

1679

1680

1681

1682

1683

1684

1685

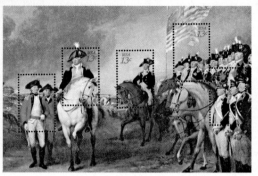

The Surrender of Lord Cornwallis at Yorktown
From a Painting by John Trumbull

1686

The Declaration of Independence, 4 July 1776 at Philadelphia
From a Painting by John Trumbull

1687

1976 continued	Un	U	FDC	Q
American Bicentennial Issue, Souvenir Sheets, May 29, 5 stamps each, Perf. 11				
1686 13¢ Surrender of Cornwallis				
at Yorktown, by John Trumbull	3.50		6.00	1,990,000
a. 13¢ Two American Officers	.65	.40		1,990,000
b. 13¢ Gen. Benjamin Lincoln	.65	.40		1,990,000
c. 13¢ George Washington	.65	.40		1,990,000
d. 13¢ John Trumbull, Col. David Cobb,				
General Friedrich von Steuben,				
Marquis de Lafayette				
and Thomas Nelson	.65	.40		1,990,000
e. 13¢ Alexander Hamilton,				
John Laurens and Walter Stewart	.65	.40		1,990,000
1687 18¢ Declaration of Independence,				
by John Trumbull	4.00		7.50	1,983,000
a. 18¢ John Adams, Roger Sherman				
and Robert R. Livingston	.80	.55		1,983,000
b. 18¢ Thomas Jefferson				
and Benjamin Franklin	.80	.55		1,983,000
c. 18¢ Thomas Nelson, Jr.,				
Francis Lewis, John Witherspoon				
and Samuel Huntington	.80	.55		1,983,000
d. 18¢ John Hancock				
and Charles Thomson	.80	.55		1,983,000
e. 18¢ George Read, John Dickinson				
and Edward Rutledge	.80	.55		1,983,000

LAFAYETTE CHAMPIONED FREEDOM

In 1777 the Marquis de Lafayette, a Frenchman, landed in America to fight for colonial independence. Soon a member of Washington's staff, he eventually helped defeat Cornwallis at Yorktown (#1686d). Lafayette returned to France, where he played an active role in the French Revolution.

	1976 continued	Un	U	PB	#	FDC	Q
	American Bicentennial Issue continued, Souvenir Sheets, May 29, 5 stamps each, Perf. 11						
1688	24¢ Washington Crossing						
	the Delaware, by Emanuel Leutze/						
	Eastman Johnson	4.50				8.50	1,953,000
	a. 24¢ Boatmen	.90	.75				1,953,000
	b. 24¢ George Washington	.90	.75				1,953,000
	c. 24¢ Flagbearer	.90	.75				1,953,000
	d. 24¢ Men in Boat	.90	.75				1,953,000
	e. 24¢ Steersman and Men on Shore	.90	.75				1,953,000
1689	31¢ Washington Reviewing Army						
	at Valley Forge, by William T. Trego	6.00				9.50	1,903,000
	a. 31¢ Two Officers	1.10	.90				1,903,000
	b. 31¢ George Washington	1.10	.90				1,903,000
	c. 31¢ Officer and Brown Horse	1.10	.90				1,903,000
	d. 31¢ White Horse and Officer	1.10	.90				1,903,000
	e. 31¢ Three Soldiers	1.10	.90				1,903,000

APPLETON STAMP BOOK MAY HAVE OLDER SIBLING

An 1863 Appleton stamp book long has been acknowledged as the oldest printed in the United States. Now it appears that this antiquarian may have an even older sibling, also published by Appleton just a few months earlier. The recent discovery surfaced after a reader saw a column about the better-known album in an August 1986 issue of Linn's Stamp News.

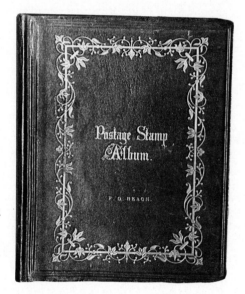

Washington Crossing the Delaware
From a Painting by Emanuel Leutze / Eastman Johnson

1688

Washington Reviewing His Ragged Army at Valley Forge
From a Painting by William T. Trego

1689

1690

1691   **1692**   **1693**   **1694**   **1694a**

1699

1700

1695   **1696**   **1698a**
1697   **1698**

1701   **1702**   **1703**

1705

1704

	1976 continued	Un	U	PB	#	FDC	Q
	American Bicentennial Issues, Benjamin Franklin, June 1, Perf. 11						
1690	13¢ Bust of Franklin						
	and Map of North America, 1776	.26	.05	1.30	(4)	.65	164,890,000
	Declaration of Independence, by John Trumbull, July 4						
1691	13¢ Delegates	.20	.08	5.75	(20)	.65	52,008,750
1692	13¢ Delegates and John Adams	.20	.08			.65	52,008,750
1693	13¢ Roger Sherman,						
	Robert R. Livingston, Thomas Jefferson						
	and Benjamin Franklin	.20	.08			.65	52,008,750
1694	13¢ John Hancock, Charles Thomson,						
	George Read, John Dickinson						
	and Edward Rutledge	.20	.08	5.75	(20)	.65	52,008,750
1694a	Strip of 4, #1691-1694	.80	.60			2.00	
	Olympic Games Issue, July 16						
1695	13¢ Diver and Olympic Rings	.30	.08	5.50	(12)	.75	46,428,750
1696	13¢ Skier and Olympic Rings	.30	.08			.75	46,428,750
1697	13¢ Runner and Olympic Rings	.30	.08	5.50	(12)	.75	46,428,750
1698	13¢ Skater and Olympic Rings	.30	.08			.75	46,428,750
1698a	Block of 4, #1695-1698	1.20	.85			2.00	
1699	13¢ Clara Maass, Aug. 18	.24	.06	3.40	(12)	.75	130,592,000
1700	13¢ Adolph S. Ochs, Sept. 18	.24	.05	1.30	(4)	.75	158,332,800
	Christmas Issue, Oct. 27						
1701	13¢ Nativity, by John Singleton Copley	.24	.05	3.40	(12)	.65	809,955,000
1702	13¢ "Winter Pastime,"						
	by Nathaniel Currier	.24	.05	3.00	(10)	.65	481,685,000
1703	13¢ as 1702	.24	.05	5.70	(20)	.65	481,685,000

#1702 has overall tagging. Lettering at base is black and usually ½mm. below design. As a rule, no "snowflaking" in sky or pond. Pane of 50 has margins on 4 sides with slogans. #1703 has block tagging the size of the printed area. Lettering at base is gray black and usually ¾mm. below design. "Snowflaking" generally in sky and pond. Pane of 50 has margin only at right or left and no slogans.

	Issues of 1977, American Bicentennial Issue, Washington at Princeton, Jan. 3						
1704	13¢ Washington, Nassau Hall,						
	Hessian Prisoners and 13-star Flag,						
	by Charles Willson Peale	.24	.05	2.90	(10)	.65	150,328,000
1705	13¢ Sound Recording, Mar. 23	.24	.05	1.30	(4)	.65	176,830,000

	1977 continued	Un	U	PB	#	FDC	Q
	American Folk Art Issue, Pueblo Pottery, Apr. 13, Perf. 11						
1706	13¢ Zia Pot	.24	.08	3.00	(10)	.75	48,994,000
1707	13¢ San Ildefonso Pot	.24	.08			.75	48,994,000
1708	13¢ Hopi Pot	.24	.08	5.00	(16)	.75	48,994,000
1709	13¢ Acoma Pot	.24	.08			.75	48,994,000
1709a	Block of 4, #1706-1709	1.00	.60			2.00	
1710	13¢ Solo Transatlantic Flight, May 20	.24	.05	3.65	(12)	.75	208,820,000
1711	13¢ Colorado Statehood, May 21	.24	.05	3.65	(12)	.65	192,250,000
	Butterflies Issue, June 6						
1712	13¢ Swallowtail	.24	.08	3.65	(12)	.75	54,957,500
1713	13¢ Checkerspot	.24	.08	3.65	(12)	.75	54,957,500
1714	13¢ Dogface	.24	.08			.75	54,957,500
1715	13¢ Orange-Tip	.24	.08			.75	54,957,500
1715a	Block of 4, #1712-1715	1.00	.60			2.00	
	American Bicentennial Issues, Lafayette's Landing In South Carolina, June 13						
1716	13¢ Marquis de Lafayette	.24	.05	1.30	(4)	.65	159,852,000
	Skilled Hands for Independence, July 4						
1717	13¢ Seamstress	.24	.08	3.65	(12)	.65	47,077,500
1718	13¢ Blacksmith	.24	.08	3.65	(12)	.65	47,077,500
1719	13¢ Wheelwright	.24	.08			.65	47,077,500
1720	13¢ Leatherworker	.24	.08			.65	47,077,500
1720a	Block of 4, #1717-1720	1.00	.60			1.75	
	Perf. 11x10½						
1721	13¢ Peace Bridge, Aug. 4	.24	.05	1.30	(4)	.65	163,625,000

Butterfly Bears
"Dogface"
The dogface butterfly is named for its unusual markings, a "dogface" with a black eye on the upper side of its forewing. Only the males of Colias eurydice, *the California dogface (#1714), bear this mark. The dogface is a "patrolling" species, the male flying all day to attract females.*

1710

1711

1706 **1707** **1709a**
1708 **1709**

1716

1712 **1713** **1715a**
1714 **1715**

1721

1717 **1718** **1720a**
1719 **1720**

187

1722

1723   **1723a**

1724

1725

1726

1727

1728

1729

1730

1731

1732   **1732a**

1733

1734

1735

1737

1738   **1739**   **1740**   **1741**   **1742**

1742a

	1977 continued	Un	U	PB/LP	#	FDC	Q
	American Bicentennial Issue, Battle of Oriskany, Aug. 6, Perf. 11						
1722	13¢ Herkimer at Oriskany,						
	by Frederick Yohn	.24	.05	3.10	(10)	.65	156,296,000
	Energy Issue, Oct. 20						
1723	13¢ Energy Conservation	.24	.08	4.00	(12)	.65	79,338,000
1723a	Attached pair, #1723-1724	.50	.35			1.00	
1724	13¢ Energy Development	.24	.08			.65	79,338,000
1725	13¢ First Civil Settlement-						
	Alta, California, Sept. 9	.24	.05	1.30	(4)	.65	154,495,000
	American Bicentennial Issue, Articles of Confederation, Sept. 30						
1726	13¢ Members						
	of Continental Congress in Conference	.24	.05	1.30	(4)	.65	168,050,000
1727	13¢ Talking Pictures, Oct. 6	.24	.05	1.30	(4)	.75	156,810,000
	American Bicentennial Issue, Surrender at Saratoga, Oct. 7						
1728	13¢ Surrender of Burgoyne,						
	by John Trumbull	.24	.05	3.10	(10)	.65	153,736,000
	Christmas Issue, Oct. 21						
1729	13¢ Washington at Valley Forge,						
	by J. C. Leyendecker	.24	.05	7.50	(20)	.65	882,260,000
1730	13¢ Rural Mailbox	.24	.05	3.10	(10)	.65	921,530,000
	Issues of 1978						
1731	13¢ Carl Sandburg, Jan. 6	.24	.05	1.30	(4)	.65	156,560,000
	Capt. Cook Issue, Jan. 20						
1732	13¢ Capt. James Cook-Alaska,						
	by Nathaniel Dance	.24	.08	1.30	(4)	.75	101,095,000
1732a	Attached pair, #1732-1733	.50	.30			1.50	
1733	13¢ *Resolution* and *Discovery*-Hawaii,						
	by John Webber	.24	.08	1.30	(4)	.75	101,095,000
1734	13¢ Indian Head Penny, Jan. 11	.24	.10	2.50	(4)	1.00	
1735	(15¢) A Stamp, May 22	.24	.05	1.50	(4)	.65	
	Perf. 11x10½						
1736	(15¢) orange Eagle (1735),						
	Single from booklet	.24	.05			.65	
1736a	Booklet pane of 8, May 22	2.25	*.60*			3.00	
	Roses Booklet Issue, July 11, Perf. 10						
1737	15¢ Roses, Single from booklet	.24	.06			.65	
1737a	Booklet pane of 8	2.40	*.60*			3.00	
	Issue of 1980, Windmills Booklet Issue, Feb. 7, Perf. 11						
1738	15¢ Virginia, 1720	.30	.05			.65	
1739	15¢ Rhode Island, 1790	.30	.05			.65	
1740	15¢ Massachusetts, 1793	.30	.05			.65	
1741	15¢ Illinois, 1860	.30	.05			.65	
1742	15¢ Texas, 1890	.30	.05			.65	
1742a	Booklet pane of 10, #1738-42	3.25	*.60*			3.75	
	#1737-42 issued only in booklets. All stamps have one or two straight edges.						
	Issue of 1978, Coil Stamp, Perf. 10 Vertically						
1743	(15¢) orange Eagle (1735), May 22	.24	.05	1.00	(2)	.65	

A Reminder: Beginning with this edition, catalog values for all stamps listed reflect (as accurately as possible) actual retail values as found in the marketplace.

	1978 continued	Un	U	PB	#	FDC	Q
	Black Heritage Issue, Harriet Tubman, Feb. 1, Perf. 10½x11						
1744	13¢ Harriet Tubman						
	and Cart Carrying Slaves	.24	.05	3.65	(12)	1.00	156,525,000
	American Folk Art Issue, Quilts, Mar. 8, Perf. 11						
1745	13¢ Basket design, red & orange	.24	.08	3.65	(12)	.75	41,295,600
1746	13¢ Basket design, red	.24	.08	3.65	(12)	.75	41,295,600
1747	13¢ Basket design, orange	.24	.08			.75	41,295,600
1748	13¢ Basket design, brown	.24	.08			.75	41,295,600
1748a	Block of 4, #1745-1748	1.00	.60			2.00	
	American Dance Issue, Apr. 26						
1749	13¢ Ballet	.24	.08	3.65	(12)	.75	39,399,600
1750	13¢ Theater	.24	.08	3.65	(12)	.75	39,399,600
1751	13¢ Folk	.24	.08			.75	39,399,600
1752	13¢ Modern	.24	.08			.75	39,399,600
1752a	Block of 4, #1749-1752	1.00	.60			1.75	
	American Bicentennial Issue, French Alliance, May 4						
1753	13¢ King Louis XVI						
	and Benjamin Franklin,						
	by Charles Gabriel Sauvage	.24	.05	1.30	(4)	.65	102,920,000
	Perf. 10½x11						
1754	13¢ Early Cancer Detection, May 18	.24	.05	1.30	(4)	.65	152,355,000
	Performing Arts Issues, Jimmie Rodgers, May 24, and George M. Cohan, July 3, Perf. 11						
1755	13¢ Jimmie Rodgers with Locomotive,						
	Guitar and Brakeman's Cap	.24	.05	3.65	(12)	.65	94,625,000
1756	15¢ George M. Cohan,						
	"Yankee Doodle Dandy" and Stars	.24	.05	4.20	(12)	.65	151,570,000

AN AMERICAN ART FORM
American pioneer women originally made quilts as a way of salvaging cloth from old garments. By quilting with neighbors they created the quilting bee, a welcome opportunity for socializing. Today quilting is a flourishing craft and an art form (#1745-1748).

1744

1745
1747

1746
1748

1748a

1749

1750

1752

1751

1752a

1753

1754

1755

1756

1757a, b, c, d

1757e, f, g, h

1757

1758

1759

1763a

1760   1761

1762   1763

1768   **1769**

1764   1765   1767a

1766   1767

	1978 continued	Un	U	PB	#	FDC	Q
	CAPEX '78, Souvenir Sheet, June 10, Perf. 11						
1757	13¢ Souvenir sheet of 8	2.10	1.75	2.75	(8)	2.75	15,170,400
1757a	13¢ Cardinal	.25	.10				
1757b	13¢ Mallard	.25	.10				
1757c	13¢ Canada Goose	.25	.10				
1757d	13¢ Blue Jay	.25	.10				
1757e	13¢ Moose	.25	.10				
1757f	13¢ Chipmunk	.25	.10				
1757g	13¢ Red Fox	.25	.10				
1757h	13¢ Raccoon	.25	.10				
1758	15¢ Photography, June 26	.26	.05	4.20	(12)	.65	163,200,000
1759	15¢ Viking Missions to Mars, July 20	.28	.05	1.50	(4)	1.10	158,880,000
	Wildlife Conservation Issue, American Owls, Aug. 26						
1760	15¢ Great Gray Owl	.28	.08	1.50	(4)	.75	46,637,500
1761	15¢ Saw-Whet Owl	.28	.08	1.50	(4)	.75	46,637,500
1762	15¢ Barred Owl	.28	.08	1.50	(4)	.75	46,637,500
1763	15¢ Great Horned Owl	.28	.08	1.50	(4)	.75	46,637,500
1763a	Block of 4, #1760-1763	1.20	.85			2.00	
	American Trees Issue, Oct. 9						
1764	15¢ Giant Sequoia	.28	.08	4.20	(12)	.75	42,034,000
1765	15¢ White Pine	.28	.08	4.20	(12)	.75	42,034,000
1766	15¢ White Oak	.28	.08			.75	42,034,000
1767	15¢ Gray Birch	.28	.08			.75	42,034,000
1767a	Block of 4, #1764-1767	1.20	.85			2.00	
	Christmas Issue, Oct. 18						
1768	15¢ Madonna and Child with Cherubim, by Andrea della Robbia	.28	.05	4.20	(12)	.65	963,370,000
1769	15¢ Child on Hobby Horse and Christmas Trees	.28	.05	4.20	(12)	.65	916,800,000

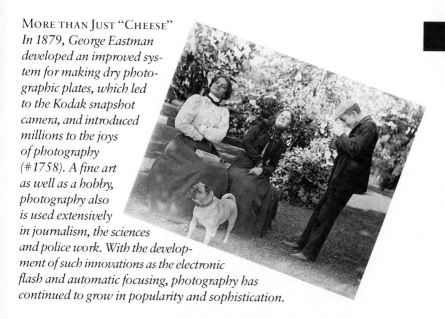

MORE THAN JUST "CHEESE"
In 1879, George Eastman developed an improved system for making dry photographic plates, which led to the Kodak snapshot camera, and introduced millions to the joys of photography (#1758). A fine art as well as a hobby, photography also is used extensively in journalism, the sciences and police work. With the development of such innovations as the electronic flash and automatic focusing, photography has continued to grow in popularity and sophistication.

	Issues of 1979, Perf. 11	Un	U	PB	#	FDC	Q
1770	15¢ Robert F. Kennedy, Jan. 12	.28	.05	1.75	(4)	.65	159,297,600
	Black Heritage Issue, Martin Luther King, Jr., Jan. 13						
1771	15¢ Martin Luther King, Jr.,						
	and Civil Rights Marchers	.28	.05	4.75	(12)	.65	166,435,000
1772	15¢ International Year of the Child,						
	Feb. 15	.28	.05	1.50	(4)	.65	162,535,000
	Literary Arts Issue, John Steinbeck, Feb. 27, Perf. 10½x11						
1773	15¢ John Steinbeck,						
	by Philippe Halsman	.28	.05	1.50	(4)	.65	155,000,000
1774	15¢ Albert Einstein, Mar. 4	.28	.05	1.50	(4)	.65	157,310,000
	American Folk Art Issue, Pennsylvania Toleware, Apr. 19, Perf. 11						
1775	15¢ Coffeepot	.28	.08	3.50	(10)	.75	43,524,000
1776	15¢ Tea Caddy	.28	.08			.75	43,524,000
1777	15¢ Sugar Bowl	.28	.08			.75	43,524,000
1778	15¢ Coffeepot	.28	.08			.75	43,524,000
1778a	Block or strip of 4, #1775-1778	1.20	.85			2.00	
	American Architecture Issue, June 4						
1779	15¢ Virginia Rotunda,						
	by Thomas Jefferson	.28	.08	1.70	(4)	.75	41,198,400
1780	15¢ Baltimore Cathedral,						
	by Benjamin Latrobe	.28	.08	1.70	(4)	.75	41,198,400
1781	15¢ Boston State House,						
	by Charles Bulfinch	.28	.08	1.70	(4)	.75	41,198,400
1782	15¢ Philadelphia Exchange,						
	by William Strickland	.28	.08	1.70	(4)	.75	41,198,400
1782a	Block of 4, #1779-1782	1.20	.85			2.00	
	Endangered Flora Issue, June 7						
1783	15¢ Persistent Trillium	.28	.08	4.20	(12)	.75	40,763,750
1784	15¢ Hawaiian Wild Broadbean	.28	.08			.75	40,763,750
1785	15¢ Contra Costa Wallflower	.28	.08	4.20	(12)	.75	40,763,750
1786	15¢ Antioch Dunes Evening Primrose	.28	.08			.75	40,763,750
1786a	Block of 4, #1783-1786	1.20	.85			2.00	

1770

1771

1772

1773

1774

| **1775** | **1776** | **1778a** |
| **1777** | **1778** | |

| **1779** | **1780** | **1782a** |
| **1781** | **1782** | |

| **1783** | **1784** | **1786a** |
| **1785** | **1786** | |

USA 15c

Seeing For Me

1787

Special Olympics

Skill · Sharing · Joy
USA 15c

1788

I have not yet begun to fight

John Paul Jones
US Bicentennial 15c

1789

Olympics 1980 Decathlon

USA 10c

1790

USA 15c

USA 15c
Olympics 1980

Olympics 1980 USA 15c

Olympics 1980 USA 15c

1791   **1792**   **1794a**
1793   **1794**

USA Olympics 1980 15c

USA 15c
Olympics 1980

USA Olympics 1980 15c

USA Olympics 1980 15c

1795   **1796**   **1798b**
1797   **1798**

Gerard David: National Gallery
Christmas USA 15c

Christmas
15c USA

1799   **1800**

WILL ROGERS

Performing Arts USA 15c

1801

USA·15c·
HONORING VIETNAM VETERANS
NOV·11·1979

1802

W.C. FIELDS

Performing Arts USA 15c

1803

Benjamin Banneker

Black Heritage USA 15c

1804

	1979 continued, Perf. 11	Un	U	PB	#	FDC	Q
1787	15¢ Seeing Eye Dogs, June 15	.28	.05	6.50	(20)	.65	161,860,000
1788	15¢ Special Olympics, Aug. 9	.28	.05	3.50	(10)	.65	165,775,000
	American Bicentennial Issue, John Paul Jones, Sept. 23, Perf. 11x12						
1789	15¢ John Paul Jones,						
	by Charles Willson Peale	.28	.05	3.50	(10)	.65	160,000,000
	Olympic Summer Games Issues, Sept. 5, Perf. 11 (see also #C97)						
1790	10¢ Javelin Thrower	.20	.22	4.50	(12)	1.00	67,195,000
1791	15¢ Runner	.28	.08	4.75	(12)	.75	46,726,250
1792	15¢ Swimmer	.28	.08	4.75	(12)	.75	46,726,250
1793	15¢ Rowers	.28	.08			.75	46,726,250
1794	15¢ Equestrian Contestant	.28	.08			.75	46,726,250
1794a	Block of 4, #1791-1794	1.20	.85			2.00	
	Issues of 1980, Olympic Winter Games Issue, Feb. 1, Perf. 11x10½						
1795	15¢ Speed Skater	.35	.08	6.50	(12)	.75	52,073,750
1796	15¢ Downhill Skier	.35	.08	6.50	(12)	.75	52,073,750
1797	15¢ Ski Jumper	.35	.08			.75	52,073,750
1798	15¢ Hockey Goaltender	.35	.08			.75	52,073,750
1798b	Block of 4, #1795-1798	1.50	1.00			2.00	
	1979 continued, Christmas Issue, Oct. 18, Perf. 11						
1799	15¢ Virgin and Child with Cherubim,						
	by Gerard David	.28	.05	4.25	(12)	.65	873,710,000
1800	15¢ Santa Claus,						
	Christmas Tree Ornament	.28	.05	4.25	(12)	.65	931,880,000
	Performing Arts Issue, Will Rogers, Nov. 4						
1801	15¢ Will Rogers Portrait						
	and Rogers as a Cowboy Humorist	.28	.05	4.25	(12)	.65	161,290,000
1802	15¢ Vietnam Veterans, Nov. 11	.28	.05	3.50	(10)	1.25	172,740,000
	1980 continued, Performing Arts Issue, W.C. Fields, Jan. 29						
1803	15¢ W.C. Fields Portrait						
	and Fields as a Juggler	.28	.05	4.25	(12)	.65	168,995,000
	Black Heritage Issue, Benjamin Banneker, Feb. 15						
1804	15¢ Benjamin Banneker Portrait						
	and Banneker as Surveyor	.28	.05	4.25	(12)	.65	160,000,000

	1980 continued	Un	U	PB/LP	#	FDC	Q
	Letter Writing Issue, Feb. 25, Perf. 11						
1805	15¢ Letters Preserve Memories	.30	.08	16.50	(36)	.65	38,933,000
1806	15¢ P.S. Write Soon	.30	.08			.65	38,933,000
1807	15¢ Letters Lift Spirits	.30	.08			.65	38,933,000
1808	15¢ P.S. Write Soon	.30	.08			.65	38,933,000
1809	15¢ Letters Shape Opinions	.30	.08			.65	38,933,000
1810	15¢ P.S. Write Soon	.30	.08	16.50	(36)	.65	38,933,000
1810a	Vertical Strip of 6, #1805-1810	1.90	1.50			3.00	
	Issues of 1980-81, Americana Issue, Coil Stamps, Perf. 10 Vertically						
1811	1¢ dark blue, *greenish*						
	Inkwell & Quill (1581), May 6, 1980	.05	.05	.15	(2)	.60	
1812, 1814-15, 1817 not assigned.							
1813	3.5¢ Weaver Violins, June 23, 1980	.09	.05	.30	(2)	.60	
1816	12¢ red brown Torch from						
	Statue of Liberty (1594), Apr. 8, 1981	.20	.05	.75	(2)	.60	
	Issues of 1981, Perf. 11x10½						
1818	(18¢) B Stamp, Mar. 15	.30	.05	1.80	(4)	.75	
	Perf. 10						
1819	(18¢) B Stamp (1818),						
	Single from booklet	.38	.05			.75	
1819a	Booklet pane of 8, Mar. 15	4.50	*1.50*				
	Coil Stamp, Perf. 10 Vertically						
1820	(18¢) B Stamp (1818), Mar. 15	.35	.05	1.50	(2)	.75	
	1980 continued, Perf. 10½x11						
1821	15¢ Frances Perkins, April 10	.28	.05	1.50	(4)	.65	163,510,000
	Perf. 11						
1822	15¢ Dolley Madison, May 20	.28	.05	1.50	(4)	.65	256,620,000
1823	15¢ Emily Bissell, May 31	.28	.05	1.50	(4)	.65	95,695,000
1824	15¢ Helen Keller/Anne Sullivan,						
	June 27	.28	.05	1.50	(4)	.80	153,975,000
1825	15¢ Veterans Administration, July 21	.28	.05	1.50	(4)	.65	160,000,000
	American Bicentennial Issue, General Bernardo de Galvez, July 23						
1826	15¢ General Bernardo de Galvez						
	and Revolutionary Flag at Battle of Mobile	.28	.05	1.50	(4)	.65	103,855,000
	Coral Reefs Issue, Aug. 26						
1827	15¢ Brain Coral, Beaugregory Fish	.28	.08	4.50	(12)	.85	51,291,250
1828	15¢ Elkhorn Coral, Porkfish	.28	.08			.85	51,291,250
1829	15¢ Chalice Coral, Moorish Idol	.28	.08	4.50	(12)	.85	51,291,250
1830	15¢ Finger Coral, Sabertooth Blenny	.28	.08			.85	51,291,250
1830a	Block of 4, #1827-1830	1.10	.85			2.00	

A Reminder: Beginning with this edition, catalog values for all stamps listed reflect (as accurately as possible) actual retail values as found in the marketplace.

1813

1816

1805
1806

1807
1808

1809
1810

1818

Frances Perkins
USA 15c
1821

1822

Emily Bissell
Crusader Against Tuberculosis
USA 15c
1823

HELEN KELLER
ANNE SULLIVAN
1824

1825

1826

1827
1829

1828
1830

1830a

Organized Labor Proud and Free

USA 15¢

1831

1832

Glow by Josef Albers USA 15¢

Learning never ends

1833

Heiltsuk, Bella Bella
Indian Art USA 15¢

Chilkat Tlingit
Indian Art USA 15¢

Tlingit
Indian Art USA 15¢

Bella Coola
Indian Art USA 15¢

1834   **1835**   **1837a**

1836   **1837**

Renwick 1818-1895 Smithsonian Washington
Architecture USA 15¢

Richardson 1838-1886 Trinity Church Boston
Architecture USA 15¢

Furness 1839-1912 Penn Academy Philadelphia
Architecture USA 15¢

A.J. Davis 1803-1892 Lyndhurst Tarrytown NY
Architecture USA 15¢

1838   **1839**   **1841a**

Christmas USA 15¢

1842

USA 15¢
Season's Greetings

1843

	1980 continued, Perf. 11	Un	U	PB	#	FDC	Q
1831	15¢ Organized Labor, Sept. 1	.28	.05	4.50	(12)	.65	166,590,000
	Literary Arts Issue, Edith Wharton, Sept. 5, Perf. 10½x11						
1832	15¢ Edith Wharton Reading Letter	.28	.05	1.50	(4)	.65	163,275,000
	Perf. 11						
1833	15¢ Education, Sept. 12	.28	.05	2.25	(6)	.65	160,000,000
	American Folk Art Issue, Pacific Northwest Indian Masks, Sept. 25						
1834	15¢ Heiltsuk, Bella Bella Tribe	.28	.08			.75	38,101,000
1835	15¢ Chilkat Tlingit Tribe	.28	.08			.75	38,101,000
1836	15¢ Tlingit Tribe	.28	.08			.75	38,101,000
1837	15¢ Bella Coola Tribe	.28	.08			.75	38,101,000
1837a	Block of 4, #1834-1837	1.10	.85	3.50	(10)	2.00	
	American Architecture Issue, Oct. 9						
1838	15¢ Smithsonian Institution,						
	by James Renwick	.28	.08			.75	38,756,000
1839	15¢ Trinity Church,						
	by Henry Hobson Richardson	.28	.08			.75	38,756,000
1840	15¢ Pennsylvania Academy						
	of Fine Arts, by Frank Furness	.28	.08			.75	38,756,000
1841	15¢ Lyndhurst,						
	by Alexander Jefferson Davis	.28	.08			.75	38,756,000
1841a	Block of 4, #1838-1841	1.10	.85	1.75	(4)	2.00	
	Christmas Issue, Oct. 31						
1842	15¢ Madonna and Child,						
	from Epiphany Window,						
	Washington Cathedral	.28	.05	4.25	(12)	.65	693,250,000
1843	15¢ Wreath and Toys	.28	.05	6.50	(20)	.65	718,715,000

WASHINGTON CATHEDRAL
GRACES U.S. CAPITAL
*The Cathedral Church of Saint
Peter and Saint Paul was built in
Washington, D.C. between 1907 and
1912. Also known as the Washington
Cathedral and the National Cathedral, the church is adorned with
beautiful stained-glass windows,
including the Epiphany Window
(#1842). The Washington Cathedral
is the final resting place of such well-
known individuals as President
Woodrow Wilson and Admiral
George Dewey.*

	Issues of 1980-85	Un	U	PB	#	FDC	Q
	Great Americans Issue, Perf. 11 (see also # 2168-72, 2176-80, 2182-84, 2188, 2191-95)						
1844	1¢ Dorothea Dix, Sept. 23, 1983	.05	.05	1.00	(20)	.60	
	Perf. 10½x11						
1845	2¢ Igor Stravinsky, Nov. 18, 1982	.05	.05	.25	(4)	.60	
1846	3¢ Henry Clay, July 13, 1983	.06	.05	.40	(4)	.60	
1847	4¢ Carl Schurz, June 3, 1983	.07	.05	.50	(4)	.60	
1848	5¢ Pearl Buck, June 25, 1983	.09	.05	.60	(4)	.60	
	Perf. 11						
1849	6¢ Walter Lippman, Sept. 19, 1985	.12	.05	2.75	(20)	.60	
1850	7¢ Abraham Baldwin, Jan. 25, 1985	.12	.05	3.00	(20)	.60	
1851	8¢ Henry Knox, July 25, 1985	.14	.05	.80	(4)	.60	
1852	9¢ Sylvanus Thayer, June 7, 1985	.16	.05	4.00	(20)	.60	
1853	10¢ Richard Russell, May 31, 1984	.18	.05	5.00	(20)	.65	
1854	11¢ Alden Partridge, Feb. 12, 1985	.20	.05	1.10	(4)	.65	
	Perf. 10½x11						
1855	13¢ Crazy Horse, Jan. 15, 1982	.22	.05	1.50	(4)	.65	
	Perf. 11						
1856	14¢ Sinclair Lewis, Mar. 21, 1985	.25	.05	7.00	(20)	.65	
	Perf. 10½x11						
1857	17¢ Rachel Carson, May 28, 1981	.30	.05	2.10	(4)	.75	
1858	18¢ George Mason, May 7, 1981	.32	.05	2.20	(4)	.75	
1859	19¢ Sequoyah, Dec. 27, 1980	.35	.07	2.00	(4)	.80	
1860	20¢ Ralph Bunche, Jan. 12, 1982	.38	.05	2.50	(4)	.75	
1861	20¢ Thomas H. Gallaudet, June 10, 1983	.38	.05	2.50	(4)	.75	
	Perf. 11						
1862	20¢ Harry S. Truman, Jan. 26, 1984	.38	.05	10.00	(20)	.75	
1863	22¢ John J. Audubon, Apr. 23, 1985	.40	.05	10.00	(20)	.80	
1864	30¢ Frank C. Laubach, Sept. 2, 1984	.52	.08	14.00	(20)	.85	
	Perf. 10½x11						
1865	35¢ Charles R. Drew, MD, June 3, 1981	.60	.08	3.50	(4)	1.00	
1866	37¢ Robert Millikan, Jan. 26, 1982	.70	.05	3.75	(4)	1.00	
	Perf. 11						
1867	39¢ Grenville Clark, May 20, 1985	.70	.08	20.00	(20)	1.00	
1868	40¢ Lillian M. Gilbreth, Feb. 24, 1984	.70	.10	17.50	(20)	1.00	
1869	50¢ Chester W. Nimitz, Feb. 22, 1985	.85	.10	5.00	(4)	1.25	

1870-74 not assigned.

Dorothea Dix — USA 1c — **1844**

Igor Stravinsky — USA 2c — **1845**

Henry Clay — USA 3c — **1846**

Carl Schurz — 4c USA — **1847**

Pearl Buck — USA 5c — **1848**

Walter Lippmann — 6 USA — **1849**

Abraham Baldwin — 7 USA — **1850**

Henry Knox — USA 8 — **1851**

Sylvanus Thayer — USA 9 — **1852**

Richard Russell — USA 10c — **1853**

Alden Partridge — USA 11 — **1854**

Crazy Horse — USA 13c — **1855**

Sinclair Lewis — USA 14 — **1856**

Rachel Carson — USA 17c — **1857**

George Mason — USA 18c — **1858**

Sequoyah — USA 19c — **1859**

Ralph Bunche — USA 20c — **1860**

Thomas H Gallaudet — USA 20c — **1861**

Harry S. Truman — USA 20c — **1862**

John J. Audubon — USA 22 — **1863**

Frank C. Laubach — USA 30c — **1864**

Charles R Drew MD — USA 35c — **1865**

Robert Millikan — 37c USA — **1866**

Grenville Clark — USA 39 — **1867**

Lillian M. Gilbreth — USA 40c — **1868**

Chester W. Nimitz — USA 50 — **1869**

1874 1875

1876   1877 1879a
1878   1879

1890

1891

1889a

1880 1881
1882 1883
1884 1885
1886 1887
1888 1889

1892   1893a
1893

1894

	Issues of 1981, Perf. 11	Un	U	PB/LP	#	FDC	Q
1874	15¢ Everett Dirksen, Jan. 4	.28	.05	1.50	(4)	.65	160,155,000
	Black Heritage Issue, Whitney Moore Young, Jan. 30						
1875	15¢ Whitney Moore Young at Desk	.28	.05	1.50	(4)	.65	159,505,000
	Flower Issue, April 23						
1876	18¢ Rose	.32	.08			.75	52,658,250
1877	18¢ Camellia	.32	.08			.75	52,658,250
1878	18¢ Dahlia	.32	.08			.75	52,658,250
1879	18¢ Lily	.32	.08			.75	52,658,250
1879a	Block of 4, #1876-1879	1.30	.85	2.10	(4)	2.50	
	Wildlife Booklet Issue, May 14						
1880	18¢ Bighorn Sheep	.32	.05			.75	
1881	18¢ Puma	.32	.05			.75	
1882	18¢ Harbor Seal	.32	.05			.75	
1883	18¢ Bison	.32	.05			.75	
1884	18¢ Brown Bear	.32	.05			.75	
1885	18¢ Polar Bear	.32	.05			.75	
1886	18¢ Elk (Wapiti)	.32	.05			.75	
1887	18¢ Moose	.32	.05			.75	
1888	18¢ White-Tailed Deer	.32	.05			.75	
1889	18¢ Prong Horned Antelope	.32	.05			.75	
1889a	Booklet pane of 10, #1880-1889	7.00				7.00	

#1880-89 issued only in booklets. All stamps are imperf. at one side or imperf. at one side and bottom.

	Flag and Anthem Issue, April 24						
1890	18¢ Flag and Anthem,						
	"…for amber waves of grain"	.32	.05	10.00	(20)	.75	
	Coil Stamp, Perf. 10 Vertically						
1891	18¢ Flag and Anthem,						
	"…from sea to shining sea"	.32	.05	6.50	(3)	.75	

Beginning with #1891, all coil stamps except #1947 feature a small plate number at the bottom of the design on stamps at varying intervals in a roll, depending on the press used. The basic collecting unit is a strip of three stamps, with the plate number appearing on the middle stamp.

	Perf. 11						
1892	6¢ USA Circle of Stars,						
	Single from booklet (1893a)	.55	.10			.75	
1893	18¢ Flag and Anthem,						
	"…for purple mountain majesties,"						
	Single from booklet (1893a)	.32	.05			.75	
1893a	Booklet pane of 8,						
	(2 #1892 & 6 #1893)	3.00				3.00	

#1892-93 issued only in booklets. All stamps are imperf. at one side or imperf. at one side and bottom.

	Flag over Supreme Court Issue, Dec. 17 (except #1896b, issued June 1, 1982)						
1894	20¢ Flag over Supreme Court	.35	.05	9.50	(20)	.75	
	Coil Stamp, Perf. 10 Vertically						
1895	20¢ Flag over Supreme Court (1894)	.35	.05	6.50	(3)	.75	
	Perf. 11x10½						
1896	20¢ Flag over Supreme Court (1894),						
	Single from booklet	.35	.05			.75	
1896a	Booklet pane of 6	2.50				8.00	
1896b	Booklet pane of 10	4.00				12.00	

	Issues of 1981-84	Un	U	PB/LP	#	FDC	Q
	Transportation Issue, Coil Stamps, Perf. 10 Vertically (See also #2123-36,						
	2225-26, 2228, 2231, 2252-66)						
1897	1¢ Omnibus 1880s, Aug. 19, 1983	.05	.05	.70	(3)	.60	
1897A	2¢ Locomotive 1870s,						
	May 20, 1982	.10	.05	.65	(3)	.60	
1898	3¢ Handcar 1880s, Mar. 25, 1983	.09	.05	1.00	(3)	.60	
1898A	4¢ Stagecoach 1890s, Aug. 19, 1982	.09	.05	1.50	(3)	.60	
1898Ab	Bureau precanceled		.09	2.25	(3)	.60	
1899	5¢ Motorcycle 1913, Oct. 10, 1983	.12	.05	1.50	(3)	.60	
1900	5.2¢ Sleigh 1880s, Mar. 21, 1983	.12	.05	9.00	(3)	.60	
1900a	Bureau precanceled		.12	8.00	(3)	.60	
1901	5.9¢ Bicycle 1870s, Feb. 17, 1982	.18	.05	12.00	(3)	.60	
1901a	Bureau precanceled		.18	15.00	(3)	.60	
1902	7.4¢ Baby Buggy 1880s,						
	April 7, 1984	.18	.08	10.00	(3)	.65	
1902a	Bureau precanceled		.18	4.00	(3)	.65	
1903	9.3¢ Mail Wagon 1880s,						
	Dec. 15, 1981	.22	.08	15.00	(3)	.65	
1903a	Bureau precanceled		.22	5.00	(3)	.65	
1904	10.9¢ Hansom Cab 1890s,						
	Mar. 26, 1982	.24	.05	20.00	(3)	.65	
1904a	Bureau precanceled		.24	20.00	(3)	.65	
1905	11¢ RR Caboose 1890s,						
	Feb. 3, 1984	.24	.08	6.00	(3)	.65	
1905a	Bureau precanceled		.24	5.00	(3)	.65	
1906	17¢ Electric Auto 1917, June 25, 1981	.32	.05	4.50	(3)	.75	
1906a	Bureau precanceled		.35	6.00	(3)	.75	
1907	18¢ Surrey 1890s, May 18, 1981	.34	.05	5.00	(3)	.75	
1908	20¢ Fire Pumper 1860s, Dec. 10, 1981	.32	.05	5.00	(3)	.65	
	Issue of 1983, Express Mail Booklet Issue, Perf. 10 Vertically, Aug. 12						
1909	$9.35 Eagle and Moon,						
	Single from booklet	26.00	7.50			25.00	
1909a	Booklet pane of 3	80.00				90.00	
	#1909 issued only in booklets. All stamps are imperf. at top and bottom or imperf. at top, bottom and one side.						
	Issues of 1981, Perf. 11x10½						
1910	18¢ American Red Cross, May 1	.32	.05	1.80	(4)	.75	165,175,000
	Perf. 11						
1911	18¢ Savings and Loans, May 8	.32	.05	1.80	(4)	.75	107,240,000

Omnibus 1880s
USA 1c

Locomotive 1870s
USA 2c

Handcar 1880s
USA 3c

Stagecoach 1890s
USA 4c

1897   **1897A**   **1898**   **1898A**

Motorcycle
1913
USA 5c

Sleigh 1880s
USA 5.2c
Auth
Nonprofit
Org

Bicycle 1870s
USA 5.9c

Baby Buggy 1880s
USA 7.4c

Mail Wagon 1880s
USA 9.3c
Bulk
Rate

1899   **1900**   **1901**   **1902**   **1903**

Hansom Cab 1890s
USA 10.9c
Bulk
Rate

RR Caboose 1890s
USA 11c
Bulk Rate

Electric Auto 1917
USA 17c

Surrey 1890s
USA 18c

Fire Pumper
1860s
USA 20c

1904   **1905**   **1906**   **1907**   **1908**

USA $9.35

The Gift of Self
USA
18c
American Red Cross
1881-1981

SAVINGS AND LOANS
SAVE
USA 18c

1909   **1910**   **1911**

Exploring the Moon USA 18c
Benefiting Mankind USA 18c
Benefiting Mankind USA 18c
Understanding the Sun USA 18c
Probing the Planets USA 18c
USA 18c
USA 18c
Comprehending the Universe USA 18c
Benefiting Mankind
Benefiting Mankind

1919a

| 1912 | 1913 | 1914 | 1915 |
| 1916 | 1917 | 1918 | 1919 |

Professional Management
USA 18c
Joseph Wharton

1920

Save Wetland Habitats USA 18c
Save Grassland Habitats USA 18c
Save Mountain Habitats USA 18c
Save Woodland Habitats USA 18c

1924a

| 1921 | 1922 |
| 1923 | 1924 |

USA 18c
Disabled doesn't mean Unable

1925

Edna St. Vincent Millay
American Poet USA 18c

1926

Alcoholism
You can beat it!
USA 18c

1927

	1981 continued	Un	U	PB	#	FDC	Q
	Space Achievement Issue, May 21, Perf 11						
1912	18¢ Exploring the Moon-						
	Moon Walk	.32	.10			.75	42,227,375
1913	18¢ Benefiting Mankind (upper right)-						
	Columbia Space Shuttle	.32	.10			.75	42,227,375
1914	18¢ Benefiting Mankind (upper left)	.32	.10			.75	42,227,375
1915	18¢ Understanding the Sun-Skylab	.32	.10			.75	42,227,375
1916	18¢ Probing the Planets-Pioneer II	.32	.10			.75	42,227,375
1917	18¢ Benefiting Mankind (lower right)-						
	Columbia Space Shuttle	.32	.10			.75	42,227,375
1918	18¢ Benefiting Mankind (lower left)	.32	.10			.75	42,227,375
1919	18¢ Comprehending						
	the Universe-Telescope	.32	.10			.75	42,227,375
1919a	Block of 8, #1912-1919	3.00	2.75	4.25	(8)	5.00	
1920	18¢ Professional Management,						
	June 18	.32	.05	1.80	(4)	.75	99,420,000
	Preservation of Wildlife Habitats Issue, June 26						
1921	18¢ Save Wetland Habitats-						
	Great Blue Heron	.32	.08	2.10	(4)	.75	44,732,500
1922	18¢ Save Grassland Habitats-						
	Badger	.32	.08			.75	44,732,500
1923	18¢ Save Mountain Habitats-						
	Grizzly Bear	.32	.08	2.10	(4)	.75	44,732,500
1924	18¢ Save Woodland Habitats-						
	Ruffled Grouse	.32	.08	2.10	(4)	.75	44,732,500
1924a	Block of 4, #1921-1924	1.40	1.00	2.10	(4)	2.50	
1925	18¢ International Year						
	of the Disabled, June 29	.32	.05	1.80	(4)	.75	100,265,000
1926	18¢ Edna St. Vincent Millay,						
	July 10	.32	.05	1.80	(4)	.75	99,615,000
1927	18¢ Alcoholism, Aug. 19	.42	.05	42.50	(20)	.75	97,535,000

3...2...1...LIFTOFF!
The pioneering of space (#1912-1919) is one of the crowning achievements of the 20th century. U.S. contributions include the placing in orbit of the space station Skylab and the launching of numerous scientific space probes. Particularly noteworthy is the 1969 U.S. landing of men on the moon, an event commemorated last July by the U.S. Postal Service with a 20th anniversary stamp issue.

1981 continued	Un	U	PB	#	FDC	Q
American Architecture Issue, Aug. 28, Perf. 11						
1928 18¢ NYU Library,						
by Sanford White	.32	.08			.75	41,827,000
1929 18¢ Biltmore House,						
by Richard Morris Hunt	.32	.08			.75	41,827,000
1930 18¢ Palace of the Arts,						
by Bernard Maybeck	.32	.08			.75	41,827,000
1931 18¢ National Farmer's Bank,						
by Louis Sullivan	.32	.08			.75	41,827,000
1931a Block of 4, #1928-1931	1.40	1.00	1.80	(4)	2.00	
American Sports Issues, Babe Zaharias and Bobby Jones, Sept. 22, Perf. 10½x11						
1932 18¢ Babe Zaharias Holding Trophy	.32	.05	1.80	(4)	.75	101,625,000
1933 18¢ Bobby Jones Teeing Off	.32	.05	1.80	(4)	.75	99,170,000
Perf. 11						
1934 18¢ Frederic Remington, Oct. 9	.32	.05	1.80	(4)	.75	101,155,000
1935 18¢ James Hoban, Oct. 13	.32	.25	3.00	(4)	.75	101,200,000
1936 20¢ James Hoban, Oct. 13	.35	.05	2.00	(4)	.75	167,360,000
American Bicentennial Issue, Yorktown-Virginia Capes, Oct. 16						
1937 18¢ Battle of Yorktown 1781	.32	.06	2.00	(4)	.75	81,210,000
1938 18¢ Battle of the Virginia Capes 1781	.32	.06			.75	81,210,000
1938a Attached pair, #1937-1938	.70	.15	2.00	(4)	1.00	
Christmas Issue, Oct. 28						
1939 20¢ Madonna and Child,						
by Botticelli	.35	.05	2.00	(4)	.75	597,720,000
1940 20¢ Felt Bear on Sleigh	.35	.05	2.00	(4)	.75	792,600,000
1941 20¢ John Hanson, Nov. 5	.35	.05	2.00	(4)	.75	167,130,000

BATTLE OF VIRGINIA CAPES HASTENED VICTORY
On September 5, 1781, the French fleet repelled the British at the Battle of Virginia Capes (#1938), gaining control of the Chesapeake Bay. General George Washington's troops then besieged Cornwallis at Yorktown (#1937). The surrender of Cornwallis traditionally marks the end of the American Revolutionary War.

1932

1933

1928

1930

1929

1931

1931a

1934

1935

1936

1937

1938

1938a

1939

1940

1941

1946

1942   **1943**   **1945**

1944

1945a

1950

1949a

1951

1952

212

	1981 continued	Un	U	PB/LP	#	FDC	Q
	Desert Plants Issue, Dec. 11, Perf. 11						
1942	20¢ Barrel Cactus	.35	.06			.75	47,890,000
1943	20¢ Agave	.35	.06			.75	47,890,000
1944	20¢ Beavertail Cactus	.35	.06			.75	47,890,000
1945	20¢ Saguaro	.35	.06			.75	47,890,000
1945a	Block of 4, #1942-1945	1.40	.85	2.50	(4)	2.50	
	Perf. 11x10½						
1946	(20¢) C Stamp, Oct. 11	.35	.05	2.25	(4)	.75	
	Coil Stamp, Perf. 10 Vertically						
1947	(20¢) brown Eagle (1946), Oct. 11	.38	.05	1.10	(2)	.75	
	Perf. 11x10½						
1948	(20¢) brown Eagle (1946),						
	Single from booklet	.38	.05			.75	
1948a	Booklet pane of 10, Oct. 11	4.00				4.00	
	Issues of 1982, Bighorn Sheep Booklet Issue, Jan. 8, Perf. 11						
1949	20¢ Bighorn Sheep,						
	Single from booklet	.42	.05			.75	
1949a	Booklet pane of 10	4.75				8.00	
	#1949 issued only in booklets. All stamps are imperf. at one side or imperf. at one side and bottom.						
1950	20¢ Franklin D. Roosevelt, Jan. 30	.38	.05	2.00	(4)	.75	163,939,200
	Perf. 11x10½						
1951	20¢ Love, Feb. 1	.42	.05	2.25	(4)	.75	446,745,000
	Perf. 11						
1952	20¢ George Washington, Feb. 22	.38	.05	2.25	(4)	.75	180,700,000

HANDY STAMP BOOKLETS ARE POPULAR COLLECTIBLES *Developed around the turn of the century, the stamp booklet is collectible and convenient. U.S. booklets contain bound panes of between 3 and 10 stamps. Collectors save panes, covers and even entire booklets.*

	1982 continued	Un	U	FDC	Q
	State Birds & Flowers Issue, Apr. 14, Perf. 10½x11				
1953	20¢ Alabama	.38	.20	1.00	13,339,900
1954	20¢ Alaska	.38	.20	1.00	13,339,900
1955	20¢ Arizona	.38	.20	1.00	13,339,900
1956	20¢ Arkansas	.38	.20	1.00	13,339,900
1957	20¢ California	.38	.20	1.00	13,339,900
1958	20¢ Colorado	.38	.20	1.00	13,339,900
1959	20¢ Connecticut	.38	.20	1.00	13,339,900
1960	20¢ Delaware	.38	.20	1.00	13,339,900
1961	20¢ Florida	.38	.20	1.00	13,339,900
1962	20¢ Georgia	.38	.20	1.00	13,339,900
1963	20¢ Hawaii	.38	.20	1.00	13,339,900
1964	20¢ Idaho	.38	.20	1.00	13,339,900
1965	20¢ Illinois	.38	.20	1.00	13,339,900
1966	20¢ Indiana	.38	.20	1.00	13,339,900
1967	20¢ Iowa	.38	.20	1.00	13,339,900
1968	20¢ Kansas	.38	.20	1.00	13,339,900
1969	20¢ Kentucky	.38	.20	1.00	13,339,900
1970	20¢ Louisiana	.38	.20	1.00	13,339,900
1971	20¢ Maine	.38	.20	1.00	13,339,900
1972	20¢ Maryland	.38	.20	1.00	13,339,900
1973	20¢ Massachusetts	.38	.20	1.00	13,339,900
1974	20¢ Michigan	.38	.20	1.00	13,339,900
1975	20¢ Minnesota	.38	.20	1.00	13,339,900
1976	20¢ Mississippi	.38	.20	1.00	13,339,900
1977	20¢ Missouri	.38	.20	1.00	13,339,900

A Reminder: Beginning with this edition, catalog values for all stamps listed reflect (as accurately as possible) actual retail values as found in the marketplace.

Alabama USA 20c	Alaska USA 20c	Arizona USA 20c	Arkansas USA 20c	California USA 20c
Yellowhammer & Camellia	Willow Ptarmigan & Forget-Me-Not	Cactus Wren & Saguaro Cactus Blossom	Mockingbird & Apple Blossom	California Quail & California Poppy
1953	1954	1955	1956	1957

Colorado USA 20c	Connecticut USA 20c	Delaware USA 20c	Florida USA 20c	Georgia USA 20c
Lark Bunting & Rocky Mountain Columbine	Robin & Mountain Laurel	Blue Hen Chicken & Peach Blossom	Mockingbird & Orange Blossom	Brown Thrasher & Cherokee Rose
1958	1959	1960	1961	1962

Hawaii USA 20c	Idaho USA 20c	Illinois USA 20c	Indiana USA 20c	Iowa USA 20c
Hawaiian Goose & Hibiscus	Mountain Bluebird & Syringa	Cardinal & Violet	Cardinal & Peony	Eastern Goldfinch & Wild Rose
1963	1964	1965	1966	1967

Kansas USA 20c	Kentucky USA 20c	Louisiana USA 20c	Maine USA 20c	Maryland USA 20c
Western Meadowlark & Sunflower	Cardinal & Goldenrod	Brown Pelican & Magnolia	Chickadee & White Pine Cone and Tassel	Baltimore Oriole & Black-Eyed Susan
1968	1969	1970	1971	1972

Massachusetts USA 20c	Michigan USA 20c	Minnesota USA 20c	Mississippi USA 20c	Missouri USA 20c
Black-Capped Chickadee & Mayflower	Robin & Apple Blossom	Common Loon & Showy Lady Slipper	Mockingbird & Magnolia	Eastern Bluebird & Red Hawthorn
1973	1974	1975	1976	1977

Montana
USA 20c

Western Meadowlark & Bitterroot

1978

Nebraska
USA 20c

Western Meadowlark & Goldenrod

1979

Nevada
USA 20c

Mountain Bluebird & Sagebrush

1980

New Hampshire
USA 20c

Purple Finch & Lilac

1981

New Jersey
USA 20c

American Goldfinch & Violet

1982

New Mexico
USA 20c

Roadrunner & Yucca Flower

1983

New York
USA 20c

Eastern Bluebird & Rose

1984

North Carolina
USA 20c

Cardinal & Flowering Dogwood

1985

North Dakota
USA 20c

Western Meadowlark & Wild Prairie Rose

1986

Ohio
USA 20c

Cardinal & Red Carnation

1987

Oklahoma
USA 20c

Scissor-tailed Flycatcher & Mistletoe

1988

Oregon
USA 20c

Western Meadowlark & Oregon Grape

1989

Pennsylvania
USA 20c

Ruffed Grouse & Mountain Laurel

1990

Rhode Island
USA 20c

Rhode Island Red & Violet

1991

South Carolina
USA 20c

Carolina Wren & Carolina Jessamine

1992

South Dakota
USA 20c

Ring-Necked Pheasant & Pasqueflower

1993

Tennessee
USA 20c

Mockingbird & Iris

1994

Texas
USA 20c

Mockingbird & Bluebonnet

1995

Utah
USA 20c

California Gull & Sego Lily

1996

Vermont
USA 20c

Hermit Thrush & Red Clover

1997

Virginia
USA 20c

Cardinal & Flowering Dogwood

1998

Washington
USA 20c

American Goldfinch & Rhododendron

1999

West Virginia
USA 20c

Cardinal & Rhododendron Maximum

2000

Wisconsin
USA 20c

Robin & Wood Violet

2001

Wyoming
USA 20c

Western Meadowlark & Indian Paintbrush

2002

	1982 continued	Un	U	FDC	Q
	State Birds and Flowers Issue continued, Apr. 14, Perf. 10½x11				
1978	20¢ Montana	.38	.20	1.00	13,339,900
1979	20¢ Nebraska	.38	.20	1.00	13,339,900
1980	20¢ Nevada	.38	.20	1.00	13,339,900
1981	20¢ New Hampshire	.38	.20	1.00	13,339,900
1982	20¢ New Jersey	.38	.20	1.00	13,339,900
1983	20¢ New Mexico	.38	.20	1.00	13,339,900
1984	20¢ New York	.38	.20	1.00	13,339,900
1985	20¢ North Carolina	.38	.20	1.00	13,339,900
1986	20¢ North Dakota	.38	.20	1.00	13,339,900
1987	20¢ Ohio	.38	.20	1.00	13,339,900
1988	20¢ Oklahoma	.38	.20	1.00	13,339,900
1989	20¢ Oregon	.38	.20	1.00	13,339,900
1990	20¢ Pennsylvania	.38	.20	1.00	13,339,900
1991	20¢ Rhode Island	.38	.20	1.00	13,339,900
1992	20¢ South Carolina	.38	.20	1.00	13,339,900
1993	20¢ South Dakota	.38	.20	1.00	13,339,900
1994	20¢ Tennessee	.38	.20	1.00	13,339,900
1995	20¢ Texas	.38	.20	1.00	13,339,900
1996	20¢ Utah	.38	.20	1.00	13,339,900
1997	20¢ Vermont	.38	.20	1.00	13,339,900
1998	20¢ Virginia	.38	.20	1.00	13,339,900
1999	20¢ Washington	.38	.20	1.00	13,339,900
2000	20¢ West Virginia	.38	.20	1.00	13,339,900
2001	20¢ Wisconsin	.38	.20	1.00	13,339,900
2002	20¢ Wyoming	.38	.20	1.00	13,339,900
2002b	Pane of 50	19.00			

PHEASANT HAS ORIENTAL ANCESTRY

Originally from China, the ring-necked pheasant (#1993) is the state bird of South Dakota. A 1989 stamp issue commemorates the South Dakota centennial.

	1982 continued, Perf. 11	Un	U	PB/LP	#	FDC	Q
2003	20¢ USA/The Netherlands, Apr. 20	.38	.05	12.50	(20)	.75	109,245,000
2004	20¢ Library of Congress, Apr. 21	.38	.05	2.00	(4)	.75	112,535,000
	Coil Stamp, Perf. 10 Vertically						
2005	20¢ Consumer Education, Apr. 27	.50	.05	60.00	(3)	.75	
	Knoxville World's Fair Issue, Apr. 29, Perf. 11						
2006	20¢ Solar Energy	.38	.08			.75	31,160,000
2007	20¢ Synthetic Fuels	.38	.08			.75	31,160,000
2008	20¢ Breeder Reactor	.38	.08			.75	31,160,000
2009	20¢ Fossil Fuels	.38	.08			.75	31,160,000
2009a	Block of 4, #2006-2009	1.60	1.00	2.50	(4)	2.50	
2010	20¢ Horatio Alger, Apr. 30	.38	.05	2.00	(4)	.75	107,605,000
2011	20¢ Aging Together, May 21	.38	.05	2.00	(4)	.75	173,160,000
	Performing Arts Issue, The Barrymores, June 8						
2012	20¢ Portraits						
	of John, Ethel and Lionel Barrymore	.38	.05	2.00	(4)	.75	107,285,000
2013	20¢ Dr. Mary Walker, June 10	.38	.05	2.00	(4)	.75	109,040,000
2014	20¢ International Peace Garden,						
	June 30	.38	.05	2.00	(4)	.75	183,270,000
2015	20¢ America's Libraries, July 13	.38	.05	2.00	(4)	.75	169,495,000
	Black Heritage Issue, Jackie Robinson, Aug. 2, Perf. 10½x11						
2016	20¢ Jackie Robinson Portrait,						
	and Robinson Stealing Home Plate	.38	.05	2.25	(4)	.75	164,235,000
	Perf. 11						
2017	20¢ Touro Synagogue, Aug. 22	.38	.05	12.50	(20)	.85	110,130,000
2018	20¢ Wolf Trap Farm Park, Sept. 1	.38	.05	2.00	(4)	.75	110,995,000
	American Architecture Issue, Sept. 30						
2019	20¢ Fallingwater,						
	by Frank Lloyd Wright	.38	.08			.75	41,335,000
2020	20¢ Illinois Institute of Technology,						
	by Mies van der Rohe	.38	.08			.75	41,335,000
2021	20¢ Gropius House,						
	by Walter Gropius	.38	.08			.75	41,335,000
2022	20¢ Dulles Airport,						
	by Eeno Saarinen	.38	.08			.75	41,335,000
2022a	Block of 4, #2019-2022	1.60	1.00	2.75	(4)	2.50	

2003

2004

2005

2006
2008

2007
2009

2009a

2010

2012

2011

2013

2014

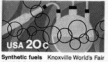

2015

2016

2017

2018

2019
2021

2020
2022

2022a

2023

2024

2025

2026

2027

2029

2028

2030

2030a

2031

2032

2033

2034

2035

2035a

2036

2037

	1982 continued, Perf. 11	Un	U	PB	#	FDC	Q
2023	20¢ Francis of Assisi, Oct. 7	.38	.05	2.00	(4)	.75	174,180,000
2024	20¢ Ponce de Leon, Oct. 12	.38	.05	12.50	(20)	.75	110,261,000
	Christmas Issue						
2025	13¢ Puppy and Kitten, Nov. 3	.24	.05	1.30	(4)	.75	234,010,000
2026	20¢ Madonna and Child,						
	by Tiepolo, Oct. 28	.38	.05	11.50	(20)	.75	703,295,000
	Seasons Greetings Issue, Oct. 28						
2027	20¢ Children Sledding	.38	.05			.75	197,220,000
2028	20¢ Children Building a Snowman	.38	.05			.75	197,220,000
2029	20¢ Children Skating	.38	.05			.75	197,220,000
2030	20¢ Children Trimming a Tree	.38	.05			.75	197,220,000
2030a	Block of 4, #2027-2030	1.60	1.00	3.00	(4)	2.50	
	Issues of 1983						
2031	20¢ Science & Industry, Jan. 19	.38	.05	2.00	(4)	.75	118,555,000
	Balloons Issue, March 31						
2032	20¢ Intrepid, 1861	.38	.08			.75	56,557,000
2033	20¢ Hot Air Ballooning	.38	.08			.75	56,557,000
2034	20¢ Hot Air Ballooning	.38	.08			.75	56,557,000
2035	20¢ Explorer II, 1935	.38	.08			.75	56,557,000
2035a	Block of 4, #2032-2035	1.60	1.00	2.30	(4)	2.50	
2036	20¢ U.S./Sweden Treaty, Mar. 24	.38	.05	2.00	(4)	.75	118,225,000
2037	20¢ Civilian Conservation Corps,						
	Apr. 5	.38	.05	2.00	(4)	.75	114,290,000

THOSE BEAUTIFUL BALLOONS

Ever since the Montgolfier brothers of France sent a duck, a rooster and a sheep for a balloon ride in 1783, balloons have been a source of great fascination. Used for everything from the observation of Civil War troops to stratospheric exploration, balloons also afford peaceful and picturesque recreation. Today there are about 1,000 sport balloonists in the United States alone (#2033-34).

1983 continued, Perf. 11	Un	U	PB	#	FDC	Q
2038	20¢ Joseph Priestley, Apr. 13	.38	.05	2.00	(4)	.75	165,000,000
2039	20¢ Voluntarism, Apr. 20	.38	.05	11.50	(20)	.75	120,430,000
2040	20¢ Concord-German Immigration,						
	Apr. 29	.38	.05	2.00	(4)	.75	117,025,000
2041	20¢ Brooklyn Bridge, May 5	.38	.05	2.00	(4)	.75	181,700,000
2042	20¢ Tennessee Valley Authority, May 18	.38	.05	11.50	(20)	.75	114,250,000
2043	20¢ Physical Fitness, May 14	.38	.05	11.50	(20)	.75	111,775,000
	Black Heritage Issue, Scott Joplin, June 9						
2044	20¢ Scott Joplin Portrait						
	and Joplin Playing the Piano	.38	.05	2.00	(4)	.75	115,200,000
2045	20¢ Medal of Honor, June 7	.38	.05	2.00	(4)	.75	108,820,000
	American Sports Issue, Babe Ruth, July 6, Perf. 10½x11						
2046	20¢ Babe Ruth Hitting a Home Run	.38	.05	2.25	(4)	.75	184,950,000
	Literary Arts Issue, Nathaniel Hawthorne, July 8, Perf. 11						
2047	20¢ Nathaniel Hawthorne,						
	by Cephus Giovanni Thompson	.38	.05	2.00	(4)	.75	110,925,000
	Olympic Summer Games Issue, July 28 (see also #2082-85, C101-112)						
2048	13¢ Discus Thrower	.24	.05			.75	98,856,250
2049	13¢ High Jumper	.24	.05			.75	98,856,250
2050	13¢ Archer	.24	.05			.75	98,856,250
2051	13¢ Boxers	.24	.05			.75	98,856,250
2051a	Block of 4, #2048-2051	1.00	.80	1.75	(4)	2.50	
	American Bicentennial Issue, Treaty of Paris, Sept. 2						
2052	20¢ Signing of Treaty of Paris						
	(John Adams, Benjamin Franklin						
	and John Jay observing David Hartley),						
	by Benjamin West	.38	.05	2.00	(4)	.75	104,340,000
2053	20¢ Civil Service, Sept. 9	.38	.05	11.50	(20)	.75	114,725,000
2054	20¢ Metropolitan Opera, Sept. 14	.38	.05	2.00	(4)	.75	112,525,000

Lincoln Center Home to Met

Known throughout the world as "the Met," the Metropolitan Opera Association (#2054) is one of the world's premier opera companies. Having performed in the Metropolitan Opera House since 1883, the Met moved in 1966 to new quarters of the same name in the Lincoln Center for the Performing Arts in New York City. Built at a cost of $14.5 million, the current 14-story facility seats more than 3,700 people.

Joseph Priestley
USA 20c

2038

2039

2040

2041

2042

2043

2044

2045

2046

2047

2048
2050

2049   **2051a**
2051

Treaty of Paris 1783
US Bicentennial 20 cents

2052

2053

2054

223

2055 **2056** **2058a**
2057 **2058**

2059 **2060** **2062a**
2061 **2062**

2063 **2065**

2064

1983 continued	Un	U	PB	#	FDC	Q
American Inventors Issue, Sept. 21, Perf. 11						
2055 20¢ Charles Steinmetz						
and Curve on Graph	.38	.08			.70	48,263,750
2056 20¢ Edwin Armstrong						
and Frequency Modulator	.38	.08			.75	48,263,750
2057 20¢ Nikola Tesla						
and Induction Motor	.38	.08			.75	48,263,750
2058 20¢ Philo T. Farnsworth						
and First Television Camera	.38	.08			.75	48,263,750
2058a Block of 4, #2055-2058	1.60	1.00	2.50	(4)	2.50	
Streetcars Issue, Oct. 8						
2059 20¢ First American Streetcar	.38	.08			.75	51,931,250
2060 20¢ Early Electric Streetcar	.38	.08			.75	51,931,250
2061 20¢ "Bobtail" Horsecar	.38	.08			.75	51,931,250
2062 20¢ St. Charles Streetcar	.38	.08			.75	51,931,250
2062a Block of 4, #2059-2062	1.60	1.00	2.50	(4)	2.50	
Christmas Issue, Oct. 28						
2063 20¢ Niccolini-Cowper Madonna,						
by Raphael	.38	.05	2.00	(4)	.75	715,975,000
2064 20¢ Santa Claus	.38	.05	11.50	(20)	.75	848,525,000
2065 20¢ Martin Luther, Nov. 11	.38	.05	2.00	(4)	.75	165,000,000

BEARER OF JOY
HAS MANY NAMES
*Santa Claus (#2064)
is known throughout
the world by many
names—Pelz Nichol,
Kris Kringle and Father
Christmas, among oth-
ers. All trace their ori-
gins to Saint Nicholas,
a kindly bishop who
lived in the 300s A.D.
in what is now Turkey
and who brought pres-
ents to those in need.
American cartoonist
Thomas Nast popular-
ized Santa Claus as a
jolly fat man who
drives a sleigh pulled
by flying reindeer.*

	Issues of 1984, Perf. 11	Un	U	PB	#	FDC	Q
2066	20¢ Alaska Statehood, Jan. 3	.38	.05	2.00	(4)	.75	120,000,000
	Olympic Winter Games Issue, Jan. 6, Perf. 10½x11						
2067	20¢ Ice Dancers	.38	.08			.75	79,918,750
2068	20¢ Alpine Skiers	.38	.08			.75	79,918,750
2069	20¢ Nordic Skiers	.38	.08			.75	79,918,750
2070	20¢ Hockey Player	.38	.08			.75	79,918,750
2070a	Block of 4, #2067-2070	1.60	1.00	2.75	(4)	2.50	
	Perf. 11						
2071	20¢ Federal Deposit Insurance						
	Corporation, Jan. 12	.38	.05	2.00	(4)	.75	103,975,000
	Perf. 11x10½						
2072	20¢ Love, Jan. 31	.38	.05	12.50	(20)	.75	554,675,000
	Black Heritage Issue, Carter G. Woodson, Feb. 1						
2073	20¢ Carter G. Woodson						
	Holding History Book	.38	.05	2.00	(4)	.75	120,000,000
2074	20¢ Soil and Water Conservation,						
	Feb. 6	.38	.05	2.00	(4)	.75	106,975,000
2075	20¢ Credit Union Act, Feb. 10	.38	.05	2.00	(4)	.75	107,325,000
	Orchids Issue, Mar. 5						
2076	20¢ Wild Pink	.38	.08			.75	76,728,000
2077	20¢ Yellow Lady's-Slipper	.38	.08			.75	76,728,000
2078	20¢ Spreading Pogonia	.38	.08			.75	76,728,000
2079	20¢ Pacific Calypso	.38	.08			.75	76,728,000
2079a	Block of 4, #2076-2079	1.60	1.00	2.25	(4)	2.50	
2080	20¢ Hawaii Statehood, Mar. 12	.38	.05	2.00	(4)	.75	120,000,000
2081	20¢ National Archives, Apr. 16	.38	.05	2.00	(4)	.75	108,000,000

CREDIT UNIONS MAKE GOOD CENTS
Credit unions (#2075) are a type of cooperative—a business owned by those who use its services. Members of a credit union pool their savings in order to borrow from the union at a low interest rate. Credit union members usually either work for the same employer, belong to the same labor union or have some other common bond.

A Reminder: Beginning with this edition, catalog values for all stamps listed reflect (as accurately as possible) actual retail values as found in the marketplace.

2066

2070a

2071

2067 2068
2069 2070

2072

2073

2074

2075

2080

2081

2079a

2076 2077
2078 2079

2086

2087

2082   **2083**   **2085a**
2084   **2085**

2088

2089

2090

2091

2092

2093

2094

2095

	1984 continued	Un	U	PB	#	FDC	Q
	Olympic Summer Games Issue, May 4, Perf. 11 (see also #2048-52, C101-112)						
2082	20¢ Diver	.38	.08			.75	78,337,500
2083	20¢ Long Jumper	.38	.08			.75	78,337,500
2084	20¢ Wrestlers	.38	.08			.75	78,337,500
2085	20¢ Kayaker	.38	.08			.75	78,337,500
2085a	Block of 4, #2082-2085	1.60	1.00	3.25	(4)	2.50	
2086	20¢ Louisiana World Exposition,						
	May 11	.38	.05	2.00	(4)	.75	130,320,000
2087	20¢ Health Research, May 17	.38	.05	2.00	(4)	.75	120,000,000
	Performing Arts Issue, May 23						
2088	20¢ Douglas Fairbanks Portrait						
	and Fairbanks in Swashbuckling						
	Pirate Role	.38	.05	12.50	(20)	.75	117,050,000
	American Sports Issue, Jim Thorpe, May 24						
2089	20¢ Jim Thorpe on Football Field	.38	.05	2.00	(4)	.75	115,725,000
	Performing Arts Issue, John McCormack, June 6						
2090	20¢ John McCormack Portrait						
	and McCormack in Tenor Role	.38	.05	2.00	(4)	.75	116,600,000
2091	20¢ St. Lawrence Seaway, June 26	.38	.05	2.00	(4)	.75	120,000,000
2092	20¢ Migratory Bird Hunting						
	& Preservation Act, July 2	.38	.05	2.00	(4)	.75	123,575,000
2093	20¢ Roanoke Voyages, July 13	.38	.05	2.00	(4)	.75	120,000,000
	Literary Arts Issue, Herman Melville, Aug. 1						
2094	20¢ Herman Melville,						
	by Joseph Eaton	.38	.05	2.00	(4)	.75	117,125,000
2095	20¢ Horace Moses, Aug. 6	.38	.05	11.50	(20)	.75	117,225,000

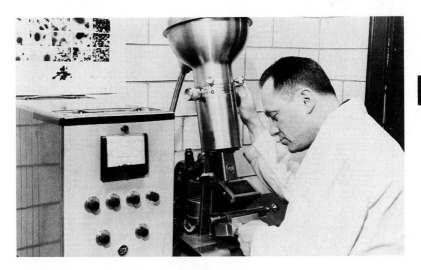

HEALTH RESEARCH PROMOTES LIFE

Thanks to research, we are continually learning more about how to maintain and improve health. Discoveries have led to the control of many diseases, such as tuberculosis and whooping cough. The World Health Organization supports health research (#2087), as does the U.S. Department of Health and Human Services.

	1984 continued, Perf. 11	Un	U	PB	#	FDC	Q
2096	20¢ Smokey the Bear, Aug. 13	.38	.05	2.00	(4)	.75	95,525,000
	American Sports Issue, Roberto Clemente, Aug. 17						
2097	20¢ Roberto Clemente Wearing						
	Pittsburgh Pirates Cap,						
	Puerto Rican Flag in Background	.38	.05	2.25	(4)	.75	119,125,000
	American Dogs Issue, Sept. 7						
2098	20¢ Beagle and Boston Terrier	.38	.08			.75	54,065,000
2099	20¢ Chesapeake Bay Retriever						
	and Cocker Spaniel	.38	.08			.75	54,065,000
2100	20¢ Alaskan Malamute and Collie	.38	.08			.75	54,065,000
2101	20¢ Black and Tan Coonhound						
	and American Foxhound	.38	.08			.75	54,065,000
2101a	Block of 4, #2098-2101	1.60	1.00	2.50	(4)	2.50	
2102	20¢ Crime Prevention, Sept. 26	.38	.05	2.00	(4)	.75	120,000,000
2103	20¢ Hispanic Americans, Oct. 31	.38	.05	2.00	(4)	.75	108,140,000
2104	20¢ Family Unity, Oct. 1	.38	.05	12.50	(20)	.75	117,625,000
2105	20¢ Eleanor Roosevelt, Oct. 11	.38	.05	2.00	(4)	.75	112,896,000
2106	20¢ A Nation of Readers, Oct. 16	.38	.05	2.00	(4)	.75	116,500,000
	Christmas Issue, Oct. 30						
2107	20¢ Madonna and Child,						
	by Fra Filippo Lippi	.38	.05	2.00	(4)	.75	751,300,000
2108	20¢ Santa Claus	.38	.05	2.00	(4)	.75	786,225,000
	Perf. 10½						
2109	20¢ Vietnam Veterans' Memorial,						
	Nov. 10	.38	.05	2.00	(4)	.75	105,300,000

JOHNNY CAN READ

With the advance of technology in the United States, the ability to read is becoming more and more essential. Many states have developed strong programs for increasing literacy among adults. In school, on the job, for information and for pleasure, reading (#2106) is one of the most vital skills for everyday life.

2096   **2097**

2098   **2099**   **2101a**
2100   **2101**

2103

2102   **2104**   **2105**

2109

2106   **2107**   **2108**

2111

2110

2114

2115b

2116

2122

2117	**2121a**
2118	
2119	
2120	
2121	

	Issues of 1985	Un	U	PB/LP	#	FDC	Q
	Performing Arts Issue, Jerome Kern, Jan. 23, Perf. 11						
2110	22¢ Jerome Kern Portrait						
	and Kern Studying Sheet Music	.40	.05	2.20	(4)	.80	124,500,000
2111	(22¢) D Stamp, Feb. 1	.40	.05	12.00	(20)	.80	
	Coil Stamp, Perf. 10 Vertically						
2112	(22¢) green Eagle (2111), Feb. 1	.40	.05	6.00	(3)	.80	
	Perf. 11						
2113	(22¢) green Eagle (2111),						
	Single from booklet	.40	.05			.80	
2113a	Booklet pane of 10, Feb. 1	4.50				9.00	
	Flag over Capitol Issue, Mar. 29 (except #2115b, issued May 23, 1987)						
2114	22¢ Flag over Capitol	.40	.05	2.20	(4)	.80	
	Coil Stamp, Perf. 10 Vertically						
2115	22¢ Flag over Capitol (2114)	.40	.05	5.00	(3)	.80	
2115b	22¢ Flag over Capitol	.40	.08	4.50	(3)		
	Test on pre-phosphored paper. Paper is whiter and colors are brighter than on #2115.						
	Perf. 10 Horizontally						
2116	22¢ Flag over Capitol						
	Single from booklet	.40	.05			.80	
2116a	Booklet pane of 5	2.20				4.50	
	#2116 issued only in booklets. Stamps are imperf. at one side or imperf. at one side and bottom.						
	Seashells Booklet Issue, Apr. 4, Perf. 10						
2117	22¢ Frilled Dogwinkle	.40	.05			.80	
2118	22¢ Reticulated Helmet	.40	.05			.80	
2119	22¢ New England Neptune	.40	.05			.80	
2120	22¢ Calico Scallop	.40	.05			.80	
2121	22¢ Lightning Whelk	.40	.05			.80	
2121a	Booklet pane of 10, #2117-21	4.00				9.00	
	#2117-21 issued only in booklets. All stamps are imperf. at one side or imperf. at one side and bottom.						
	Express Mail Booklet Issue, Apr. 29, Perf. 10 Vertically						
2122	$10.75 Eagle and Moon,						
	Single from booklet	19.00				30.00	
2122a	Booklet pane of 3	57.50					
	#2122 issued only in booklets. All stamps are imperf. at top and bottom or imperf. at top, bottom and one side.						

233

	Issues of 1985-87, Coil Stamps, Transportation Issue, Perf. 10 Vertically	Un	U	PB/LP	#	FDC	Q
2123	3.4¢ School Bus 1920s,						
	June 8, 1985	.07	.05	1.50	(3)	.70	
2123a	Bureau precanceled		.15	1.75	(3)	.70	
2124	4.9¢ Buckboard 1880s,						
	June 21, 1985	.10	.05	1.25	(3)	.70	
2124a	Bureau precanceled		.10	2.00	(3)	.70	
2125	5.5¢ Star Route Truck 1910s,						
	Nov. 1, 1986	.11	.05	1.75	(3)	.70	
2125a	Bureau precanceled		.11	1.75	(3)	.70	
2126	6¢ Tricycle 1880s, May 6, 1985	.12	.05	2.00	(3)	.60	
2126a	Bureau precanceled		.12	2.50	(3)	.60	
2127	7.1¢ Tractor 1920s, Feb. 6, 1987	.15	.05	2.25	(3)	.70	
2127a	Bureau precanceled		.15	2.25	(3)	.70	
2128	8.3¢ Ambulance 1860s,						
	June 21, 1985	.18	.05	1.90	(3)	.70	
2128a	Bureau precanceled		.16	2.00	(3)	.70	
2129	8.5¢ Tow Truck, Jan. 24, 1987	.18	.05	2.50	(3)	.70	
2129a	Bureau precanceled		.18	3.00	(3)	.70	
2130	10.1¢ Oil Wagon 1890s,						
	Apr. 18, 1985	.22	.05	2.50	(3)	.75	
2130a	Bureau precanceled, black		.22	2.75	(3)	.70	
	Bureau precanceled, red		.22	3.50	(3)	.70	
2131	11¢ Stutz Bearcat 1933,						
	June 11, 1985	.22	.05	2.50	(3)	.75	
2132	12¢ Stanley Steamer 1909,						
	Apr. 2, 1985	.24	.05	2.75	(3)	.75	
2132a	Bureau precanceled		.24	3.00	(3)	.75	
2133	12.5¢ Pushcart 1880s, Apr. 18, 1985	.25	.05	3.00	(3)	.75	
2133a	Bureau precanceled		.25	3.00	(3)	.75	
2134	14¢ Iceboat 1880s, Mar. 23, 1985	.28	.05	2.00	(3)	.80	
2135	17¢ Dog Sled 1920s, Aug. 20, 1986	.34	.05	3.25	(3)	.80	
2136	25¢ Bread Wagon 1880s,						
	Nov. 22, 1986	.45	.05	5.00	(3)		
	Issues of 1985, Black Heritage Issue, Mary McLeod Bethune, Mar. 5, Perf. 11						
2137	22¢ Mary McLeod Bethune Portrait	.40	.05	2.20	(4)	.80	120,000,000
	American Folk Art Issue, Duck Decoys, Mar. 22						
2138	22¢ Broadbill Decoy	.40	.08			.80	75,000,000
2139	22¢ Mallard Decoy	.40	.08			.80	75,000,000
2140	22¢ Canvasback Decoy	.40	.08			.80	75,000,000
2141	22¢ Redhead Decoy	.40	.08			.80	75,000,000
2141a	Block of 4, #2138-2141	1.60	1.00	2.75	(4)	2.75	
2142	22¢ Winter Special Olympics, Mar. 25	.40	.05	2.20	(4)	.80	120,580,000
2143	22¢ Love, Apr. 17	.40	.05	2.20	(4)	.80	729,700,000
2144	22¢ Rural Electrification						
	Administration, May 11	.40	.05	11.50	(20)	.80	124,750,000

School Bus 1920s
3.4 USA

2123

Buckboard 1880s
USA
4.9

2124

Star Route Truck
5.5 USA 1910s

2125

Tricycle 1880s
6 USA

2126

Tractor 1920s
7.1 USA

2127

Ambulance 1860s
8.3 USA

2128

Tow Truck 1920s
8.5 USA

2129

Oil Wagon 1890s
10.1 USA

2130

Stutz Bearcat 1933
11 USA

2131

Stanley Steamer 1909
USA
12

2132

Pushcart 1880s
12.5
USA

2133

Iceboat 1880s
USA
14

2134

Dog Sled 1920s
17 USA

2135

Bread Wagon 1880s
25 USA

2136

Mary McLeod Bethune
Black Heritage USA 22

2137

Broadbill Decoy
Folk Art USA 22

Mallard Decoy
Folk Art USA 22

Canvasback Decoy
Folk Art USA 22

Redhead Decoy
Folk Art USA 22

2138   **2139**   **2141a**
2140   **2141**

22 USA
Winter Special Olympics

2142

LOVE
USA 22

2143

22 USA
Rural
Electrification
Administration   1935   1985

2144

2145

2146

F.A. Bartholdi, Statue of Liberty Sculptor

2147

2149

2150

2152

2153

2154

Quarter horse   Morgan

Saddlebred   Appaloosa

2155   2156   2158a
2157   2158

Public Education

2159

YMCA Youth Camping   USA   Boy Scouts   USA

Big Brothers/Big Sisters   USA   Camp Fire   USA

2160   2161   2163a
2162   2163

	1985 continued, Perf. 11	Un	U	PB/LP	#	FDC	Q
2145	22¢ AMERIPEX 86, May 25	.40	.05	2.20	(4)	.80	203,496,000
2146	22¢ Abigail Adams, June 14	.40	.05	2.20	(4)	.80	126,325,000
2147	22¢ Frederic A. Bartholdi, July 18	.40	.05	2.20	(4)	.80	130,000,000
2148 not assigned.							
	Coil Stamps, Perf. 10 Vertically						
2149	18¢ George Washington,						
	Washington Monument, Nov. 6	.32	.08	3.25	(3)	.80	
2149a	Bureau precanceled		.32	4.00	(3)	.80	
2150	21.1¢ Sealed Envelopes, Oct. 22	.42	.08	4.50	(3)	.80	
2150a	Bureau precanceled		.42	5.00	(3)	.80	
2151 not assigned.							
	Perf. 11						
2152	22¢ Korean War Veterans, July 26	.40	.05	2.20	(4)	.80	119,975,000
2153	22¢ Social Security Act, Aug. 14	.40	.05	2.20	(4)	.80	120,000,000
2154	22¢ World War I Veterans, Aug. 26	.40	.05	2.20	(4)	.80	119,975,000
	American Horses Issue, Sept. 25						
2155	22¢ Quarter Horse	.40	.08			.80	36,985,000
2156	22¢ Morgan	.40	.08			.80	36,985,000
2157	22¢ Saddlebred	.40	.08			.80	36,985,000
2158	22¢ Appaloosa	.40	.08			.80	36,985,000
2158a	Block of 4, #2155-2158	1.60	1.00	2.50	(4)	2.75	
2159	22¢ Public Education, Oct. 1	.40	.05	2.20	(4)	.80	120,000,000
	International Youth Year Issue, Oct. 7						
2160	22¢ YMCA Youth Camping	.40	.08			.80	32,500,000
2161	22¢ Boy Scouts	.40	.08			.80	32,500,000
2162	22¢ Big Brothers/Big Sisters	.40	.08			.80	32,500,000
2163	22¢ Camp Fire	.40	.08			.80	32,500,000
2163a	Block of 4, #2160-2163	1.60	1.00	2.50	(4)	2.75	

SEALED ENVELOPES SERVE US WELL
Sealed envelopes (#2150) preserve our privacy and protect our messages. Whereas letters once were sealed with wax, the founding of the U.S. glue industry in 1827 by Peter Cooper made possible the development of envelopes sealed with glue.

	1985 continued, Perf. 11	Un	U	PB	#	FDC	Q
2164	22¢ Help End Hunger, Oct. 15	.40	.05	2.20	(4)	.80	120,000,000
	Christmas Issue, Oct. 30						
2165	22¢ Genoa Madonna,						
	by Luca della Robbia	.40	.05	2.20	(4)	.80	759,200,000
2166	22¢ Poinsettia Plants	.40	.05	2.20	(4)	.80	757,600,000
	Issue of 1986						
2167	Arkansas Statehood, Jan. 3	.40	.05	2.25	(4)	.80	130,000,000
	Issues of 1986-88, Great Americans Issue						
2168	1¢ Margaret Mitchell, June 30, 1986	.05	.05	.25	(4)	.80	
2169	2¢ Mary Lyon, Feb. 28, 1987	.05	.05	.25	(4)	.80	
2170	3¢ Paul Dudley White, MD,						
	Sept. 15, 1986	.06	.05	.30	(4)	.80	
2171	4¢ Father Flanagan, July 14, 1986	.07	.05	.40	(4)	.80	
2172	5¢ Hugo L. Black, Feb. 27, 1986	.09	.05	.50	(4)	.80	
2173-75 not assigned.							
2176	10¢ Red Cloud, Aug 15, 1987	.16	.05	1.00	(4)	.80	
2177	14¢ Julia Ward Howe, Feb 12, 1987	.24	.05	1.40	(4)	.80	
2178	15¢ Buffalo Bill Cody, June 6, 1988	.25	.05	1.50	(4)	.75	
2179	17¢ Belva Ann Lockwood,						
	June 18, 1986	.28	.06	1.75	(4)	.80	
2180	21¢ Chester Carlson, Oct. 21, 1988	.32	.05	2.10	(4)	.80	
2181 not assigned.							
2182	23¢ Mary Cassatt, Nov. 4, 1988	.35	.05	2.30	(4)	.80	
2183	25¢ Jack London, Jan. 11, 1986	.38	.06	2.50	(4)	.85	
2183a	Booklet pane of 10, May 3, 1988	4.00				8.50	
2185-87 not assigned.							
2188	45¢ Harvey Cushing, MD, June 17, 1988	.70	.05	4.50	(4)	1.05	
2189-90 not assigned.							
2191	56¢ John Harvard, Sept. 3, 1986	.80	.08	5.50	(4)	1.25	
2192	65¢ H.H. 'Hap' Arnold, Nov. 5, 1988	.95	.18	6.50	(4)	1.50	
2193 not assigned.							
2194	$1 Bernard Revel, Sept. 23, 1986	1.40	.50	10.00	(4)	2.00	
2195	$2 William Jennings Bryan,						
	Mar. 19, 1986	3.00	.50	20.00	(4)	4.00	
2196	$5 Bret Harte, Aug. 25, 1987	7.00	1.00	50.00	(4)	10.00	
	Perf. 10 Vertically and Horizontally						
2197	25¢ Jack London (2183),						
	Single from booklet	.50	.05				
2197a	Booklet pane of 6	3.00				5.25	
	Issues of 1986, United States-Sweden Stamp Collecting Booklet Issue, Jan. 23, Perf. 10 Vertically						
2198	22¢ Handstamped Cover	.40	.05			.80	948,860,000
2199	22¢ Boy Examining Stamp Collection	.40	.05			.80	16,999,200
2200	22¢ #836 Under Magnifying Glass	.40	.05			.80	16,999,200
2201	22¢ 1986 Presidents Miniature Sheet	.40	.05			.80	16,999,200
2201a	Booklet pane of 4, #2198-2201	1.70				3.75	

#2198-2201 issued only in booklets. All stamps are imperf. at top and bottom or imperf. at top, bottom and one side.

A Reminder: Beginning with this edition, catalog values for all stamps listed reflect (as accurately as possible) actual retail values as found in the marketplace.

Help End Hunger USA22

2164

CHRISTMAS
USA 22
Luca della Robbia, Detroit Institute of Arts

2165

Season's Greetings USA22

2166

Arkansas Statehood 1836-1986
Old State House Little Rock
USA22

2167

Margaret Mitchell USA 1

2168

Mary Lyon USA 2

2169

Paul Dudley White MD USA 3

2170

Father Flanagan USA 4

2171

Hugo L. Black 5 USA

2172

Red Cloud 10 USA

2176

14 USA Julia Ward Howe

2177

Buffalo Bill Cody USA 15

2178

Belva Ann Lockwood USA 17

2179

Chester Carlson USA 21

2180

USA 23 Mary Cassatt

2182

USA 25 Jack London

2183

Harvey Cushing MD USA 45

2188

John Harvard USA 56

2191

H.H.'Hap' Arnold USA 65

2192

Bernard Revel USA $1

2194

Bryan $2 USA William Jennings

2195

Bret Harte USA $5

2196

STAMP COLLECTING
USA 22

2198

STAMP COLLECTING
USA 22

2199

STAMP COLLECTING
USA 22

2200

STAMP COLLECTING
Ameripex 86 USA 22

2201   **2201a**

1986

2202

2203

2204

2205

2206

2207

2208

2209

2210

2211

	1986 continued, Perf. 11	Un	U	PB	#	FDC	Q
2202	22¢ Love, Jan. 30	.40	.05	2.25	(4)	.80	948,860,000
	Black Heritage Issue, Sojourner Truth, Feb. 4						
2203	22¢ Sojourner Truth Portrait						
	and Truth Lecturing	.40	.05	2.25	(4)	.80	130,000,000
2204	22¢ Republic of Texas						
	150th Anniversary, Mar. 2	.40	.05	2.20	(4)	.80	136,500,000
	Fish Booklet Issue, Mar. 21, Perf. 10 Horizontally						
2205	22¢ Muskellunge	.40	.05			.80	43,998,000
2206	22¢ Atlantic Cod	.40	.05			.80	43,998,000
2207	22¢ Largemouth Bass	.40	.05			.80	43,998,000
2208	22¢ Bluefin Tuna	.40	.05			.80	43,998,000
2209	22¢ Catfish	.40	.05			.80	43,998,000
2209a	Booklet pane of 5, #2205-09	2.25				4.00	
	#2205-09 issued only in booklets. All stamps are imperf. at sides or imperf. at sides and bottom.						
	Perf. 11						
2210	22¢ Public Hospitals, Apr. 11	.40	.05	2.20	(4)	.80	130,000,000
	Performing Arts Issue, Duke Ellington, Apr. 29						
2211	22¢ Duke Ellington Portrait						
	and Piano Keys	.40	.05	2.20	(4)	.80	130,000,000

SOJOURNER STOOD FOR TRUTH, FREEDOM *Originally named Isabella Baumfree, Sojourner Truth (#2203) was the first black woman to speak out publicly against slavery. Born a slave in New York's Ulster County around 1797, she was freed in 1828. After receiving what she believed to be a command from God, Baumfree changed her name and began to lecture.*

	1986 continued	Un	U	FDC	Q
	AMERIPEX '86 Issue, Presidents Miniature Sheets, May 22, Perf. 11				
2216	Sheet of 9	3.75		4.00	5,825,050
2216a	22¢ George Washington				
2216b	22¢ John Adams				
2216c	22¢ Thomas Jefferson				
2216d	22¢ James Madison				
2216e	22¢ James Monroe				
2216f	22¢ John Quincy Adams				
2216g	22¢ Andrew Jackson				
2216h	22¢ Martin Van Buren				
2216i	22¢ William H. Harrison				
	a-i, any single	.40	.20	.80	
2217	Sheet of 9	3.75		4.00	5,825,050
2217a	22¢ John Tyler				
2217b	22¢ James Polk				
2217c	22¢ Zachary Taylor				
2217d	22¢ Millard Fillmore				
2217e	22¢ Franklin Pierce				
2217f	22¢ James Buchanan				
2217g	22¢ Abraham Lincoln				
2217h	22¢ Andrew Johnson				
2217i	22¢ Ulysses S. Grant				
	a-i, any single	.40	.20	.80	

PIERCE PRESIDENCY WAS PROSPEROUS, CHAOTIC

Franklin Pierce, 14th president of the United States (#2217e), served from 1853 to 1857. This was a prosperous period for the country, marked by the California gold rush and the acquisition of the Kansas and Nebraska Territories. However, Pierce's support of the Kansas-Nebraska Act— which gave states the option to enter the Union as either slave states or free states—resulted in much chaos and bitterness.

George Washington 1789-1797
2216a

John Adams 1797-1801
2216b

Thomas Jefferson 1801-1809
2216c

James Madison 1809-1817
2216d

James Monroe 1817-1825
2216e

John Quincy Adams 1825-1829
2216f

Andrew Jackson 1829-1837
2216g

Martin Van Buren 1837-1841
2216h

William Henry Harrison 1841-1841
2216i

John Tyler 1841-1845
2217a

James K. Polk 1845-1849
2217b

Zachary Taylor 1849-1850
2217c

Millard Fillmore 1850-1853
2217d

Franklin Pierce 1853-1857
2217e

James Buchanan 1857-1861
2217f

Abraham Lincoln 1861-1865
2217g

Andrew Johnson 1865-1869
2217h

Ulysses S. Grant 1869-1877
2217i

2218a   **2218b**   **2218c**   **2218d**   **2218e**

Rutherford B. Hayes 1877-1881   James A. Garfield 1881-1881   Chester A. Arthur 1881-1885   Grover Cleveland 1885-89, 1893-97   Benjamin Harrison 1889-1893

2218f   **2218g**   **2218h**   **2218i**

William McKinley 1897-1901   Theodore Roosevelt 1901-1909   William H. Taft 1909-1913   Woodrow Wilson 1913-1921

2219a   **2219b**   **2219c**   **2219d**   **2219e**

Warren G. Harding 1921-1923   Calvin Coolidge 1923-1929   Herbert C. Hoover 1929-1933   Franklin D. Roosevelt 1933-1945

2219f   **2219g**   **2219h**   **2219i**

Harry S. Truman 1945-1953   Dwight D. Eisenhower 1953-1961   John F. Kennedy 1961-1963   Lyndon B. Johnson 1963-1969

	1986 continued	Un	U	FDC	Q
	AMERIPEX '86 Issue continued, Presidents Miniature Sheets, May 22, Perf. 11				
2218	Sheet of 9	3.75		4.00	5,825,050
2218a	22¢ Rutherford B. Hayes				
2218b	22¢ James A. Garfield				
2218c	22¢ Chester A. Arthur				
2218d	22¢ Grover Cleveland				
2218e	22¢ Benjamin Harrison				
2218f	22¢ William McKinley				
2218g	22¢ Theodore Roosevelt				
2218h	22¢ William H. Taft				
2218i	22¢ Woodrow Wilson				
	a-i, any single	.40	.20	.80	
2219	Sheet of 9	3.75		4.00	5,825,050
2219a	22¢ Warren G. Harding				
2219b	22¢ Calvin Coolidge				
2219c	22¢ Herbert Hoover				
2219d	22¢ Franklin D. Roosevelt				
2219e	22¢ White House				
2219f	22¢ Harry S. Truman				
2219g	22¢ Dwight D. Eisenhower				
2219h	22¢ John F. Kennedy				
2219i	22¢ Lyndon B. Johnson				
	a-i, any single	.40	.20	.80	

CIVIL SERVICE CREATED UNDER ARTHUR

On September 20, 1881, Chester Alan Arthur (#2218c) was sworn in as the 21st President of the United States. Sometimes called the "Gentleman Boss," Arthur was elected Vice President in 1880. He soon succeeded President James Garfield, who died from an assassin's bullet. The Civil Service Act was passed during Arthur's administration.

	1986 continued	Un	U	PB/LP	#	FDC	Q
	Polar Explorers Issue, May 28, Perf. 11						
2220	22¢ Elisha Kent Kane	.40	.05			.80	32,500,000
2221	22¢ Adolphus W. Greely	.40	.05			.80	32,500,000
2222	22¢ Vilhjalmur Stefansson	.40	.05			.80	32,500,000
2223	22¢ Robert E. Peary, Matthew Henson	.40	.05			.80	32,500,000
2223a	Block of 4, #2220-23	1.60	1.00			2.75	
2224	22¢ Statue of Liberty, July 4	.40	.05	2.75	(4)	.80	220,725,000
	Issues of 1986-87, Reengraved Transportation Issues, Coil Stamps, Perf. 10 Vertically						
2225	1¢ Omnibus, Nov. 26, 1986	.05	.05	.90	(3)	.70	
2226	2¢ Locomotive, Mar. 6, 1987	.05	.05	.95	(3)	.70	
2227 not assigned.							
2228	4¢ Stagecoach, Aug. 1986	.08	.05	1.75	(3)		
2231	8.3¢ Ambulance, (precancel),						
	Aug. 29, 1986		.16	2.75	(3)		
2232-34 not assigned.							

On #2228, "Stagecoach 1890s" is 17 mm long; on #1898A, it is 19½ mm long. On #2231, "Ambulance 1860s" is 18 mm long; on #2128, it is 18½ mm long.

		Un	U	PB/LP	#	FDC	Q
	American Folk Art Issue, Navajo Blankets, Sept. 4, Perf. 11						
2235	22¢ Navajo Blanket,						
	black-and-white lines dominate	.40	.08			.80	60,131,250
2236	22¢ Navajo Blanket,						
	black and white diamonds dominate	.40	.08			.80	60,131,250
2237	22¢ Navajo Blanket,						
	white diamonds dominate	.40	.08			.80	60,131,250
2238	22¢ Navajo Blanket, black-and-white						
	bordered patterns dominate	.40	.08			.80	60,131,250
2238a	Block of 4, #2235-38	1.60	1.00	2.20	(4)	2.75	
	Literary Arts Issue, T.S. Eliot, Sept. 26						
2239	22¢ T.S. Eliot Portrait	.40	.05	2.20	(4)	.80	131,700,000
	American Folk Art Issue, Wood-Carved Figurines, Oct. 1						
2240	22¢ Highlander Figure	.40	.08			.80	60,000,000
2241	22¢ Ship Figurehead	.40	.08			.80	60,000,000
2242	22¢ Nautical Figure	.40	.08			.80	60,000,000
2243	22¢ Cigar-Store Figure	.40	.08			.80	60,000,000
2243a	Block of 4, #2240-43	1.60	1.00	2.20	(4)	2.75	
	Christmas Issue, Oct. 24						
2244	22¢ Madonna and Child, by Perugino	.40	.05	2.20	(4)	.80	690,100,000
2245	22¢ Village Scene	.40	.05	2.20	(4)	.80	882,150,000
	Issues of 1987, Perf. 11						
2246	22¢ Michigan Statehood, Jan. 26	.40	.05	2.20	(4)	.80	167,430,000
2247	22¢ Pan American Games, Jan. 29	.40	.05	2.20	(4)	.80	166,550,000
	Perf 11½x11						
2248	22¢ Love, Jan. 30	.40	.05	2.20	(4)	.80	842,360,000
	Black Heritage Issue, Jean Baptiste Point Du Sable, Feb. 20, Perf. 11						
2249	22¢ Chicago Settlement						
	and Portrait of Du Sable	.40	.05	2.20	(4)	.80	142,905,000
	Performing Arts Issue, Enrico Caruso, Feb. 27						
2250	22¢ Caruso						
	as the Duke of Mantua in *Rigoletti*	.40	.05	2.20	(4)	.80	130,000,000
2251	22¢ Girl Scouts, Mar. 12	.40	.05	2.20	(4)	.80	149,980,000

2225

2224

2226

2220
2222

2221
2223

2223a

2239

2235
2237

2236
2238

2238a

2240
2242

2241
2243

2243a

2244

2245

2247

2246

2248

2249

2250

2251

Conestoga Wagon 1800s
USA 3

2252

Milk Wagon 1900s
5 USA

2253

Elevator 1900s
5.3 USA
Nonprofit Carrier Route Sort

2254

Congratulations! USA 22

Carreta 1770s
7.6 USA
Nonprofit

2255

Wheel Chair 1920s
8.4 USA
Nonprofit

2256

Canal Boat 1880s
10 USA

2257

Get Well!
USA 22
USA 22

Thank You!

Patrol Wagon 1880s
USA 13
Presorted First-Class

2258

Coal Car 1870s
13.2 Bulk Rate
USA

2259

Tugboat 1900s
USA 15

2260

Love You, Dad! USA 22

Best Wishes! USA 22

Happy Birthday! USA 22

Popcorn Wagon
16.7 USA 1902
Bulk Rate

2261

Racing Car 1911
USA 17.5

2262

USA 20
Cable Car 1880s

2263

USA 22

Love You, Mother!

Keep In Touch! USA 22

Happy Birthday! USA 22

Fire Engine 1900s
20.5 USA
ZIP+4 Presort

2264

Railroad Mail Car 1920s
Presorted First-Class
21 USA

2265

Tandem Bicycle
1890s 24.1 USA
ZIP+4

2266

Congratulations! USA 22

2274a

2267
2268   **2269**
2270
2271   **2272**
2273

	Issues of 1987-88	Un	U	LP	#	FDC	Q
	Transportation Issue, Perf. 10 Vertically						
2252	3¢ Conestoga Wagon 1800s, Feb. 29, 1988	.06	.05	1.00	(3)	.65	
2253	5¢ Milk Wagon 1900s, Sept. 25, 1987	.09	.05	1.75	(3)	.70	
2254	5.3¢ Elevator 1900s,						
	Bureau precanceled, Sept. 16, 1988		.10	1.85	(3)	.70	
2255	7.6¢ Carreta 1770s,						
	Bureau precanceled, Aug. 30, 1988		.14	2.25	(3)	.70	
2256	8.4¢ Wheel Chair 1920s,						
	Bureau precanceled, Aug. 12, 1988		.15	2.50	(3)	.70	
2257	10¢ Canal Boat 1880s, Apr. 11, 1987	.18	.05	2.75	(3)	.75	
2258	13¢ Patrol Wagon 1880s,						
	Bureau precanceled, Oct. 29, 1988		.22	3.00	(3)	.75	
2259	13.2¢ Coal Car 1870s,						
	Bureau precanceled, July 19, 1988		.22	3.00	(3)	.75	
2260	15¢ Tugboat 1900s, July 12, 1988	.24	.05	1.50	(3)	.75	
2261	16.7¢ Popcorn Wagon 1902,						
	Bureau precanceled, July 7, 1988		.28	3.25	(3)	.75	
2262	17.5¢ Racing Car 1911, Sept. 25, 1987	.30	.05	3.50	(3)	.80	
2262a	Bureau precanceled		.30	4.00	(3)	.80	
2263	20¢ Cable Car 1880s, Oct. 28, 1988	.35	.05	3.75	(3)	.80	
2264	20.5¢ Fire Engine 1920s,						
	Bureau precanceled, Sept. 28, 1988		.38	3.75	(3)	.80	
2265	21¢ Railroad Mail Car 1920s,						
	Bureau precanceled, Aug. 16, 1988		.38	4.00	(3)	.80	
2266	24.1¢ Tandem Bicycle 1890s,						
	Bureau precanceled, Oct. 26, 1988		.42	4.25	(3)	.80	
	Special Occasions Booklet Issue, Apr. 20, 1987 Perf. 10						
2267	22¢ Congratulations!	.40	.05			.80	1,222,140,000
2268	22¢ Get Well!	.40	.05			.80	611,070,000
2269	22¢ Thank You!	.40	.05			.80	611,070,000
2270	22¢ Love You, Dad!	.40	.05			.80	611,070,000
2271	22¢ Best Wishes!	.40	.05			.80	611,070,000
2272	22¢ Happy Birthday!	.40	.05			.80	1,222,140,000
2273	22¢ Love You, Mother!	.40	.05			.80	611,070,000
2274	22¢ Keep In Touch!	.40	.05			.80	611,070,000
2274a	Booklet pane of 10, #2268-2271,						
	2273-2274, and 2 each						
	of #2267, 2272	4.00				7.00	

#2267-74 issued only in booklets. All stamps are imperf. at sides or imperf. at sides and bottom.

	1987 continued, Perf. 11	Un	U	PB/LP	#	FDC	Q
2275	United Way, Apr. 28	.40	.05	2.20	(4)	.80	156,995,000
2276	Flag with Fireworks, May 9	.40	.05	2.20	(4)	.80	
2276a	Booklet pane of 20, Nov. 30	8.00				15.00	
	Issues of 1988						
2277	(25¢) E Stamp, Mar. 22	.40	.05	2.50	(4)	.85	
2278	25¢ Flag with Clouds, May 6	.40	.05	2.50	(4)	.85	
	Coil Stamps, Perf. 10 Vertically						
2279	(25¢) E Stamp (2277), Mar. 22	.40	.05	2.25	(3)	.85	
2280	25¢ Flag over Yosemite, May 20	.40	.05	2.25	(3)	.85	
2281	25¢ Honeybee, Sept. 2	.40	.05	2.25	(3)	.85	
	Perf. 10						
2282	(25¢) E Stamp (2277),						
	Single from booklet	.40	.05			.85	
2282a	Booklet pane of 10, Mar. 22	4.00				8.50	
2283	25¢ Pheasant,						
	Single from booklet	.40	.05			.85	
2283a	Booklet pane of 10, Apr. 29	4.00				8.50	
2284	25¢ Owl,						
	Single from booklet	.40	.05			.85	
2285	25¢ Grosbeak,						
	Single from booklet	.40	.05			.85	
2285b	Booklet pane of 10, 5 each of 2284,						
	2285, May 28	4.00				8.50	
2285A	25¢ Flag with Clouds (2278),						
	Single from booklet	.40	.05			.85	
2285Ac	Booklet pane of 6, July 5	2.50				5.25	

HONEYBEES ARE
BUSY BEES
*Thousands of honey-
bees (#2281) live in
a single, organized
colony. Together they
build and maintain
their hive and gather
nectar for honey. The
colony's workers feed
and protect the queen,
whose only function
is to create more bees
by laying eggs.*

2275

2276

2277

2278

2280

2281

2283

2283a

2284

2285

2285a

	1987 continued	Un	U	FDC	Q
	American Wildlife Issue, June 13, Perf. 11				
2286	22¢ Barn Swallow	.40	.05	.80	12,952,500
2287	22¢ Monarch	.40	.05	.80	12,952,500
2288	22¢ Bighorn Sheep	.40	.05	.80	12,952,500
2289	22¢ Broad-tailed Hummingbird	.40	.05	.80	12,952,500
2290	22¢ Cottontail	.40	.05	.80	12,952,500
2291	22¢ Osprey	.40	.05	.80	12,952,500
2292	22¢ Mountain Lion	.40	.05	.80	12,952,500
2293	22¢ Luna Moth	.40	.05	.80	12,952,500
2294	22¢ Mule Deer	.40	.05	.80	12,952,500
2295	22¢ Gray Squirrel	.40	.05	.80	12,952,500
2296	22¢ Armadillo	.40	.05	.80	12,952,500
2297	22¢ Eastern Chipmunk	.40	.05	.80	12,952,500
2298	22¢ Moose	.40	.05	.80	12,952,500
2299	22¢ Black Bear	.40	.05	.80	12,952,500
2300	22¢ Tiger Swallowtail	.40	.05	.80	12,952,500
2301	22¢ Bobwhite	.40	.05	.80	12,952,500
2302	22¢ Ringtail	.40	.05	.80	12,952,500
2303	22¢ Red-winged Blackbird	.40	.05	.80	12,952,500
2304	22¢ American Lobster	.40	.05	.80	12,952,500
2305	22¢ Black-tailed Jack Rabbit	.40	.05	.80	12,952,500
2306	22¢ Scarlet Tanager	.40	.05	.80	12,952,500
2307	22¢ Woodchuck	.40	.05	.80	12,952,500
2308	22¢ Roseate Spoonbill	.40	.05	.80	12,952,500
2309	22¢ Bald Eagle	.40	.05	.80	12,952,500
2310	22¢ Alaskan Brown Bear	.40	.05	.80	12,952,500

LOBSTERS' LIVES SHORTENED BY GREEDY GOURMETS
Often called the American lobster (#2304), the common lobster of North America is a crustacean—an animal without backbones. Lobsters weigh from 1 to 20 pounds and, if not eaten prematurely by seafood fans, may live for 15 years. The lobster was immortalized by "The Lobster Quadrille," a poem by Lewis Carroll in his book, Alice in Wonderland.

	1987 continued	Un	U	FDC	Q
	American Wildlife Issue continued, June 13, Perf. 11				
2311	22¢ Iiwi	.40	.05	.80	12,952,500
2312	22¢ Badger	.40	.05	.80	12,952,500
2313	22¢ Pronghorn	.40	.05	.80	12,952,500
2314	22¢ River Otter	.40	.05	.80	12,952,500
2315	22¢ Ladybug	.40	.05	.80	12,952,500
2316	22¢ Beaver	.40	.05	.80	12,952,500
2317	22¢ White-tailed Deer	.40	.05	.80	12,952,500
2318	22¢ Blue Jay	.40	.05	.80	12,952,500
2319	22¢ Pika	.40	.05	.80	12,952,500
2320	22¢ Bison	.40	.05	.80	12,952,500
2321	22¢ Snowy Egret	.40	.05	.80	12,952,500
2322	22¢ Gray Wolf	.40	.05	.80	12,952,500
2323	22¢ Mountain Goat	.40	.05	.80	12,952,500
2324	22¢ Deer Mouse	.40	.05	.80	12,952,500
2325	22¢ Black-tailed Prairie Dog	.40	.05	.80	12,952,500
2326	22¢ Box Turtle	.40	.05	.80	12,952,500
2327	22¢ Wolverine	.40	.05	.80	12,952,500
2328	22¢ American Elk	.40	.05	.80	12,952,500
2329	22¢ California Sea Lion	.40	.05	.80	12,952,500
2330	22¢ Mockingbird	.40	.05	.80	12,952,500
2331	22¢ Raccoon	.40	.05	.80	12,952,500
2332	22¢ Bobcat	.40	.05	.80	12,952,500
2333	22¢ Black-footed Ferret	.40	.05	.80	12,952,500
2334	22¢ Canada Goose	.40	.05	.80	12,952,500
2335	22¢ Red Fox	.40	.05	.80	12,952,500
2335a	Pane of 50, #2286-2335	20.00			

WOLVERINE NOTED FOR GLUTTONY

The wolverine (#2327) is a fur-bearing animal inhabiting the northern woods of Europe, Asia and North America. With its long, shaggy coat and tan markings, the wolverine resembles a small bear but actually belongs to the weasel family. Because of its habit of killing more animals than it needs for food, the wolverine is known in Europe as the glutton.

22 USA *Iiwi*	22 USA *Badger*	22 USA *Pronghorn*	22 USA *River Otter*	22 USA *Ladybug*
2311	2312	2313	2314	2315
22 USA *Beaver*	22 USA *White-tailed Deer*	22 USA *Blue Jay*	22 USA *Pika*	22 USA *Bison*
2316	2317	2318	2319	2320
22 USA *Snowy Egret*	22 USA *Gray Wolf*	22 USA *Mountain Goat*	22 USA *Deer Mouse*	22 USA *Black-tailed Prairie Dog*
2321	2322	2323	2324	2325
22 USA *Box Turtle*	22 USA *Wolverine*	22 USA *American Elk*	22 USA *California Sea Lion*	22 USA *Mockingbird*
2326	2327	2328	2329	2330
22 USA *Raccoon*	22 USA *Bobcat*	22 USA *footed Ferret*	22 USA *nada Goose*	22 USA *Red Fox*

Dec 7, 1787 USA
Delaware 22

2336

Dec 12, 1787
Pennsylvania 22

2337

Dec 18, 1787 USA
New Jersey 22

2338

22 USA
January 2, 1788
Georgia

2339

22 USA
January 9, 1788
Connecticut

2340

Feb 6, 1788 USA
Massachusetts 22

2341

April 28, 1788 USA
Maryland 22

2342

25 USA
May 23, 1788
South Carolina

2343

25 USA
June 21, 1788
New Hampshire

2344

June 25, 1788 USA
Virginia 25

2345

July 26, 1788 USA
New York 25

2346

Friendship
with Morocco
1787-1987
USA 22

2349

William Faulkner
USA 22

2350

The Bicentennial
of the Constitution
of the United States
of America
1787-1987
USA 22

We the people
of the United States,
in order to form
a more perfect Union...
Preamble, U.S. Constitution USA 22

Establish justice,
insure domestic tranquility,
provide for the common defense,
promote the general welfare...
Preamble, U.S. Constitution USA 22

And secure
the blessings of liberty
to ourselves
and our posterity...
Preamble, U.S. Constitution USA 22

Do ordain
and establish this
Constitution for the
United States of America.
Preamble, U.S. Constitution USA 22

Lacemaking USA 22
Lacemaking USA 22
Lacemaking USA 22
Lacemaking USA 22

2351   2352   2354a
2353   2354

2355   2359a
2356

Issues of 1987-88	Un	U	PB	#	FDC	Q
Constitution Bicentennial Issues, Statehood, Perf. 11						
2336 22¢ Delaware Statehood, July 4, 1987	.40	.05	2.20	(4)	.80	168,000,000
2337 22¢ Pennsylvania Statehood,						
Aug. 26, 1987	.40	.05	2.20	(4)	.80	186,575,000
2338 22¢ New Jersey Statehood, Sept. 11, 1987	.40	.05			.80	184,325,000
2339 22¢ Georgia, Jan. 6, 1988	.40	.05	2.20	(4)	.80	168,845,000
2340 22¢ Connecticut, Jan. 9, 1988	.40	.05	2.20	(4)	.80	155,170,000
2341 22¢ Massachusetts, Feb. 6, 1988	.40	.05	2.20	(4)	.80	102,100,000
2342 22¢ Maryland, Feb. 15, 1988	.40	.05	2.20	(4)	.80	103,325,000
2343 25¢ South Carolina, May 23, 1988	.40	.05	2.20	(4)	.85	162,045,000
2344 25¢ New Hampshire, June 21, 1988	.40	.05	2.20	(4)	.85	153,295,000
2345 25¢ Virginia, June 25, 1988	.40	.05	2.20	(4)	.85	160,245,000
2346 25¢ New York, July 26, 1988	.40	.05	2.20	(4)	.85	183,290,000
2348 not assigned.						
Issues of 1988						
2349 22¢ Friendship with Morocco, July 17	.40	.05			.80	157,475,000
Literary Arts Issue, William Faulkner, Aug. 3						
2350 22¢ Portrait of Faulkner	.40	.05	2.20	(4)	.80	156,225,000
American Folk Art Issue, Lacemaking, Aug. 14						
2351 22¢ Squash Blossoms	.40	.08			.80	40,995,000
2352 22¢ Floral Piece	.40	.08			.80	40,995,000
2353 22¢ Floral Piece	.40	.08			.80	40,995,000
2354 22¢ Dogwood Blossoms	.40	.08			.80	40,995,000
2354a Block of 4, #2351-2354	1.60	1.00	2.20	(4)	2.75	
Constitution Bicentennial Issue, Drafting of the Constitution, Aug. 28, Perf. 10 Horizontally						
2355 22¢ "The Bicentennial..."	.40	.08			.80	121,944,000
2356 22¢ "We the people..."	.40	.08			.80	121,944,000
2357 22¢ "Establish justice..."	.40	.08			.80	121,944,000
2358 22¢ "And secure..."	.40	.08			.80	121,944,000
2359 22¢ "Do ordain..."	.40	.08			.80	121,944,000
2359a Booklet pane of 5, #2355-2359	2.00				4.00	

#2355-59 issued only in booklets. All stamps are imperf. at sides or imperf. at sides and bottom.

20TH CENTURY REVIVES ANCIENT ART

The painstaking process of lace-making is so time-consuming that for centuries lace was worn only by royalty. In the 1800s the invention of lacemaking machines rendered lace much more affordable. There currently is a resurgence of interest in the lacemaker's art, with many people learning the ancient techniques of needlepoint and bobbin lace (#2351-2354).

	1987 continued	Un	U	PB	#	FDC	Q
	Constitution Bicentennial Issue, Signing of the Constitution, Sept. 17, Perf. 11						
2360	22¢ Constitution and Signer's Hand						
	Holding Quill Pen, Sept. 17	.40	.05	2.20	(4)	.80	168,995,000
2361	22¢ Certified Public Accountants,						
	Sept. 21	.40	.05	2.20	(4)	.80	163,145,000
	Locomotives Booklet Issue, Oct. 1, Perf. 10 Horizontally						
2362	22¢ Stourbridge Lion, 1829	.40	.08			.80	142,501,200
2363	22¢ Best Friend of Charleston, 1830	.40	.08			.80	142,501,200
2364	22¢ John Bull, 1831	.40	.08			.80	142,501,200
2365	22¢ Brother Jonathan, 1832	.40	.08			.80	142,501,200
2366	22¢ Gowan & Marx, 1839	.40	.08			.80	142,501,200
2366a	Booklet pane of 5, #2362-2366	2.00				4.00	
	#2362-66 issued only in booklets. All stamps are imperf. at sides or imperf. at sides and bottom.						
	Christmas Issue, Oct. 23, Perf. 11						
2367	22¢ Madonna, by Moroni	.40	.05	2.20	(4)	.80	528,790,000
2368	22¢ Christmas Ornaments	.40	.05	2.20	(4)	.80	978,340,000
	Issues of 1988, Olympic Winter Games Issue, Jan. 10						
2369	22¢ Skier	.40	.05	2.20	(4)	.80	158,870,000
2370	22¢ Australia Bicentennial, Jan. 26	.40	.05	2.20	(4)	.80	145,560,000
	Black Heritage Issue, James Weldon Johnson, Feb. 2						
2371	22¢ Portrait of Johnson						
	and music from "Lift Ev'ry Voice and Sing"	.40	.05	2.20	(4)	.80	97,300,000
	American Cats Issue, Feb. 5						
2372	22¢ Siamese and Exotic Shorthair	.40	.05	2.20	(4)	.80	39,639,000
2373	22¢ Abyssinian and Himalayan	.40	.05			.80	39,639,000
2374	22¢ Maine Coon and Burmese	.40	.05	2.20	(4)	.80	39,639,000
2375	22¢ American Shorthair and Persian	.40	.05			.80	39,639,000
2375a	Block of 4, #2372-75	1.60	1.00	2.20	(4)	2.75	

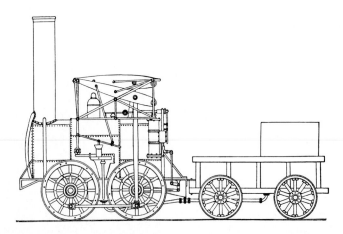

I'VE BEEN WORKING ON THE…

The Stourbridge Lion *(#2362) helped launch the railroad era in America. The Postal Service benefitted tremendously from that progress. Although much mail is carried by air transport today, locomotive stamps carry the trains that once carried them.*

2360

2361

2362

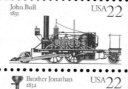

2363

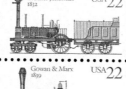

2364

2365

2366

2366a

2367

2368

2369

2370

2371

2372
2374

2373
2375

2375a

22 USA

KNUTE ROCKNE

2376

Francis Ouimet

USA 25

US Open Champion, 1913

2377

USA 25

LOVE

2378

LOVE

USA 45

2379

OLYMPICS 88

25 USA

2380

USA 25 — 1928 Locomobile

USA 25 — 1929 Pierce-Arrow

USA 25 — 1931 Cord

USA 25 — 1932 Packard

USA 25 — 1935 Duesenberg

2381
2382
2383
2384
2385

2385a

USA 25 — Nathaniel Palmer

USA 25 — Lt. Charles Wilkes

USA 25 — Richard E. Byrd

USA 25 — Lincoln Ellsworth

2386   **2387**   **2389a**
2388   **2389**

25 USA

25 USA

25 USA

25 USA

2393a

2390   **2391**
2392   **2393**

	1988 continued	Un	U	PB	#	FDC	Q
	American Sports Issues, Knute Rockne, Mar. 9, Perf. 11						
2376	22¢ Rockne Holding Football on Field	.40	.05	2.20	(4)	.80	97,300,000
	Francis Ouimet, June 13						
2377	25¢ Portrait of Ouimet						
	and Ouimet Hitting Fairway Shot	.40	.08	2.50	(4)	.85	153,045,000
2378	25¢ Love, July 4	.40	.05	2.50	(4)	.85	753,640,000
2379	45¢ Love, Aug. 8	.65	.05	4.50	(4)	1.05	154,115,000
	Olympic Summer Games Issue, Aug. 19						
2380	25¢ Gymnast on Rings	.40	.08	2.50	(4)	.85	157,215,000
	Classic Cars Booklet Issue, Aug. 25, Perf. 10 Horizontally						
2381	25¢ 1928 Locomobile	.40	.08			.85	127,047,600
2382	25¢ 1929 Pierce-Arrow	.40	.08			.85	127,047,600
2383	25¢ 1931 Cord	.40	.08			.85	127,047,600
2384	25¢ 1932 Packard	.40	.08			.85	127,047,600
2385	25¢ 1935 Duesenberg	.40	.08			.85	127,047,600
2385a	Booklet pane of 5, #2381-85	2.00				4.00	
	Antarctic Explorers Issue, Sept. 14, Perf. 11						
2386	25¢ Nathaniel Palmer	.50	.08	2.50	(4)	.85	40,535,000
2387	25¢ Lt. Charles Wilkes	.50	.08			.85	40,535,000
2388	25¢ Richard E. Byrd	.50	.08	2.50	(4)	.85	40,535,000
2389	25¢ Lincoln Ellsworth	.50	.08			.85	40,535,000
2389a	Block of 4, #2386-89	2.00	.32			3.00	
	American Folk Art Issue, Carousel Animals, Oct. 1						
2390	25¢ Deer	.50	.08	2.50	(4)	.85	
2391	25¢ Horse	.50	.08	2.50	(4)	.85	
2392	25¢ Camel	.50	.08			.65	
2393	25¢ Goat	.50	.08			.85	
2393a	Block of 4, #2390-93	2.00	1.25			3.00	

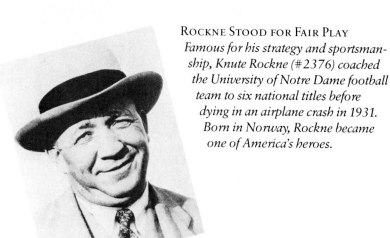

ROCKNE STOOD FOR FAIR PLAY
Famous for his strategy and sportsman-
ship, Knute Rockne (#2376) coached
the University of Notre Dame football
team to six national titles before
dying in an airplane crash in 1931.
Born in Norway, Rockne became
one of America's heroes.

	1988 continued, Perf. 11	Un	U	PB	#	FDC
2394	$8.75 Express Mail, Oct. 4	17.50		84.50	(4)	25.00
	Special Occasions Booklet Issue, Oct. 22, Perf. 10					
2395	25¢ Happy Birthday	.50	.05			.85
2396	25¢ Best Wishes	.50	.05			.85
2396a	Booklet pane of 6, 3 #2395					
	and 3 #2396 with gutter between	3.00				5.25
2397	25¢ Thinking of You	.50	.05			.85
2398	25¢ Love You	.50	.05			.85
2398a	Booklet pane of 6, 3 #2397					
	and 3 #2398 with gutter between	3.00				5.25
	Christmas Issue, Oct. 20, Perf. 11					
2399	25¢ Madonna and Child, by Botticelli	.50	.05	2.50	(4)	.85
2400	25¢ One-Horse Open Sleigh					
	and Village Scene	.50	.05	2.50	(4)	.85

MADONNA AND CHILD: BOTTICELLI MASTERPIECE *Sandro Botticelli (1445-1510) was one of the foremost artists of the Italian Renaissance. At once serious and playful in subject matter, his masterpieces include* Madonna and Child *(#2395),* Birth of Venus *and* Saint Sebastian. *Botticelli spent most of his life in Florence, Italy.*

A Reminder: Beginning with this edition, catalog values for all stamps listed reflect (as accurately as possible) actual retail values as found in the marketplace.

2394

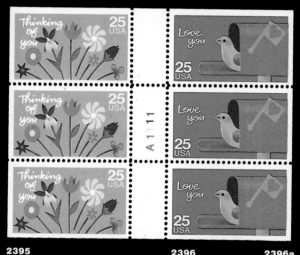

2395 **2396** **2396a**

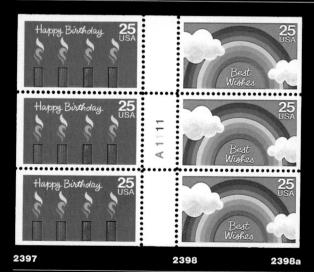

2397 **2398** **2398a**

2399

2400

Montana Statehood (25¢, #2401)
Date of Issue: January 15, 1989
Place of Issue: Helena, Montana
Designer: Bradbury Thompson
Printing: Offset/Intaglio
Montana's rugged, rewarding terrain has
created a respect for the land among inhabitants
and visitors.

A. Philip Randolph (25¢, #2402)
Date of Issue: February 3, 1989
Place of Issue: New York, New York
Designer: Thomas Blackshear
Printing: Gravure
Randolph was a respected leader of minority
labor and civil rights movements for more than
50 years.

North Dakota Statehood (25¢, #2403)
Date of Issue: February 21, 1989
Place of Issue: Bismarck, North Dakota
Designer: Wendell Minor
Printing: Gravure
Early North Dakotans triumphed over physical
hardships in a stubborn but resource-rich land.

Washington Statehood (25¢, #2404)
Date of Issue: February 22, 1989
Place of Issue: Olympia, Washington
Designer: Howard Rogers
Printing: Gravure
Washington has maintained its outdoor wonder-
land while prospering through agriculture
and industry.

Steamboats (25¢, #2405-9)
Date of Issue: March 3, 1989
Place of Issue: New Orleans, Louisiana
Designer: Richard Schlecht
Printing: Offset/Intaglio
These new booklet stamps portray five of the earliest and most innovative steamboats. Steamboats transformed uncharted waterways into America's first superhighways, shifting the country from domination by eastern coastal interests to growth and westward expansion.

WORLD STAMP EXPO '89 (25¢, #2410)
Date of Issue: March 16, 1989
Place of Issue: New York, New York
Designer: Richard D. Sheaff
Printing: Offset/Intaglio
WORLD STAMP EXPO '89, an international stamp show, was slated for Washington, DC.

Arturo Toscanini (25¢, #2411)
Date of Issue: March 25, 1989
Place of Issue: New York, New York
Designer: Jim Sharpe
Printing: Gravure
Toscanini's musical genius and inspiring standards made him one of the world's greatest conductors.

U.S. House of Representatives (25¢, #2412)
Date of Issue: April 4, 1989
Place of Issue: Washington, DC
Designer: Howard Koslow
Printing: Offset/Intaglio
This stamp commemorates the bicentennial of the House, where representation is based on population.

U.S. Senate (25¢, #2413)
Date of Issue: April 6, 1989
Place of Issue: Washington, DC
Designer: Howard Koslow
Printing: Offset/Intaglio
The Senate, with two members from each state, is part of the Legislative Branch along with the House.

Executive Branch (25¢, #2414)
Date of Issue: April 16, 1989
Place of Issue: Mount Vernon, Virginia
Designer: Howard Koslow
Printing: Offset/Intaglio
The Inauguration of George Washington as President brought the Executive Branch into being in 1789.

South Dakota Statehood (25¢, #2416)
Date of Issue: May 3, 1989
Place of Issue: Pierre, South Dakota
Designer: Marian Henjum
Printing: Gravure
South Dakota's scenic wonders are reflected in the Black Hills, the Badlands and Mount Rushmore.

Lou Gehrig (25¢, #2417)
Date of Issue: June 10, 1989
Place of Issue: Cooperstown, New York
Designer: Bart Forbes
Printing: Gravure
Lou Gehrig, one of baseball's greatest hitters, played in an incredible 2,130 consecutive games.

Ernest Hemingway (25¢, #2418)
Date of Issue: July 17, 1989
Place of Issue: Key West, Florida
Designer: Greg Rudd
Printing: Gravure
His spare, gripping prose earned Hemingway recognition as one of the great authors of the 20th century.

North Carolina Statehood (25¢, #2347)
Date of Issue: August 22, 1989
Place of Issue: Raleigh, North Carolina
Designer: Bob Timberlake
Printing: Gravure
The state and its official flower, the dogwood, blossomed after ratification of the Constitution.

Letter Carriers (25¢, #2420)
Date of Issue: August 30, 1989
Place of Issue: Milwaukee, Wisconsin
Designer: Jack Davis
Printing: Gravure
The vital contributions of hundreds of thousands of letter carriers are commemorated through this stamp.

Drafting of the Bill of Rights (25¢, #2421)
Date of Issue: September 25, 1989
Place of Issue: Philadelphia, Pennsylvania
Designer: Lou Nolan
Printing: Offset/Intaglio
The Bill of Rights was developed to supplement the Constitution by outlining individual rights.

Prehistoric Animals
(25¢, #2422-25)
Date of Issue:
October 1, 1989
Place of Issue:
Orlando, Florida
Designer: John Gurche
Printing: Gravure
This block of four
stamps portrays three
dinosaurs and a pte-
ranodon, a winged
creature that ruled the skies while dinosaurs ruled the land during the
Mesozoic Era, or Age of Reptiles, which lasted some 100 million years.

America (25¢, #2426)
Date of Issue: October 12, 1989
Place of Issue: San Juan, Puerto Rico
Designer: Lon Busch
Printing: Gravure
Pre-Columbian artifacts and the Postal Union
of the Americas and Spain are linked on
this stamp.

Christmas Traditional (25¢, #2427)
Date of Issue: October 19, 1989
Place of Issue: Washington, DC
Designer: Bradbury Thompson
Printing: Gravure
The Madonna and Child detail is from Lodovico
Carracci's *The Dream of Saint Catherine of
Alexandria*, circa 1590, now in the National
Gallery of Art.

Christmas Contemporary (25¢, #2428)
Date of Issue: October 19, 1989
Place of Issue: Westport, Connecticut
Designer: Stevan Dohanos
Printing: Offset/Intaglio
This fanciful image, developed as a composite
of turn-of-the-century sleighs, evokes nostalgia
for oldtime American holiday activities.

WORLD STAMP EXPO '89

The classic 1869 U.S. Abraham Lincoln stamp is reborn in these four larger versions commemorating World Stamp Expo'89, held in Washington, D.C. during the 20th Universal Postal Congress of the UPU. These stamps show the issued colors and three of the trial proof color combinations.
©USPS 1989

WORLD STAMP EXPO '89

($3.60, #2433)
Date of Issue:
November 17, 1989
Place of Issue:
Washington, DC
Designer:
Richard Sheaff
Printing:
Offset/Intaglio
This souvenir sheet was planned to help honor and publicize its namesake, the mammoth international stamp show and exhibition sponsored by the Postal Service in Washington, DC.

Classic Mail Transportation

(25¢, #2434-37)
Date of Issue:
November 20, 1989
Place of Issue:
Washington, DC
Designer: Mark Hess
Printing:
Offset/Intaglio
These four designs, which recognize the 20th Congress of the Universal Postal Union, pay tribute to early methods of mail transportation: the stagecoach, the steamboat, the biplane and the automobile.

20th Universal Postal Congress

A review of historical methods of delivering the mail in the United States is the theme of these four stamps issued in commemoration of the convening of the 20th Universal Postal Congress in Washington, D.C. from November 13 through December 15, 1989. The United States, as host nation to the Congress for the first time in ninety-two years, welcomed more than 1,000 delegates from most of the member nations of the Universal Postal Union to the major international event.

Classic Mail Transportation

($1, #2438)
Date of Issue:
November 27, 1989
Place of Issue:
Washington, DC
Designer:
Richard Sheaff
Printing:
Offset/Intaglio
This souvenir sheet is one of three that honors the 20th Congress of the Universal Postal Union, set in the United States (in Washington, DC) for the first time in 92 years.

Flag Over Yosemite (25¢, #2280b)
Date of Issue: February 14, 1989
Place of Issue: Yosemite, California
Designer: Peter Cocci
Printing: Offset/Intaglio
First issued in 1988, this design was reprinted
on prephosphored paper, which gives it a
brighter look and better absorbs and holds
cancellations.

Tractor (7.1¢, #2127b)
Date of Issue: May 26, 1989
Place of Issue: Rosemont, Illinois
Designer: Ken Dallison
Printing: Intaglio
First issued in 1987 in both mint and precanceled
versions, this design was reprinted with a
different precancel to meet a new mailing rate.

Johns Hopkins ($1, #2194A)
Date of Issue: June 7, 1989
Place of Issue: Baltimore, Maryland
Designer: Bradbury Thompson
Printing: Intaglio
Johns Hopkins revolutionized the teaching of
American medicine by requiring that rigid study
be combined with research and patient care.

French Revolution (45¢, #C120)
Date of Issue: July 14, 1989
Place of Issue: Washington, DC
Designer: Richard D. Sheaff
Printing: Offset/Intaglio
The French people's pursuit of democracy, inspired by the American Revolution, received a bicentennial salute from France's longtime ally.

Moon Landing ($2.40, #2419)
Date of Issue: July 20, 1989
Place of Issue: Washington, DC
Designer: Christopher Calle
Printing: Offset/Intaglio
Issued for use at the Priority Mail rate, the Moon Landing stamp celebrates the 20th anniversary of the initial steps taken on the lunar surface by American astronaut Neil Armstrong, first man on the moon.

Sitting Bull (28¢, #2184)
Date of Issue: September 28, 1989
Place of Issue: Pierre, South Dakota
Designer: Robert Anderson
Printing: Intaglio
Best known for his defeat of General Custer at the Battle of Little Bighorn, Sitting Bull was a symbol of Indian opposition to white encroachment.

America (45¢, #C121)
Date of Issue: October 12, 1989
Place of Issue: San Juan, Puerto Rico
Designer: Lon Busch
Printing: Gravure
A kachina-like altar figure graces this Postal Union of the Americas and Spain airmail.

*Design not available
at press time.*

Eagle and Shield

(25¢, #2431)
Date of Issue:
Undetermined
Place of Issue:
Undetermined
Designer: Jay Haiden
Printing: Gravure
This self-adhesive,
issued on foldable
liners containing
18 stamps, was to be
tested in 15 cities.

Future Mail Transportation

(45¢, #C122-125)
Date of Issue:
November 24, 1989
Place of Issue:
Washington, D.C.
Designer: Ken Hodges
Printing:
Offset/Intaglio
These four designs
commemorating the

Universal Postal Union's 20th Congress offer a glimpse of future mail
transportation methods: a hypersonic airliner, an air-cushion vehicle, a
surface rover and a shuttle.

Future Mail Transportation

($1.80, #C126)
Date of Issue:
November 28, 1989
Place of Issue:
Washington, D.C.
Designer:
Richard Sheaff
Printing:
Offset/Intaglio
This souvenir sheet
is one of three honor-

ing the 20th Congress of the Universal Postal Union and its more than
1,000 delegates from most of its 169 member nations.

Souvenirs Become Philatelic Collectibles

- Special programs published for First Day Ceremonies, now available by mail order
- Issued for all philatelic items—stamps, postal cards and stamped envelopes

New in 1989

Virtually every time a new stamp or stationery item is issued, a First Day Dedication Ceremony is held. These ceremonies have taken place in cities and towns all over the country; complimentary First Day of Issue programs usually accompany the festivities.

What's new is that collectors can sign up to receive a full set of these official Souvenir Programs from First Day Ceremonies through mail order. The subscription price will average out to less than $6.00 per program (unless the face value of the postage affixed exceeds this amount); a limited production run of approximately 10,000 will be made available. Colorful, top-quality programs include a list of participants in the ceremonies, a biography or background on the stamp subject and the stamp, postal card or stamped envelope, which is affixed and postmarked with the First Day of Issue cancellation.

How to Subscribe

For more information, use the postage-paid request card in this book or write:

USPS GUIDE
CEREMONY PROGRAMS
 SUBSCRIPTION PROGRAM
US ENVELOPE AGENCY
ROUTE 866
WILLIAMSBURG PA 16693-9989

1918-1938

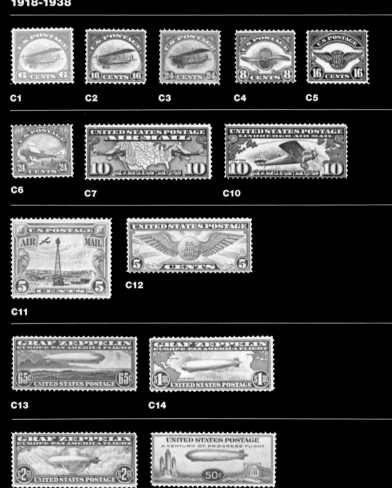

C1   C2   C3   C4   C5

C6   C7   C10

C11   C12

C13   C14

C15   C18

C20   C21   C23

	Airmail Stamps	Un	U	PB	#	FDC	Q
	For prepayment of postage on all mailable matter sent by airmail. All unwatermarked.						
	Issues of 1918, Perf. 11						
C1	6¢ Curtiss Jenny, Dec. 10	70.00	30.00	1,200.00	(6)	*17,500.00*	3,395,854
C2	16¢ Curtiss Jenny, July 11	100.00	32.50	2,250.00	(6)	*22,500.00*	3,793,887
C3	24¢ Curtiss Jenny, May 13	100.00	35.00	2,600.00	(12)	*27,500.00*	2,134,888
C3a	Center Inverted	*135,000.00*					
	Issues of 1923						
C4	8¢ Airplane Radiator						
	and Wooden Propeller, Aug. 15	25.00	11.00	600.00	(6)	450.00	6,414,576
C5	16¢ Air Service Emblem, Aug. 17	95.00	30.00	3,250.00	(6)	850.00	5,309,275
C6	24¢ De Havilland Biplane, Aug.21	100.00	25.00	4,250.00	(6)	1,000.00	5,285,775
	Issues of 1926-27						
C7	10¢ Map of U.S.						
	and Two Mail Planes, Feb. 13, 1926	2.25	.25	55.00	(6)	65.00	42,092,800
C8	15¢ olive brown (C7), Sept. 18, 1926	2.50	1.65	65.00	(6)	110.00	15,597,307
C9	20¢ yel. grn. (C7), Jan. 25, 1927	8.00	1.25	165.00	(6)	115.00	17,616,350
	Issues of 1927-28						
C10	10¢ Lindbergh's						
	"Spirit of St. Louis," June 18, 1927	6.00	1.50	200.00	(6)	25.00	20,379,179
C10a	Booklet pane of 3, May 26, 1928	110.00	*60.00*			925.00	
	#C1-10 inclusive also were available for ordinary postage.						
	Issue of 1928						
C11	5¢ Beacon on Rocky Mountains,						
	July 25	3.00	.25	65.00	(6)	50.00	106,887,675
	Issues of 1930						
C12	5¢ Winged Globe, Feb. 10	8.00	.22	250.00	(6)	20.00	97,641,200
	Graf Zeppelin Issue, Apr. 19						
C13	65¢ Zeppelin over Atlantic Ocean	250.00	175.00	3,850.00	(6)	1,850.00	93,536
C14	$1.30 Zeppelin						
	Between Continents	700.00	485.00	8,250.00	(6)	1,400.00	72,428
C15	$2.60 Zeppelin Passing Globe	1,050.00	550.00	13,000.00	(6)	2,000.00	61,296
	Issued for use on mail carried on the first Europe Pan-American round-trip flight of Graf Zeppelin, May 1930.						
	Issues of 1931-32, Perf. 10½x11						
C16	5¢ violet (C12), Aug. 19, 1931	4.75	.30	135.00	(4)	200.00	57,340,050
C17	8¢ olive bistre (C12), Sept. 26, 1932	1.90	.20	45.00	(4)	20.00	76,648,803
	Issue of 1933, Century of Progress Issue, Oct. 2, Perf. 11						
C18	50¢ Zeppelin, Federal Building						
	at Chicago Exposition						
	and Hangar at Friedrichshafen	90.00	75.00	1,050.00	(6)	275.00	324,070
	Issue of 1934, Perf. 10½x11						
C19	6¢ dull orange (C12), June 30	2.25	.12	27.50	(4)	*200.00*	302,205,100
	Issue of 1935-37, Trans-Pacific Issue, Perf. 11						
C20	25¢ China Clipper over Pacific,						
	Nov. 22, 1935	1.10	.75	20.00	(6)	40.00	10,205,400
C21	20¢ China Clipper over Pacific,						
	Feb. 15, 1937	8.00	1.25	150.00	(6)	40.00	12,794,600
C22	50¢ carmine (C21), Feb. 15, 1937	7.75	3.25	140.00	(6)	40.00	9,285,300
	Issue of 1938						
C23	6¢ Eagle Holding Shield,						
	Olive Branch and Arrows, May 14	.50	.06	11.00	(4)	15.00	349,946,500

	Issue of 1939	Un	U	PB/LP	#	FDC	Q
	Trans-Atlantic Issue, May 16, Perf. 11						
C24	30¢ Winged Globe	6.00	1.25	200.00	(6)	45.00	19,768,150
	Issues of 1941-44, Perf. 11x10½						
C25	6¢ Twin-Motor Transport Plane, 1941	.12	.05	1.00	(4)	2.25	4,476,527,700
C25a	Booklet pane of 3, May 18, 1943	6.50	1.00			25.00	
	Singles of #C25a are imperf. at sides or imperf. at sides and bottom.						
C26	8¢ olive green (C25), Mar. 21, 1944	.16	.05	1.25	(4)	3.75	1,744,878,650
C27	10¢ violet (C25), Aug. 15, 1941	1.10	.20	12.50	(4)	10.00	67,117,400
C28	15¢ brown carmine (C25),						
	Aug. 19, 1941	2.25	.35	19.00	(4)	12.00	78,434,800
C29	20¢ bright green (C25), Aug. 27, 1941	1.65	.30	16.50	(4)	15.00	42,359,850
C30	30¢ blue (C25), Sept. 25, 1941	2.00	.30	17.50	(4)	22.50	59,880,850
C31	50¢ orange (C25), Oct. 29, 1941	10.00	4.00	100.00	(4)	45.00	11,160,600
	Issue of 1946						
C32	5¢ DC-4 Skymaster, Sept. 25	.10	.05	.75	(4)	2.00	864,753,100
	Issues of 1947, Perf. 10½x11						
C33	5¢ DC-4 Skymaster, Mar. 26	.10	.05	.75	(4)	2.00	971,903,700
	Perf. 11x10½						
C34	10¢ Pan American Union Building,						
	Washington, D.C. and Martin 2-0-2,						
	Aug. 30	.20	.06	2.25	(4)	2.00	207,976,550
C35	15¢ Statue of Liberty, N.Y. Skyline						
	and Lockheed Constellation, Aug. 20	.30	.05	2.50	(4)	2.75	756,186,350
C36	25¢ San Francisco-Oakland Bay Bridge						
	and Boeing Stratocruiser, July 30	.75	.12	8.00	(4)	3.75	132,956,100
	Issues of 1948, Coil Stamp, Perf. 10 Horizontally						
C37	5¢ carmine (C33), Jan. 15	.80	.75	13.50	(2)	2.00	
	Perf. 11x10½						
C38	5¢ New York City, July 31	.10	.10	13.50	(4)	1.75	38,449,100
	Issues of 1949, Perf. 10½x11						
C39	6¢ carmine (C33), Jan. 18	.12	.05	.90	(4)	1.50	5,070,095,200
C39a	Booklet pane of 6, Nov. 18	12.00	5.00			10.00	
	Perf. 11x10½						
C40	6¢ Alexandria, Virginia, May 11	.12	.10	.85	(4)	1.25	75,085,000
	Coil Stamp, Perf. 10 Horizontally						
C41	6¢ carmine (C33), Aug. 25	2.75	.05	20.00	(2)	1.25	
	Universal Postal Union Issue, Perf. 11x10½						
C42	10¢ Post Office Dept. Bldg., Nov. 18	.20	.20	2.50	(4)	1.75	21,061,300
C43	15¢ Globe and Doves						
	Carrying Messages, Oct. 7	.28	.28	2.50	(4)	2.25	36,613,100
C44	25¢ Boeing Stratocruiser						
	and Globe, Nov. 30	.48	.48	10.00	(4)	3.00	16,217,100
C45	6¢ Wright Brothers, Dec. 17	.14	.10	.85	(4)	4.25	80,405,000
	Issue of 1952						
C46	80¢ Diamond Head,						
	Honolulu, Hawaii, Mar. 26	6.00	1.50	50.00	(4)	17.50	18,876,800
	Issue of 1953						
C47	6¢ Powered Flight, May 29	.14	.10	.85	(4)	1.50	78,415,000

C24

C25

C32

C33

C34

C35

C36

C38

C40

C42

C43

C44

C45

C46

C47

C48

C49

C51

C53

C54

C55

C56

C57

C58

C59

C62

C63

C64

C66

C67

C69

C68

		Un	U	PB/LP	#	FDC	Q
	Issue of 1954, Perf. 11x10½						
C48	4¢ Eagle in Flight, Sept. 3	.08	.08	3.75	(4)	.75	50,483,977
	Issue of 1957						
C49	6¢ Air Force, Aug. 1	.12	.10	1.25	(4)	1.75	63,185,000
	Issues of 1958						
C50	5¢ rose red (C48), July 31	.14	.12	5.00	(4)	.80	72,480,000
	Perf. 10½x11						
C51	7¢ Jet Airliner, July 31	.14	.05	1.30	(4)	.75	1,326,960,000
C51a	Booklet pane of 6, July 31	15.00	6.50			9.50	
	Coil Stamp, Perf. 10 Horizontally						
C52	7¢ blue (C51), July 31	2.00	.10	22.50	(2)	.90	157,035,000
	Issues of 1959, Perf. 11x10½						
C53	7¢ Alaska Statehood, Jan. 3	.15	.12	1.50	(4)	.65	90,055,200
	Perf. 11						
C54	7¢ Balloon Jupiter, Aug. 17	.15	.12	1.50	(4)	1.10	79,290,000
	Perf. 11x10½						
C55	7¢ Hawaii Statehood, Aug. 21	.15	.12	1.50	(4)	1.00	84,815,000
	Perf. 11						
C56	10¢ Pan American Games, Aug. 27	.30	.30	3.00	(4)	.90	38,770,000
	Issue of 1959-60						
C57	10¢ Liberty Bell, June 10, 1960	1.50	1.00	14.00	(4)	1.25	39,960,000
C58	15¢ Statue of Liberty, Nov. 20, 1959	.40	.06	3.25	(4)	1.25	98,160,000
C59	25¢ Abraham Lincoln, Apr. 22, 1960	.50	.06	4.00	(4)	1.75	
	Issues of 1960, Perf. 10½x11						
C60	7¢ Jet Airliner, Aug. 12	.14	.05	1.50	(4)	.70	1,289,460,000
C60a	Booklet pane of 6, Aug. 19	20.00	7.00			9.50	
	Coil Stamp, Perf. 10 Horizontally						
C61	7¢ carmine (C60), Oct. 22	3.75	.25	50.00	(2)	1.00	87,140,000
	Issues of 1961, Perf. 11						
C62	13¢ Liberty Bell, June 28	.35	.10	3.50	(4)	.80	
C63	15¢ Statue of Liberty, Jan. 13	.30	.08	2.25	(4)	1.00	
	#C63 has a gutter between the two parts of the design; #C58 does not.						
	Issues of 1962, Perf. 10½x11						
C64	8¢ Jetliner over Capitol, Dec. 5	.18	.05	1.10	(4)	.60	
C64b	Booklet pane of 5 + label	7.50	1.25			2.00	
	Coil Stamp, Perf. 10 Horizontally						
C65	8¢ carmine (C64), Dec. 5	.35	.08	4.00	(2)	.80	
	Issues of 1963, Perf. 11						
C66	15¢ Montgomery Blair, May 3	.52	.50	6.00	(4)	1.35	42,245,000
	Perf. 11x10½						
C67	6¢ Bald Eagle, July 12	.12	.10	3.50	(4)	.50	
	Perf. 11						
C68	8¢ Amelia Earhart, July 24	.20	.15	2.50	(4)	2.75	63,890,000
	Issue of 1964						
C69	8¢ Robert H. Goddard, Oct. 5	.40	.15	4.00	(4)	2.75	62,255,000

A Reminder: Beginning with this edition, catalog values for all stamps listed reflect (as accurately as possible) actual retail values as found in the marketplace.

		Un	U	PB/LP	#	FDC	Q
	Issues of 1967, Perf. 11						
C70	8¢ Alaska Purchase, Mar. 30	.20	.20	3.50	(4)	.70	55,710,000
C71	20¢ "Columbia Jays," by Audubon,						
	Apr. 26 (see also #1241)	.80	.15	7.50	(4)	2.00	165,430,000
	Issues of 1968, Perf. 11x10½						
C72	10¢ 50-Star Runway, Jan. 5	.22	.05	2.25	(4)	.60	
C72b	Booklet pane of 8, Jan. 5	4.00	.75			3.00	
C72c	Booklet pane of 5 + label, Jan. 6	2.50	.75			115.00	
	Coil Stamp, Perf. 10 Vertically						
C73	10¢ carmine (C72), Jan. 5	.32	.05	3.50	(2)	.60	
	Perf. 11						
C74	10¢ U.S. Air Mail Service, May 15	.25	.15	5.00	(4)	1.50	
C75	20¢ USA and Jet, Nov. 22	.50	.06	4.25	(4)	1.10	
	Issue of 1969						
C76	10¢ Moon Landing, Sept. 9	.20	.15	1.75	(4)	3.50	152,364,800
	Issues of 1971-73, Perf. 10½x11, 11x10½						
C77	9¢ Plane, May 15, 1971	.16	.15	1.50	(4)	.50	
C78	11¢ Silhouette of Jet, May 7, 1971	.22	.05	1.75	(4)	.50	
C78a	Booklet pane of 4 + 2 labels,						
	May 7, 1971	1.50	.40			1.75	
C79	13¢ Winged Airmail Envelope,						
	Nov. 16, 1973	.22	.10	1.65	(4)	.55	
C79a	Booklet pane of 5 + label,						
	Dec. 27, 1973	1.35	.70			1.75	
	Perf. 11						
C80	17¢ Statue of Liberty, July 13, 1971	.35	.15	2.75	(4)	.60	
	Perf. 11x10½						
C81	21¢ USA and Jet, May 21, 1971	.38	.10	2.75	(4)	.75	
	Coil Stamps, Perf. 10 Vertically						
C82	11¢ Silhouette of Jet (C78),						
	May 7, 1971	.25	.06	2.25	(2)	.50	
C83	13¢ red (C79), Dec. 27, 1973	.28	.10	2.10	(2)	.50	
	Issues of 1972, National Parks Centennial Issue, May 3, Perf. 11 (see also #1448-54)						
C84	11¢ Kii Statue and Temple						
	at City of Refuge Historical National Park,						
	Honaunau, Hawaii	.20	.15	1.75	(4)	.65	78,210,000
	Olympic Games Issue, Aug. 17, Perf. 11x10½ (see also #1460-62)						
C85	11¢ Skiers and Olympic Rings	.22	.15	3.50	(10)	.50	96,240,000
	Issue of 1973, Progress in Electronics Issue, July 10, Perf. 11 (see also #1500-02)						
C86	11¢ De Forest Audions	.20	.15	1.75	(4)	.50	58,705,000
	Issues of 1974						
C87	18¢ Statue of Liberty, Jan. 11	.35	.35	2.50	(4)	.65	
C88	26¢ Mount Rushmore						
	National Memorial, Jan. 2	.45	.15	3.00	(4)	.85	
	Issues of Jan. 2, 1976						
C89	25¢ Plane and Globes	.45	.18	3.25	(4)	.85	
C90	31¢ Plane, Globes and Flag	.55	.10	3.25	(4)	.85	

C70

C71

C72

C74

C75

C76

C77

C78

C79

C80

C81

C84

C85

C86

C87

C88

C89

C90

C97

C98

C91 C92a C93 C94a C95 C96a
C92 C94 C96

C99 **C100**

C105 C106 C108a
C107 C108

C101 C102 C104a
C103 C104

C109 C110 C112a

		Un	U	PB	#	FDC	Q
	Issue of 1978, Wright Brothers Issue, Sept. 23, Perf. 11						
C91	31¢ Orville and Wilbur Wright						
	and Flyer A	.65	.15			1.15	157,445,000
C92	31¢ Wright Brothers,						
	Flyer A and Shed	.65	.15			1.15	157,445,000
C92a	Attached pair, #C91-C92	1.40	1.25	4.50	(4)	2.30	
	Issues of 1979, Octave Chanute Issue, March 29						
C93	21¢ Chanute and Biplane Hang-Glider	.85	.32			1.00	29,012,500
C94	21¢ Biplane Hang-Glider and Chanute	.85	.32			1.00	29,012,500
C94a	Attached pair, #C93-C94	1.75	.75	6.50	(4)	2.00	
	Wiley Post Issue, Nov. 20						
C95	25¢ Wiley Post and "Winnie Mae"	1.15	.35			1.00	32,005,000
C96	25¢ NR-105-W,						
	Post in Pressurized Suit and Portrait	1.15	.35			1.00	32,005,000
C96a	Attached pair, #C95-C96	2.50	.85	12.50	(4)	2.00	
	Olympic Summer Games Issue, Nov. 1 (see also #1790-94)						
C97	31¢ High Jumper	.70	.30	12.00	(12)	1.15	47,200,000
	Issues of 1980						
C98	40¢ Philip Mazzei, Oct. 13	.75	.30	12.00	(12)	1.35	80,935,000
C99	28¢ Blanche Stuart Scott, Dec. 30	.55	.15	9.25	(12)	1.10	20,190,000
C100	35¢ Glenn Curtiss, Dec. 30	.65	.15	10.00	(12)	1.25	22,945,000
	Issues of 1983, Olympic Summer Games Issue, June 17, Perf. 11 (see also #2048-51, 2082-85)						
C101	28¢ Gymnast	.56	.28			1.10	42,893,750
C102	28¢ Hurdler	.56	.28			1.10	42,893,750
C103	28¢ Basketball Player	.56	.28			1.10	42,893,750
C104	28¢ Soccer Player	.56	.28	3.75	(4)	1.10	42,893,750
C104a	Block of 4, #C101-C104	2.75	1.75			3.75	
	Olympic Summer Games Issue, April 8 (see also #2048-51 and 2082-85)						
C105	40¢ Shotputter	.80	.40			1.35	66,573,750
C106	40¢ Gymnast	.80	.40			1.35	66,573,750
C107	40¢ Swimmer	.80	.40			1.35	66,573,750
C108	40¢ Weightlifter	.80	.40	5.25	(4)	1.35	66,573,750
C108a	Block of 4, #C105-C108	3.75	2.00			5.00	
	Olympic Summer Games Issue, Nov. 4 (see also #2048-51 and 2082-85)						
C109	35¢ Fencer	.70	.35			1.25	42,587,500
C110	35¢ Bicyclist	.70	.35			1.25	42,587,500
C111	35¢ Volleyball Players	.70	.35			1.25	42,587,500
C112	35¢ Pole Vaulter	.70	.35	5.00	(4)	1.25	42,587,500
C112a	Block of 4, #C109-C112	3.25	1.85			4.50	

	Issues of 1985, Perf. 11	Un	U	PB	#	FDC	Q
C113	33¢ Alfred V. Verville, Feb. 13	.66	.20	3.50	(4)	1.25	168,125,000
C114	39¢ Lawrence & Elmer Sperry,						
	Feb. 13	.78	.20	4.00	(4)	1.35	167,825,000
C115	44¢ Transpacific Airmail, Feb. 15	.88	.20	4.50	(4)	1.35	209,025,000
C116	44¢ Junipero Serra, Aug. 22	1.00	.20	6.50	(4)	1.35	164,350,000
	Issues of 1988						
C117	44¢ New Sweden, Mar. 29	.88	.20	4.50	(4)	1.35	136,900,000
C118	45¢ Samuel P. Langley, May 14	.90	.20	4.50	(4)	1.40	
C119	36¢ Igor Sikorsky, June 23	.72	.20	3.60	(4)	1.30	
	Airmail Special Delivery Stamps						
	Issue of 1934						
CE1	16¢ Great Seal						
	of the United States, Aug. 30	.65	.85	20.00	(6)	25.00	
	For imperforate variety see #771.						
	Issue of 1936						
CE2	16¢ carmine and blue						
	Great Seal of the United States, Feb. 10	.40	.25	8.50	(4)	17.50	

SPERRYS INSTRUMENTAL IN STABILIZING AIRCRAFT
American inventor Elmer Ambrose Sperry (1860-1930) greatly improved aircraft navigation. In collaboration with his son, Lawrence (1892-1937), Sperry developed a gyroscopic stabilizer used to keep airplanes steady in flight (#C114).

C113

C114

C115

C116

C117

C118

C119

CE1

E1 **E3** **E4**

E6 **E7** **E12**

E13 **E14**

E17 **E18**

E20 **E21**

E22 **E23**

	Special Delivery Stamps	Un	U	PB	#	FDC
	Issue of 1885, Oct. 1, Unwmkd., Perf. 12					
E1	10¢ Messenger Running	175.00	20.00	*12,000.00*	(8)	*8,000.00*
	Issue of 1888, Sept. 6					
E2	10¢ blue Messenger Running (E3)	175.00	5.00	*12,000.00*	(8)	
	Issue of 1893, Jan. 24					
E3	10¢ Messenger Running	110.00	11.00	*7,250.00*	(8)	
	Issue of 1894, Line under "Ten Cents," Oct. 10					
E4	10¢ Messenger Running	450.00	12.50	*14,500.00*	(6)	
	Issue of 1895, Aug. 16, Wmkd. (191)					
E5	10¢ blue Messenger Running (E4)	85.00	1.50	*4,500.00*	(6)	
	Issue of 1902, Dec. 9					
E6	10¢ Messenger on Bicycle	52.50	1.50	*2,750.00*	(6)	
	Issue of 1908, Dec. 12					
E7	10¢ Mercury Helmet and Olive Branch	57.50	21.00	925.00	(6)	
	Issue of 1911, Jan., Wmkd. (190)					
E8	10¢ ultramarine					
	Messenger on Bicycle (E6)	55.00	2.25	*2,750.00*	(6)	
	Issue of 1914, Sept., Perf. 10					
E9	10¢ ultramarine					
	Messenger on Bicycle (E6)	110.00	2.50	*5,000.00*	(6)	
	Issue of 1916, Oct. 19, Unwmkd.					
E10	10¢ ultramarine					
	Messenger on Bicycle (E6)	200.00	12.50	6,250.00	(6)	
	Issue of 1917, May 2, Perf. 11					
E11	10¢ ultramarine					
	Messenger on Bicycle (E6)	10.00	.20	200.00	(6)	
	Issue of 1922, July 12					
E12	10¢ Postman and Motorcycle	18.00	.15	375.00	(6)	500.00
	Issues of 1925					
E13	15¢ Postman and Motorcycle, Apr. 11	15.00	.40	250.00	(6)	250.00
E14	20¢ Post Office Truck, Apr. 25	1.90	.85	37.50	(6)	125.00
	Issue of 1927, Nov. 29, Perf. 11x10½					
E15	10¢ gray violet					
	Postman and Motorcycle (E12)	.60	.05	6.50	(4)	90.00
	Issue of 1931, Aug. 13					
E16	15¢ orange Postman and Motorcycle (E16)	.70	.08	5.50	(4)	125.00
	Issues of 1944, Oct. 30					
E17	13¢ Postman and Motorcycle	.60	.06	4.00	(4)	12.00
E18	17¢ Postman and Motorcycle	2.75	1.25	28.50	(4)	12.00
	Issue of 1951, Nov. 30					
E19	20¢ black Post Office Truck (E14)	1.50	.12	10.00	(4)	5.00
	Issues of 1954-57					
E20	20¢ Delivery of Letter, Oct. 13, 1954	.38	.08	4.00	(4)	3.00
E21	30¢ Delivery of Letter, Sept. 3, 1957	.48	.05	5.00	(4)	2.25
	Issues of 1969-71, Perf. 11					
E22	45¢ Arrows, Nov. 21, 1969	.90	.12	11.50	(4)	3.50
E23	60¢ Arrows, May 10, 1971	.85	.10	6.00	(4)	3.50

> **A Reminder:** Beginning with this edition, catalog values for all stamps listed reflect (as accurately as possible) actual retail values as found in the marketplace.

1879-1959

F1

FA1

J2

J19

J25

J33

J69

J78

J88

J98

J101

Registration Stamp

Issued for the prepayment of registry; not usable for postage. Sale discontinued May 28, 1913.

	Issue of 1911, Wmkd. (190), Perf. 12	Un	U	PB	#	FDC	Q
F1	10¢ Bald Eagle, Dec. 1	55.00	2.25	1,850.00	(6)	8,000.00	

Certified Mail Stamp

For use on First-Class mail for which no indemnity value was claimed, but for which proof of mailing and proof of delivery were available at less cost than registered mail.

	Issue of 1955, Perf. 10½x11						
FA1	15¢ Letter Carrier, June 6	.28	.20	6.25	(4)	3.25	54,460,300

Postage Due Stamps

For affixing by a postal clerk to any mail to denote amount to be collected from addressee because of insufficient prepayment of postage.

	Issues of 1879, Printed by American Bank Note Co., Design of J2, Perf. 12, Unwmkd.	Un	U
J1	1¢ brown	30.00	5.00
J2	2¢ Figure of Value	200.00	4.00
J3	3¢ brown	25.00	2.50
J4	5¢ brown	300.00	25.00
J5	10¢ brown, Sept. 19	350.00	12.50
J6	30¢ brown, Sept. 19	175.00	20.00
J7	50¢ brown, Sept. 19	225.00	30.00
	Special Printing, Soft, Porous Paper		
J8	1¢ deep brown	5,750.00	—
J9	2¢ deep brown	3,750.00	—
J10	3¢ deep brown	3,500.00	—
J11	5¢ deep brown	3,000.00	—
J12	10¢ deep brown	1,850.00	—
J13	30¢ deep brown	1,850.00	—
J14	50¢ deep brown	2,000.00	—

	Issues of 1884-89, Design of J19	Un	U
J15	1¢ red brown	30.00	2.50
J16	2¢ red brown	37.50	2.50
J17	3¢ red brown	500.00	100.00
J18	5¢ red brown	250.00	12.50
J19	10¢ Figure of Value, Mar. 15, 1887	225.00	7.00
J20	30¢ red brown	110.00	22.50
J21	50¢ red brown	1,000.00	125.00
	Issues of 1891, Design of J25		
J22	1¢ bright claret	12.50	.50
J23	2¢ bright claret	15.00	.45
J24	3¢ bright claret	27.50	4.00
J25	5¢ Figure of Value	35.00	4.00
J26	10¢ bright claret	70.00	10.00
J27	30¢ bright claret	250.00	85.00
J28	50¢ bright claret	275.00	85.00
	Issues of 1894, Printed by the Bureau of Engraving and Printing, Design of J33, Perf. 12		
J29	1¢ vermilion	575.00	100.00
J30	2¢ vermilion	250.00	50.00

	Issues of 1894-95, Design of J33, Perf. 12, Unwmkd.	Un	U	PB	#
J31	1¢ deep claret, Aug. 14, 1894	20.00	3.00	375.00	(6)
J32	2¢ deep claret, July 20, 1894	15.00	1.75	325.00	(6)
J33	3¢ Figure of Value, Apr. 27, 1895	75.00	20.00	850.00	(6)
J34	5¢ deep claret, Apr. 27, 1895	100.00	22.50	950.00	(6)
J35	10¢ deep rose, Sept. 24, 1894	85.00	17.50	950.00	(6)
J36	30¢ deep claret, Apr. 27, 1895	255.00	50.00	2,100.00	(6)
J37	50¢ deep claret, Apr. 27, 1895	500.00	120.00	5,000.00	(6)
	Issues of 1895-97, Design of J33, Wmkd. (191)				
J38	1¢ deep claret, Aug. 29, 1895	5.00	.30	190.00	(6)
J39	2¢ deep claret, Sept. 14, 1895	5.00	.20	190.00	(6)
J40	3¢ deep claret, Oct. 30, 1895	35.00	1.00	425.00	(6)
J41	5¢ deep claret, Oct. 15, 1895	37.50	1.00	450.00	(6)
J42	10¢ deep claret, Sept. 14, 1895	40.00	2.00	550.00	(6)
J43	30¢ deep claret, Aug. 21, 1897	300.00	22.50	3,750.00	(6)
J44	50¢ deep claret, Mar. 17, 1896	190.00	20.00	2,250.00	(6)
	Issues of 1910-12, Design of J33, Wmkd. (190)				
J45	1¢ deep claret, Aug. 30, 1910	20.00	2.00	400.00	(6)
J46	2¢ deep claret, Nov. 25, 1910	20.00	.15	350.00	(6)
J47	3¢ deep claret, Aug. 31, 1910	350.00	17.50	3,850.00	(6)
J48	5¢ deep claret, Aug. 31, 1910	60.00	3.50	600.00	(6)
J49	10¢ deep claret, Aug. 31, 1910	75.00	7.50	1,150.00	(6)
J50	50¢ deep claret, Sept. 23, 1912	600.00	75.00	7,500.00	(6)
	Issues of 1914-15, Design of J33, Perf. 10				
J52	1¢ carmine lake	40.00	7.50	550.00	(6)
J53	2¢ carmine lake	32.50	.20	350.00	(6)
J54	3¢ carmine lake	425.00	20.00	4,500.00	(6)
J55	5¢ carmine lake	25.00	1.50	285.00	(6)
J56	10¢ carmine lake	40.00	1.00	600.00	(6)
J57	30¢ carmine lake	140.00	12.00	2,100.00	(6)
J58	50¢ carmine lake	*5,500.00*	375.00	*40,000.00*	(6)
	Issues of 1916, Design of J33, Unwmkd.				
J59	1¢ rose	1,100.00	175.00	8,750.00	(6)
J60	2¢ rose	85.00	10.00	800.00	(6)
	Issues of 1917, Design of J33, Perf. 11				
J61	1¢ carmine rose	1.75	.08	40.00	(6)
J62	2¢ carmine rose	1.50	.05	35.00	(6)
J63	3¢ carmine rose	8.50	.08	100.00	(6)
J64	5¢ carmine	8.50	.08	85.00	(6)
J65	10¢ carmine rose	12.50	.20	125.00	(6)
J66	30¢ carmine rose	55.00	.40	525.00	(6)
J67	50¢ carmine rose	75.00	.12	750.00	(6)

	Issue of 1925, Design of J33	Un	U	PB	#
J68	½¢ dull red, Apr. 13	.65	.06	11.00	(6)
	Issues of 1930-31, Design of J69				
J69	½¢ Figure of Value	2.00	.70	35.00	(6)
J70	1¢ carmine	2.50	.15	27.50	(6)
J71	2¢ carmine	2.00	.15	40.00	(6)
J72	3¢ carmine	12.50	1.00	250.00	(6)
J73	5¢ carmine	13.00	1.50	225.00	(6)
J74	10¢ carmine	30.00	.50	425.00	(6)
J75	30¢ carmine	85.00	1.00	1,000.00	(6)
J76	50¢ carmine	100.00	.30	1,250.00	(6)
	Design of J78				
J77	$1 carmine	20.00	.06	275.00	(6)
J78	$5 "FIVE" on $	27.50	.12	375.00	(6)
	Issues of 1931-56, Design of J69, Perf. 11x10½				
J79	½¢ dull carmine	1.00	.08	22.50	(4)
J80	1¢ dull carmine	.15	.05	2.00	(4)
J81	2¢ dull carmine	.15	.05	2.00	(4)
J82	3¢ dull carmine	.25	.05	3.00	(4)
J83	5¢ dull carmine	.35	.05	4.00	(4)
J84	10¢ dull carmine	1.10	.05	8.50	(4)
J85	30¢ dull carmine	8.50	.08	45.00	(4)
J86	50¢ dull carmine	9.50	.06	57.50	(4)
	Design of J78, Perf. 10½x11				
J87	$1 scarlet	40.00	.20	300.00	(4)
	Issues of 1959, June 19, Design of J88 and J98, Perf. 11x10½				
J88	½¢ Figure of Value	1.25	.85	150.00	(4)
J89	1¢ carmine rose	.05	.05	.50	(4)
J90	2¢ carmine rose	.06	.05	.60	(4)
J91	3¢ carmine rose	.07	.05	.70	(4)
J92	4¢ carmine rose	.08	.05	1.25	(4)
J93	5¢ carmine rose	.10	.05	.75	(4)
J94	6¢ carmine rose	.12	.05	1.40	(4)
J95	7¢ carmine rose	.14	.06	1.60	(4)
J96	8¢ carmine rose	.16	.05	1.75	(4)
J97	10¢ carmine rose	.20	.05	1.25	(4)
J98	30¢ Figure of Value	.70	.05	5.50	(4)
J99	50¢ carmine rose	1.10	.05	6.50	(4)
	Design of J101				
J100	$1 carmine rose	2.00	.05	10.00	(4)
J101	$5 Outline Figure of Value	8.00	.15	40.00	(4)
	Issues of 1978-85, Design of J88 and J98				
J102	11¢ carmine rose, Jan. 2, 1978	.22	.05	3.50	(4)
J103	13¢ carmine rose, Jan. 2, 1978	.26	.05	3.00	(4)
J104	17¢ carmine rose, June 10, 1985	.34	.05	12.50	(4)

OFFICIAL AND PENALTY MAIL STAMPS

1873-1988

07

O14

O18

O34

O44

O52

O57

O71

O76

O91

O121

O127

O129A

O132

O135

O136

O138

O139

O140

Official Stamps

The franking privilege having been abolished as of July 1, 1873, these stamps were provided for each of the departments of government for the prepayment on official matter.

These stamps were supplanted on May 1, 1879 by penalty envelopes and on July 5, 1884 were declared obsolete.

Issues of 1873
Printed by the Continental Bank Note Co., Thin Hard Paper, Perf. 12, Unwmkd. Department of Agriculture: Yellow

		Un	U
O1	1¢ Franklin	65.00	30.00
O2	2¢ Jackson	45.00	13.50
O3	3¢ Washington	40.00	3.50
O4	6¢ Lincoln	50.00	12.50
O5	10¢ Jefferson	110.00	47.50
O6	12¢ Clay	140.00	70.00
O7	15¢ Webster	110.00	47.50
O8	24¢ Scott	125.00	55.00
O9	30¢ Hamilton	165.00	85.00

Executive Dept.: Carmine

O10	1¢ Franklin	250.00	85.00
O11	2¢ Jackson	165.00	70.00
O12	3¢ Washington	190.00	65.00
O13	6¢ Lincoln	300.00	140.00
O14	10¢ Jefferson	275.00	140.00

Dept. of the Interior: Vermilion

O15	1¢ Franklin	17.50	3.50
O16	2¢ Jackson	15.00	2.00
O17	3¢ Washington	22.50	2.00
O18	6¢ Lincoln	17.50	2.00
O19	10¢ Jefferson	16.00	5.00
O20	12¢ Clay	25.00	4.00
O21	15¢ Webster	40.00	10.00
O22	24¢ Scott	30.00	7.00
O23	30¢ Hamilton	40.00	8.00
O24	90¢ Perry	90.00	15.00

Dept. of Justice: Purple

O25	1¢ Franklin	40.00	17.50
O26	2¢ Jackson	65.00	20.00
O27	3¢ Washington	65.00	8.00
O28	6¢ Lincoln	60.00	11.00
O29	10¢ Jefferson	70.00	25.00
O30	12¢ Clay	50.00	14.00
O31	15¢ Webster	110.00	47.50
O32	24¢ Scott	300.00	120.00
O33	30¢ Hamilton	275.00	85.00
O34	90¢ Perry	400.00	175.00

		Un	U
	Navy Dept.: Ultramarine		
O35	1¢ Franklin	35.00	10.00
O36	2¢ Jackson	25.00	9.00
O37	3¢ Washington	27.50	4.00
O38	6¢ Lincoln	25.00	6.00
O39	7¢ Stanton	165.00	65.00
O40	10¢ Jefferson	35.00	11.00
O41	12¢ Clay	45.00	10.00
O42	15¢ Webster	75.00	25.00
O43	24¢ Scott	75.00	30.00
O44	30¢ Hamilton	65.00	15.00
O45	90¢ Perry	300.00	80.00

Post Office Dept.: Black

O47	1¢ Figure of Value	7.25	3.00
O48	2¢ Figure of Value	7.00	2.50
O49	3¢ Figure of Value	2.50	.75
O50	6¢ Figure of Value	8.00	1.65
O51	10¢ Figure of Value	40.00	16.50
O52	12¢ Figure of Value	22.50	5.00
O53	15¢ Figure of Value	25.00	8.50
O54	24¢ Figure of Value	32.50	10.00
O55	30¢ Figure of Value	32.50	9.00
O56	90¢ Figure of Value	47.50	12.50

Dept. of State: Green

O57	1¢ Franklin	42.50	13.00
O58	2¢ Jackson	85.00	25.00
O59	3¢ Washington	32.50	9.00
O60	6¢ Lincoln	32.50	9.00
O61	7¢ Stanton	60.00	18.50
O62	10¢ Jefferson	50.00	15.00
O63	12¢ Clay	75.00	27.50
O64	15¢ Webster	70.00	20.00
O65	24¢ Scott	175.00	75.00
O66	30¢ Hamilton	160.00	60.00
O67	90¢ Perry	300.00	125.00
O68	$2 green and black		
	Seward	550.00	250.00
O69	$5 green and black		
	Seward	4,250.00	2,000.00
O70	$10 green and black		
	Seward	2,750.00	1,300.00
O71	$20 Seward	2,250.00	1,100.00

1873 continued, Perf. 12	Un	U
Treasury Dept.: Brown		
O72 1¢ Franklin	17.50	1.75
O73 2¢ Jackson	20.00	1.75
O74 3¢ Washington	12.50	1.00
O75 6¢ Lincoln	17.50	1.00
O76 7¢ Stanton	42.50	12.50
O77 10¢ Jefferson	42.50	4.50
O78 12¢ Clay	42.50	3.00
O79 15¢ Webster	37.50	4.50
O80 24¢ Scott	185.00	60.00
O81 30¢ Hamilton	62.00	5.00
O82 90¢ Perry	67.50	5.00
War Dept.: Rose		
O83 1¢ Franklin	60.00	4.00
O84 2¢ Jackson	55.00	6.00
O85 3¢ Washington	50.00	1.50
O86 6¢ Lincoln	240.00	4.00
O87 7¢ Stanton	52.50	30.00
O88 10¢ Jefferson	19.00	5.00
O89 12¢ Clay	52.50	4.00
O90 15¢ Webster	15.00	2.50
O91 24¢ Scott	15.00	3.00
O92 30¢ Hamilton	17.50	2.50
O93 90¢ Perry	40.00	12.50

Issues of 1879
Printed by the American Bank Note Co., Soft, Porous Paper
Dept. of Agriculture: Yellow

O94 1¢ Franklin, issued		
without gum	1,350.00	
O95 3¢ Washington	125.00	37.50
Dept. of the Interior: Vermilion		
O96 1¢ Franklin	125.00	65.00
O97 2¢ Jackson	2.50	.75
O98 3¢ Washington	2.00	.60
O99 6¢ Lincoln	3.00	1.00
O100 10¢ Jefferson	32.50	17.50
O101 12¢ Clay	65.00	30.00
O102 15¢ Webster	150.00	70.00
O103 24¢ Scott	1,200.00	
Dept. of Justice: Bluish Purple		
O106 3¢ Washington	50.00	17.50
O107 6¢ Lincoln	110.00	60.00
Post Office Dept.: Black		
O108 3¢ Figure of Value	7.50	1.40
Treasury Dept.: Brown		
O109 3¢ Washington	27.50	3.50
O110 6¢ Lincoln	50.00	17.50
O111 10¢ Jefferson	65.00	15.00
O112 30¢ Hamilton	750.00	135.00
O113 90¢ Perry	775.00	135.00

	Un	U
War Dept.: Rose Red		
O114 1¢ Franklin	2.00	.75
O115 2¢ Jackson	3.00	1.00
O116 3¢ Washington	3.00	.65
O117 6¢ Lincoln	2.50	.70
O118 10¢ Jefferson	20.00	6.00
O119 12¢ Clay	15.00	3.00
O120 30¢ Hamilton	47.50	25.00

Official Postal Savings Mail
These stamps were used to prepay postage on official correspondence of the Postal Savings Division of the Post Office Department.
Discontinued Sept. 23, 1914.

Issues of 1911, Perf. 12, Wmkd. (191)		
O121 2¢ Postal Savings	9.00	1.10
O122 50¢ dark green		
Postal Savings	110.00	32.50
O123 $1 ultramarine		
Postal Savings	100.00	9.50
Wmkd. (190)		
O124 1¢ dark violet		
Postal Savings	4.00	1.00
O125 2¢ black		
Postal Savings	30.00	3.50
O126 10¢ carmine		
Postal Savings	8.50	1.00

Penalty Mail Stamps
Stamps for use by government departments were reinstituted in 1983. Now known as Penalty Mail stamps, they help provide a better accounting of actual mail costs for official departments and agencies, etc.

Issues of 1983-88, Perf. 11 x 10½, Unwmkd.		
O127 1¢, Jan. 12, 1983	.05	
O128 4¢, Jan. 12, 1983	.08	
O129 13¢, Jan. 12, 1983	.26	
O129A 14¢, May 15, 1985	.28	
O130 17¢, Jan. 12, 1983	.34	
O131 not assigned.		
O132 $1, Jan. 12, 1983	1.75	
O133 $5, Jan. 12, 1983	9.00	
O134 not assigned.		
Coil Stamps, Perf. 10 Vertically		
O135 20¢, Jan. 12, 1983	2.00	.40
O136 22¢, May 15, 1985	.44	
O137 not assigned.		
Perf. 11		
O138 (14¢) D Stamp, Feb. 4, 1985	3.00	
Coil Stamps, Perf. 10 Vertically		
O138A 15¢, June 11, 1988	.30	
O138B 20¢, May 19, 1988	.40	
O139 (22¢) D Stamp, Feb. 4, 1985	3.00	
O140 (25¢) E Stamp, Mar. 22, 1988	.50	
O141 25¢, June 11, 1988	.50	

Newspaper, Parcel Post and Special Handling Stamps

PR1   PR2   PR3

Newspaper Stamps

A total of 125 Newspaper Stamps were issued between 1865 and 1897. Represented is a partial listing of those issues.

	Issues of 1865 **Printed by the National Bank Note Co.,** **Thin, Hard Paper, No Gum, Perf. 12,** **Unwmkd., Colored** **Borders**	Un	U
PR1	5¢ Washington	150.00	

	White Border, **Yellowish Paper**	Un	U
PR4	5¢ light blue (PR1)	35.00	30.00
	Reprints of 1875 **Printed by the Continental Bank Note Co.,** **Hard, White Paper, No Gum**		
PR5	5¢ dull blue (PR1),		
	white border	60.00	
PR6	10¢ dark bluish green		

PR15   **PR18**   **PR24**   **PR25**   **PR26**

PR28   **PR29**   **PR30**   **PR78**   **PR79**

Issue of 1875
Printed by the Continental Bank Note Co., Thin, Hard Paper

		Un	U
PR9	2¢ black (PR15)	12.50	11.00
PR10	3¢ black (PR15)	16.00	14.00
PR14	9¢ black (PR15)	55.00	55.00
PR15	10¢ Statue of Freedom	75.00	20.00
PR16	12¢ rose (PR18)	55.00	40.00
PR18	36¢ "Commerce"	72.50	50.00
PR21	72¢ rose (PR18)	165.00	110.00
PR24	$1.92 Ceres	130.00	90.00
PR25	$3 "Victory"	240.00	135.00
PR26	$6 Clio	400.00	165.00
PR28	$12 Vesta	500.00	250.00
PR29	$24 "Peace"	650.00	325.00
PR30	$36 "Commerce"	675.00	375.00

Special Printing, Hard, White Paper, Without Gum

PR33	2¢ gray black (PR15)	70.00	
PR34	3¢ gray black (PR15)	75.00	

Issue of 1879
Printed by the American Bank Note Co., Soft, Porous Paper

		Un	U
PR57	2¢ black (PR15)	6.00	4.5
PR58	3¢ black (PR15)	7.50	5.0
PR59	4¢ black (PR15)	7.50	5.0
PR60	6¢ black (PR15)	15.00	11.0
PR61	8¢ gray black (PR15)	15.00	11.0
PR62	10¢ black (PR15)	15.00	11.0
PR63	12¢ red (PR15)	45.00	25.0
PR64	24¢ red (PR18)	45.00	22.5
PR65	36¢ red (PR18)	150.00	95.0
PR66	48¢ red	115.00	60.0
PR67	60¢ red (PR18)	85.00	60.0
PR68	72¢ red (PR18)	185.00	115.0
PR69	84¢ red (PR18)	140.00	85.0
PR70	96¢ red (PR18)	100.00	60.0
PR71	$1.92 pale brn. (PR24)	80.00	55.0
PR72	$3 red vermilion (PR25)	80.00	55.0
PR73	$6 blue (PR26)	114.00	90.0

PR116

PR118

PR119

PR120

PR121

PR122

PR123

PR124

PR125

		Un		U
	Issue of 1883			
	Special Printing			
PR80	2¢ intense blk. (PR15)	175.00		
	Issue of 1885			
	Printed by the American Bank Note Co.			
PR81	1¢ black (PR15)	8.50		5.00
PR82	12¢ carmine (PR18)	27.50		12.50
PR83	24¢ carmine (PR18)	30.00		15.00
PR84	36¢ carmine (PR18)	42.50		17.50
PR85	48¢ carmine (PR18)	60.00		30.00
PR87	72¢ carmine (PR18)	95.00		45.00
PR88	84¢ carmine (PR18)	140.00		85.00

All values of the 1885 issue exist imperforate but were not regularly issued.

	Issue of 1894		
	Printed by the Bureau of Engraving and Printing, Soft Wove Paper		
PR90	1¢ intense blk. (PR15)	42.50	
PR91	2¢ intense blk. (PR15)	42.50	
PR92	4¢ intense blk. (PR15)	60.00	
PR94	10¢ intense blk. (PR15)	110.00	
PR95	12¢ pink (PR18)	500.00	
PR96	24¢ pink (PR18)	400.00	
PR97	36¢ pink (PR18)	2,750.00	
PR98	60¢ pink (PR18)	2,750.00	
PR100	$3 scarlet (PR25)	5,500.00	
PR101	$6 pale blue (PR26)	6,250.00	

	Issue of 1895, Unwmkd.		
PR102	1¢ black (PR116)	25.00	7.50
PR103	2¢ black (PR116)	25.00	7.50
PR104	5¢ black (PR116)	35.00	12.50

		Un	U
PR105	10¢ black (PR116)	75.00	32.50
PR106	25¢ carmine (PR118)	100.00	35.00
PR107	50¢ carmine (PR118)	235.00	95.00
PR108	$2 scarlet (PR120)	275.00	65.00
PR109	$5 ultramarine (PR121)	375.00	150.00
PR110	$10 green	350.00	165.00
PR111	$20 slate	675.00	300.00
PR112	$50 dull rose (PR124)	700.00	300.00
PR113	$100 purple (PR125)	775.00	350.00
	Issue of 1895-97		
	Wmkd. (191), Yellowish Gum		
PR114	1¢ black (PR116)	3.50	2.00
PR115	2¢ black (PR116)	4.00	1.50
PR116	5¢ State of Freedom		
	on Capitol Dome	6.00	5.00
PR117	10¢ black (PR116)	4.00	3.50
PR118	25¢ "Justice"	8.00	8.00
PR119	50¢ "Justice"	8.00	3.50
PR120	$2 "Victory"	12.00	15.00
PR121	$5 Clio	20.00	25.00
PR122	$10 Vesta	20.00	25.00
PR123	$20 "Peace"	20.00	27.50
PR124	$50 "Commerce"	25.00	30.00
PR125	$100 Indian Maiden	30.00	37.50

In 1899, the Government sold 26,989 sets of these stamps, but because the stock of the high values was not sufficient to make up the required number, the $5, $10, $20, $50 and $100 were reprinted. These are virtually indistinguishable from earlier printings.

Parcel Post Stamps

Issued for the prepayment of postage on parcel post packages only.

Beginning July 1, 1913 these stamps were valid for all postal purposes.

	Issue of 1912-13, Perf. 12, Wmkd. (190)	Un	U
Q1	1¢ Post Office Clerk,		
	Nov. 27, 1912	2.75	.90
Q2	2¢ City Carrier,		
	Nov. 27, 1912	3.25	.70
Q3	3¢ Railway Postal Clerk,		
	Apr. 5, 1913	6.50	5.00
Q4	4¢ Rural Carrier,		
	Dec. 12, 1912	17.50	2.00
Q5	5¢ Mail Train,		
	Nov. 27, 1912	13.50	1.25
Q6	10¢ Steamship		
	and Mail Tender,		
	Dec. 9, 1912	25.00	1.75
Q7	15¢ Automobile Service,		
	Dec. 16, 1912	40.00	9.00
Q8	20¢ Aeroplane Carrying		
	Mail, Dec. 16, 1912	90.00	17.50
Q9	25¢ Manufacturing,		
	Nov. 27, 1912	40.00	4.50
Q10	50¢ Dairying,		
	Mar. 15, 1913	175.00	35.00
Q11	75¢ Harvesting,		
	Dec. 18, 1912	55.00	30.00
Q12	$1 Fruit Growing,		
	Jan. 3, 1913	300.00	20.00

Special Handling Stamps

For use on parcel post packages to secure the same expeditious handling accorded to First-class mail matter.

	Issue of 1925-29, Perf. 11	Un	U
QE1	10¢ Special Handling,		
	June 25, 1928	1.25	.90
QE2	15¢ Special Handling,		
	June 25, 1928	1.40	.90
QE3	20¢ Special Handling,		
	June 25, 1928	2.25	1.75
QE4	25¢ Special Handling,		
	1929	15.00	7.50
QE4a	25¢ deep green,		
	April 11, 1925	25.00	4.50

Parcel Post Postage Due Stamps

For affixing by a postal clerk to any parcel post package to denote the amount to be collected from the addressee because of insufficient prepayment of postage.

Beginning July 1, 1913 these stamps were valid for use as regular postage due stamps.

	Issues of 1912, Design of JQ1 and JQ5, Perf. 12, Wkmd. (190)		
JQ1	1¢ Figure of Value,		
	Nov. 27	5.00	3.00
JQ2	2¢ dark green,		
	Dec. 9	40.00	15.00
JQ3	5¢ dark green,		
	Nov. 27	6.00	3.50
JQ4	10¢ dark green,		
	Dec. 12	110.00	35.00
JQ5	25¢ Figure of Value,		
	Dec. 16	50.00	3.50

A Reminder: Beginning with this edition, catalog values for all stamps listed reflect (as accurately as possible) actual retail values as found in the marketplace.

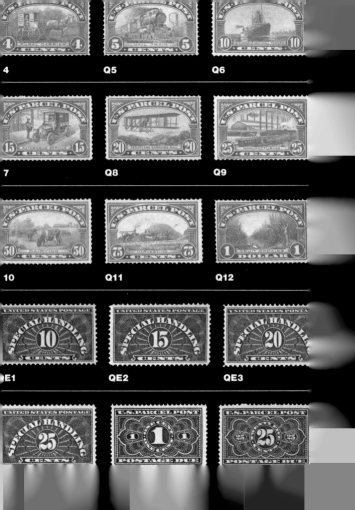

U172

U348

U523

U576

U609

UC14

Represented below is only a partial listing of stamped envelopes. Values are for cut squares. Prices for entire envelopes are higher. Color in italics is the color of the envelope paper.

		Un	U
1853-1871			
U1	3¢ red Washington,		
	die 1, *white*	175.00	15.00
U6	3¢ red, die 3, *buff*	125.00	25.00
U9	3¢ red, die 5, *white*	15.00	1.50
U13	6¢ green, *white*	165.00	85.00
U18	10¢ grn., die 2, *buff*	90.00	50.00
U19	1¢ blue, die 1, *buff*	22.50	10.00
U34	3¢ pink, *white*	14.00	4.00
U39	3¢ pink, *buff*	55.00	55.00
U42	12¢ red and brown, *buff*	175.00	140.00
U52	2¢ black Jackson,		

		Un	U
U84	3¢ green Washington,		
	cream	6.50	2.5
U97	15¢ red orange		
	Webster, *white*	140.00	175.0
1874-86			
U109	1¢ light blue Franklin,		
	die 2, *orange*	.40	.3
U147	2¢ vermilion Jackson,		
	die 5, *fawn*	5.00	3.5
U163	3¢ green Washington,		
	die 2, *white*	.75	.2
U166	3¢ green, die 2, *blue*	5.00	3.0
U172	5¢ Taylor, die 1, *white*	7.00	6.0
U183	6¢ red Lincoln, *cream*	14.00	9.0

1874-86 continued		Un	U
U250	4¢ green Jackson,		
	die 1, *white*	2.00	2.00
U262	2¢ brown Washington,		
	blue	8.50	4.00
U277	2¢ brown, die 1, *white*	.25	.15
U289	2¢ brown, die 2, *amber*	10.00	9.00
U293	2¢ green Grant,		
	white, entire	20.00	8.50

1887-94

U294	1¢ blue Franklin, *white*	.40	.20
U305	2¢ green Washington		
	die 1, *white*	7.00	6.00
U314	2¢ green, die 2, *blue*	.40	.20
U327	4¢ carm. Jackson, *blue*	3.00	3.00
U331	5¢ blue Grant,		
	die 1, *amber*	3.00	1.50
U348	1¢ Columbus		
	& Liberty, *white*	1.75	.75
U350	5¢ chocolate, *white*	7.50	6.50

1899

U352	1¢ grn. Franklin, *white*	.40	.20
U362	2¢ carmine Washington,		
	die 2, *white*	.25	.20
U377	5¢ blue Grant, *white*	7.50	7.00

1903

U379	1¢ grn. Franklin, *white*	.50	.10
U386	2¢ carm. Wash., *amber*	1.25	.20
U390	4¢ choc. Grant, *white*	14.00	8.00

1904

U398	2¢ carm. Wash., *blue*	2.50	.75

1907-16

U404	1¢ green Franklin,		
	die 1, *manila*	2.25	1.75
U408	2¢ brn. red Washington,		
	die 1, *oriental buff*	5.50	1.25
U414	2¢ carmine, die 1, *blue*	.30	.10

1916-32

U423	1¢ green Franklin,		
	die 1, *blue*	.35	.08
U429	2¢ carmine Washington,		
	die 1, *white*	.05	.05
U436	3¢ dk. vio., die 1, *white*	.40	.15
U447	2¢ on 3¢, *white*	4.75	5.00
U468	2¢ on 3¢, w/bars, *white*	.45	.30
U481	1½¢ brown Washington,		
	die 1, *white*	.10	.06
U510	1½¢ on 1¢ green, *white*	1.50	1.00
U522	2¢ carmine Liberty Bell,		
	die 1, *white*	1.50	.50
U523	1¢ Mount Vernon,		
	die 1, *white*	1.75	1.25
U528	5¢ dark blue, *white*	5.00	4.00
U531	6¢ orange Washington,		
	die 7, *blue*	10.00	7.50

		Un	U

1950-88

From 1950 on, envelopes white except as noted.

U534	3¢ dk. vio. Wash., die 4	.35	.10
U543	4¢ brn. Pony Express Rider	.60	.30
U547	1¼¢ brown Liberty Bell		.15
U551	6¢ grn. Statue of Liberty	.70	.05
U557	8¢ ultramarine Eagle	.40	.05
U564	8¢ light blue		
	Aging Conference	.50	.15
U569	10¢ yellow, blue and green		
	Tennis Centenary	.24	.15
U572	13¢ brown and blue green		
	Quilt Pattern, *lt. brown*	.30	.15
U576	13¢ Liberty Tree	.30	.13
U578	2.1¢ green Nonprofit		.05
U581	15¢ red Uncle Sam	.35	.15
U591	5.9¢ brown Nonprofit		.08
U594	(20¢) brown Eagle, C	.40	.10
U599	15¢ brown, green		
	and yellow Honeybee	.35	.15
U601	20¢ maroon Capitol Dome	.45	.10
U604	5.2¢ orange Nonprofit		.10
U608	22¢ brown Bison	.55	.12
U609	6¢ bl. grn. USS Constitution		.06
U611	25¢ dk. red, dp. bl. Stars	.60	.14

Airmail Envelopes and Aerogrammes, 1929-88

UC1	5¢ blue Airplane, die 1	3.00	1.75
UC2	5¢ blue, die 2	12.50	5.00
UC3	6¢ orange, die 2a	1.25	.25
UC6	6¢ orange, die 3	1.00	.35
UC14	5¢ carmine DC-4, die 1	.75	.20
UC25	6¢ red Eagle	.75	.50
UC40	10¢ red Jet Liner	.50	.06
UC47	13¢ red Bird in Flight	.28	.10
UC53	30¢ blue, red, brown Tourism,		
	blue	1.50	.22
UC57	30¢ Olympic Games, *blue*	.60	.30
UC60	36¢ Mark Twain/		
	Halley's Comet	.72	.36

Official Envelopes, 1873-79
Post Office Department (Numeral 9½mm high)

UO1	2¢ black, *lemon*	9.00	5.00
(Numeral 10½mm high)			
UO5	2¢ black, *lemon*	3.00	2.50

Postal Service

UO16	blue, *amber*	25.00	16.00

War Department

UO20	3¢ dk. red Wash., *white*	45.00	30.00
UO48	2¢ red Jackson, *amber*	20.00	6.00

Postal Savings Envelopes, 1911

UO72	2¢ carmine, *white*	6.00	1.50

Penalty Mail Envelopes, 1983-88 (Entires)

UO73	20¢ blue Great Seal	.50	
UO74	22¢ blue Great Seal	.55	
UO76	(25¢) Great Seal, E	.60	
UO77	25¢ black, blue Seal	.60	

1873-1988

UX14

UX27

UX56

UX64

UX83

UX94

UXC19

Represented below is only a partial listing of postal cards. Values are for entire cards.

		Un	U
UX1	1¢ brn. Liberty, wmkd.	275.00	17.50
UX4	1¢ black, unwmkd.	50.00	.40
UX10	1¢ black Grant	25.00	1.25
UX14	1¢ Jefferson	20.00	.25
UX22	1¢ blue McKinley	11.00	.25
UX27	1¢ Jefferson	.25	.10
UX32	1¢ on 2¢ red		
	Jefferson, cream	6.00	1.25
UX38	2¢ carm. rose Franklin	.30	.25
UX46	3¢ pur. Statue of Liberty	.40	.20
UX51	4¢ red and blue		
	U.S. Customs Service	.40	.50
UX56	5¢ Women Marines	.35	.20
UX61	6¢ black Tourism Year/		
	USF Constellation	.30	.50
UX64	6¢ John Hanson	.25	.15
UX71	9¢ Federal Court House,		
UX77	(10¢) Molly Pitcher,		
	Monmouth	.25	.16
UX80	10¢ Olympic Games	.50	.25
UX83	10¢ Salt Lake Temple	.22	.15
UX88	(12¢) violet Eagle	.28	.18
UX94	13¢ "Swamp Fox"		
	Francis Marion	.30	.20
UX100	13¢ Olympic Games	.30	.20

		Un	U
UX107	25¢ Clipper Flying Cloud	.60	5.00
UX110	14¢ Stamp Collecting	.28	.18
UX116	14¢ Constitutional		
	Convention	.28	.18
UX122	28¢ Yorkshire	.60	.28
Paid Reply Postal Cards (Prices are: Un = unsevered, U = severed card)			
UY1	1¢ + 1¢ black Grant	30.00	7.50
UY7	1¢ + 1¢ green		
	G. and M. Washington	1.00	.50
UY31	(12¢ + 12¢) purple		
	1981 Eagle	.75	.25
Airmail Postal Cards			
UXC1	4¢ orange red Eagle	.40	.35
UXC4	6¢ red Bald Eagle	.40	.20
UXC7	6¢ Boy Scout		
	World Jamboree	.40	.20
UXC11	15¢ Commerce Dept.		
	Travel Service	1.50	8.00
UXC17	21¢ Curtiss Jenny	.75	3.00
UXC19	28¢ First Transpacific		
	Flight	.75	1.00
UXC22	33¢ China Clipper	.66	1.00
Official Postal Cards			
UZ1	1¢ black Numeral	300.00	150.00
UZ2	13¢ blue Great Seal	.40	
UZ3	14¢ blue	.45	
UZ4	15¢ blue	.30	

Souvenir Cards

These cards were issued as souvenirs of the philatelic gatherings at which they were distributed by the United States Postal Service or its predecessor, the United States Post Office Department. They were not valid for postage.

The forerunner of the souvenir cards is the 1939 Philatelic Truck souvenir sheet which the Post Office Department issued and distributed in various cities visited by the Philatelic Truck. It depicts the White House, printed in blue on white paper. Issued with and without gum. Price with gum, *$65,* without gum, *$10.*

First values listed are for uncancelled cards; values in italics are for cards bearing USPS first-day-of-show or first-day-of-sale cancels. The absence of a value for a cancelled card indicates that its price varies according to the type of cancel applied. Descriptions include the Scott Catalogue numbers for the U.S. and foreign stamp designs reproduced on the cards, as well as text in languages in addition to English. Prices are courtesy of Brookman Stamp Co. of Bedford, New Hampshire.

United States Post Office & United States Postal Service

1960 BARCELONA 1st International Philatelic Congress, Mar. 26-Apr. 5. Card of 1. #231.   300.00

1968 EFIMEX, International Philatelic Exhibition, Nov. 1-9, Mexico City. Card of 1. #292. Inscribed in Spanish.   3.00

1970 PHILYMPIA, London International Stamp Exhibition, Sept. 18-26. Card of 3. #548-550.   3.00

1971 EXFILIMA '71, 3rd Inter-American Philatelic Exhibition, Nov. 6-14, Lima, Peru. Card of 3, #1111 and 1126, Peru #360. Card inscribed in Spanish.   2.00

1972 BELGICA '72, Brussels International Philatelic Exhibition, June 24-July 9, Brussels, Belgium. Card of 3. #914, 1026 and 1104. Card inscribed in Flemish and French.   1.50

OLYMPIA PHILATELIC MUNCHEN '72, Aug. 18-Sept. 10, Munich, Germany. Card of 4. #1460-1462 and C85. Card inscribed in German.   2.00

EXFILBRA '72, 4th Inter-American Philatelic Exhibition, Aug. 26-Sept. 2, Rio de Janeiro, Brazil. Card of 3. #C14, Brazil #C18-C19. Card inscribed in Portuguese.   2.00

NATIONAL PHILATELIC FORUM VI, Aug. 28-30, Washington, D.C. Card of 4. #1396.   2.00

1973 IBRA '73 Internationale Briefmarken Ausstellung, May 11-20, Munich, Germany. Card of 1. #C13.   2.75

APEX '73, International Airmail Exhibition, July 4-7, Manchester, England. Card of 3, #C3a, Honduras #C12 and Newfoundland #C4.   2.75

POLSKA '73, Swiatowa Wystawe Filatelistyczna, Aug. 19-Sept. 2, Poznan, Poland. Card of 3. #1488 and Poland #1944-1945. Card inscribed in Polish.   2.75

POSTAL PEOPLE, Card of 10. (11" x 14") #1489-1498. Distributed to Postal Service employees. Not available to public. $125.00

1974 HOBBY, The Hobby Industry Association of America Convention and Trade Show, Feb. 3-6, Chicago, Illinois. Card of 4. #1456-1459.   3.50

INTERNABA, International Philatelic Exhibition, June 7-16, Basel, Switzerland. Card of 8. #1530-1537. Card inscribed in French, German and Italian.   3.50

STOCKHOLMIA '74, International Frimarksustailning, Sept. 21-29, Stockholm, Sweden. Card of 3. #836 and Sweden #300 and 765. Card inscribed in Swedish.   3.50

EXFILMEX '74 Philatelic Exposition Inter-Americana, Oct. 26-Nov. 3, Mexico City, Mexico. Card of 2. #1157 and Mexico #910. Card inscribed in Spanish.   3.50

1975 ESPANA '75, World Stamp Exhibition, Apr. 4-13, Madrid, Spain. Card of 3. #233 and 1271 and Spain #1312. Card inscribed in Spanish.   2.75

ARPHILA '75, June 6-16, Paris, France. Card of 3. #1187 and 1207 and France #1117. Card inscribed in French.   2.75

1976 WERABA '76, Third International Space Stamp Exhibition, Apr. 1-4, Zurich, Switzerland. Card of 2. #1434 and 1435 se-tenant. 5.00 *6.50*

BICENTENNIAL EXPOSITION on Science and Technology, May 30-Sept. 6, Kennedy Space Center, Fla. Card of 1. #C76. 4.00 *7.50*

COLORADO STATEHOOD CENTENNIAL, Aug. 1. Card of 3. #288, 743 and 1670. 4.00 *6.50*

HAFNIA '76, International Stamp Exhibition, Aug. 20-29, Copenhagen, Denmark. Card of 2. #5 and Denmark #2. Card inscribed in Danish. 4.00 *5.50*

ITALIA '76, International Philatelic Exhibition, Oct. 14-24, Milan, Italy. Card of 3. #1168 and Italy #578 and 601. Card inscribed in Italian. 4.00 *5.50*

NORDPOSTA '76, North German Stamp Exhibition, Oct 30-31, Hamburg, Germany. Card of 3. #689 and Germany #B366 and B417. Card inscribed in German. 4.00 *5.50*

1977 AMPHILEX '77, International Philatelic Exhibition, May 26-June 5, Amsterdam, Netherlands. Card of 3. #1027 and Netherlands #41 and 294. Card inscribed in Dutch. 4.00 *5.50*

SAN MARINO '77, International Philatelic Exhibition, Aug. 28-Sept. 4, San Marino. Card of 3. #1-2 and San Marino #1. Card inscribed in Italian. 4.00 *5.50*

1978 ROCPEX '76, International Philatelic Exhibition, Mar. 20-29, Taipei, Taiwan. Card of 6. #1706-1709 and Taiwan #1812 and 1816. Card inscribed in Chinese. 5.00

NAPOSTA '78, International Philatelic Exhibition, May 20-25, Frankfurt, Germany. Card of 3. # 555 and 563 and Germany #1216. Card inscribed in German. 4.00 *5.50*

1979 BRASILIANA '79, International Philatelic Exhibition, Sept. 15-23. Rio de Janeiro, Brazil. Card of 3. #C91-C92 (C92a) and Brazil #1295. Card inscribed in Portuguese. 6.00 *7.50*

JAPEX '79, International Philatelic Exhibition, Nov. 2-4, Tokyo, Japan. Card of 2. #1158 and Japan #1024. Card inscribed in Japanese. 6.00 *7.50*

1980 LONDON '80, International Philatelic Exposition, May 6-14, London, England. Card of 1. #329. 6.00

NORWEX '80, International Philatelic Exposition, June 13-22, Oslo, Norway. Card of 3. #620-621 and Norway #658. Card inscribed in Norwegian. 5.00 *6.50*

ESSEN '80, International Philatelic Exposition, Nov. 15-19, Essen, Germany. Card of 2. #1014 and Germany #723. Card inscribed in German. 5.00 *6.50*

1981 WIPA '81, International Philatelic Exhibition, May 22-31, Vienna, Austria. Card of 2. #1252 and Austria #789. 5.00 *6.50*

NSCM, National Stamp Collecting Month. October. Card of 2. #245 and 1918. 5.00 *6.50*

PHILATOKYO '81, International Philatelic Exhibition, Oct. 9-18, Tokyo, Japan. Card of 2. #1531 and Japan #800. Card inscribed in Japanese. 5.00 *6.50*

NORDPOSTA '81, North German Stamp Exhibition, Nov. 7-8, Hamburg, Germany. Card of 2. #923 and Germany #B538. Card inscribed in German. 5.00 *7.50*

1982 CANADA '82, International Philatelic Youth Exhibition, May 20-24, Toronto, Ontario, Canada. Card of 2. #116 and Canada #15. Card inscribed in French. 5.00 *6.50*

PHILEXFRANCE '82, International Philatelic Exposition, June 11-21, Paris, France. Card of 2. #1753 and France #1480. Card inscribed in French. 4.00 *5.50*

NSCM, National Stamp Collecting Month, Oct. Card of 1. #C3a. 5.00 *6.00*

ESPAMER '82, International Philatelic Exposition, Oct. 12-17, San Juan, Puerto Rico. Card of 3. #810, 1437 and 2024. Card inscribed in Spanish. 5.00 *6.00*

1983 Sweden/U.S. joint stamp issues, Mar. 24, Philadelphia, PA. Card of 3. #958 and 2036 and Sweden #1453. Card inscribed in Swedish. 5.00 *6.00*

GERMAN/U.S. JOINT STAMP ISSUES, Apr. 29, Germantown, PA. Card of 2. #2040 and Germany #1397. Card inscribed in German. 5.00 *6.00*

TEMBAL '83, International Philatelic Exposition, May 21-29, Basil, Switzerland. Card of 2. #C71 and Switzerland #3L1. Card inscribed in German. 5.00 *6.00*

BRASILIANA '83, International Philatelic Exhibition, July 29-Aug. 7, Rio de Janeiro, Brazil. Card of 2. #1 and Brazil #1. 5.00 *6.00*

BANGKOK '83, International Philatelic Exposition, Aug. 4-13, Bangkok, Thailand. Card of 2. #210 and Thailand #1. Card inscribed in Thai. 5.00 *6.00*

International Philatelic Memento, 1983-84. Card of 1. #1387. 2.50 *4.50*

NSCM, National Stamp Collecting Month, October. Card of 1. #293. 5.00 *6.00*

1984 ESPANA '84, International Philatelic Exhibition, Apr. 27-May 6, Madrid, Spain. Card of 2. #223 and Spain #428. Card inscribed in Spanish. 5.00 *6.00*

HAMBURG '84, International Philatelic Exhibition, June 19-26, Hamburg, Germany. Card of 2. #C66 and Germany #669. Card inscribed in French and German. 5.00 *6.00*

CANADA/U.S. JOINT STAMP ISSUES, June 26, Massena, N.Y. Card of 2. #1131 and Canada #387. Card inscribed in French.   4.50 *5.50*

AUSIPEX '84, International Philatelic Exhibition, Sept. 21-30, Melbourne, Australia. Card of 2. #290 and Western Australia #1.   4.50 *5.50*

NSCM, National Stamp Collecting Month, October. Card of 1. #2104.   4.50 *5.50*

PHILAKOREA '84, Oct. 22-31, Seoul, Korea. Card of 2. #741 and Korea #994. Card inscribed in Korean.   4.50 *5.50*

1985 INTERNATIONAL PHILATELIC MEMENTO, 1985. Card of 1. #2.   4.50 *5.50*

OLYMPHILEX '85, International Philatelic Exhibition, Mar. 18-24, Lausanne, Switzerland. Card of 2. #C106 and Switzerland #746. Card inscribed in French.   4.50 *5.50*

ISRAPHIL '85, International Philatelic Exhibition, May 14-22, Tel Aviv, Israel. Card of 2. #566 and Israeli #33. Card inscribed in Hebrew.   4.50 *5.50*

ARGENTINA '85, International Philatelic Exhibition, July 5-14, Buenos Aires, Argentina. Card of 2. #1737 and Argentina #B27. Card inscribed in Spanish.   4.50 *5.50*

MOPHILA '85, International Philatelic Exhibition, Sept. 11-15, Hamburg, Germany. Card of 2. #296 and Germany #B595. Card inscribed in German.   5.50 *6.50*

ITALIA '85, International Philatelic Exhibition, Oct. 25-Nov. 3, Rome, Italy. #1107 and Italy #830. Card inscribed in Italian.   4.50 *5.50*

1986 MEMENTO '86, Statue of Liberty Centennial, Feb. 21. Card of 1. #C87.   6.50 *4.50*

STOCKHOLMIA '86, International Philatelic Exhibition, Aug. 28-Sept. 7, Stockholm, Sweden. Card of 2. #113 and Sweden #253. Card inscribed in Swedish.   6.50 *6.50*

1987 CAPEX '87, International Philatelic Exhibition, June 13-21, Toronto, Canada. Card of 2. #569 and Canada #883. Card inscribed in French.   4.50 *5.50*

HAFNIA '87, International Philatelic Exhibition, Oct. 16-25, Copehagen, Denmark. Card of 2. #299 and Denmark #B52. Inscribed in Danish.   4.50 *5.50*

EXPOSITION PHILATELIQUE, Nov. 13-17, Monte Carlo, Monaco. Card of 3. #2287 and 2300 and Monaco #1589. Card inscribed in French.   4.50 *5.50*

1988 FINLANDIA '88, June 1-12, Helsinki, Finland. Card of 2. #836 and Finland's 1988 New Sweden issue. Card inscribed in Finnish.   4.50 *5.50*

1989 PHILEXFRANCE '89, July 7-17, Paris, France. Card of 2. #C120 and "Egalite" stamp from France's Revolution Bicentennial issue. Card inscribed in French.   4.00 *5.00*

On July 14, 1989, the French Ministry of Posts, Telecommunications and Space and the United States Postal Service issued stamps commemorating the anniversary of the French Revolution. First day of issue ceremonies were held in Washington, D.C. and Paris.

In 1789, King Louis XVI lost most of his power to a new governing body in France, the National Assembly, which published a document entitled, "The Rights of Man and the Citizen." This declaration described the basic freedoms to which all people are entitled. The French Revolution was under way. Inspired in part by the American Revolution, this movement in France brought remarkable changes not only to that country, but to all of Europe, and eventually much of the world.

The U.S. Postal Service is pleased to issue this souvenir card to honor the PHILEXFRANCE 89 International Philatelic Exhibition.

Le 14 juillet 1989, le Ministère français des Postes, des Télécommunications et de l'Espace et le Service postal des Etats-Unis ont émis des timbres commémorant l'anniversaire de la Révolution française. Les manifestations de premier jour eurent lieu à Washington, D.C. et à Paris.

En 1789, le roi Louis XVI perdit la plus grande partie de son pouvoir au profit du nouveau gouvernement de France : l'Assemblée nationale qui publia un document intitulé "Les Droits de l'homme et du citoyen". Cette déclaration définit les libertés individuelles de chacun. La Révolution française était en route. S'inspirant en partie de la Révolution américaine, ce mouvement s'est apporté des changements considérables non seulement en France, mais dans toute l'Europe et finalement dans une grande partie du monde.

Le Service postal des Etats-Unis a le plaisir de publier cette carte-souvenir en l'honneur de l'Exposition philatélique mondiale PHILEXFRANCE 89.

Souvenir Pages Subscription Program

Your Ticket to the Entire Year's Issues

- Featuring every stamp issued each year
- Complete with First Day cancellation and informative text
- A convenient, affordable way to collect

The U.S. Postal Service's Souvenir Pages Subscription Program is your ticket to all the year's stamp issues. It's a great way to collect and learn about the stamps and stamp subjects honored during the year.

Comprehensive And Inexpensive
A Souvenir Page is issued for every stamp—all definitives and commemoratives, as well as airmails, coil stamps and booklet panes. Each Souvenir Page includes the featured stamp(s), postmarked with a First Day of Issue cancellation, mounted on an 8" x 10½" page. Information on relevant philatelic specifications and a lively narrative about the history of the stamp's subject are included.

Affordable Collectibles
Souvenir Pages are printed in a limited quantity each year. Subscribers receive monthly letters with information on upcoming issues, new designs and other postal products. And the cost of a Souvenir Page is just $1.00 per page. (In the rare event that the face value of the stamp[s] affixed exceeds $1.00, the price will be the face value.)

Money-back Guarantee
If you are ever dissatisfied, return your Souvenir Pages within 30 days of receipt for a *full* refund. For more information and an order form, fill out the postage-paid request card in this book or write to:

USPS GUIDE
SOUVENIR PAGES PROGRAM
PHILATELIC SALES DIVISION
UNITED STATES POSTAL SERVICE
POST OFFICE BOX 9995
WASHINGTON DC 20265-9995

Souvenir Pages

With First Day Cancellations

The Postal Service offers Souvenir Pages for new stamps. The series began with a page for the Yellowstone Park Centennial stamp issued March 1, 1972. The pages feature one or more stamps tied by the first day cancel, along with technical data and information on the subject of the issue. More than just collectors' items, Souvenir Pages make wonderful show and conversation pieces. Souvenir Pages are issued in limited editions.

1972
- **1** Yellowstone Park, FDC with Eagle 1971 watermark — 100.00
- **1a** Same with Parsons wmk. — 100.00
- **1b** Same without any wmk. — 100.00
- **1c** Yellowstone Park with Washington, DC first day cancel and Eagle 1971 wmk. — 600.00
- **1d** Same without any wmk. — 600.00
- **1A** Family Planning (ASDA) with Eagle 1971 wmk. — 600.00
- **1Aa** Same without any wmk. — 400.00
- **2** Cape Hatteras, with Eagle 1971 wmk. — 100.00
- **2a** Same with Parsons wmk. — 100.00
- **2b** Same without any wmk. — 100.00
- **3** Fiorello LaGuardia, with Eagle 1971 wmk. — 120.00
- **3a** Same with Parsons wmk. — 175.00
- **3b** Same without any wmk. — 100.00
- **4** City of Refuge, with 1971 Eagle wmk. — 100.00
- **4a** Same with Parsons wmk. — 100.00
- **4b** Same without any wmk. — 100.00
- **5** Wolf Trap Farm, with 1971 Eagle wmk. (No star before (GPO #) — 40.00
- **5a** Same with 1972 Eagle wmk. — 50.00
- **5b** Wolf Trap Farm with Parsons wmk. and Star before GPO # — 40.00
- **6** Colonial Craftsmen — 20.00

- **7** Mount McKinley — 25.00
- **8** Olympic Games — 12.00
- **8E** Olympic Games with broken red circle on 6¢ stamp — 800.00
- **9** PTA — 8.00
- **10** Wildlife Conservation — 10.00
- **11** Mail Order — 8.00
- **11E** Mail Order with double-tailed cat on stamp — 200.00
- **12** Osteopathic Medicine — 8.00
- **13** Tom Sawyer — 8.00
- **14** Benjamin Franklin — 8.00
- **15** Christmas — 10.00
- **16** Pharmacy — 8.00
- **17** Stamp Collecting — 8.00

1973
- **18** Eugene O'Neill coil, with 1972 Eagle wmk. and U.S. GPO # 1972-0-491-478 — 15.00
- **18E** Same with 1973 Eagle wmk. and U.S. GPO # 1973-0-509-757 — 600.00
- **19** Love — 10.00
- **20** Pamphleteers — 6.00
- **21** George Gershwin — 7.00
- **22** Posting a Broadside — 20.00
- **22E** Same with 1971 Eagle wmk. — 300.00
- **23** Copernicus — 6.00
- **23a** Same with 1973 Eagle wmk. — 8.00
- **24** Postal Service Employees — 8.00
- **25** Harry S. Truman — 6.00
- **26** Post Rider — 6.00
- **27** Amadeo Gianninni — 6.00
- **27a** Same without wmk. — 8.00
- **28** Boston Tea Party — 8.00
- **29** Progress in Electronics — 7.00
- **30** Robinson Jeffers — 5.00
- **30a** Same without wmk. — 8.00
- **30T** Same on "thin" paper — 15.00

- **31** Lyndon B. Johnson — 5.00
- **32** Henry O. Tanner — 5.00
- **33** Willa Cather — 5.00
- **33T** Same on "thin" paper — 8.00
- **34** Colonial Drummer — 8.00
- **34T** Same on "thin" paper — 5.00
- **35** Cattle — 5.00
- **36** Christmas — 7.00
- **37** 13¢ Winged Envelope airmail sheet stamp — 4.00
- **38** 10¢ Crossed Flags — 4.00
- **39** Jefferson Memorial — 4.00
- **40** 13¢ Winged Envelope airmail coil — 4.00

1974
- **41** Mount Rushmore airmail — 6.00
- **41a** Mount Rushmore with wmk. — 40.00
- **42** ZIP Code — 5.00
- **42E** ZIP Code, date error — 600.00
- **43** Statue of Liberty airmail — 6.00
- **43a** Statue of Liberty with wmk. — 40.00
- **44** Elizabeth Blackwell — 3.00
- **45** VFW — 3.00
- **46** Robert Frost — 3.00
- **47** EXPO '74 — 3.00
- **47a** Same with 1974 Eagle wmk. — 6.00
- **48** Horse Racing — 3.00
- **49** Skylab with wmk. — 6.00
- **49a** Skylab without wmk. — 20.00
- **50** Universal Postal Union — 6.00
- **51** Mineral Heritage — 6.00
- **52** First Kentucky Settlement — 3.00
- **53** First Continental Congress — 5.00

53a	Same with 1974 Eagle wmk.	25.00
54	Chautauqua	3.00
55	Kansas Wheat	3.00
56	Energy Conservation	3.00
57	6.3¢ Liberty Bell coil	5.00
58	Sleepy Hollow	4.00
59	Retarded Children	3.00
60	Christmas	6.00
	1975	
61	Benjamin West	3.00
62	Pioneer/Jupiter	7.00
63	Collective Bargaining	3.00
64	8¢ Sybil Ludington	4.00
65	Salem Poor	5.00
66	Haym Salomon	4.00
67	18¢ Peter Francisco	4.00
68	Mariner 10	6.00
69	Lexington & Concord	3.00
70	Paul Laurence Dunbar	7.00
70a	Same with 1974 Eagle wmk.	5.00
70b	Same without wmk.	8.00
71	D.W. Griffith	4.00
71a	Same without wmk.	8.00
72	Bunker Hill	3.00
73	Military Uniforms	7.00
74	Apollo Soyuz	7.00
75	International Women's Year	3.00
76	Postal Service Bicentennial	5.00
77	World Peace Through Law	3.00
77a	Same with 1975 Eagle wmk.	6.00
78	Banking and Commerce	3.00
79	Christmas	5.00
80	3¢ Francis Parkman	4.00
81	11¢ Freedom of the Press	3.00
82	24¢ Old North Church	3.00
83	Flag over Independence Hall	3.00
84	9¢ Freedom to Assemble	3.00
85	Liberty Bell coil	3.00
86	American Eagle and Shield	3.00
86a	Same with Parsons wmk.	5.00
	1976	
87	Spirit of '76	5.00
87a	Same with Parsons wmk.	10.00
87b	Same with Weston 1974 wmk.	20.00
87c	Same with Weston 1975 wmk.	20.00
87E	Spirit of '76 with error cancellation	800.00
88	25¢ & 31¢ Plane and Globes airmails	4.00
89	Interphil 76	4.00
89a	Same with Parsons wmk.	8.00
90	Fifty State Flag Series, (5 pages)	45.00
91	9¢ Freedom to Assemble coil	3.00

91a	Same with 1974 Weston wmk.	10.00
91b	Same with 1975 Weston wmk.	10.00
92	Telephone	3.00
93	Commercial Aviation	3.00
94	Chemistry	3.00
94a	Same with 1975 Weston wmk.	10.00
95	7.9¢ Drum coil	3.00
96	Benjamin Franklin	3.00
97	Bicentennial SS, (4 pages)	40.00
97E	31¢ Souvenir Sheet with missing 31¢ values	800.00
98	Declaration of Independence	5.00
99	Olympics	5.00
100	Clara Maass	3.00
101	Adolph S. Ochs	3.00
102	Christmas	4.00
103	7.7¢ Saxhorns coil	3.00
	1977	
104	Washington at Princeton	3.00
105	$1 Flag over Capitol booklet, perf. 10	20.00
106	Sound Recording	3.00
107	Pueblo Pottery	4.00
108	Lindbergh Flight	4.00
109	Colorado Statehood	3.00
110	Butterflies	4.00
111	Lafayette	3.00
112	Skilled Hands	4.00
113	Peace Bridge	3.00
114	Battle of Oriskany	3.00
115	Alta, CA, First Civil Settlement	3.00
115a	Same with Parsons wmk.	3.00
116	Articles of Confederation	3.00
117	Talking Pictures	3.00
118	Surrender at Saratoga	3.00
118a	Same with Fox River wmk.	3.00
119	Energy	3.00
120	Christmas, Mailbox	3.00
121	Christmas, Valley Forge	3.00
122	10¢ Petition for Redress coil	3.00
123	10¢ Petition for Redress sheet stamp	3.00
124	1¢, 2¢, 3¢, 4¢ Americana Issues	3.00
	1978	
125	Carl Sandburg	3.00
125a	Same without wmk.	5.00
126	Indian Head Penny	3.00
127	Captain Cook, Anchorage cancel	4.00
128	Captain Cook, Honolulu cancel	4.00
129	Harriet Tubman	5.00
130	Quilts	4.00
131	16¢ Statue of Liberty	3.00
132	29¢ Lighthouse	3.00
133	Dance	4.00
134	French Alliance	3.00
135	Early Cancer Detection	3.00

136	A Stamps	5.00
137	Jimmie Rodgers	4.00
138	CAPEX '78, SS	9.00
139	Oliver Wendell Holmes coil	10.00
140	Photography	3.00
141	Fort McHenry Flag	4.00
142	George M. Cohan	3.00
143	Rose booklet single	3.00
144	8.4¢ Piano coil	4.00
145	Viking Missions	6.00
146	28¢ Remote Outpost	3.00
147	Owls	4.00
148	Wright Brothers airmails	4.00
149	Trees	4.00
150	Christmas, Hobby Horse	3.00
151	Christmas, Madonna	3.00
152	$2 Kerosene Lamp	7.00
	1979	
153	Robert F. Kennedy	3.00
154	Martin Luther King, Jr.	6.00
155	Year of the Child	3.00
156	John Steinbeck	3.00
157	Albert Einstein	3.00
158	Octave Chanute airmails	4.00
159	Pennsylvania Toleware	4.00
160	Architecture	4.00
161	Endangered Flora	4.00
162	Seeing Eye Dogs	3.00
163	$1 Candle	6.00
164	Special Olympics	3.00
165	$5 Lantern	15.00
166	30¢ Schoolhouse	4.00
167	10¢ Olympics	4.00
168	50¢ Lamp	4.00
169	John Paul Jones	3.00
170	15¢ Olympics	5.00
171	Christmas, Madonna	4.00
172	Christmas, Santa Claus	4.00
173	3.1¢ Guitar coil with Parsons wmk., 100% cotton paper	10.00
173a	Same with Scotch linen paper	15.00
173b	Same with Parsons #1 Record wmk.	15.00
173c	Same with Parsons 1974 wmk.	15.00
173d	Same with Parsons 1975 wmk.	15.00
173e	Same with Parsons 1976 wmk.	10.00
173f	Same with Gilbert wmk.	15.00
173g	Same without wmk.	15.00
174	31¢ Olympics airmail	6.00
175	Will Rogers	3.00
176	Vietnam Veterans	3.00
177	Wiley Post airmails	5.00

1980

178	W. C. Fields	3.00
179	Winter Olympics	6.00
180	Windmills booklet	6.00
181	Benjamin Banneker	5.00
181a	Same with	
	Gilbert wmk.	10.00
182	Letter Writing	3.00
183	1¢ Ability to Write	3.00
184	Frances Perkins	3.00
185	Dolley Madison	3.00
185a	Same with	
	Parsons wmk.	4.00
186	Emily Bissell	3.00
187	3.5¢ Violins coil	4.00
188	Helen Keller/	
	Anne Sullivan	3.00
189	Veterans	
	Administration	3.00
190	General Galvez	3.00
191	Coral Reefs	4.00
191a	Same without wmk.	6.00
192	Organized Labor	4.00
192a	Same with Parsons wmk.,	
	100% cotton paper	8.00
192b	Same with Parsons wmk.,	
	Scotch linen paper	6.00
192c	Same without wmk.	8.00
193	Edith Wharton	4.00
193a	Same with Parsons wmk.,	
	100% cotton paper	8.00
193b	Same with Parsons wmk.,	
	Scotch linen paper	6.00
193c	Same with	
	Weston 1975 wmk.	8.00
193d	Same without wmk.	8.00
194	Education	4.00
194a	Same with Parsons wmk.,	
	100% cotton paper	8.00
194b	Same with Parsons wmk.,	
	Scotch linen paper	8.00
195	Indian Masks	4.00
196	Architecture	4.00
197	Philip Mazzei	
	airmail	4.00
198	Christmas,	
	Madonna	4.00
198a	Same without wmk.	10.00
199	Christmas,	
	Wreath and Toys	4.00
199a	Same without wmk.	10.00
200	Sequoyah	3.00
201	Blanche Scott	
	airmail	3.00
202	Glenn Curtiss	
	airmail	3.00

1981

203	Everett Dirksen	3.00
204	Whitney M. Young	5.00
205	B sheet and coil	4.00
206	B booklet	3.00
207	12¢ Freedom	
	of Conscience	
	sheet and coil	4.00
208	Flowers	4.00
209	Flag and Anthem	
	sheet and coil	4.00
210	Flag and Anthem	
	booklet	4.00
211	Red Cross	3.00
212	George Mason	3.00
213	Savings and Loans	3.00
214	Wildlife Booklet	5.00
215	Surrey coil	5.00
216	Space Achievement	10.00
217	Rachel Carson	3.00
218	35¢ Charles Drew,	
	MD	3.00

219	Professional	
	Management	3.00
220	17¢ Electric Auto	
	coil	5.00
221	Wildlife Habitats	4.00
222	Year of Disabled	3.00
223	Edna St. Vincent	
	Millay	5.00
223E	Same with broken	
	Vi"n"cent	8.00
224	Alcoholism	4.00
225	Architecture	4.00
226	Babe Zaharias	4.00
227	Bobby Jones	4.00
228	Frederic	
	Remington	3.00
229	C sheet and coil	4.00
230	C booklet	4.00
231	18¢/20¢ Hoban	3.00
232	Yorktown,	
	Virginia Capes	3.00
233	Christmas,	
	Bear on Sleigh	5.00
234	Christmas,	
	Madonna	4.00
235	John Hanson	3.00
236	Fire Pumper coil	7.00
237	Desert Plants	15.00
238	9.3¢ Mail Wagon	
	coil	15.00
238a	Same with	
	Weston 1982 wmk.	5.00
239	Flag over Supreme Court	
	sheet and coil	10.00
239a	Same with	
	Weston 1982 wmk.	5.00
240	Flag over Supreme Court	
	booklet	5.00

1982

241	Sheep booklet	4.00
242	Ralph Bunche	7.00
243	13¢ Crazy Horse	3.00
244	37¢ Robert Millikan	3.00
245	Franklin Roosevelt	3.00
246	Love	3.00
247	5.9¢ Bicycle coil	10.00
247a	Same with	
	Weston 1981 wmk.	6.00
247b	Same with	
	Weston 1982 wmk.	8.00
248	George Washington	8.00
248a	Same with	
	Weston 1981 wmk.	5.00
248b	Same wtih	
	Weston 1982 wmk.	12.00
249	10.9¢ Hansom Cab	
	coil	5.00
250	Birds & Flowers Series,	
	(5 pages)	60.00
250A	Birds & Flowers with	
	all 10½ x 11 perfs.	100.00
250B	Birds & Flowers with	
	all 11 x 11 perfs.	150.00
251	U.S./Netherlands	3.00
252	Library of Congress	3.00
253	Consumer Education	
	coil	4.00
254	Knoxville World's	
	Fair	3.00
255	Horatio Alger	3.00
256	2¢ Locomotive coil	4.00
257	Aging Together	3.00
258	The Barrymores	3.00
259	Dr. Mary Walker	3.00
260	Peace Garden	3.00
261	America's Libraries	3.00
261a	Same with	
	Parsons wmk.	5.00
262	Jackie Robinson	15.00
263	4¢ Stagecoach coil	5.00
264	Touro Synagogue	3.00
265	Wolf Trap	
	Farm Park	3.00

266	Architecture	3.00
267	Francis of Assisi	3.00
268	Ponce de Leon	3.00
269	Christmas, Seasons	
	Greetings	4.00
270	Christmas,	
	Madonna	3.00
271	13¢ Kitten	
	and Puppy	3.00
272	2¢ Igor Stravinsky	3.00

1983

273	Penalty Mail,	
	(7 stamps, 5 pgs.)	25.00
273A	Same with all	
	Weston 1982 wmks.	30.00
273B	Same with all	
	Weston 1983 wmks.	50.00
274	Science & Industry	15.00
274a	Same with	
	Weston 1982 wmk.	3.00
274b	Same with	
	Weston 1983 wmk.	15.00
275	5.2¢ Sleigh coil	5.00
276	Sweden/USA	
	Treaty	3.00
276a	Same with	
	Weston 1982 wmk.	15.00
277	3¢ Handcar coil	5.00
278	Balloons	3.00
279	Civilian Conservation	
	Corps	3.00
280	40¢ Olympics	
	airmails	4.00
281	Joseph Priestley	3.00
282	Voluntarism	3.00
283	Concord/German	
	Immigration	3.00
284	Physical Fitness	3.00
284a	Same with	
	Weston 1983 wmk.	10.00
285	Brooklyn Bridge	3.00
286	TVA	3.00
287	4¢ Carl Schurz	3.00
288	Medal of Honor	3.00
289	Scott Joplin	5.00
290	Thomas H.	
	Gallaudet	3.00
291	28¢ Olympics	
	airmails	5.00
292	5¢ Pearl Buck	3.00
293	Babe Ruth	10.00
294	Nathaniel	
	Hawthorne	3.00
295	3¢ Henry Clay	3.00
296	13¢ Olympics	5.00
297	$9.35 Eagle	
	booklet single	125.00
297A	$9.35 Eagle	
	booklet pane of 3	200.00
298	1¢ Omnibus coil	5.00
299	Treaty of Paris	3.00
300	Civil Service	3.00
301	Metropolitan	
	Opera	3.00
302	Inventors	4.00
303	1¢ Dorothea Dix	3.00
304	Streetcars	4.00
305	5¢ Motorcycle coil	5.00
306	Christmas,	
	Santa Claus	3.00
307	Christmas,	
	Madonna	3.00
308	35¢ Olympics	
	airmails	5.00
309	Martin Luther	3.00
310	Flag over Supreme Court	
	booklet	4.00

1984

311	Alaska Statehood	3.00
312	Winter Olympics	5.00
313	FDIC	3.00
314	Harry S. Truman	3.00
315	Love	3.00
316	Carter G. Woodson	5.00
317	11¢ RR Caboose coil	5.00
318	Soil and Water Conservation	3.00
319	Credit Union Act	3.00
320	40¢ Lillian M. Gilbreth	3.00
321	Orchids	4.00
322	Hawaii Statehood	3.00
323	7.4¢ Baby Buggy coil	5.00
324	National Archives	3.00
325	20¢ Olympics	5.00
326	Louisiana World Exposition	3.00
327	Health Research	3.00
328	Douglas Fairbanks	3.00
329	Jim Thorpe	8.00
329a	Same with 1984 large wmk.	10.00
330	10¢ Richard Russell	3.00
331	John McCormack	3.00
332	St. Lawrence Seaway	3.00
333	Migratory Bird Hunting and Conservation Stamp Act	6.00
333a	Same with 1984 large wmk.	10.00
334	Roanoke Voyages	3.00
335	Herman Melville	3.00
336	Horace Moses	3.00
337	Smokey Bear	8.00
337a	Same with Weston 1984 wmk.	10.00
338	Roberto Clemente	10.00
339	30¢ Frank Laubach	3.00
340	Dogs	5.00
341	Crime Prevention	3.00
342	Family Unity	3.00
343	Eleanor Roosevelt	3.00
344	Nation of Readers	3.00
345	Christmas, Santa Claus	4.00
346	Christmas, Madonna	4.00
347	Hispanic Americans	3.00
348	Vietnam Veterans Memorial	4.00

1985

349	Jerome Kern	5.00
349a	Same with 1984 small wmk.	8.00
350	7¢ Abraham Baldwin	5.00
350a	Same with 1984 small wmk.	8.00
351	D sheet and coil	4.00
351a	Same with 1984 small wmk.	15.00
352	D booklet	5.00
352a	Same with 1984 small wmk.	15.00
353	D Penalty Mail sheet and coil	4.00
354	11¢ Alden Partridge	3.00
355	Alfred Verville airmail	3.00
356	Lawrence & Elmer Sperry airmail	3.00
357	Transpacific airmail	3.00
358	50¢ Chester Nimitz	3.00

359	Mary McLeod Bethune	4.00
360	39¢ Grenville Clark	3.00
361	6¢ Sinclair Lewis	3.00
362	Duck Decoys	4.00
363	14¢ Iceboat coil	5.00
364	Winter Special Olympics	3.00
365	Flag over Capitol sheet and coil	4.00
366	Flag over Capitol booklet	4.00
367	12¢ Stanley Steamer coil	5.00
368	Seashells booklet	6.00
369	Love	4.00
370	10.1¢ Oil Wagon coil	5.00
371	12.5¢ Pushcart coil	5.00
372	John J. Audubon	3.00
373	$10.75 Eagle booklet single	40.00
373A	Eagle booklet pane of 3	90.00
374	5.9¢ Tricycle coil	5.00
375	Rural Electrification Administration	3.00
376	14¢ and 22¢ Penalty Mail sheet and coil	5.00
377	AMERIPEX '86	3.00
378	9¢ Sylvanus Thayer	3.00
379	3.4¢ School Bus coil	5.00
380	11¢ Stutz Bearcat coil	5.00
381	Abigail Adams	3.00
382	4.9¢ Buckboard coil	5.00
383	8.3¢ Ambulance coil	5.00
384	Frederic Bartholdi	3.00
385	8¢ Henry Knox	5.00
386	Korean War Veterans	4.00
387	Social Security Act	3.00
388	Father Serra airmail	3.00
389	Veterans, World War I	3.00
390	6¢ Walter Lippmann	3.00
391	Horses	5.00
392	Public Education	3.00
393	Youth	3.00
394	Help End Hunger	3.00
395	21.1¢ Letters	4.00
396	Christmas, Poinsettias	3.00
397	Christmas, Madonna	3.00
398	18¢ Washington coil	4.00

1986

399	Arkansas Statehood	3.00
400	25¢ Jack London	2.50
401	Stamp Collecting booklet	6.00
401E	Stamp booklet with missing colors	800.00
402	Love	3.00
403	Sojourner Truth	5.00
404	5¢ Hugo L. Black	2.50
405	Republic of Texas	2.50
406	$2 William J. Bryan	5.00
407	Fish booklet	5.00
408	Public Hospitals	2.50
409	Duke Ellington	5.00
410	Presidents SS	20.00
411	Polar Explorers	5.00
412	17¢ Belva Ann Lockwood	3.50
413	1¢ Margaret Mitchell	2.50
414	Statue of Liberty	3.00
415	4¢ Father Flanagan	2.50
416	17¢ Dog Sled coil	4.00

417	56¢ John Harvard	2.50
418	Navajo Blankets	4.00
419	3¢ Dr. Paul Dudley White	2.50
420	$1 Bernard Revel	3.00
421	T.S. Eliot	2.50
422	Wood-Carved Figurines	3.50
423	Christmas, Village Scene	2.50
424	Christmas, Madonna	2.50
425	5.5¢ Star Route Truck coil	5.00
426	25¢ Bread Wagon coil	5.00

1987

427	8.5¢ Tow Truck coil	5.00
427a	Same with Weston 1986 wmk.	3.00
428	Michigan Statehood	8.00
428a	Same with Weston 1986 wmk.	3.00
429	Pan American Games	8.00
429a	Same with Weston 1986 wmk.	3.00
430	1987 Love	6.00
430a	Same with Weston 1986 wmk.	6.00
431	7.1¢ Tractor coil	8.00
431a	Same with Weston 1986 wmk.	5.00
432	14¢ Julia Ward Howe	3.00
433	Jean Baptiste Pointe Du Sable	10.00
434	Enrico Caruso	3.00
435	2¢ Mary Lyon	2.50
436	2¢ Reengraved Locomotive coil	4.00
437	Girl Scouts	5.00
438	10¢ Canal Boat coil	4.00
439	Special Occasions booklet	6.00
440	United Way	2.50
441	Flag with Fireworks	2.50
442	Flag coil with pre-phosphored paper	4.00
443	American Wildlife Series, (5 pages)	25.00
444	Delaware Statehood	3.00
445	U.S./Morocco Diplomatic Relations	2.50
446	William Faulkner	2.50
447	Lacemaking	4.00
448	10¢ Red Cloud	2.50
449	$5 Bret Harte	12.00
450	Pennsylvania Statehood	3.00
451	Constitution booklet	5.00
452	New Jersey Statehood	3.00
453	Signing of Constitution	3.00
454	Certified Public Accountants	3.00
455	17.5¢ Racing Car and 5¢ Milk Wagon coils	4.00
456	Locomotives booklet	8.00
457	Christmas, Madonna	2.50
458	Christmas, Ornaments	2.50
459	Flag with Fireworks booklet	3.00

1988

No.	Description	Price
460	Georgia Statehood	3.00
461	Connecticut Statehood	3.00
462	1988 Winter Olympics	3.00
463	Australia Bicentennial	2.50
464	James Weldon Johnson	5.00
464a	Same with Weston 1987 wmk.	10.00
465	Cats	5.00
465a	Same with Weston 1987 wmk.	10.00
466	Massachusetts Statehood	4.00
466a	Same with Weston 1987 wmk.	10.00
467	Maryland Statehood	4.00
467a	Same with Weston 1987 wmk.	10.00
468	3¢ Conestoga Wagon coil	4.00
469	Knute Rockne	4.00
470	E sheet and coil	4.00
471	E booklet	6.00
472	E Penalty Mail coil	3.50
473	New Sweden airmail	3.00
474	Pheasant booklet	6.00
475	Jack London booklet (6)	4.50
476	Jack London booklet (10)	6.00
477	Flag with Clouds	2.50
478	Samuel Langley airmail	3.00
479	20¢ Penalty Mail coil	3.00
480	Flag over Yosemite coil	3.50
481	South Carolina Statehood	3.00
482	Owl/Grosbeak booklet	6.00
483	15¢ Buffalo Bill Cody	3.00
484	15¢ & 25¢ Penalty Mail coils	4.00
485	Francis Ouimet	3.00
486	45¢ Dr. Harvey Cushing	2.50
487	New Hampshire Statehood	3.00
488	Igor Sikorsky airmail	3.00
489	Virginia Statehood	3.00
490	10.1¢ Oil Wagon precancel coil	4.00
491	25¢ Love	3.00
492	Flag with Clouds booklet	5.00
493	16.7¢ Popcorn Wagon coil	4.00
494	15¢ Tugboat coil	4.00
495	13.2¢ Coal Car coil	4.00
496	New York Statehood	3.00
497	45¢ Love	3.00
498	8.4¢ Wheelchair coil	4.00
499	21¢ RR Mail Car coil	4.00
500	Summer Olympics	2.50
501	Classic Cars booklet	7.00
502	7.6¢ Carretta coil	4.00
503	Honeybee coil	3.00
504	Antarctic Explorers	4.00
505	5.3¢ Elevator coil	4.00
506	20.5¢ Fire Engine coil	4.00
507	Carousel Animals	3.50
508	$8.75 Eagle	20.00
509	Christmas, Snow Scene	2.50
510	Christmas, Madonna	2.50
510E	Same with missing curlicue	800.00
511	21¢ Chester Carlson	2.50
512	Special Occasions Love You booklet pane	10.00
513	Special Occasions Happy Birthday booklet pane	10.00
514	24.1¢ Tandem Bicycle coil	4.00
515	20¢ Cable Car coil	4.00
516	13¢ Patrol Wagon coil	4.00
517	65¢ General H.H. "Hap" Arnold	3.00
518	23¢ Mary Cassatt	2.50

1989*

No.	Description	Price
519	Montana Statehood	2.50
520	A. Philip Randolph	2.50
521	Flag over Yosemite coil, prephosphored	3.00
522	North Dakota Statehood	2.50
523	Washington Statehood	2.50
524	Steamboats booklet	6.00
525	WORLD STAMP EXPO '89	2.50
526	Arturo Toscanini	2.50
527	U.S. House of Representatives	2.50
528	U.S. Senate	2.50
529	Executive Branch	2.50
530	South Dakota Statehood	2.50
531	7.1¢ Tractor coil, precancel	4.00
532	$1 Johns Hopkins	3.50
533	Lou Gehrig	3.50
534	1¢ Penalty Mail	2.50
535	French Revolution airmail	2.50
536	$2.40 Moon Landing	7.00
537	Ernest Hemingway	2.50
538	North Carolina Statehood	3.00
539	Letter Carriers	2.50
540	28¢ Sitting Bull	2.50
541	Drafting of the Bill of Rights	2.50
542	Prehistoric Animals	3.50
543	25¢ and 45¢ PUAS-America	3.00
	Christmas, Madonna	2.50
	Same, booklet	6.00
	Christmas, Antique Sleigh	2.50
	Same, booklet	6.00
	$3.60 WORLD STAMP EXPO '89 souvenir sheet	10.00
	Classic Mail Transportation	3.50
	Future Mail Transportation airmail	4.00
	$1 Classic Mail Transportation souvenir sheet	4.00
	$1.80 Future Mail Transportation souvenir sheet	6.00

*Numbers and pricing for 1989 issues subject to change.

Prices are courtesy of Charles D. Simmons, a stamp dealer specializing in Souvenir Pages.

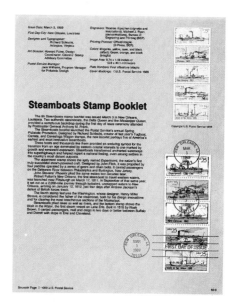

Steamboats Stamp Booklet

The 85 Steamboats stamp booklet was issued March 3 in New Orleans, Louisiana. Two authentic steamboats, the Delta Queen and the Mississippi Queen, provided a sumptuous backdrop during the first day of issue ceremony attended by Postmaster General Anthony M. Frank.

The Steamboats booklet launched the Postal Service's annual Spring Philatelic Promotion. Designed by Richard Schlecht, creator of last year's Tugboat, Carreta, and Conestoga Wagon stamps, the new booklet portrays five of America's earliest and most innovative steamboats.

These boats and thousands like them provided an enduring symbol for the transition from an age dominated by eastern coastal interests to one marked by growth and westward expansion. Steamboats transformed uncharted waterways into superhighways and helped impart a national feeling, even among settlers in the country's most distant outposts.

The uppermost stamp shows the aptly named Experiment, the nation's first truly successful steam-powered craft. Designed by John Fitch, it was propelled by four paddles operated by a series of gears and chain belts. It carried passengers on the Delaware River between Philadelphia and Burlington, New Jersey.

The second stamp shows the Phoenix. John Stevens' Phoenix plied the same waters ten decades later. Robert Fulton's New Orleans, the next steamboat to travel western waters, was launched near Pittsburgh on March 17, 1811. In September of that same year, it set out on a 2,000-mile journey through turbulent, unexplored waters to New Orleans, arriving on January 12, 1812, just four days after Andrew Jackson's defeat of British forces there.

The fourth stamp features the Washington, movie designer, Henry Miller Shreve, is considered the father of the steamboat, both for his design innovations and for clearing the most treacherous sections of the Mississippi. Steamboats plied these as well as rivers, and the bottom stamp shows the Walk in the Water, the first steam vessel on Lake Erie. Built in 1818 by Noah Brown, it carried passengers, mail and cargo in two days or better between Buffalo and Detroit, with stops in Erie and Cleveland.

Souvenir Page © 1989 U.S. Postal Service

AMERICAN COMMEMORATIVE PANELS

The Postal Service offers American Commemorative Panels for each new commemorative stamp and special Christmas and Love stamp issued. The series began in 1972 with the Wildlife Commemorative Panel and will total 344 panels by the end of 1989. The panels feature mint stamps complemented by fine reproductions of steel line engravings and the stories behind the commemorated subjects.

1972
1 Wildlife — 9.00
2 Mail Order — 8.00
3 Osteopathic Medicine — 9.00
4 Tom Sawyer — 8.00
5 Pharmacy — 9.00
6 Christmas, Angels — 11.00
7 Christmas, Santa Claus — 11.00
7E Same with error date (1882) — 750.00
8 Stamp Collecting — 8.00

1973
9 Love — 12.00
10 Pamphleteers — 10.00
11 George Gershwin — 11.00
12 Posting of the Broadside — 10.00
13 Copernicus — 10.00
14 Postal People — 9.00
15 Harry S. Truman — 11.00
16 Post Rider — 11.00
17 Boston Tea Party — 32.00
18 Electronics — 9.00
19 Robinson Jeffers — 9.00
20 Lyndon B. Johnson — 11.00
21 Henry O. Tanner — 9.00
22 Willa Cather — 9.00
23 Drummer — 13.00
24 Angus Cattle — 9.00
25 Christmas, Madonna — 13.00
26 Christmas, Needlepoint Tree — 13.00

1974
27 VFW — 9.00
28 Robert Frost — 9.00
29 EXPO '74 — 11.00
30 Horse Racing — 11.00
31 Skylab — 13.00
32 Universal Postal Union — 9.00
33 Mineral Heritage — 11.00
34 First Kentucky Settlement — 9.00
35 Continental Congress — 11.00

35A Same with corrected Logo — 150.00
36 Chautauqua — 9.00
37 Kansas Wheat — 9.00
38 Energy Conservation — 9.00
39 Sleepy Hollow — 9.00
40 Retarded Children — 9.00
41 Christmas, Currier & Ives — 13.00
42 Christmas, Angel Altarpiece — 13.00

1975
43 Benjamin West — 9.00
44 Pioneer — 13.00
45 Collective Bargaining — 9.00
46 Contributors to the Cause — 9.00
47 Mariner 10 — 13.00
48 Lexington & Concord — 10.00
49 Paul Laurence Dunbar — 9.00
50 D. W. Griffith — 9.00
51 Bunker Hill — 10.00
52 Military Uniforms — 10.00
53 Apollo Soyuz — 13.00
54 World Peace Through Law — 9.00
54A Same with August 15, 1975 date — 150.00
55 Women's Year — 9.00
56 Postal Service Bicentennial — 11.00
57 Banking and Commerce — 10.00
58 Christmas, Prang Card — 13.00
59 Christmas, Madonna — 13.00

1976
60 Spirit of '76 — 16.00
61 Interphil 76 — 15.00
62 State Flags — 35.00
63 Telephone — 12.00
64 Commercial Aviation — 16.00
65 Chemistry — 13.00
66 Benjamin Franklin — 13.00
67 Declaration of Independence — 13.00
68 Olympics — 17.00

69 Clara Maass — 13.00
70 Adolph Ochs — 13.00
70A Same with Charter Logo — 18.00
71 Christmas, Winter Pastime — 21.00
71A Same with Charter Logo — 21.00
72 Christmas, Nativity — 17.00
72A Same with Charter Logo — 21.00

1977
73 Washington at Princeton — 23.00
73A Same with Charter Logo — 18.00
74 Sound Recording — 41.00
74A Same with Charter Logo — 33.00
75 Pueblo Pottery — 110.00
75A Same with Charter Logo — 110.00
76 Solo Transatlantic Flight — 120.00
77 Colorado Statehood — 22.00
78 Butterflies — 25.00
79 Lafayette — 22.00
80 Skilled Hands — 22.00
81 Peace Bridge — 22.00
82 Battle of Oriskany — 22.00
83 Alta, CA, Civil Settlement — 22.00
84 Articles of Confederation — 22.00
85 Talking Pictures — 32.00
86 Surrender at Saratoga — 22.00
87 Energy — 27.00
88 Christmas, Valley Forge — 27.00
89 Christmas, Mailbox — 46.00

1978
90 Carl Sandburg — 14.00
91 Captain Cook — 23.00
92 Harriet Tubman — 14.00
93 Quilts — 25.00

NO POSTAGE
NECESSARY IF
MAILED IN THE
UNITED STATES

BUSINESS REPLY MAIL
First Class, Permit No. 73026, Washington, D.C.

UNITED STATES POSTAL SERVICE
PHILATELIC SALES DIVISION
WASHINGTON, DC 20265-9980

Additional Information on Stamp Collecting Products

Item #8864
Price $5.95

You can expand your stamp collection and keep it updated with philatelic products from the USPS. Check the box next to the products you'd like to learn more about.

☐ *American Commemorative Panels*
☐ *Commemorative Mint Sets*
☐ *Commemorative Stamp Club*
☐ *Definitive Mint Sets*

☐ *FDC Souvenir Programs*
☐ *Souvenir Pages Program*
☐ *Standing Order Service*
☐ *UPU Topical Mint Set*

...And FREE Offers!

Let us know which complimentary offers you're interested in receiving:

☐ *Two tickets to WORLD STAMP EXPO '89 (request must be mailed by October 21)*
☐ *A copy of the **Philatelic Catalog***

Neatly print your name and address below, and drop this card in the mail—no postage necessary.

Information that you provide is protected and only disclosed in accordance with the Privacy Act of 1974.

Mr./Mrs./Ms. _____

Street Address _____
(Include P.O. Box, Apt. No., R.D. Route, etc. where appropriate)

City _____ State _____ ZIP Code _____

Please detach at perforation.

94	Dance	18.00	125	Frances Perkins	12.00	156	U.S. Desert Plants	14.00

#	Name	Price
94	Dance	18.00
95	French Alliance	18.00
96	Early Cancer Detection	14.00
97	Jimmie Rodgers	20.00
98	Photography	14.00
99	George M. Cohan	25.00
100	Viking Missions	44.00
101	Owls	44.00
102	Trees	44.00
103	Christmas, Madonna	20.00
104	Christmas, Hobby Horse	20.00
1979		
105	Robert F. Kennedy	13.00
106	Martin Luther King, Jr.	12.00
107	International Year of the Child	12.00
108	John Steinbeck	12.00
109	Albert Einstein	13.00
110	Pennsylvania Toleware	12.00
111	Architecture	12.00
112	Endangered Flora	13.00
113	Seeing Eye Dogs	13.00
114	Special Olympics	17.00
115	John Paul Jones	12.00
116	15¢ Olympics	18.00
117	Christmas, Madonna	17.00
118	Christmas, Santa Claus	17.00
119	Will Rogers	16.00
120	Vietnam Veterans	17.00
121	10¢, 31¢ Olympics	18.00
1980		
122	W.C. Fields	11.00
123	Winter Olympics	18.00
124	Benjamin Banneker	13.00

#	Name	Price
125	Frances Perkins	12.00
126	Emily Bissell	12.00
127	Helen Keller/ Anne Sullivan	12.00
128	Veterans Administration	12.00
129	General Bernardo de Galvez	12.00
130	Coral Reefs	14.00
131	Organized Labor	11.00
132	Edith Wharton	11.00
133	Education	11.00
134	Indian Masks	14.00
135	Architecture	11.00
136	Christmas, Epiphany Window	17.00
137	Christmas, Toys	17.00
1981		
138	Everett Dirksen	12.00
139	Whitney Moore Young	12.00
140	Flowers	14.00
141	Red Cross	13.00
142	Savings & Loans	12.00
143	Space Achievement	16.00
144	Professional Management	12.00
145	Wildlife Habitats	17.00
146	Int'l. Year Disabled Persons	10.00
147	Edna St. Vincent Millay	10.00
148	Architecture	11.00
149	Babe Zaharias/ Bobby Jones	13.00
150	James Hoban	11.00
151	Frederic Remington	11.00
152	Battle of Yorktown/ Virginia Capes	11.00
153	Christmas, Bear and Sleigh	16.00
154	Christmas, Madonna	16.00
155	John Hanson	10.00

#	Name	Price
156	U.S. Desert Plants	14.00
1982		
157	Roosevelt	13.00
158	Love	16.00
159	G. Washington	13.00
160	State Birds & Flowers	34.00
161	U.S./ Netherlands	15.00
162	Library of Congress	16.00
163	Knoxville World's Fair	16.00
164	Horatio Alger	13.00
165	Aging Together	18.00
166	The Barrymores	20.00
167	Dr. Mary Walker	16.00
168	Peace Garden	18.00
169	America's Libraries	19.00
170	Jackie Robinson	34.00
171	Touro Synagogue	18.00
172	Architecture	18.00
173	Wolf Trap Farm Park	20.00
174	Francis of Assisi	20.00
175	Ponce de Leon	20.00
176	Christmas, Madonna	29.00
177	Christmas, Season's Greetings	29.00
178	Kitten & Puppy	29.00
1983		
179	Science and Industry	9.00
180	Sweden/USA Treaty	9.00
181	Balloons	12.00
182	Civilian Conservation Corps	9.00
183	40¢ Olympics	11.00
184	Joseph Priestley	9.00

313

185	Voluntarism	8.00	**219**	Jim Thorpe	14.00	
186	Concord/German		**220**	John		
	Immigration	9.00		McCormack	8.00	
187	Physical		**221**	St. Lawrence		
	Fitness	8.00		Seaway	10.00	
188	Brooklyn		**222**	Preserving		
	Bridge	10.00		Wetlands	13.00	
189	TVA	9.00	**223**	Roanoke		
190	Medal			Voyages	8.00	
	of Honor	12.00	**224**	Herman		
191	Scott Joplin	14.00		Melville	8.00	
192	28¢ Olympics	12.00	**225**	Horace Moses	8.00	
193	Babe Ruth	20.00	**226**	Smokey Bear	11.00	
194	Nathaniel		**227**	Roberto		
	Hawthorne	9.00		Clemente	16.00	
195	13¢ Olympics	16.00	**228**	Dogs	11.00	
196	Treaty of Paris	11.00	**229**	Crime		
197	Civil Service	11.00		Prevention	8.00	
198	Metropolitan		**230**	Family Unity	8.00	
	Opera	11.00	**231**	Christmas,		
199	Inventors	11.00		Madonna	11.00	
200	Streetcars	13.00	**232**	Christmas,		
201	Christmas,			Santa Claus	11.00	
	Madonna	15.00	**233**	Eleanor		
202	Christmas,			Roosevelt	9.00	
	Santa Claus	15.00	**234**	Nation		
203	35¢ Olympics	16.00		of Readers	9.00	
204	Martin Luther	13.00	**235**	Hispanic		
	1984			Americans	9.00	
205	Alaska		**236**	Vietnam Veterans		
	Statehood	8.00		Memorial	12.00	
206	Winter			**1985**		
	Olympics	11.00	**237**	Jerome Kern	9.00	
207	FDIC	8.00	**238**	Mary McLeod		
208	Love	9.00		Bethune	9.00	
209	Carter G.		**239**	Duck Decoys	11.00	
	Woodson	11.00	**240**	Winter Special		
210	Soil and Water			Olympics	9.00	
	Conservation	8.00	**241**	Love	9.00	
211	Credit Union		**242**	Rural Electrification		
	Act	8.00		Administration	8.00	
212	Orchids	11.00	**243**	AMERIPEX	11.00	
213	Hawaii		**244**	Abigail Adams	7.00	
	Statehood	10.00	**245**	Frederic Auguste		
214	National			Bartholdi	13.00	
	Archives	8.00	**246**	Korean War		
215	20¢ Olympics	11.00		Veterans	9.00	
216	Louisiana World		**247**	Social Security		
	Exposition	10.00		Act	8.00	
217	Health		**248**	World War I		
	Research	8.00		Veterans	8.00	
218	Douglas		**249**	Horses	11.00	
	Fairbanks	8.00				

250	Public	
	Education	8.00
251	Youth	9.00
252	Help End	
	Hunger	8.00
253	Christmas,	
	Poinsettias	13.00
254	Christmas,	
	Madonna	13.00
	1986	
255	Arkansas	
	Statehood	7.00
256	Stamp	
	Collecting	9.00
257	Love	9.00
258	Sojourner Truth	9.00
259	Republic	
	of Texas	9.00
260	Fish	9.00
261	Public Hospitals	7.00
262	Duke Ellington	9.00
263	U.S. Presidents'	
	Sheet #1	9.00
264	U.S. Presidents'	
	Sheet #2	9.00
265	U.S. Presidents'	
	Sheet #3	9.00
266	U.S. Presidents'	
	Sheet #4	9.00
267	Polar	
	Explorers	9.00
268	Statue	
	of Liberty	10.00
269	Navajo Blankets	9.00
270	T.S. Eliot	7.00
271	Woodcarved	
	Figurines	9.00
272	Christmas,	
	Madonna	9.00
273	Christmas,	
	Village Scene	9.00
	1987	
274	Michigan	
	Statehood	7.00
275	Pan American	
	Games	7.00
276	Love	8.00
277	Jean Baptiste	
	Du Sable	8.00
278	Enrico Caruso	8.00
279	Girl Scouts	9.00
280	Special	
	Occasions	7.00

281	United Way	7.00	**310** Francis Ouimet	7.00	Classic Transportation
282	#1 American		**311** New Hampshire		stamps and
	Wildlife	10.00	Statehood	7.00	souvenir sheet 9.00
283	#2 American		**312** Virginia		Future Transportation
	Wildlife	10.00	Statehood	7.00	stamps and
284	#3 American		**313** Love	7.00	souvenir sheet 9.00
	Wildlife	10.00	**314** New York		WORLD STAMP
285	#4 American		Statehood	7.00	EXPO '89
	Wildlife	10.00	**315** Classic Cars	9.00	souvenir sheet 9.00

281 United Way 7.00
282 #1 American Wildlife 10.00
283 #2 American Wildlife 10.00
284 #3 American Wildlife 10.00
285 #4 American Wildlife 10.00
286 #5 American Wildlife 10.00
287 Delaware Statehood 7.00
288 Morocco/U.S. Diplomatic Relations 7.00
289 William Faulkner 7.00
290 Lacemakers 7.00
291 Pennsylvania Statehood 7.00
292 Constitution Booklet 7.00
293 New Jersey Statehood 7.00
294 Signing of the Constitution 7.00
295 Certified Public Accountants 9.00
296 Locomotives 9.00
297 Christmas, Madonna 9.00
298 Christmas, Ornaments 9.00

1988
299 Georgia Statehood 7.00
300 Connecticut Statehood 7.00
301 Winter Olympics 9.00
302 Australia 7.00
303 James Weldon Johnson 7.00
304 Cats 9.00
305 Massachusetts Statehood 7.00
306 Maryland Statehood 7.00
307 Knute Rockne 9.00
308 New Sweden 7.00
309 South Carolina Statehood 7.00

310 Francis Ouimet 7.00
311 New Hampshire Statehood 7.00
312 Virginia Statehood 7.00
313 Love 7.00
314 New York Statehood 7.00
315 Classic Cars 9.00
316 Summer Olympics 9.00
317 Antarctic Explorers 7.00
318 Carousel Animals 7.00
319 Christmas, Traditional 9.00
320 Christmas, Contemporary 7.00

1989*
Montana Statehood 7.00
A. Philip Randolph 7.00
North Dakota Statehood 7.00
Washington Statehood 7.00
Steamboats Booklet 9.00
WORLD STAMP EXPO '89 10.00
Arturo Toscanini 7.00
U.S. House 7.00
U.S. Senate 7.00
Executive Branch South Dakota Statehood 7.00
Lou Gehrig 9.00
French Revolution 7.00
Ernest Hemingway 7.00
Moon Landing 15.00
North Carolina Statehood 7.00
Letter Carriers 7.00
Drafting of the Bill of Rights 7.00
Prehistoric Animals 9.00
America/PUAS 7.00
Christmas, Traditional and Contemporary 9.00

Classic Transportation stamps and souvenir sheet 9.00
Future Transportation stamps and souvenir sheet 9.00
WORLD STAMP EXPO '89 souvenir sheet 9.00

*1989 issues subject to change.

Prices are courtesy of the American Society of Philatelic Pages and Panels, an organization specializing in Commemorative Panels.

AMERICAN COMMEMORATIVES

statehood of MONTANA

AMERICAN COMMEMORATIVES

Washington Statehood

SUBJECT INDEX

IMPORTANT NOTE: This Index covers all issues from the 1893 Columbian Exposition issues (#230) through 1989. Listings in italic typeface refer to Definitive or Regular issues. The numbers listed next to the stamp description are the Scott numbers, and the numbers in parenthesis are the numbers of the pages on which the stamps are illustrated.

317

Postmasters General of the United States

1789 Samuel Osgood, MA
1791 Timothy Pickering, PA
1795 Joseph Habersham, GA
1801 Gideon Granger, CT
1814 Return J. Meigs, Jr., OH
1823 John McLean, OH
1829 William T. Barry, KY
1835 Amos Kendall, KY
1840 John M. Niles, CT
1841 Francis Granger, NY
1841 Charles A. Wickliffe, KY
1845 Cave Johnson, TN
1849 Jacob Collamer, VT
1850 Nathan K. Hall, NY
1852 Samuel D. Hubbard, CT
1853 James Campbell, PA
1857 Aaron V. Brown, TN
1859 Joseph Holt, KY
1861 Horatio King, ME
1861 Montgomery Blair, DC
1864 William Dennison, OH
1866 Alexander W. Randall, WI
1869 John A.J. Creswell, MD
1874 James W. Marshall, NJ
1874 Marshall Jewell, CT
1876 James N. Tyner, IN
1877 David McK. Key, TN
1880 Horace Maynard, TN
1881 Thomas L. James, NY
1882 Timothy O. Howe, WI
1883 Walter Q. Gresham, IN
1884 Frank Hatton, IA
1885 William F. Vilas, WI

1888 Don M. Dickinson, MI
1889 John Wanamaker, PA
1893 Wilson S. Bissell, NY
1895 William L. Wilson, WV
1897 James A. Gary, MD
1898 Charles Emory Smith, PA
1902 Henry C. Payne, WI
1904 Robert J. Wynne, PA
1905 George B. Cortelyou, NY
1907 George von L. Meyer, MA
1909 Frank H. Hitchcock, MA
1913 Albert S. Burleson, TX
1921 Will H. Hays, IN
1922 Hubert Work, CO
1923 Harry S. New, IN
1929 Walter F. Brown, OH
1933 James A. Farley, NY
1940 Frank C. Walker, PA
1945 Robert E. Hannegan, MO
1947 Jesse M. Donaldson, IL
1953 Arthur E. Summerfield, MI
1961 J. Edward Day, CA
1963 John A. Gronouski, WI
1965 Lawrence F. O'Brien, MA
1968 W. Marvin Watson, TX
1969 Winton M. Blount, AL
1972 E. T. Klassen, MA
1975 Benjamin Franklin Bailar, MD
1978 William F. Bolger, CT
1985 Paul N. Carlin, WY
1986 Albert V. Casey, MA
1986 Preston R. Tisch, NY
1988 Anthony M. Frank, CA